soul power

soul power

•

CULTURE, RADICALISM, AND THE MAKING OF A U.S. THIRD WORLD LEFT

CYNTHIA A. YOUNG

•

DUKE UNIVERSITY PRESS

Durham and London

2006

© 2006 DUKE UNIVERSITY PRESS
All rights reserved. Printed in the
United States of America on acid-free
paper ∞ Designed by Amy Ruth
Buchanan. Typeset in Minion and
Frutiger by Keystone Typesetting, Inc.
Library of Congress Cataloging-in-
Publication data and republication
acknowledgments appear on the last
printed pages of this book.

*Duke University Press gratefully
acknowledges the support of the Department of English at the University of
Southern California, which provided
funds toward the production of this book.*

For Betty J. Young
and the late Melvin F. Young
for teaching me what it means
to be accountable to others.

Contents

●

Preface

●

Too often, academic writers enjoy the pretense that our books are solely the result of painstakingly conducted research rather than the product of deeply held personal beliefs and prejudices that drive our careful research. The more we deny a personal investment that mars a supposedly unclouded objectivity, the more validation we get, as if the lines between the personal and the professional do not always cross and converge. Instead of relying on this thin subterfuge, I acknowledge up front that this story of boundary crossers, of activists and artists, workers and students who reimagined national, racial, and individual identities in the 1960s and 1970s is deeply connected to my personal history.

Born in a Midwestern suburb, the child of a black and white union, I have always been fascinated by the sixties. Perhaps this is because I turned one in 1970 and so experienced them from an increasingly nostalgic distance; the drama of Woodstock or Haight-Ashbury seemed as far away from Shaker Heights, Ohio, as the moon. Perhaps I became obsessed with the sixties because my parents were Popular Front rather than flower children with stories of protest marches and pot smoking to retell. Or maybe it is because my parents, the daughter of an Irish coal miner and union activist and the son of a black electrician, understood themselves to be living Martin Luther King Jr.'s dream. Whatever the reason, the nostalgia-dripped, one-dimensional images of the sixties—peace, love, and freedom—provided the backdrop against which my family and I negotiated suburban Cleveland. In 1974, interracial unions were still rare there, drawing prolonged stares, stage whispers, and the occasional congratulations from strangers to my mother for having fostered a black child. Such episodes always prompted brief lectures to me on integration and its difficulties.

My childhood sense of identity, multivalent and far from fixed, never matched the binary racial categories with which I was constantly confronted. In those early years, I repeatedly learned that certain kinds of boundary crossings had to be explained. The Sesame Street song "One of These Things (Is Not Like the Other)" took on new meaning once I entered elementary school. I quickly figured out that the complexity of my racial identity was best left unspoken. Blending in was the best way to avoid conflict, and so for much of my childhood I lived vicariously. I became an obsessive reader and devoted TV watcher. I inhabited the personas of Scarlett O' Hara in Gone With the Wind or of Jake Barnes in The Sun Also Rises as easily as I did those of Starsky, JJ, or Sanford's son Lamont. This odd assortment of characters mingled effortlessly in my head. Popular culture afforded me a certain kind of freedom; it plunged me into a landscape where strange behavior, freakish identities, and general nonconformity were tolerated, even prized.

It was only much later that I would realize that my experience was not unique, nor that it was not reserved for those of us with differently raced parents. Understanding identity in complicated, hybrid, and strategically essentialist terms was the norm among my black friends. This always seemed much less true of my white friends whose possessive investment in whiteness made it difficult for them to see the privilege they enjoyed by virtue of whiteness's supposed invisibility.[1] If my college reading of W. E. B. Du Bois's The Souls of Black Folk captured the conflicting imperatives of being what my mother called "mixed," "double consciousness" did not seem sufficient to encompass the range of political and cultural identities intersecting within my family and me. Written in 1903, Souls could not fully explain why my white mother felt most comfortable in a black social world or why that same world would reject her when my father died. It could not account for the fact that she, a secretary, was much more likely than my attorney father to "go up to that school" whenever she believed racism was at work. Though distant from sixties' cultural forms, my parents' racial and class identities, shot through with their progressive and conservative elements, were only possible in the wake of the social, cultural, and political upheavals of the sixties and seventies. Even for those at a considerable cultural distance those decades forged a space, sometimes imaginary and sometimes real, that was deeply utopian even as its racial egalitarianism was intensely and frequently contested. As their child, I learned that identity works in obvious as well as unmarked, contradictory, and confusing ways long before I had the language to express it. I learned that identities involve a range of political and cultural choices, that they are both foisted on us and chosen, that they are shaped by our ideals, values, and actions. Often people, particularly marginalized peoples, recognize and act on this knowledge in ways misunderstood, even ignored by theorists and politicians. My mother still has much to teach me about racial equality and class solidarity.

The people with which this book is concerned, the writers, organizers, filmmakers, and unionists that I call U.S. Third World Leftists, transgressed various boundaries—most particularly those of race, nation, and class. In telling their story, I, too, have been forced to breach various scholarly and disciplinary boundaries. This is a book informed by several disciplines and interdisciplines, most immediately literary studies, cultural studies, history, American studies, ethnic studies, anthropology, and philosophy. It also relies on an enormous range of sources: fictional, nonfictional, and autobiographical writing, conventional and oral histories, manifestos, popular music, narrative and documentary film, organizational archives, and personal interviews. As a result, this book is, I hope, a cultural history in the richest and broadest sense. I have put various texts, individuals, and organizations in conversation with one another in order to challenge conventional interpretations of politics and culture in the sixties and seventies. I do this not to impose another partial and limiting understanding of the period, but rather to clear the ground for more nuanced investigations of this intriguing period in recent history.

As I look back over the years it took me to complete this project, one thing is clear: though I did not intend it, I assembled an archive. It involved unearthing sources that have rarely been examined, let alone in connection with this period, or juxtaposing known and unknown sources in ways that defy the cultural and political apartheid many sixties critics endorse. In building this archive, I have met profound generosity and incredible resistance, most often from people who "lived through" the period. These survivors do not recognize the figures and organizations I discuss, or if they do recognize them, they do not feel they warrant scholarly attention. This attitude, laden with racial and class biases, is particularly vehement because so much of this book is concerned with women of color and the working class. In addition, the sixties were a uniquely sectarian era, and so some movement veterans are still invested in battles over organizational or political integrity. Reminders that people whom I group under the rubric U.S. Third World Left hated each other or worked against one another have consistently dogged this project, making it difficult for some to see the forest for the trees. The advantage of distance, however, is that it allows one to see how people who saw themselves working in opposition to one another agreed about more than they disagreed.

In addition to political and intellectual resistance, I also faced challenges unique to the sixties. Because of the intense state repression faced by activists and those they loved, critical participants in this story did not want to talk "on the record." They either felt it was too risky or found it too painful to rehearse struggles and victories that came at considerable personal or professional cost. Overcoming such understandable resistance sometimes proved impossible, and no doubt this book is poorer without their stories. In other instances, the passage of time had made participants' recall unstable and unreliable, a challenge facing anyone doing oral histories, but perhaps one more acute given the enormous backlash that followed the sixties. The political and cultural Right has so effectively demonized and discredited the sixties era that it was often difficult to get informants to detail their activities without simultaneously hearing commentary about how "foolish" or "unrealistic" or just "plain wrong" they must seem from today's vantage point. In that sense, the intervening years of political backlash always remained with this project and its protagonists.

Had I known how much labor this project would eventually entail, I might not have embarked on it. In this case, ignorance was truly bliss. Certainly, I would have scaled back my ambitions. However, the complexity of the period and its struggles required me to expand rather than narrow my critical focus. It pushed me to continually boundary-cross, attain new expertise, and let go of the assumptions—about the people, the period, and the lessons to be drawn from them—that had lived in my head for so long. Now that I am at the end, I find myself frustrated that I could not include even more people and events. The U.S. Third World Left was a diverse and important cultural formation, every bit as significant as the New Left or the civil rights mainstream. For some who "were there," this book may look like a detour off the main road of sixties and seventies history, but those willing to follow this path may realize that what looks like a detour might just be a more interesting and varied route through the period.

Acknowledgments

•

This project was shelved at least a dozen times. The fact that it did not stay on the shelf is due to the financial and intellectual support I have received over the years. For support during the dissertation phase of the project, I thank the Ford Foundation for awarding me a Dissertation Fellowship for Minorities. Without that award, I would have abandoned the PhD and this book in its infancy. The Ford Foundation revived this project again when they awarded me a Postdoctoral Fellowship for Minorities without which I might not have completed the manuscript. The Rockefeller Foundation also supported this project by awarding me two postdoctoral fellowships. The first fellowship year was spent at New York University's International Center for Advanced Studies Project on Cities and Urban Knowledges. In addition to the generous hosting by Thomas Bender and Allan Hunter, I had lively conversations with the center fellows, especially Manu Goswami, Srirupa Roy, and Rebeccah Welch, for which I am profoundly grateful. I also held a Rockefeller Foundation fellowship at the University of California, Riverside's Center for Ideas and Society, directed with true grace and unbelievable heart by Emory Elliot. His support and that of his amazing staff Marilyn Davis, Laura Lozon, and Antonette Toney made the time there both productive and fun. While there, I also found three lifetime friends and critics in Toby Miller, Amitava Kumar, and Mona Ahmad Ali. Throughout the years of research, many people opened up their archives and their lives to me, including Allan Siegel, Ada Gay Griffin, Norman Fruchter, Susan Robeson, the late Moe Foner, Charles Burnett, and Ntongela Masilela. I could not have completed this project without them. In particular, I want to single out Allan. Without his frank and detailed recollections and his personal introductions, the Newsreel and Third World Newsreel chapters would have foundered. Thanks also to the courageous example of Amiri Baraka, Harold Cruse, Robert F. Williams, Local 1199, the Attica rebels, Operation Move-In activists, Third World Newsreel, and the L.A. Rebellion for making a history worth writing about.

This project has been enriched by commentary on various versions of chapters, articles, and conference papers. In particular, I would like to thank the anonymous readers at Duke University Press who enriched the manuscript with their thorough, intellectually generous critiques. During my time at SUNY Binghamton, I was fortunate to have great colleagues including Darryl Thomas, Christopher Fynsk, Mahua Sarkar, and the members of my writing group, Michael Hames-Garcia, Benita Roth, Deborah Cahalen, and Carlos Riobó. At the University of Southern California, my work and life has benefited from the timely advice and unstinting encouragement of Cathy Cooper, Judith Jackson Fossett, Judith Halberstam, Jane Iwamura, Carla Kaplan, Roberto Lint-Sagarena, David Lloyd, Fred Moten, David Roman, John C. Rowe, Brian Story, and Janelle Wong. In the final stages of editing, Jane and Janelle worked tirelessly to edit the manuscript, Judith Jackson Fossett provided countless meals and access to her amazing family, while David Román supplied numerous pep talks. I am also indebted to my fabulous research assistants Reina Prado, Carol Bunch, Jesús Hernandez, and Ambre Ivol, without whom there would be numerous bibliographical errors. Much of this manuscript has been read and critiqued by my dissertation committee members Michael Denning, Hazel Carby, and Robin D. G. Kelley. In particular, I want to thank Robin for sharing his inexhaustible knowledge of black radicalism without which I would not have even known where to look. Chapters of this manuscript have also been workshopped in the L.A. Women's Group for the Collaborative Study of Race and Gender in Culture. The group, whose members include Gabrielle Foreman, Alexandra Juhasz, Laura Hyun Yi Kang, Rachel Lee, and Eve Oishi, theorizes, writes, and produces scholarship within a progressive, collective feminist framework. I would like to express my thanks to the members of the group and encourage other scholars to create collaborative networks that support this too often alienating way of life.

Through all of the geographic and personal shifts, the following people have remained constants: Prudence Cumberbatch, Joseph Entin, Jacqueline

Goldsby, Rebecca Schreiber, Jennifer Philips, Doreen Chen, and Gaspar González. I am glad you all came into my orbit. Thanks also to Whelan, Nika, and Joseph McPeak who got me out of my own head and into the sunshine at least once a day. In the home stretch, I was fortunate to have been warmly embraced by the Morgan clan, Emma and Jennifer Morgan, Herman Bennett, Maymette Carter, the late Claudia Morgan, and John Paul Morgan. Most especially, I wish to thank Zachary Morgan. He has pulled me out of more than one ditch in the road, for which I am profoundly and inexpressibly grateful. Finally, I wish to thank my mother, Betty J. Young, whose love and support gives new meaning to the word *unqualified*.

Go awaken my people from Texas to Virginia,

Tell them of our glorious brothers in the colony of Kenya

Go tell my people that the dawn has come,

Sound the trumpet, beat the drum!

Let the tyrant shudder, let the oppressor tremble at the thunder,

For the tide of humanity rises to sweep the despot under.

Go awaken my people wherever they sleep,

Tell them that we have a rendezvous that we must keep.

—Robert F. Williams, "Go Awaken My People"

Introduction

●

We colored folk of America have long lived with you yellow, brown and black folk
of the world under the intolerable arrogance and assumptions of the white race. We
beg you to close ranks against men in America, Britain, France, Spain, Belgium and the
Netherlands, so long as they fight and scheme for the colonial system, for color, caste
and class exploitation.

—W. E. B. Du Bois, "The Bandung Conference"

On the occasion of the 1955 Asian-African Conference in Bandung, Indo-
nonesia, W. E. B. Du Bois sent these fiery words to the assembled delegates.
Unable to attend because the U.S. State Department had denied passports to
him and Paul Robeson, Du Bois was nonetheless enthusiastic about this unprecedented gathering of representatives from twenty-nine developing nations. Writing as formal decolonization accelerated throughout the Third
World, he echoed the militant mood of the delegates: "Let the white world keep
its missionaries at home to teach the Golden Rule to its corporate thieves.
Damn the God of slavery, exploitation, and war."[1] Organized by India, Paki-
stan, Ceylon (Sri Lanka), Burma (Myanmar), and Indonesia, the Bandung
Conference was a meeting of Third World nations dedicated to "the elimina-
tion of colonialism and the 'color line.'"[2] Defying the Cold War era's division
of the globe into anticommunist and communist spheres, the Bandung Con-

ference sought to craft an independent, nonaligned identity for the Third World by fostering alliances among the decolonizing and newly decolonized nations of Africa and Asia.

If Bandung heralded the entrance of Third World nations onto the world stage, it also spurred the transformation of leftists of color in the United States. Du Bois suggests as much when he links African Americans to colonized peoples, anti-imperialism to antiracism, forcefully arguing that "color, caste and class" are interconnected. In doing so, Du Bois defines "colored" identity as a global identity, one profoundly shaped by racism, colonialism, and imperialism. Bandung served as a symbol of international coalition and anticolonial resistance that challenged the very foundation of Western power. Participating nations sought to wrest the term *Third World* out of the geopolitical context in which it was first coined by the French demographer Alfred Sauvy in 1952. Sauvy derived *Third World* from *Third Estate*, the French revolutionary-era term used to describe those at the bottom of the social hierarchy. Reclaiming the term meant inverting that political, economic, and social hierarchy; it meant challenging a global order in which the vast majority of nations pursued the ever-shrinking horizon of First World status.

In its denunciation of Western imperialism, economic exploitation, and the racism on which it thrives, in its urgent appeal to all the "yellow, brown, and black folk of the world," Du Bois's words epitomize the ideals animating a diverse group of U.S.-based intellectuals, artists, and activists mobilizing in the 1960s and 1970s. *Soul Power: Cultural Radicalism and the Formation of a U.S. Third World Left* analyzes the ideas, art forms, and cultural rituals of a group of African Americans, Latino/as, Asian Americans, and Anglos who, inspired by events in the decolonizing world, saw their own plight in global terms. Writers, filmmakers, hospital workers, students, and grassroots activists turned to Third World anticolonial struggles for ideas and strategies that might aid their own struggles against the poverty, discrimination, and brutality facing peoples of color.

There was, of course, significant precedent for their activities. Not only did they follow in the footsteps of the two black Americans absent from Bandung, Robeson and Du Bois, but they were also part of a long and distinguished history of anticolonial, antiracist, and anticapitalist agitation among leftists of color in the United States.[3] In addition to organizations like the African Blood Brotherhood, the League of Struggle for Negro Rights, and the International Labor Defense, there were Hubert Henry Harrison, Cyril Briggs, A. Philip Randolph, Hosea Hudson, Grace Campbell, William Patterson, Louise Thompson Patterson, Claudia Jones, Benjamin Davis Jr., and countless workers, intellectuals, and organizers who worked within Communist Party chapters, New Deal–era unions, civil rights groups, and grassroots organizations. During the McCarthy era, however, the shape of this activism shifted as radicals adapted to the political repression of Cold War (North) America. Penny Von Eschen reads this shift as a turn away from politics toward culture. As evidence, she cites the 1956 Congress of Colored Writers' decision to shy away from "concretely examin[ing] the increasing similarities in the plight of Africans and of black Americans" and focus instead on "the contributions of African culture to American life."[4] Von Eschen's view is one shared by many U.S. historians. Rebeccah Welch breaks with this historiography suggesting that the turn toward culture produced both antiracist critiques and innovative art.[5]

If the impact of the McCarthy era on leftist activism has been a matter of considerable debate, most critics agree that cultural production and cultural identity assumed a new prominence during the 1950s. Indeed, some leftists used the turn toward culture as a way of combining cultural critiques with antiracist and anticolonial ones. That interstitial approach paved the way for U.S. Third World Leftists in the 1960s who created cultural artifacts that would not only register the Third World's influence, but speak back to it in powerful ways. Inspired by a host of Third World leaders including Kwame Nkrumah in Ghana, Fidel Castro and Che Guevara in Cuba, Mao Tse-Tung in the People's Republic of China, and Amílcar Cabral in Guinea-Bissau, *Soul Power*'s protagonists—LeRoi Jones (later Amiri Baraka), Harold Cruse, and Angela Y. Davis, as well as filmmakers in Third World Newsreel and at the University of California at Los Angeles (UCLA), unionists in the hospital workers' 1199 union, squatters in Operation Move-In, and students in the Young Lords Party crafted what Arjun Appadurai has called "new diasporic public spheres," insisting on the interconnections between U.S. minorities and Third World majorities in a moment of global decolonization.[6]

Forged in the interstices between the New Left and the civil rights movement, between the counterculture and the Black Arts movements, this U.S. Third World Left created cultural, material, and ideological links to the Third World as a mode through which to contest U.S. economic, racial, and cultural arrangements. The appellation *Third World* served as a shorthand for leftists of color in the United States, signifying their opposition to a particular economic and racial world order. This diverse group of organizations and individuals fostered the creation and circulation of a sophisticated cultural lexicon, one characterized by its innovative stylistics, ideological hybridity, and a sense of political urgency. Just as the Port Huron Statement, the Freedom Summer, and the music of Bob Dylan helped craft what Raymond Williams has called a "structure of feeling" for the New Left, certain events, individuals, and ideologies forged a U.S. Third World Left that was simultaneously committed to transnational political resistance and cultural innovation. Linking the social justice struggles of U.S. peoples of color to liberation struggles in Africa and Asia, U.S. Third World Leftists wrote essays, made films, and engaged in activism that created a distinct cultural and political formation. This formation melded the civil rights movement's focus on racial inequality, the Old Left's focus on class struggle and anticolonialism, and the New Left's focus on grassroots, participatory democracy.

Challenging Western liberalism's tendency to view politically engaged art as simply propaganda, U.S. Third World Leftists developed new aesthetic techniques and vocabularies. Newsreel's groundbreaking films combined the models offered by the Russian documentarian Dziga Vertov and French and American cinema verité to capture the frenzy, confusion, and spontaneous community that characterized the 1967 march on the Pentagon and the 1968 Columbia University student strike. Third World Newsreel was influenced by the documentary films of Instituto Cubano del Arte e Industria Cinematográficos (ICAIC), Cuba's film institute, mixing cartoon footage, personal interviews, and newsreel footage in *Teach Our Children* (1972), a film about the 1971 Attica prison rebellion. Filmmakers Haile Gerima and Charles Burnett, based at UCLA, turned to the narrative examples offered by Brazilian Cinema Novo, using them to explore the impact of state repression on individual and community identity in Los Angeles. The U.S. Third World Leftists' interest in aesthetic experimentation was always informed by a commitment to a diverse set of political ideals, but such experimentation was never sacrificed to the exigencies of ongoing political struggle. For this group, cultural production and political activism complemented rather than opposed each other.

In addition to its formal innovations, this group also articulated a powerful antiracist and anti-imperialist critique of the United States, developing an analysis of state violence and refining the internal-colony model popularized by the Communist Party International. These twin foci emphasized the parallels between urban communities of color and Third World colonies. The group's ability to imagine and claim common cause with a radical Third World subject involved multiple translations and substitutions; it required the production of an imagined terrain able to close the multiple gaps between First and Third World subjects. The analysis of how U.S. state violence produced internal colonies created a distinct framework with its own set of assumptions and biases. For one, U.S. Third World Leftists privileged urban over rural communities; in the cases considered here, these included New York, Newark, and Los Angeles. They emphasized solidarity based on material circumstance rather than racial, ethnic, or geographic kinship; they understood internal colonies to be racially and ethnically diverse communities whose members faced certain forms of state violence. The internal colony was no longer solely a description of the Southern Black Belt, as it had been for earlier leftists, but was also a term for black, Asian American, and Latino enclaves. Rather than using race as a means of spurring class identification or using race and class interchangeably, the revision of the internal-colony thesis combined Third World colonial status with both class and race.

Both Angela Y. Davis and Haile Gerima, for instance, analyzed the ways in which state practices of containment—incarceration, housing segregation, welfare bureaucracies—constitute powerful forms of state violence that echo colonial practices and produce forms of individual alienation that can either impede or ignite political resistance. They showed that state violence directed at peoples of color not only defines U.S. democracy but also provides an insidious blueprint for U.S. imperial designs. After their visit to Castro's Cuba, the writers Harold Cruse, LeRoi Jones, and Robert F. Williams debated the suitability of the colonial model for black Americans. Jones and Williams argued that U.S. urban communities were segregated, brutally suppressed, and exploited in ways that mimicked the conditions defining Third World colonies. Consequently, they viewed armed struggle as a primary path to black liberation. Cruse, on the other hand, disagreed, believing that black Americans' First World status meant that armed revolution would never prove viable. For Cruse, this was not simply a question of demographics; it also stemmed from his sense that the complexity of black American struggle required an assault on the cultural and ideological foundations of the United States. This led him to advocate for a "cultural revolution" that would challenge U.S. state practices from within and offer a powerful ideological and cultural alternative.[7] Charles Burnett's brilliant *Killer of Sheep* (1977) depicts the daily life of Stan, a meat-factory worker struggling to find his way out of his dead-end Watts existence. By juxtaposing the helpless sheep being led to slaughter with Stan's children, Burnett suggests that internal colonization results from a set of violent state practices that lead to the death of hope and human connection. Though they did not always articulate their demands in terms of state violence, the 1199ers' fight for better wages and fairer workplaces consistently linked those demands to improvement in the overall living conditions of hospital workers. Their campaigns demonstrated the fact that discrimination and exploitation constitute forms of state violence endemic to working-class black and Puerto Rican life. In doing so, they exposed the gap between the rhetoric of U.S.

democracy and its grim reality. In explicit and implicit ways, U.S. Third World Leftists used a focus on state violence and the internal colony to provide the ideological glue connecting U.S. minorities and Third World majorities.

The example offered by U.S. Third World Leftists challenges extant historiographies of sixties activism, many of which focus on the New Left: the Berkeley Free Speech Movement, Students for a Democratic Society (SDS), and other white-dominated groups. Through this lens, middle-class white students and their issues—the draft, student rights—define the decade.[8] Characterized by racial myopia and North American exceptionalism, this New Left–centric historiography has diminished the influence of domestic movements for racial and economic equality and international liberation struggles. Another set of histories focuses on civil rights and Black Power; in those narratives, the Southern Christian Leadership Conference (SCLC), the Student Nonviolent Coordinating Committee (SNCC), the Congress on Racial Equality (CORE), and the Black Panther Party take center stage. Often such histories divide the period's historical actors into integrationists and separatists, Martin Luther King Jr. versus Malcolm X. They overemphasize race as a rallying point, ignoring the fact that assaults against Jim Crow segregation and equality were also assaults on entrenched class and gender exploitation.

Both historiographic tendencies foreground middle-class men and their organizations and underplay struggles to overturn capitalism or imperialism. They overinvest in youth as the catalyst for social change, reinforcing the perception that sixties activism emerged because of a generational conflict between conformist parents and their rebellious kids. Though the Vietnam War certainly made for a primary focus of both the New Left and civil rights, histories of them tend to underestimate the enormous influence of decolonization, thus reducing the international context solely to Vietnam. Finally, these historiographic traditions reify the divide between culture and politics, as if the culture of the period, symbolized by the so-called turn on, tune in, drop out ethos, offered an escape from politics. If we primarily conceive of the period in phallocentric, youth-oriented, and hypersexualized terms—the black jacketed Panther, the male white student—then we continue to mystify a historical moment rather than decode it.

In turning to grassroots organizations, cultural producers, and union members, *Soul Power* defies such easy categorizations, revealing what they obscure: that the boundaries between political philosophies and organizations were often more permeable and fluid than scholars acknowledge, that the working class, women of color, and older people also played an important role in this history. Indeed, the one point is related to the other. If one expands the lens beyond the New Left and civil rights/Black Power, then one recognizes that this set of marginalized actors created new ideological and political formations to which we need to attend. This expanded focus helps shift our understanding of the sixties and seventies, offering new tools for analyzing and acting in our current historical moment.

This perspective also calls into question the way in which the sixties, themselves, have been periodized.[9] A concentration on the New Left and civil rights has led to a focus on the period between 1960 and 1968. Such an abbreviated timeline supports the familiar truism that 1968 constituted a watershed year after which activism on college campuses and in city streets ground to a halt. However, this periodization obscures the fact that some of the largest U.S. demonstrations of the era occurred after 1968, including the 1970 Mobilization against the War, which drew seven hundred thousand people to a protest in Washington.[10] After 1968, notes historian Terry Anderson, "social activism reached its zenith . . . as millions of baby boomers . . . took to the streets."[11] The Third World strikes in San Francisco, the Moratorium to End the War in Vietnam, the so-called blowouts in East Los Angeles all confirm the fact that grassroots protest exceeded the limits placed on it by chronological markers.

In considering the sixties' importance as a historical period in the United States, I find it useful to defy decade and national markers. I take my cue from Fredric Jameson's contention in "Periodizing the Sixties" that the sixties began in 1957 with the independence of Ghana and concluded somewhere between 1972 and 1974.[12] I would amend his periodization slightly, pushing the decade's beginning back to 1955 and the Montgomery Bus Boycotts and extending its end to 1973, with the completion of the U.S. troop withdrawal from Vietnam, the CIA-sponsored coup in Chile, and the beginning of the five-month OPEC oil embargo. My amendments, however, illustrate Jameson's larger point: namely, that one's historical interpretation of an era determines one's periodization, rather than the other way around. I have extended my discussion into the late 1970s to discuss the UCLA filmmakers because I see the Watts films as a eulogy for the era.

If the formation, consolidation, and decline of the U.S. Third World Left stretched across two decades, two significant factors sparked its emergence. The first factor was decolonization. During the 1960s alone, almost thirty countries in Africa, Asia, and Latin America declared formal independence after long, sometimes bloody struggles. In a relatively short period of time, the political and economic contours of Africa and much of the Caribbean transformed, as did those of their former colonizers, none more dramatically than those of France and Britain. For U.S. Third World Leftists, events in Ghana,

Cuba, China, Algeria, Kenya, and Vietnam appeared particularly resonant. As the first independent African nation, Ghana became a beacon for many black Americans including Nina Simone, Stokely Carmichael, and W. E. B. Du Bois, who died there at the age of ninety-five. In the cases of Kenya, Algeria, and Vietnam, armed struggle proved central to their national independence movements, making the Mau Mau in Kenya, the Vietcong in Vietnam, and the Front de Libération Nationale (FLN) in Algeria mythic heroes to U.S. Third World and other leftists. Though it occurred in the 1940s, Mao Tse-tung's revolution in China also wielded considerable influence in U.S. Third World Left circles. Maoism, Chairman Mao's unique interpretation of Marxism-Leninism, held particular sway among leftists of color, as did the ideas of Vladimir Lenin and Ernesto "Che" Guevara.[13]

Of seminal importance to U.S. Third World Leftists, however, was the 1959 Cuban Revolution. "The Cuban Revolution," Paul Lyons asserts, "provided young American dissidents with revolutionary inspiration, while the response of the United States imperialism to that revolution played a significant role in breaking down Cold War mythologies."[14] For a brief period before United States–Cuba relations soured, a generation of young men identified with the romantic figure cut by revolutionaries Fidel Castro and Che Guevara and dreamed of taking up arms in Cuba's name. North Americans as disparate as the theorists C. Wright Mills and Paul Sweezy, the Beats Allen Ginsberg and Lawrence Ferlinghetti, and the mainstream journalist Herbert Matthews were united in their support for Castro, whom they saw as a "rebel with a cause."[15] If young men gravitated toward Castro as the embodiment of the triumphant nonconformist, they also envied his ability to craft his own history and that of a nation. "Young, bearded, defiant," John Diggins argues, "Castro became the symbol of rebellious young Americans in search of a John Wayne of the Left, a guerrilla who could shoot his way to power and at the same time remain virtually uncorrupted by the temptations of power."[16] If that image (even more than its reality) proved compelling for a generation of white leftists "bred in at least modest comfort . . . looking uncomfortably into the world [they] inherit[ed]," it proved equally so for many of the critics, activists, and artists who were part of the U.S. Third World Left.[17]

In Cuba, many of these leftists found a way to connect domestic struggles for racial equality to Third World liberation movements. The Cuban Revolution served as a powerful emblem for writers and activists, as well as the masses of black and Latino/a peoples. When Castro appeared in New York City's Central Park in 1959, several thousand Latinos came to see him receive keys to the city. The following year, a triumphant Castro returned to the United States and stayed at Harlem's Theresa Hotel, causing a throng of African Americans, Cubans, Dominicans, Puerto Ricans, and other Spanish-speaking Caribbean peoples to surround the hotel.[18] For writers and intellectuals, Castro's Cuba held a special appeal because it offered a model for integrating cultural production and radical politics. Cuba's investment in film, literature, and art demonstrated the centrality of cultural production and its creators to the attainment of national autonomy.

The second primary factor in the U.S. Third World Left's formation was a time-space compression that helped bridge geographic, ideological, and experiential gaps between U.S. minorities and Third World majorities.[19] Print culture proved an absolutely essential technology of time-space compression by helping to disseminate Third World ideas across the globe. Max Elbaum notes that by the mid 1960s, inexpensive copies of Mao's *Little Red Book*, as well as the writings of Guevara, Castro, Marx, Engels, Lenin, and Stalin were "available in every large city and college town." Vigorous publishing and distribution industries in both Cuba and China assisted this circulation, primarily targeting the United States.[20] Mao's *Little Red Book* vied for shelf space with Frantz Fanon's *The Wretched of the Earth*, Amílcar Cabral's *Return to the Source*, Robert F. Williams's *Negros with Guns*, Ngugi wa Thiong'o's *Homecoming*, Georg Lukács's *History and Class Consciousness*, and Herbert Marcuse's *An Essay on Liberation*, to name only a select few. The worldwide convulsions caused by the decolonization movement not only transformed the geopolitics of the era but changed the ways in which people understood global arrangements of power and dominance. The greater circulation of radical literature from around the globe depended on print and media technologies, national infrastructures, and transnational networks that, in a very real sense, shrank the distance between national contexts and the people in them. Conversely, the circulation of this print media also accomplished time-space compression as people in Los Angeles, Oakland, and New York could read Fanon's account of the FLN or learn Mao's aphorisms.

Travel constituted another central technology of time-space compression. In the twentieth century generally, and particularly after World War II, people of color had greater opportunity and means to voluntarily travel. Migration from the South to the North, immigration from colonies to metropoles, and circulation to international conferences transformed local and global landscapes, simultaneously shortening and stretching ideological and demographic boundaries. These various modes of and reasons for movement and boundary crossing exposed individuals and groups to a wider array of experiences and influences than ever before as the greater circulation of bodies and texts from the Third World to the First World made its indelible mark on local political cultures.

Another technology of time-space compression was the use of image-making media and the wider circulation of images. The civil rights movement, for example, was profoundly impacted by television images of white brutality: watching dogs biting black flesh from the coziness of one's living room made an impression no verbal description ever could.[21] The development of smaller, lighter cameras enabled Cuban filmmakers to shoot and exhibit their films in rural areas, just as it allowed U.S. independent filmmakers to exercise great control over the visual representations of themselves and their communities. Not only did this technological shift mean greater autonomy but it also meant independent distribution and a larger circulation of alternative images.

If, as Michael Denning has argued, the very concept of culture shifted midcentury because of "the uneven development of a global culture out of the cultural and ideological struggles between the three worlds," then this project explores the meaning of those shifts within a twenty-year period.[22] Like Warren Susman in his essays on cultural history, I am interested in the "forms, patterns and symbols" that resulted from certain historical events, rather than the events themselves.[23] Taking its cue from Michael Denning's *The Cultural Front*, in which the author attends to both "the politics of allegiances and affiliations" and the "politics of form," *Soul Power* establishes personal links, party memberships, and political affiliations, as well as attending to the ways in which people, styles, themes, and particular forms unexpectedly converge. As Raymond Williams notes, "cultural formations" are always both "artistic forms and social locations."[24] Forms, in other words, are always social in the richest sense of the term, full of meanings that cannot be known in advance.

The fragmentary, partial, and provisional nature of the U.S. Third World Left as a cultural formation requires me to define a few terms. The emerging body of diaspora theory has profoundly influenced this project.[25] For one, I have found the well-established paradigm of "roots and routes" a necessary but not sufficient analytic frame for this project. All diasporas are characterized by the oscillation between movement and stasis, retention and innovation. Brent Edwards describes the culture of the African diaspora as one characterized by a series of *décalages*—a term he translates from the French as both spatial "gaps" and time "intervals."[26] Following this notion of disjunctures and conjunctures defining transnational identities, we might conceptualize the U.S. Third World Left as a cultural and political formation characterized by the simultaneous uncovering and suturing of multiple aporias that define the experience of diaspora. In diaspora, roots and routes are expanded and contracted, ruptured and rebuilt.

Attending to the ways in which local specificities are shaped by and shape global economic, political, and intellectual forces, Inderpal Grewal and Caren Kaplan emphasize the necessity of foregrounding gender analysis in transnational studies, though they also insist on the need to "compare multiple, overlapping, and discrete oppressions rather than to construct a theory of hegemonic oppression under a unified category of gender."[27] This holds no less true for transnational race and class analysis. The call for Third World solidarity appears on its face to depend on a unitary theory of hegemonic oppression, but analysis of its impacts and uses in individual contexts undercuts this impression. Nonetheless, I am interested in the ways in which a global analysis of race, class, gender, and national oppression, with all of its hegemonizing tendencies, helped U.S. Third World Leftists describe local concerns in more urgent, compelling, and specific terms. A complex analysis of their usage demands scholarship that is flexible, nonsectarian, and non-ideologically bound in any narrow sense.

That scholarly imperative extends to my conception of the term *radicalism*. If, as Edwards argues, "black internationalism" is a form of radicalism, then its counterhegemonic value must also be critically weighed.[28] Eager to avoid many of the sectarian debates that fractured the era and have hampered its subsequent analysis, my use of the term *radical* reflects a belief that the cultural and political forms under consideration had profound counterhegemonic effects in the social world. For one, they imagined a social world in which forms of Third World internationalism created new power blocs and dismantled imperial claims to domination. They addressed systemic inequities, entrenched forms of discrimination, and challenged the representational forms that undergirded them. One's understanding of radicalism cannot be frozen in time or space, but rather must reflect a keen assessment of how representational acts and political strategies signify in and impact specific material and ideological contexts. In other words, my project is not interested in outlining any narrow criteria for radicalism. Exercises in describing a group or person as "radical" or "reactionary" may satisfy a need to impose order on messy realities, but ultimately they run the risk of obscuring the larger historical significance of individuals and organizations.

This brings me to the most difficult and vexing problem posed by this project—the political and intellectual difficulties inherent in deploying the term *Third World* in a First World context. Strictly speaking, this book is not about the Third World. It is not an exploration of how literature, filmmaking, political movements, ideologies, agendas, and wars understood to "originate" in the Third World impacted people living there.[29] It is, however, about how the literature, films, political movements, ideologies, agendas, and wars understood to originate in the Third World impacted people of color living in the United States. Consequently, it both is and is not about the Third World. It is about how the Third World profoundly impacted the way activists, writers, thinkers, filmmakers, organizations, and individuals understood themselves, their identities, and their political, economic, social, and cultural conditions. This book considers how the discourses, ideologies, and aesthetic practices adapted from Third World anticolonialism helped leftists of color reconsider and rethink their own local context and their position within the U.S. nation-state. Simply put, it is about how the relationship between the global and local came to be understood and made new cultural and political possibilities available to a group I call U.S. Third World Leftists. That rethinking proved productive and enabling, but it also had its price, reducing the Third World in some instances to a set of icons, a set of projections and imaginaries.

Given this, *Soul Power* necessarily has its gaps and blind spots. This book does not address how people living in the Third World understood themselves in relation to people of color in the United States, though I hope it will spark such studies; it does not survey the diverse histories and outcomes of countries and communities in the Third World, though they inform them. As a result, I and U.S. Third World Leftists run the very real risk of replicating the homogenizing tendency of Western imperialism and colonialism. That tendency sees developing countries as a backward unity, bereft of regional, national, religious, ethnic, racial, and political differences, rather than entitites shaped by histories that share but cannot be collapsed into their common aspects. Indeed, the very use of the term *Third World* brings with it (among other things) a history shaped by racism, imperialism, colonialism, and a ruthless capital-accumulation drive that depends on a self/other logic ultimately about the self rather than the other. From that perspective, Third World knowledges, histories, logics—in short, Third World specificities—need not be incorporated into what "we" in the West already know about "them," no matter that the historical record tells us that the Third, Second, and First worlds are mutually constitutive. This book tries to avoid such a homogenizing tendency by focusing on how specific struggles, practices, and ideas were translated and put to ideological and political work in U.S. localities. Mindful of colonialism's heterogeneity, I take seriously Lawrence Grossberg's assessment that cultural studies often ends up "reducing it to discourses of representation and ignoring its material realities."[30]

Nonetheless, people, ideas, artifacts, and cultural practices travel, that is to say they are taken out of their context and put in others; they mutate, transform, and take on new meanings that cannot fully dislodge but do resituate earlier meanings and contexts. It is that process of mutation on which I focus because those meanings and contexts also form a part of colonialism's material reality.

I am interested in how Third World discourse and strategy was deployed by U.S. Third World Leftists and at what cost. For one, it was used to describe racially, ethnically, and nationally diverse organizations and coalitions. In some instances, it became a banner under which people of color—African Americans, Asian Americans, Latino/as—and whites worked together and formed coalitions. In other instances, it suggested parallels between U.S. citizens and Third World immigrants. The term was often used in imprecise and contradictory ways. For example, *Third World* was often conflated with *working class*, a conflation that cannot account for the existence of a relatively large Third World middle class and a powerful, if tiny, elite whose interests clash with those of the working class. It cannot account for the historical moment at which Antonio Gramsci's "class fractions" become part of the "historical bloc," helping to maintain the hegemony that dominates the working class, as well as members of more elite classes.[31] Put differently, it confuses nationalism with Marxism, a nation with a class. Yet as Fanon reminds us in "The Pitfalls of National Consciousness," the "national bourgeoisie" sees itself as the "transmission line between the nation and a capitalism, rampant though camouflaged, which today puts on the mask of neo-colonialism."[32] A less troubling reading of this conflation might be that those using the term deployed it in the name of a Fanonian "national consciousness," one that fuses with a "political and social consciousness." Certainly this reading is consistent with the Black Panther Party's denunciation of "pork chop nationalists" who fetishized and reified the rituals and artifacts of a particular (national) culture for their own conservative interests. Still another and perhaps more persuasive reading might understand the use of the term to denote an international consciousness and mode of solidarity—certainly this was also true of the Panthers who used it to claim common cause with Mao and Nkrumah, for instance. Rather than speaking and working in the name of a narrow nationalism, U.S. Third World Leftists claimed affiliation with an international anticolonial community, one in which the use of the term *Third World* offered a way of interpellating and signaling a community with certain shared interests: the commitment to eradicating colonialism, imperialism, racism, class exploitation, and, in some admittedly rare instances, homophobia and misogyny.

But this is where the metaphorical use of the term bumps up against its material limits. The specific forms of oppression faced by national minorities who are legal citizens differ considerably from that of colonized national subjects, though both were denied full citizenship rights. This raises the question, then, of what kinds of transpositions are needed in order to build a representational vocabulary that bridges—if only in the realm of the symbolic—the geographic and experiential gaps between Watts and Nairobi. The elision of specific historical conditions and their attendant consequences makes certain political and cultural possibilities available, but it also closes down others. It cannot fully address the situational privilege First World national minorities have vis-à-vis Third World national majorities; it cannot account in any real specificity for the difference that colonialism combined with enslavement makes; and it cannot account for the different forms of colonialism or the differences between colonialism and imperialism. In short, the collapsing of disparities implied in the use of the term fails to acknowledge variation, hierarchies, and gradations within the Third World itself, or between it and the First World. That is to say, the metaphor potentially works in favor of helping First World minorities demand greater rights and privileges, but the political danger exists that it might perform significant work on, rather than for, Third World majorities. It might be the case that conflating people in the First World with those in the Third World borrows the latter's legitimacy while maintaining the spotlight firmly on the First World. Clearly, there is no one simple way out of this dilemma, but there are perhaps cases where U.S. peoples of color borrow legitimacy without taking any away from Third World majorities, or where First World minorities fight to wrest concessions from the state on their own behalf and that of Third World majorities. It is these politically and culturally significant cases to which we must critically attend.

I am interested in scrutinizing the claiming of a Third World identity by First World minorities for the very forms of exchange that make what might be taken as a collapsing of differences possible. In other words, how do ideas, political strategies, styles, cultural practices, and rhetoric mutate and adapt across multiple diasporas? At the very center of this project lies the question of how the borrowing of a terminology, the claiming of a political lineage or a cultural community, has historically impacted U.S. struggles for social justice and radical transformation. Those who used the term *Third World* saw in it a way of signaling an intersectional focus on empire, race, class, and often gender that did not reduce their political struggle to any single issue. Nonetheless, its use marks a conceptual lacuna, one that reveals the inadequacy of the language readily available to U.S. Third World Leftists. It suggests a working through of intersectional approaches, a grappling with various categories of oppression that do not lend themselves to elegant rhetorical (or political) solutions. At the same time, U.S. Third World Leftists did not use the term solely in metaphoric terms, merely as a colorful backdrop against which to define themselves and their priorities. Instead, this group labored to fill in the aesthetic, cultural, and intellectual ground so that the term *Third World* captured their understanding of the global and local dynamics behind race, class, colonial, and imperial domination. In their writing, film, and activism, I decode this perspective, while acknowledging that it is one that walks the tightrope between analysis and idealization, between sophisticated differentiation and crude reduction, by conceding that it often gets the balance horribly wrong. Nonetheless, I am intrigued by the ways in which we might understand the term *Third World* as a placeholder, a contradictory edifice of ideas and concepts that expresses, as Louis Althusser wrote when defining ideology, an "imagined relation" to the material world as much as it expresses a "scientifically verifiable" reality.[33]

Over the course of this project I consider a range of figures and formations including LeRoi Jones, Angela Y. Davis, Robert F. Williams, Harold Cruse, Susan Robeson, Christine Choy, Charles Burnett, the L.A. Rebellion, Third World Newsreel, and the Young Lords Party. In doing so, I attend to the specific and unique ways each used Third World discourse and to what political and cultural ends. I have elected to incorporate specific theorists, texts, and ideas that emerged in the Third World as they arise narratively in the book, rather than separating them into a separate framing chapter. I discuss them in the context of how they were used and mobilized by groups of people or individuals for specific purposes, which is to say often in fragmentary and strategic ways. Constructing a totalizing discourse into which I fit each thinker would seem to me to violate the hybrid, provisional, and partial manner in which U.S. Third World Leftists adopted and adapted ideas and forms. To do so would rub against the grain of the project itself—though I hope that the reader will attain a concrete sense of common themes or preoccupations despite the fact that they are not reducible to a common or singular reading of any particular text or thinker.

Soul Power is organized into six chapters. "Havana Up in Harlem and Down in Monroe: Armed Revolt and the Making of a Cultural Revolution" uses a historic trip that LeRoi Jones, Harold Cruse, and Robert F. Williams made to Cuba in 1960 to investigate the impact of the Cuban Revolution on the U.S. Third World Left. Juxtaposing these three men's writings and activism, I trace the debates about culture, identity, and revolution that lie at the core of U.S. Third World Left discourse.

"Union Power, Soul Power: Class Struggle by Cultural Means" looks at the early history of 1199, the health care workers union. Examining the role that cultural production played in consolidating a racially and ethnically diverse workforce, I argue that the union's history offers us a new way of conceptualizing U.S. Third World radicalism and identity politics.

Chapter 3, "Newsreel: Rethinking the Filmmaking Arm of the New Left," considers Newsreel, an activist documentary film movement born out of the 1967 march on the Pentagon. Conventionally seen as a New Left organization, I show how Newsreel's exhibition and distribution practices, as well as two of their later films on the Young Lords Party and the squatters' rights organization Operation Move-In, preview many of the themes and concerns that found fuller articulation in its successor Third World Newsreel. Discussion of the two activist groups depicted affords me the opportunity to consider their representation in the films, as well as their forms of organization and activism.

Chapter 4, "Third World Newsreel Visualizes the Internal Colony," traces the influence of Third Cinema, particularly of Cuban film, on the collective's work. Led by women of color during this period, I analyze Third World Newsreel's 1972 film on the Attica prison rebellion, exploring the film's representation of the internal-colony thesis, which compares communities of color with Third World countries. I conclude this chapter by assessing the group's efforts to solidify national and transnational cultural networks and help construct a U.S. Third World Left imaginary.

Chapter 5, "Angela Y. Davis and U.S. Third World Left Theory and Praxis," considers the seminal figure of Angela Y. Davis. By looking at her autobiographical and theoretical work, I explore the impact of anticolonialism and Western Marxism on the production of Davis's intersectional approach to political analysis and activism. Finally, in "Shot in Watts: Film and State Violence in the 1970s," I conclude with the L.A. Rebellion, a group of African American and African filmmakers that produced narrative films on the community of Watts. In two of their films, Charles Burnett's *Killer of Sheep* and Haile Gerima's *Bush Mama* (1979), one can see the disintegration of U.S. Third World Left discourse under the pressure of an increasingly conservative political atmosphere.

This book offers by no means a definitive account of U.S. Third World Leftists. If it were definitive, it would have to include some of the following: Audre Lorde, the Black Panther Party, I Wor Kuen, the Brown Berets, Shirley Graham Du Bois, the Puerto Rican Revolutionary Workers Organization, the Third World Student Strikers, Toni Cade Bambara, the Revolutionary Action Movement, the Third World Women's Alliance, the League of Revolutionary Black Workers, the Communist Labor Party, and many others. Because this is a cultural history, I have included figures and organizations that produced literary texts, cultural works, forms of analysis, and activism that raised important issues for U.S. Third World Leftists more generally. Though many of the people I consider are African American, the reader should not take this as a sign that they dominated this cultural and political formation: Asian Americans, Puerto Ricans, Chicanos, and Native Americans were also central to this group. As I show in what follows, these leftists worked in multiracial, multiethnic, and even multinational groups. It is also true that womanism emerged as a central legacy of U.S. Third World Leftists. Analysis of the specific forms of discrimination facing women of color and a rigorous antihomophobic stance remain hallmarks of this rich feminist tradition. Though much of the activism undertaken by women of color in *Soul Power* articulates this point of view, none of the chapters explicitly theorize the specific forms of oppression facing women of color. This is due in part to the fact that numerous scholars have analyzed the textual contributions of Third World feminism, and also to the fact that archival sources on the organizations at the center of this movement were largely unavailable.

Consideration of U.S. Third World Leftists must be central to any analysis of postwar U.S. activism and theory. For just at the moment when the U.S. nation-state sought to assert its global hegemony, U.S. Third World Leftists challenged that hegemony by appealing to transnational modes of solidarity that resituated First World peoples and their struggles. What this body of counterhegemonic ideas and practices—with all of its contradictions—meant has long been overlooked. Mapping the roots and routes of ideas, cultural practices, and political strategies from Havana to Harlem, Vietnam to New York, London to Los Angeles, *Third World Power* offers important insights into how ideas and cultural products travel, mutate, and leave profound and often troubling historical traces.

1. Havana Up in Harlem
and Down in Monroe

Armed Revolt and the Making of

a Cultural Revolution

●

I came to realize that Fidel and Cuba's embrace of socialism was the key to understanding the protracted nature of the struggle, not only in the United States, but worldwide.
—LeRoi Jones, "Cuba Libre"

The fault of our artists and intellectuals lies in their original sin: they are not truly revolutionary.
—Ernesto "Che" Guevara, "Notes for the Study of Man and Socialism in Cuba"

In July of 1960, the armed self-defense advocate Robert F. Williams, the Beat poet LeRoi Jones (later Imamu Amiri Baraka), and the culture critic Harold Cruse went to Cuba to see Fidel Castro's revolution up close. With Castro barely in power a year, the three men witnessed firsthand the young rebel army transforming itself into the new Cuban government. Unlikely traveling companions, Cruse and Jones were part of a delegation organized by the journalist

Richard Gibson for the Fair Play for Cuba Committee (FPCC). The trip constituted an effort to enlist black left support for Castro and was originally to include several prominent African American artists and intellectuals such as Langston Hughes, James Baldwin, and Alice Childress.[1] Though they all declined, Jones, Cruse, and Williams eventually traveled with the writers Julian Mayfield, Sarah Wright, and John Henrik Clarke. The trip proved a pivotal one, shaping all three men's ideas about African American culture, community, and the likely prospects for black revolution.

In Cuba, the three men witnessed a new revolutionary experiment, one that sparked their own musings on the nature of African American oppression and the impact that Third World revolutions might have in crafting liberation strategies. The Cuban Revolution also propelled the three men to consider their role and that of other artists, intellectuals, and activists in confronting the forces of U.S. hegemony. In fact, their ideas shaped much of the U.S. Third World Left's political and cultural agenda. On their return from Havana, each wrote extensively about Cuba. In his autobiography, subsequent interviews, and in the 1960 essay "Cuba Libre," Jones reflected on Cuba's radicalizing influence on both his politics and art, charting his movement from disengaged Beat to black radical. For much of the 1960s, Williams filled many pages of his newsletter *The Crusader* and several speeches with praise for Cuba's racial equality. The experience transformed the somewhat older Cruse, helping to crystallize his fundamental disagreements with Jones and the rest of what he termed the "black New Left," a perspective articulated in his seminal work, *The Crisis of the Negro Intellectual*.[2]

Though at times the three found themselves at ideological odds, they also shared significant intellectual and political ground, working together in various organizations such as the FPCC. During the 1960s, Cruse and Jones not only became allies but their intellectual and political work drastically shifted the cultural terrain on which black leftists maneuvered during the decade, fueling their search for a black national culture and the belief in cultural revolution as the key to political liberation. Indeed, their activities were often intertwined. For instance, when Williams was forced into exile, Jones rallied with other writers and activists to secure his right to return to the United States. Cruse and Jones worked together in Harlem, crafting revolutionary theory and practice for the U.S. context. Guided by the Cuban example, all three men likened the relationship of African Americans to colonized peoples, debated the viability of armed struggle, and asserted culture's centrality in forging oppositional identities.

This chapter looks at each man's investment in Cuba as a way of thinking through Cuba's meaning for U.S. Third World Leftists more generally. I reflect

on the various ways that Williams, Jones, and Cruse understood the relationship between culture and politics, the First and the Third Worlds, armed
struggle and revolution. In short, I consider how the Cuban Revolution served
as one critical foundation for the formation of a U.S. Third World Left.

The Traffic to Cuba

Williams, Cruse, and Jones were by no means the only or even the first visitors
to Castro's Cuba. In December 1959, former heavyweight champ Joe Louis and
baseball stars Jackie Robinson and Roy Campanella traveled there, eating New
Year's dinner with Castro himself, one year to the day after Fulgencio Batista's
flight from Cuba.[3] That spring, Williams also went to Cuba, a trip he later
described as "a pilgrimage to the shrine of hope," offering "three weeks of the
only true freedom I have ever known."[4] On his recommendation, other members of the Armed Deacons for Self-Defense began visiting Cuba in 1961.[5] Later
in the decade, other black radicals, especially those influenced by Williams,
visited Cuba, including members of RAM, the Revolutionary Action Movement, an underground Black Nationalist organization, and the Detroit militants who subsequently formed the Dodge Revolutionary Union Movement
(DRUM) and later the League of Revolutionary Black Workers.[6] In 1967, the
Black Panther Stokely Carmichael briefly visited, and in 1972, the recently
released political prisoner Angela Y. Davis drew huge crowds when she came to
the island to thank Cubans for spearheading the international effort on her
behalf.[7] If U.S. Third World Leftists found Cuba an important site for political
education, it was also a critical outpost for those seeking political asylum.
Castro's government found itself flooded by immigration requests as U.S.
government repression against black radicals intensified. In 1961, Williams
went into exile there briefly, as did Black Panthers Eldridge Cleaver in 1968,
Huey Newton in 1974, and Assata Shakur in 1979.

What accounts for the black radical interest in and traffic to Cuba during
the sixties and seventies? First, the Cuban Revolution actively courted black
Americans from the very moment of its victory, emphasizing the new government's vanquishing of racial segregation. Waging a media war of position,
Cuba's tourism board via a U.S. public relations firm associated with Joe Louis
promoted Cuba as a land "free of racism" in advertisements flooding black
magazines and newspapers in the early 1960s.[8] This reputation was built on the
fact that Castro outlawed segregation and discrimination just two months after
the guerrillas assumed power, an extremely important act for black Americans
in light of an accelerating civil rights movement.[9] The Cuban government also

established an open-door policy for black visitors through the FPCC and other organizations. In the early 1960s, these visits were intended to publicize the Cuban Revolution's successes, but later on, they also helped train and educate black revolutionaries. When visitors returned from Havana, many praised the regime's treatment of Afro-Cubans, explicitly contrasting it with the U.S. government's support of racial segregation. Such publicity fueled a propaganda war between Havana and Washington on the race question, a war that had significant Cold War consequences and reached fever pitch during the fall of 1960, when Castro came to New York to address the United Nations.[10]

Havana Comes to Harlem

Fidel Castro's visit instantly created a crisis that exposed the omnipresence of racism in the United States. Accusing the hotel staff of discrimination, the Cuban delegation left the elite Shelbourne Hotel, where UN delegates habitually stayed, for Harlem's Hotel Theresa, a move that deliberately flouted the era's segregationist conventions. That single act cemented Castro's status as folk hero, the champion of oppressed black and U.S. Latino/a peoples. Exhilarated by his presence, thousands of African Americans, Cubans, Dominicans, Puerto Ricans, and other Spanish-speaking Caribbean peoples surrounded the hotel throughout Castro's stay.[11] During one such rally, a Harlemite held a sign that read, "U.S. Jim Crows Fidel just like U.S. Jim Crows Us Negroes."[12] On one level, this slogan mistakenly equates the Cuban delegation's onetime experience to the daily discrimination faced by African Americans. However, read within the larger context of Castro's opposition to Western imperialism generally and U.S. imperialism specifically, the slogan and the mass demonstrations suggest that protestors saw the new Cuban government as an ally of subjugated peoples in the United States and worldwide. No matter that Castro and the white Cuban middle class had defeated the mulatto Fulgencio Batista, racial "origin" was not the overriding means of identification with the Cuban Revolution. Rather, identification with Cuba marked and facilitated a growing internationalism among peoples of color in the United States, which Brenda Gayle Plummer argues challenged African Americans' binary understandings of race: "Cultural differences in racial perception, coupled with Cuba's oppositional stance, challenged taken-for-granted categories of domination."[13] As decolonization accelerated in the Third World, Harlem's black and U.S. Latino/a population increasingly understood that U.S. racial domination was intimately interconnected to global relations of economic, cultural, and, above all, territorial domination. For many during this period, mobilization against racism entailed mobilization against Western imperialism, a task that required the forging of alliances between and among U.S. national minorities and emerging postcolonial nation-states.[14]

The political impact of Castro's Harlem sojourn made this point abundantly clear. In declaring Harlem his base of operation, Castro insisted on world recognition of black Americans and their plight. Not only did the renegade leader meet with Nikita Khrushchev there but he also received Egyptian president Gamal Abdel Nasser and Indian prime minister Jawaharlal Nehru. Harlem, thus, temporarily became a center of Third World negotiation and anticolonial solidarity. *The Amsterdam News* best captured the significance of these meetings, writing, "Castro's move to the Theresa and Khrushchev's decision to visit him gave the Negroes of Harlem one of the biggest 'lifts' they have had in their cold racial war with the white man."[15] A ghetto routinely neglected by local and national officials alike had suddenly become a politically significant site. Symbolically, Castro had moved the UN uptown, centering the Third World—both Cuba and Harlem—at the very heart of the First World.

This point was further reinforced at the UN General Assembly when Castro linked the cause of African Americans to Third World struggles for national liberation. Calling for "African American nationhood," Plummer writes, Castro stressed "the need for economic self-sufficiency, and independence from white cultural and political domination" (135). These comments were not the express reason for Castro's UN address, but they proved far from tangential. They should be understood as part and parcel of his assertion that Cuba constituted a leading force in the global anticolonial movement. Castro's reference to black Americans elevated them to the level of a revolutionary force akin to Cuban guerrillas and African freedom fighters.

This assertion was strengthened by the main text of Castro's speech, which unveiled Cuba's policy toward Africa. Reminding UN delegates of the history of slavery and colonization shared by Cuba and Africa, Castro declared common cause with "the remaining colonial peoples in Africa and on the side of the Negroes against whom discrimination is exercised in the Union of South Africa" (qtd. on 142). The Cuban leader then pledged his nation's assistance to decolonizing Africa, a policy already well underway by 1960. In fact, Cuba had already lent political and military support to many of the twenty-one new nation-states formed in Africa between 1955 and 1961.[16] Thorough in its denunciations—Castro spoke for over four hours—the speech was characteristic of the Cuban's rhetoric during the 1960s. Such speeches secured Cuba's status as an active foe of Western imperialism in both its European and North American guises, resonating with an emerging group of U.S. Third World

Leftists who saw Castro as an ally in the fight against racism at home and imperialism abroad.

A New Revolutionary Experiment

Castro's uniting of antiracist rhetoric and anticolonial politics in his appeals to black Americans enabled them and other U.S. Third World Leftists to connect domestic struggles for racial equality to Third World liberation movements. If the Cuban Revolution was immensely popular among African Americans and other U.S. national minorities in the early 1960s, it stood as an especially powerful emblem for writers and intellectuals who gravitated toward it because of the centrality of cultural production to Castro's victory and subsequent rule of the nation. During the seven-year war, Castro's July Twenty-sixth Movement astutely used various cultural technologies to enlist support for its cause. Professionals in advertising agencies created campaigns for products such as Tornillo Soap that covertly challenged the legitimacy of the Batista regime by alluding to its corruption.[17] Cubans also heard news of the guerrillas' progress over Radio Rebelde, a station the rebel army had set up in the Sierra Maestra to contravene Batista's censorship codes. Even after Batista's defeat, Castro continued to use the mass media ingeniously. Television became an important means for publicizing the new government's programs and policies as the charismatic Castro often delivered speeches via the medium, a technique that visually underscored his enormous popularity by presenting the spectacle of huge and enthusiastic crowds.

The rebel army's savvy use of popular culture and media technologies is perhaps best exemplified through its development of Cuba's filmmaking tradition. Just two weeks after the rebel army's victory, Che Guevara created a military cultural school devoted to documentary filmmaking. Members of the underground filmmaking scene including Santiago Álvarez, Julio García Espinosa, and Tomás Guttiérez Alea soon joined the fledgling organization, and two months later, the Instituto Cubano de Arte y Industria Cinematográficos (ICAIC) was born. As Michael Chanan has noted, the decree establishing the ICAIC "declared cinema an art, an instrument for the creation of individual and collective consciousness" (20). The institute was initially sustained by government grants, but its acquisition of a record factory and an advertising studio soon established it as an independent cultural force to be reckoned with. In a relatively short period of time, the ICAIC was able to transform film from what Chanan has described as an "industrialized art and agent of cultural imperialism" into a truly populist art form and a "powerful new mode of perception" (81). In its first two years of production, the ICAIC completed several films, including Tomás Guttiérrez Alea and Julio García Espinosa's *Esta tierra nuestra* (1959), Néstor Almendros's *Ritmo de Cuba* (1960), and Espinosa's *La vivienda* (1959). Most of these early works were didactic treatises on the government's reforms, patriotic records of Castro's decisive battles, or films celebrating Cuba's indigenous cultural traditions and excoriating Western imperialism. The ICAIC's mobile cinema units traveled to isolated rural communities, showing these films in schools and village squares where they reached a largely illiterate populace and sparked vigorous public debate.

Under ICAIC, Chanan asserts, "Cuban cinema had become a powerful force in the collective memory of the Cuban people, popular historian of the Revolution second only to Fidel, and thus a force for social cohesion" (3). In addition to garnering widespread public appeal, Cuban films also earned extensive acclaim. In 1960, Cuban films won five international awards including ones at the Leipzig Film Festival and at the Festival of the Peoples in Florence (99). They proved compelling not only for their subject matter—the progress of a young revolution—but also for their innovative forms. Cuban filmmakers crafted a new documentary style by combining cartoon sequences, montages, newsreel footage, and reenactments. Through its film journal *Cine Cubano*, the ICAIC even began publishing a series of theoretical texts on the relationship between cinema, aesthetics, and revolution. The theoretical and cinematic language of Third Cinema slowly began to emerge, and although the roots of Third Cinema originated in the Documentary Film School in Argentina and in Brazilian Cinema Novo, Cuba was the "first territory in Latin America where it was possible to envisage a new film culture, both popular and critical, on a national scale."[18] Much more than a film production company, the ICAIC became a meeting ground for artists and intellectuals of all stripes.

This was also the case for Casa de Las Américas, the country's newly formed literary and cultural center. Casa's mission was to promote Cuban culture and pan-American exchange, and it did so in a variety of ways. It supported a literary generation and facilitated intellectual debate through the publication of prominent Latin American and Caribbean writers in its influential journal, *Revista Casa*, edited for much of its history by the renowned writer Roberto Fernández Retamar. The organization also sponsored frequent conferences, literary competitions, and cultural festivals, attracting artists, writers, and intellectuals to Cuba from all over Latin America. In its early days, Casa even hosted luminaries from the West, including the filmmaker Maya Deren and the writers Simone de Beauvoir and Jean-Paul Sartre. It is no coincidence that Casa was the primary Cuban sponsor for the FPCC trip in which Jones and Cruse participated. In addition to these activities, Casa also founded an adult education school devoted to disseminating and popularizing Cuban culture among its largely illiterate and rural populace. Challenged by Retamar's famously ironic question, "Does a Latin American culture exist?" Casa's activities helped spark a pan-American revolution in the arts and catapulted Havana onto the world cultural stage.[19]

Together the ICAIC and Casa did more than just disprove the widespread misconception that political revolution necessarily stymies cultural innovation; they redefined the relationship between North and South America. Instead of serving as a dumping ground for Hollywood's B-movies, Cuban filmmakers created internationally acclaimed films of local relevance. Instead of voraciously devouring Western literature, Latin American intellectuals focused on the works of Alfonso Reyes, José Carlos Mariátegui, and Carlos Fuentes. Though it would be a mistake to ignore the contributions of other Latin American countries, Cuba's principal role in this cultural revolution is indisputable. "From the beginning," Fredric Jameson writes, "the Cuban experience affirmed itself as an original one, as a new revolutionary model."[20] Jameson is referring here to the rebel army's successful deployment of Guevara's so-called foco theory of guerrilla warfare about which much has been written, but his words might just as easily refer to Cuba's artful blending of political and cultural concerns. It was this dual focus that rendered the Cuban example such an impressive and important one for U.S. Third World Leftists. With its insistence on both political and cultural autonomy and its commitment to Third World solidarity, Cuba inspired a generation of political and cultural activists.

From Black Rebel to Black Radical via Havana

Of all the participants in the Cuba trip, it was de facto leader Robert Williams who most powerfully connected with the Cuban Revolution. His actions prior to July 1960 garnered him a great deal of acclaim in Cuba and defined him quite literally as a physical and ideological bridge between the Cuban Revolution and the black revolt brewing in the United States. Described in Jones's "Cuba Libre" as a "strange tall man in a straw hat and feathery beard," Williams was the only member of the delegation whom the Cuban dignitaries not only recognized but revered.[21] In fact, Williams had visited Cuba prior to the Fair Play delegation's trip, touring the country with Richard Gibson and granting numerous photo ops and interviews during which he denounced the U.S. government for its refusal to support Castro and protect black civil rights. Impressed with the revolution's commitment to racial equality, Williams wrote a series of favorable articles in *The Crusader*. "There was a real drive to bring social justice to all the Cubans, including the black ones," he reflected.[22] He even hoisted a Cuban flag in his backyard, a move that earned him the ire of one Jesse Helms, the city's fire chief and father of the infamous U.S. senator.[23]

In fact, Williams was one of the first figures to directly link the Cuban Revolution to the struggle for black liberation in the United States. In late 1959, he argued, "The American white man claims to be upset by the latest developments in Cuba. Only the fool can expect to exploit and oppress peoples over an extended period of time without provoking animosity and resistance." "Castro and all other colored rulers," Williams asserted, "will do well to shun bigoted Uncle Sam's smiling false face and his racial claims of bondage."[24] His reference to Castro as a "colored ruler" underscores the anti-imperialist politics Williams assumes Cuba and black America share. *Colored* here emerges as not so much a genotypic marker as a badge of political affiliation; Castro, scion of Cuba's white-skinned bourgeoisie, is here redefined as a colored ruler because he has thwarted U.S. imperial ambitions in his country, and has declared common cause with the decolonizing nations of Africa and the Caribbean. This linguistic and ideological slippage between racial and colonial oppression would become one of the salient features of the U.S. Third World Left.

Like the Cubans, LeRoi Jones was clearly impressed with Williams. The black radical "figured very largely in the trip, certainly in my impressions of it," Jones wrote in "Cuba Libre."[25] Williams's appeal for the poet lay in his public promotion of armed self-defense, his insistence on uniting cultural and political agitation, and his consistently international perspective. It was these qualities that made Williams what Robin D. G. Kelley and Betsy Esch have called a "hero to the new wave of internationalists whose importance almost rivaled that of Malcolm X."[26] Williams first came to international prominence because of his willingness to use arms to defend against North Carolina's Ku Klux Klan. He had first encountered leftist politics in a Detroit auto factory in the early 1940s. Communists and socialists he met on the factory floor impressed Williams when they spoke of the "idea of equality, the denial of the power of one man to exploit another man, of equal justice . . . that men shouldn't be allowed to hog the money, or some men to hog the property, that it should be collectively owned." In the definitive biography of Williams, Timothy Tyson argues that these sentiments resonated with Williams because of his Christian background rather than his familiarity with communism. Speeches about ending class exploitation impressed on him the fact that there were "people who wanted to abolish racism."[27]

Enlisting in the army at the very end of World War II, Williams gained weapons training and, as he put it in *Negroes with Guns*, "a taste of discrimination."[28] He felt it acutely in everyday slights, in the segregated quarters, in the training films depicting Japanese soldiers in blackface. Put in the brig numerous times for insubordination, Williams remarked, "Prison did not scare me because black men are born in prison." The one bright spot during his eighteen months of service was a writing course in which he wrote about "life in the South, and lynching."[29] Unbelievably, Williams enlisted again in 1954, only this time in the Marine Corps, where having developed a passion for writing he dreamed of becoming a military journalist. However, he soon discovered that there "were no black marines in information services" and was made a supply sergeant instead. He wrote protest letters to President Eisenhower and others, but when these went unanswered, his righteous anger led to an undesirable discharge after sixteen months (72).

Like many black men of his generation, Williams found that military service during and immediately after World War II dramatized the gap between U.S. democratic rhetoric and the reality of U.S. white supremacy. While in the armed services, black men gained valuable training and a hard-won confidence that made them determined to reap the benefits of U.S. democracy. When asked by a reporter whether his support for Cuba meant he would be willing to give up his U.S. citizenship, Williams responded by saying, "As an Afro-American, I [have] never had American citizenship" (qtd. on 224). His astute response illustrates the immense alienation Williams felt as a U.S. citizen and soldier. In the war's aftermath, as the Cold War heated up and Western colonialism found itself under siege, men like Williams sensed an opportunity to press their case for equal rights on an international stage. If, stealing John Dittmer's unforgettable phrase, black veterans were quite literally the "shock troops of the modern civil rights movement," their pivotal role has for too long remained marginalized in narratives of the period.[30]

Williams's critical consciousness and newfound military skills were eventually put to good use fighting the Ku Klux Klan and other white extremists in his hometown of Monroe, North Carolina. Recruiting other veterans as well as "laborers, farmers, domestic workers, [and] the unemployed," Williams created an NAACP branch that was working class in orientation and militant in attitude, though there were some middle-class members, arguably including Williams himself.[31] When the Klan moved to halt the chapter's push toward integration, Williams organized sixty residents into an armed self-defense league that patrolled Monroe's black community and protected sit-in strikers. While the use of force in the name of peaceful demonstrations might sound paradoxical, Williams argued that this show of force lessened the incidence of actual violence: "Our sit-ins proved that self-defense and non-violence could be successfully combined."[32] In the Monroe context of white lawlessness, where even police officers marched in Klan parades, Williams contended, "Non-violence is a very potent weapon when the opponent is civilized but non-violence is no repellent for a sadist."[33]

Not only did Williams's militia activities pose a fundamental challenge to the county's white power structure but they also threatened much of the NAACP's central leadership. When national newspapers quoted Williams's declaration that he would "meet violence with violence, lynching with lynching," Roy Wilkins suspended him as president of the Monroe NAACP.[34] Even though the suspension was eventually shortened to six months, the incident led Williams to forge alliances with Trotskyist groups including the Socialist Workers Party and the Workers World Party. These alliances should not be understood as an indication of Williams's conversion to socialism; rather, he was a political pragmatist, seeking support wherever he could find it, particularly as the national NAACP leadership distanced itself from the militant brand of integration represented by Williams.[35]

The national debate that ensued over Williams's lynching remark had another important consequence, the founding of *The Crusader*. Convinced that one of the "most immediate needs was better communication within the race," Williams began the newsletter in June 1959 to "inform both Negroes and whites of Afro-American liberation struggles taking place in the United States." It was Williams's hope that the newsletter would unite the various liberation struggles around the United States: "The real Afro-American struggle was merely a disjointed network of pockets of resistance and the shameful thing about it was that Negroes were relying upon the white man's inaccurate reports as their sources of information about these isolated struggles."[36] Initially, *The Crusader* publicized the integration movement in Monroe, urging its readers to appeal to the U.S. government and the Justice Department to establish law and order.[37] However, Williams continued publishing the newsletter even after his exile to Cuba and later China, enabling black radicals in the United States to read about the Third World's most important revolutionary leaders. In addition to Che Guevara and Fidel Castro, *The Crusader* introduced "young Black militants to Mao Zedong and promoted the vision of Black world revolution articulated by critics such as Harold Cruse."[38] What began as an attempt to publicize national events, soon evolved into an effort to forge an international network of radicals: low-tech cultural production, a single-authored, mimeographed newsletter, effectively disseminated news censored by the mainstream media.

In 1961, Williams went into temporary exile in Cuba. During this time, he combined this low-tech newsletter with a weekly radio broadcast he called *Radio Free Dixie*. Airing Friday nights at 11:00 P.M., with a signal strength of 50,000 watts, Williams's program could be heard in California and Washington, but Southern blacks were still his primary constituency. Armed with the latest jazz and blues records sent by LeRoi Jones and Richard Gibson from the United States, the show also featured the Black Nationalist editorials of the Reverend Albert B. Cleage Jr. and gave Williams and his wife Mabel a platform from which they could espouse their belief in equality, armed self-defense, and international solidarity. A cultural innovator, Williams fused avant-garde music and his uncompromising demands for racial equality into a unique amalgam. In a fascinating discussion of the program, Tyson highlights Williams's use of free jazz, which he seems to have wielded with the sensibility of a modern-day DJ, cutting and mixing Ornette Coleman and Max Roach with news of white racial violence and voter registration campaigns. So popular was *Radio Free Dixie* that for a time "bootleg copies circulated in Watts and Harlem."[39] Even after Williams fell out of favor with Castro and was forced to decamp to China, he continued to produce *The Crusader* from exile until he returned to the United States in 1969.

Despite the fact that he eventually denounced the Castro regime for betraying its professions of racial democracy, Williams's internationalism, bound up in his belief in cultural production's centrality to political change and his investment in armed self-defense, was in some sense fundamentally shaped by his exposure to the Cuban Revolution. While on his second Cuba trip, Williams edited a special issue titled "Los Negros en USA" for *Lunes de Revolución*, a weekly literary journal. With contributions from LeRoi Jones, Langston Hughes, James Baldwin, Harold Cruse, and Alice Childress, Williams drew parallels between the U.S. civil rights struggle and the Cuban Revolution: "Pictures of white mobs in Little Rock carrying signs proclaiming 'Race Mixing is Communism,' for example, were captioned 'Los racistas son tambien anti-communistas' (the racists are also anticommunists)."[40] After his return from the Fair Play–sponsored trip, Williams received a letter from the national office of the NAACP cautioning him to avoid being "just another pawn in the present unfortunate feud between Cuba and our country." In response, Williams blasted the NAACP: "Cuba's aversion for America's inhumanity to man is not an interference in a 'native American problem.' It is common knowledge that the master race of the 'free world' is out to export North American manufactured racism. Racism in the USA is as much a world problem as was Nazism." Eschewing the labels *communist* and *Black Nationalist*, Williams professed himself an "Internationalist." He declared, "Wherever there is oppression in the world today, it is the concern of the entire race. My cause is the same as the Asians against the imperialist. It is the same as the African against the white savage. It is the same as Cuba against the white supremacist imperialist."[41]

Part of the reason Williams was so taken with Cuba had to do with the fact that it had committed to eradicating racism, even if it ultimately fell short. In the early 1960s, it seemed as if Cuba had succeeded where the United States had failed. Williams met with Castro when he visited New York and was eventually recruited by the FPCC to do a speaking tour where he spread the word about Cuba and the organizing happening in Monroe. The final date of that tour saw Williams speaking at a Harlem street rally; that would help ignite the UN demonstration against Patrice Lumumba's assassination. Gathered to protest the CIA-backed murder of Congo's prime minister, LeRoi Jones, Carlos Moore, Abby Lincoln, and Max Roach were among the protestors who fought police when they tried to disrupt the demonstration. The UN protest would become a seminal event in the "anticolonial black nationalist revival."[42]

Just a month before Williams was forced into exile in 1961, he presented a ten-point program to Monroe's city council. The program demanded an end to employment discrimination, the construction of a swimming pool for blacks, desegregation of city schools, and the increased involvement of black people in city government. Arguing that "equal employment rights were the most important of the ten points," Williams asked that black people be given the right to work in the county's new factories, most of which had moved to North Carolina to avoid labor unions and fair wages.[43] Though such changes would have ameliorated the desperate situation in which most Monroe blacks lived, Williams's program was one of reform, not revolution. However, after 1964, Williams moved even further to the left, advocating urban guerrilla warfare based on the principles of Guevara's foco theory of revolution: "This year, 1964 is going to be a violent one . . . America is a house on fire—freedom now!—or let it burn, let it burn."[44] Dispensing explicit instructions for how to make "the black power bomb," Williams had moved a long way from his days of advocating self-defense for the purposes of integration. If his methods changed, however, his belief in Third World solidarity and the defensive use of arms to overthrow racial oppression never wavered and would become a significant legacy for a younger generation of black radicals.

From Beat to Black Radical via Havana

LeRoi Jones dedicated an entire essay to the 1960 Fair Play for Cuba trip; the lengthy "Cuba Libre" charts Jones's transformation from Beat poet to black radical. In it, we are presented with a compelling conversion narrative, one that contrasts Jones's New York life of letters with the revolutionary dynamism of Cuba. Examining the way in which Jones frames that conversion narrative allows us to see why he invested his own cultural production with the same revolutionary potential evident in the new Cuban government. After Cuba, Jones is no longer a politically disengaged Beat poet—if he ever was—he is a nascent black revolutionary. Originally published in the Beat journal *Evergreen Review*, "Cuba Libre," also serves as the opening salvo in his 1966 collection of essays *Home: Social Essays*, an angry assessment of U.S. cultural and political life. If it seems striking that an essay ostensibly concerned with Cuba should frame Jones's analysis of North American life, Jones argues that traveling to Cuba brought him metaphorically home; on his return to the United States, Jones became, in his own words, the "Prodigal," growing "even blacker" under the Cuban sun.[45] Through his identification with the series of (mostly) white Cuban men he encounters on the trip, Jones forges a new black identity and a critique of the United States that depends on his newly acquired anticolonial perspective.

This profound shift in Jones's worldview has been primarily expressed through his persistent search for an African American national culture that would serve as the foundation for the revolutionary black American state. In 1965, Jones wrote, "a culturally aware black politics would use all the symbols of the culture, all the keys and images out of the black past, out of the black present, to gather the people to it."[46] As we have seen, this sentiment was perfectly in keeping with Castro's investment in revolutionary culture. By demonstrating the integral role culture plays in political change and offering literal embodiments of the male revolutionary hero, the Cuba trip enabled Jones, the Beat writer, to become Jones, the U.S. Third World Leftist.

In order to understand fully the significance of his transformation, it is necessary to situate Jones within his artistic and political milieu. Everett LeRoy Jones was born in Newark, New Jersey, on 7 October 1934, the child of Anna Lois Russ, herself the daughter of small business owners who cut short her education at Tuskegee when she found herself pregnant by Coyt LeRoy Jones, a high school graduate and itinerant laborer.[47] Jones grew up in Newark's West Ward, a section of the city populated by Eastern European immigrants and black Southern migrants. After leaving Howard University in 1954, Jones enlisted in the U.S. Air Force, where he spent the following three years. Soon he found himself permanently stationed in the U.S. colony of Puerto Rico, where he established the Ramey Air Force Base Salon, a gathering of white and black photographers, painters, and intellectuals. Although Jones has never acknowledged this, it seems to have been a familiar paradox of colonialism—a member of a dominated group enforcing U.S. imperialism abroad—that fueled his intense alienation. Decidedly ill suited for his role as colonial enforcer, Jones retreated into the world of arts and letters, self-consciously fashioning himself as an intellectual. Interestingly, his intellectual inquiries failed to encompass his own local context; Jones's memoir does not even mention San Juan's economic or political subordination, let alone describe it as a colonized city. Puerto Rico, like Cuba later on, served as a catalyst for his personal revelations. In the one instance in which Jones recalls having ventured into San Juan alone, he sits on a bench, weeping over the *New Yorker*, thinking that "he could never write like that writer . . . something in me so *out*, so unconnected with what this writer was and what that magazine was."[48] This passage reads as a measure of his own cultural alienation—"something in me so *out*"—but narratively, it also serves to explain why the *Atlantic Monthly*, the *New Yorker*, *Harper's*, and the *Saturday Review* all rejected his poetry.

Falsely accused of being a communist, Jones was dishonorably discharged from the Air Force in 1957. Soon after, he took up residence in Greenwich Village, quickly becoming a fixture in New York bohemian life along with fellow writers Diana DiPrima, Allen Ginsberg, Robert Creeley, and Frank O'Hara. With his wife, Hettie Jones, he began editing the literary magazine *Yugen* in 1958, which was devoted to the publication of Beat and Black Mountain poets. By July of 1959, Jones had made quite a name for himself in New York literary circles when suddenly the chance to visit Cuba presented itself:

> A man called me on a Saturday afternoon some months ago and asked me if I wanted to go to Cuba with some other Negroes, some of whom were also writers . . . . I hesitated for a minute, asking the man just why would we (what seemed to me to be just "a bunch of Negroes") be going. For what purpose? He said, "Oh, I thought that since you were a poet you might like to know what's *really* going on down there." Being an American poet, I suppose, I thought my function was simply to talk about everything as if I knew . . . it had never entered my mind that I might really like to find out for once what was actually happening someplace else in the world.[49]

So begins the section of "Cuba Libre" entitled "What I Brought to the Revolution." With this introduction, Jones begins to position himself and his Beat circle as skeptical libertines, arrogant enough to write about the world without experiencing its complexity firsthand. Implicit within such an assessment is the assumption that artists—at least Beat writers—consciously remain removed from contemporary politics, content to obtain their information from sources that will not say what's "really going on" in Cuba or anywhere else. This initial section proves critical to understanding Jones's narrative strategy throughout the essay; he consistently and quite self-consciously juxtaposes his cynical, arrogant persona with the people and sites he encounters in Cuba. Assuming the role of Castro devotee somewhat reluctantly, Jones presents a compelling conversion narrative, one designed to draw in his fellow skeptics.

From his vantage point as a self-described American poet, Jones steels himself against the Castro propaganda machine he imagines awaiting him in Havana. "From the very outset of the trip I was determined not be 'taken,'" he writes; "I had cautioned myself against any undue romantic persuasion and had vowed to set myself up as a completely 'objective' observer" (16). Vowing to use his knowledge of Spanish to "tramp around" and discover the real Cuba, Jones is wary of falling prey to revolutionary idealism (16). "Cuba Libre's" narrative energy is driven by this tension between Jones's posture as an objective Western journalist and his increasing fascination with Castro's revolution. However, the poet's struggle to remain at a distance from the revolutionary fervor everywhere apparent is a half-hearted one. His objective pose is merely a wily literary ruse, for he was no more neutral than Castro himself. Before Jones ever set foot in Cuba, he had already declared himself in political sympathy with Castro. In 1959, Jones broke with *Yugen's* editorial staff over his desire to publish a special issue on the Cuban Revolution. Shortly thereafter, he independently compiled and published a pro-Castro anthology entitled *Fidel Castro*.

Even before his trip, Castro and Guevara were already mythic characters for Jones. He recalls in his autobiography, "This was 1959 . . . and for the last few months I had been fascinated by the headlines from Cuba. I had been raised on Errol Flynn's *Robin Hood* and the endless hero-actors fighting against injustice and leading the people to victory over the tyrants. The Cuban thing seemed a case of classic Hollywood proportions."[50] Jones's description conjures up images of the prototypical North American hero, the white, male gunslinger defending the weak against the threat of savage Indians, rebel slaves, or men in black hats. Jones, however, inverts expectations, casting Castro and Guevara as the white-hatted heroes of Hollywood fantasy. Van Gosse has written that Fidel Castro's appearance on the U.S. scene struck a chord with middle-class young men inundated with postwar Hollywood images of the "bad boy" struggling to escape middle-class conformity and suburban uniformity. This rebel figure linked bohemian, youth, and popular cultures in a heady amalgam popularized in such 1950s films as Nicholas Ray's *Rebel without a Cause* (1955), László Benedek's *The Wild One* (1953), and Richard Brooks's *Blackboard Jungle* (1955). In Castro, Jones's generation saw a "flamboyant individualism and pure gallantry," and thus the Cuban Revolution became for them "a convenient shorthand for both individual commitment and sheer exotica, an emblem of a nascent bohemia."[51] Bound up in Jones's casting of the Cuban guerrillas as Hollywood gunslingers is at once his desire to emulate them and his recognition that he figures as a poor imitation. Nonetheless, Jones's identification with Castro enabled him to transform himself into a spokesperson for black American cultural and political revolution. In Castro's Cuba, Jones would begin to equate the mythic guerrilla fighter with the black American artist, equating the black ghetto and the Third World colony. His admiration for guerrilla fighters impressed on him the need to utilize his literary skills in the service of revolutionary change. In one sense, then, Jones's affinity for Castro and Cuba was simply an extension of his Beat life in New York. The middle-class Castro and his ragtag guerrilla army triumphing over the military might of the dictator Batista appeared a properly anarchic image. In another way, however, it clearly seemed to Jones the complete antithesis of that experience, enabling him to transform himself into a spokesperson for black cultural and political revolution.

This profound shift in Jones's worldview facilitated an already nascent identification with both a real and an imagined Third World characterized by two elements: Jones's reliance on an ultramasculinist ideology and his belief in the central importance of culture in precipitating revolution. As Kimberly Benston succinctly asserts, "the underlying topic of most Jones pieces is seen to be . . . manhood."[52] While it is easy to read this preoccupation with masculinity as simply an eccentricity—one of Jones's psychic ticks—Gosse has attributed Castro's widespread appeal to the concurrent "collapse and reinvention of traditional boyhood and manhood."[53] Castro's appearance at a moment during which codes of masculinity were undergoing an intense transformation might not only explain his attractiveness to Jones but also the author's persistent intertwining of masculine identity and violent rebellion. The literal blueprint for the Jones hero might very well be Castro, as well as Robert Williams, whom he met for the first time on the Cuba trip.

All told, "Cuba Libre" is as much an exercise in self-criticism as it is a mechanism for skewering the West. It is as much an exposé of Jones's own radical pretensions as it is an indictment of U.S. society. For all his rebellious trappings, in Cuba, Jones discovers himself to be just another "ugly American":

"The rebels among us have become merely people like myself who grow beards and will not participate in politics."[54] He reflects, "The young intellectual living in the United States inhabits an ugly void. He cannot use what is around him, neither can he revolt against it. Revolt against whom? Revolution in this country of 'due processes of law' would be literally impossible" (39–40). Jones critiques the United States for rendering revolution a seeming impossibility and for instilling in him a false dichotomy between politics and art.

In Cuba, government officials and the ordinary citizens he meets challenge these views. When a visiting, Mexican student calls him a "Yanqui Imperialist," Jones can only sputter, "I'm a poet . . . what can I do? I write, that's all, I'm not even interested in politics" (43). At this moment, a gaping aporia exists between who Jones imagines himself to be—the rebellious artist—and who people in the Third World perceive him to be—a middle-class American poet smug in his derision of politics and political art. In his memoir, Jones later recalled, "In the face of what I'd already seen in Cuba and in the faces of these young Latino activists and intellectuals, already politicized, for whom Cuba was the first payoff of a world they had already envisioned and were already working for, I was the oddball, the world weary traveler/tourist from the U.S. of A."[55]

The ideological, as well as the literary, problem for Jones, then, was how to forge a convincing and concrete affiliation between himself and the Third World rebels in his midst. The engine for this ideological magic trick is gender. It is on the basis of gender identification and not a little projection that Jones is able to effect his own transformation into a radical black man. We see this in the contrast between the passive objectivity of the Western critic and the heroic men of the Cuban Revolution. In his tours of the National Agrarian Reform Institute, the Ministry of Education, and la Casa de las Américas, Jones encounters a series of highly idealistic and extremely articulate young men. In many instances, soldiers in full dress gear flank them: "huge pearl-handled .45s" and "faultlessly polished boots."[56] These bureaucrats are Jones's Hollywood cowboys come to Cuban life. They are the rebels who appear to have beaten the West at its own game, escaping their manifest destiny.

The most impressive of these figures is Dr. Jiménez, the man responsible for implementing the government's land-reform program. As Jones describes him, Jiménez becomes the ideal politician, an amalgam of the intellectual, the soldier, and the sex symbol. A university professor, he is characterized by Jones as "beautiful, a tall, scholarly-looking man with black hair and a full black beard" (33). His attire only heightens his sexual magnetism: "The uniform of the rebel army with the black and red shoulder insignia of a captain" (33). In his belt, he carries a square-handled .45; in his hand, he proffers a copy of his latest book. In short, he is the guerrilla intellectual par excellence, the incarnation of Jones's latent literary and political fantasies.

Jiménez, however, is only the narrative understudy for Fidel Castro, who makes his appearance in the final third of "Cuba Libre." Near the end of the North Americans' visit, signs appear announcing a celebration in the Sierra Maestra at which Castro is scheduled to speak. In order to get there, Jones and the others must survive an odyssey across the island, a journey it seems the entire population is undertaking as if in one body. In crowded trains and packed trucks, through winding mountain passes and muddy rivers, Jones is repeatedly struck by the "unbelievable joy and excitement" evident despite the physical hardships of the trip (44). He sees "people moving, being moved . . . something I had never seen before, exploding all around me" (44). The experience culminates with the black poet's meeting with the "tall young Cuban" whose appearance has whipped the country into a frenzy (52). Jones, never one to be awed into silence, answers Castro's inquiries as to his occupation by firing questions at the young leader: "I told him I was a New York poet, he seemed extremely amused and asked me what the government thought about my trip. I shrugged my shoulders and asked him what did he intend to do with this revolution." His answer less than inspiring, Castro counters, "That *is* a poet's question and the only poet's answer I can give you is that I will do what I think is right, what I think the people want" (52). When asked what role communism plays in his government, Castro fires back, "I am certainly not an anti-communist. The United States likes anti-communists, especially so close to their mainland. . . . I consider myself a humanist. A radical humanist" (53). With that, Jones is swept aside as the crowd clamors for autographs, kisses, and photos, treating Castro more like a rock star than a head of state.

Castro's claim to be both a radical and a humanist surely appealed to a bohemian poet struggling to marry his creative impulses with his nagging sense of social responsibility. Despite the relentless sun and then the pouring rain in the Sierra Maestra, the crowd is transfixed by Castro's speech. For two and a half hours, he condemns Eisenhower, Nixon, and the Monroe Doctrine, his words punctuated by the Cubans' chants of "Fidel, Fidel . . ." and "Venceremos, Venceremos!!!" Though he does not describe his own reaction to Castro's speech, Jones notes that the "crowd went out of its head roaring for almost forty-five minutes." However, the celebration does not end there. Instead, it becomes what the poet describes as "a strange mixture of pop culture and mainstream highbrow *haute culture*." A choral group and ballet dancers share the stage with calypso dancers and West Indian performers who enact a carnival scene complete with "floats, huge papier-mâché figures, drummers, and masks" (55–56). Once again, the intertwining of culture and politics is represented as the primary characteristic of Castro's revolution.

"Cuba Libre" concludes with Jones's reactions to the trip, which has irrevocably altered him. "The idea of 'a revolution' had been foreign to me," Jones reflects; "it was one of those inconceivably 'romantic' and/or hopeless ideas that we Norteamericanos have been taught since public school to hold up to the cold light of 'reason.' That reason being whatever repugnant lie our usurious 'ruling class' had paid their journalists to disseminate" (61). As if to punctuate his point, Jones's first stop on U.S. soil is a Miami newsstand, where he glances at a paper. The headline reads, "Cuban Celebration Rained Out" (62). Struck by the contrast between his own experience and the mainstream U.S. media's description of the event, the growing disjuncture between his own beliefs and those of the hegemonic cultural apparatus, Jones found himself increasingly alienated from the intellectual, literary, and cultural milieu in which he had formerly thrived. Revolution or, at the very least, radical political action no longer seemed an impossible fantasy; rather, it became a concrete goal toward which to strive.

Fidel Castro and the band of guerrilla intellectuals Jones had met provided a model for incorporating thought and action, cultural work, and political revolution: "The dynamic of the revolution had touched me. Talking to Fidel or Juan Almeida, the black commander of the revolution, or to the young minister of agrarian reform, Nuñez Jiménez, or Jaime or Rubi or Pablo Fernández. Seeing youth not just turning on and dropping out, not *just* hiply cynical or cynically hip, but using their strength and energy to *change* the real world—that was too much."[57] Jones's encounter with the Cuban Revolution quite literally transformed the course of the young poet's life. In his memoir, he recalled, "When I returned I was shaken more deeply than even I realized. The arguments I'd had with my old poet comrades increased and intensified. It was not enough just to write, to feel, to think, one must act! One *could* act."[58] And act he did. Almost immediately, Jones broke with the Beat circle, serving as the New York chapter chairman of the Fair Play for Cuba Committee and working with the Monroe Defense Committee to raise money for Robert Williams's legal defense.

A Critic Takes Cultural Stock

If Jones and Williams found in Cuba a model for intellection and action, the culture critic Harold Cruse found in Havana something altogether different. Cruse garnered many lessons from that 1960 trip, but most of them were far from favorable. Although a critical supporter of the Cuban Revolution, Cruse maintained his characteristic skepticism about the relevance of Cuba for the United States. In his two major works, Cruse scorned Williams, Jones, and the black New Left for their easy identification with the Third World in general and Cuba in particular. This tension around the substance and motivation for Third World identification runs throughout U.S. Third World Leftist discourse and cultural production. For Cruse, this identification resulted in an unreasonable faith in violence as the key to liberation and an insufficient understanding of the cultural differences between black America and the Third World. In *The Crisis of the Negro Intellectual* and *Rebellion or Revolution?* Cruse thoroughly critiqued Jones's and Williams's position, setting forth his own theory for successful black American revolution. Ironically, this theory proposed a series of cultural prescriptions heavily indebted to the Cuban example.

Cruse was already a veteran writer and cultural activist by the time he visited Cuba, once describing himself as a "critical Kamikaze fighter on the cultural front."[59] A teenager during the Great Depression, Cruse came of age during the early 1940s and enlisted in the army at age twenty-one. As in the case of Williams and Jones, his military experience seems to have precipitated his move to the political Left. Cruse later wrote, "The Army was the beginning of my real education about the reality of being black" (169). Stationed in the southern United States and Western Europe, Cruse eventually found himself fighting in North Africa as part of the Allied troops landing in Oran, Algeria, later a critical front in the Third World battle for liberation. Once there, Cruse confronted the fact that while he felt himself completely alienated from the Arab inhabitants of Algeria, they assumed a certain kinship existed between themselves and black Americans. Two Algerian women once stopped him and his friends to inquire whether they "were also Arab." In response to their assertion that they were actually Americans, the women "insisted that [they] were Arab *but didn't know it because [their] fathers had been stolen from Africa many years ago*" (170).

Whether exaggerated or not, Cruse clearly wished to use this anecdote to illustrate the fraught mechanics of ideological interpellation. In this exchange, the Arab women pretend to misrecognize Cruse and his comrades and then unsuccessfully hail them as fellow colonial subjects who have access to a shared historical memory. The black soldiers, however, assert their identity as American citizens, thereby affirming their inadvertent role as the enforcers of Algeria's colonial status. This affiliation, however, is far from a secure one. While Cruse defines himself as an American soldier, he cannot help noticing the similarities between the discrimination black Americans faced from white Americans and that faced by Arabs at the hands of the French. "The resultant race conflict," Cruse reflected, "among American blacks, American whites, French and Arabs was very enlightening and had a curious amalgam of racial and political overtones." While in North Africa, Cruse became aware of Algeria's underground resistance movement but was never able to "get inside the intimate areas of native response to the colonial situation." It was this prolonged exposure to the dynamics of colonialism that made of Cruse "a changed political animal," pushing him to the radical Left on his return to the United States (171–72).

Cruse had always been an insatiable reader, consuming everything from pulp fiction to the work of Langston Hughes, Henrik Ibsen, and Karl Marx. During his Harlem childhood, he also frequented venues like the Lincoln, the Harlem Opera House, and the Apollo where he saw black vaudeville performers including Cab Calloway, Bill "Bojangles" Robinson, and Ethel Waters. It was this wealth of literary knowledge and cultural experience on which Cruse drew after his discharge from the army. Cruse began his career writing black film and theater reviews for the Communist Party's *Daily Worker*. By the early 1950s, however, he had broken with the Communist Party, wary of the communists' propensity for collapsing race into class struggle and critical of the *Daily Worker* for its scant reporting on Africa and its inability to comprehend black cultural production if it deviated from socialist realism. Cruse later explained, "I could not function in the Left as a creative writer and critic with my own convictions concerning the 'black experience' " (8). However, he was equally dissatisfied with what he perceived as the black Left's reformist demands for integration.

Cruse's failure to fit comfortably inside either paradigm led him to seek an international community of radicals. In the late 1950s, he was briefly involved with the U.S. branch of the Society of African Culture (SAC), an anticolonial organization that published the influential journal *Présence Africaine*. However, he soon left SAC, colliding with its members over the Senegalese poet Léopold Sédar Senghor's concept of Negritude. Cruse's belief that the "African concept of Negritude really applies to the American Negro" reflected his growing preoccupation with black cultural aesthetics and its potentially radical anticolonial significance. Faulting "culturally white-oriented Negroes" for not seriously engaging the relationship between black American and African culture, Cruse found himself at odds with yet another left contingent (118). For much of the 1960s, Cruse retreated to his Chelsea apartment, working as a freelance writer for the *Liberator* and *Studies on the Left* and working on *The Crisis of the Negro Intellectual*. It was during this period that the opportunity to visit Cuba presented itself.

Jones described Cruse in "Cuba Libre" as a "1930s type Negro 'essayist' who turned out to be marvelously un-lied to."[60] Though Cruse traveled to Cuba an avowed Castro supporter, his customary skepticism led him to view the new regime with a curious but cautious eye. "I was admittedly pro-Castro," he later recalled in his typically irascible fashion, "but there were too many Communists around acting imperious and important. Moreover there was the obvious and unclarified position of the Cuban Negro to consider."[61] While Jones seems to assume that the government's claims to have eradicated race prejudice are accurate, Cruse notes that the "revolutionary intelligentsia of the Castro regime" are all white Cubans (356). Nor is he altogether certain that Castro has the support of black Cubans: "It did not escape me that Havana was full of Cubans (white and black) who were visibly skeptical about the new regime and did not hesitate to say so. How the Cuban Negroes would fare it was too early to predict in 1960."[62] This was quite a prescient observation. It would take most black Americans some time before they began to question Cuba's claim to have eradicated racial discrimination. In its attempts to promote cultural assimilation, Castro's government had not only repressed efforts to establish antiracist movements in Cuba but it had also sought to extinguish Afro-Cuban religious and cultural practices.[63] Cruse's refusal to confuse antiracist rhetoric with social and material reality was undoubtedly prompted by his own struggles with communists in the United States.

Despite his misgivings about the new government's race policies, Cruse nonetheless realized the significance of the revolution for African Americans. Noting that the "effects of the Cuban Revolution, the appeal of Fidel Castro (who was not even black) penetrated even into the Negro ghettos of the United States," Cruse observed that Cuba had stirred up the latent nationalism in black Americans.[64] For him, this was not entirely undesirable: "Is it not just as valid for Negro nationalists to want to separate from American whites as it is for Cuban nationalists to want to separate economically and politically from the United States?" (95). However, he thought the comparison between African Americans and Third World peoples incorrect; the United States were not a Third World country, nor were African Americans a colonized people, although they did exist in what he saw as a "colonial" relation to white Americans. The "American Negro does not exist within an underdeveloped country with a large population of tribes and impoverished peasantry," Cruse asserted, therefore the black movement must "cast its praxis into a theoretic frame" that was neither Marxist nor integrationist (186).

After his return from Cuba, Cruse reflected on the growing sense of solidarity African Americans felt with Third World revolutions. In two 1962 essays, entitled "The New Wave of Negro Nationalism" and "Revolutionary Nationalism and the Afro-American," Cruse remarked on the potential of such an affiliation. Keenly aware of the economic and cultural differences between formal colonies and black communities in the United States, Cruse nonetheless realized that U.S. Black Nationalism "has its roots in the same kind of soil as the nationalism of the African colonies proper" (71). This nationalism was "a unique fusion of conflicting ideas," at once disdainful of mainstream civil rights groups yet viewing the Freedom Riders as revolutionaries (71). Distrustful of both Marxists and white liberals, nationalist groups were attempting to reconcile the separatist and integrationist tendencies in black political history. Lacking any coherent philosophy, a fact underscored by their confusion about what exactly constituted a revolutionary act, these nationalists were "finding themselves pulled by political gravity toward the far left" (73). In doing so, Cruse warned "Afro-Americanism" not to "become absorbed in the dead-end politics of American Marxism" (73). Instead, it should "plant itself solidly in both the Negro community and in the international politics of African liberation, else it can have no real meaning beyond a certain social or racial symbolism" (72). Although in his view politically confused and lacking any coherent philosophy, Cruse still saw the Black Nationalist movement as significant, if only because it sounded a loud denunciation to white America. The existence of Malcolm X, Robert Williams, Kwame Nkrumah, and Fidel Castro shouted: "We don't think your civilization is worth the effort of any black man to try to integrate into" (73). Such a belief at least potentially formed the foundation for a revolutionary politics.

In "Revolutionary Nationalism and the Afro-American" Cruse again emphasizes the elements that rendered African Americans a force analogous to Third World revolutionaries. Crippled by disease, poverty, urban slums, psychological impairment, and what he termed "cultural starvation," African Americans are "domestic colonials" who "experience the tyranny imposed upon the lives of those who inhabit underdeveloped countries" (76). Their unique position within U.S. society—in but not of America—explained why the Cuban Revolution resonates so strongly with black Americans. "The revolutionary initiative," Cruse wrote, "has passed to the colonial world, and in the United States is passing to the Negro, while Western Marxists theorize, temporize and debate" (75). Cruse's distrust of Western Marxists reverberated with U.S. Third World Leftists who were often unwilling to fully commit to a Western Marxist tradition to which many Third World revolutions were indebted.

Cruse's brand of Third World identification depended on him distancing himself from the Old Left's brand of Marxism. Castigating Marxists for what he saw as their lukewarm support for Cuba, Ghana, and revolutionary nationalism generally, Cruse postulated that this response stemmed from the fact that former colonies were liberating themselves despite the stalled progress of socialist revolution in the West. In doing so, these nations had not only violated a basic principle of orthodox Marxism, namely that revolution will spread to the Third World only after its triumph in the West, but had also challenged the racial hierarchy implicit in this theory. "From underdevelopment itself," Cruse asserts, "have come the indigenous schools of theory and practice for achieving independence" (75). Instead of following the West's lead, Third World nations are in the revolutionary vanguard, forging new theories of social change that Cruse calls "Maoism or Castroism" (75). Though Cruse does not describe in any detail what those philosophies entail, we know from "Negro Nationalism's New Wave" that both Maoism and Castroism describe the process of defining theory through revolutionary praxis. Besides, Cruse is not actually interested in the specifics of that theory, despite the presence of *revolutionary nationalism* in the essay's title.

His real target is Western Marxists and so he sets out the reasons black radicals should avoid alliances with U.S. communists. Just as Western Marxism has no adequate theory for Third World revolution, Cruse maintains, it has little to offer African Americans in their quest for liberation. Disputing one of the basic premises of U.S. Marxism by arguing that black Americans do not even form part of the working class, Cruse maintains: "Negroes have never been equal to whites of any class in economic, social, cultural or political status, and very few whites of any class have ever regarded them as such. The Negro is not really an integral part of the American nation beyond the convenient formal recognition that he lives within the borders of the United States." As a "domestic colonial," then, the African American cannot be seen as a legitimate part of the U.S. proletariat (78). In other words, Cruse redefines the structural position of black Americans, arguing that they are far more similar to other colonized peoples than they are to white workers. Given the choice between class-based and nation-based radicalism, he seems to choose the latter. However, Cruse's conclusion appears highly problematic, particularly because he never actually deals with the logistical issues attendant to such a position: What land will African Americans occupy? How will formal secession occur? What resources will form the economic base for this new nation's economy? Cruse skirts these issues by merely saying, "[The Negro's] national boundaries are the color of his skin, his racial characteristics and the social conditions within his subcultural world" (78). Clearly, then, the black nation depends on phenotypic, sociohistorical, and especially cultural qualities rather than actual geographic borders.

Having established that U.S. Marxists have fundamentally misapprehended the structural position of black Americans, Cruse goes on to discuss the rising phenomena of Black Nationalism. Although he admits that the latest upsurge in this philosophy is a "reflection of the revolutionary nationalism that is changing the world," Cruse traces the roots of this Black Nationalism back to the debates between Booker T. Washington and W. E. B. Du Bois, and then to Marcus Garvey's Back to Africa movement (77). It is this history that Western Marxists have failed to understand, ignoring what Cruse describes as the "bourgeois origins" of Black Nationalism (78). Communists in 1928 promulgated the Black Belt–nation thesis, which declared black Southerners members of a separate nation but did not adequately account for black Northerners. As a result of this ideological shift, U.S. communists crudely lumped the various strands of black activism under the umbrella term of the "Negro liberation movement" (78). This oversimplification in turn has led Marxists to focus little attention on class stratification within the black community and—and this is critical for Cruse— to miss the schism between the NAACP and pro-integration forces and Black Muslims and other separatist wings within the black community.

For Cruse, this distinction between integrationists and separatists represents "two main wings of racial ideology," roughly delineating a widening gap between the black middle and working classes (89). Ultimately, then, Cruse's foregrounding of this conflict is not so much the supplanting of class analysis— as one might think given the ire he directs at Marxists—as it is the extension of that analysis to black Americans. "What we must ask," Cruse writes, "is why these classes are not all striving in the same directions and with the same degrees of intensity. Why are some lagging behind the integration movement, and still others in conflict with it"? (89). He continues, "To attempt to answer these questions we must consider why the interests of the Negro bourgeoisie have become separated from those of the Negro working class" (90). Integration, an essentially bourgeois movement, could not guarantee economic and political equality for all African Americans and consequently did not have their unanimous support, and so Cruse predicted that the conflict between middle-class integrationists and working-class separatists would fracture the black movement into contentious wings.

It is striking that in 1962 Cruse was able to so clearly forecast the ideological conflict that would define black political life in the 1960s. After all, it was not until 1966 that Stokely Carmichael would coin the phrase *black power*, thereby ushering in an era of militant separatism. However, Cruse astutely read the cultural and political landscape, predicting in 1962 that African Americans would "make a lot of noise in militant demonstrations, cultivate beards and sport their Negroid hair in various degrees of la mode au naturel, and tend to be cultish with African- and Arab-style dress" (73). Beyond such acerbic fashion forecasts, Cruse also identified the emergence of a political and cultural formation, a group neither wholly integrationist nor separatist, equally concerned with U.S. civil rights and Third World human rights, radical politics and cultural innovation. In other words, a formation of which he was a distinguished example—though he might not have seen it that way. Cruse called this group the "third trend—young social rebels who [were] followers of Williams' Monroe Movement." Uncharacteristically optimistic about such a group's potential, Cruse was still loath to consider it radical, arguing that its members did "not have revolutionary objectives" (80). In making this assessment, Cruse drew on his critiques of both Robert Williams and LeRoi Jones with whom he became closely acquainted during the trip to Cuba. Convinced that both Williams and Jones were foolishly enamored with the armed guerrilla figure so compellingly incarnated in the Cuban Revolution, Cruse based much of his subsequent analysis of this "third trend" on his impressions of Williams and Jones.

In his 1967 work *The Crisis of the Negro Intellectual*, Cruse offered his assessment of Williams, Jones, and the third trend of which they formed an integral part. Though primarily concerned with the contemporary state of black culture and politics, *Crisis* leveled a sweeping indictment of the black political and cultural movements in which Cruse had participated during the previous fifty years. Beginning in the 1920s, Cruse considers several cultural figures including Paul Robeson, Richard Wright, and Lorraine Hansberry whose association with white leftists, according to Cruse, prevented them from founding independent cultural institutions, thus precipitating the current crisis in black intellectual life. The inheritors of this crisis are, of course, the young members of Cruse's third trend. In a chapter entitled, "The Intellectuals and Force and Violence," Cruse begins his lengthy discussion of this formation with reflections on the Cuba trip. It should come as no surprise that Cruse's consideration of these U.S. Third World Leftists arcs back to Cuba, for Cruse uses the Fair Play for Cuba trip as a springboard for his critique of Williams, Jones, and other members of his generation.

Born between the two World Wars, Jones and his cohort, Cruse argues, have been indelibly marked by Third World nationalist movements. He writes, "This generation grew up in time to be deeply impressed by the emergence of the African states, the Cuban Revolution, Malcolm X and Robert Williams himself. They were witnessing a revolutionary age of the liberation of oppressed peoples. Thus, they were led to connect their American situation with those foreign revolutionary situations."[65] In the late 1950s, a heightened awareness of the relationship between Western imperialism and domestic racism prompted this interwar generation to enter a "new era of black ideological transformation" (356). This emergent group of U.S. Third World Leftists began reorienting themselves toward the Third World and away from mainstream civil rights concerns. For Cruse, the Cuban Revolution stands as a pivotal moment in that transformation, and Jones emerges as the quintessential exemplar of this third trend. Describing Jones as the "most interesting personality" in the delegation, Cruse confesses: "During the whole time I watched him closely and wondered what he was thinking. I wondered how this Beat poet would relate politically, artistically, ideologically to this foreign revolution" (356). Soon enough Cruse has his answer. "The great transformation in LeRoi Jones," he concludes, "was brought on by the Cuban Revolution" (356). Faced with the Castroites' euphoria and elevated to the "rank of visiting dignitaries," the delegation (save Cruse, of course) quickly falls victim to "revolutionary indoctrination, this ideological enchantment" that has made them enthusiastic, if naive, supporters of Cuba and Williams's Monroe activities (357). Though Cruse is hardly unsympathetic to their position, he remains the prodding gadfly, wondering if Cuba's ideology and tactics can be transplanted to the U.S. context: "What did it all mean and how did it relate to the Negro in America?" (357). Ultimately, the transplant would prove more difficult than U.S. Third World Leftists anticipated; the third trend, Cruse writes, "did not know, of course, that to attempt to apply foreign ideologies to the United States was more easily imagined than accomplished" (354). It is one thing to imagine Black Berets storming the White House, quite another to successfully execute such a maneuver. Nonetheless, Cruse asserts, young intellectuals like Jones have become ardent believers in "force and violence," romanticizing guerrillas and armed warfare, without seriously considering whether such an approach can succeed in the United States.

Cruse believes that it cannot, offering as proof positive the example of Robert Williams. Williams's Monroe movement could easily have been construed as the Third World chickens coming home to roost. With his calls for armed self-defense and his defiance of the civil rights mainstream, Williams became a cause célèbre for both white leftists and young members of the U.S.

Third World Left: "[Williams's] armed self-defense tactic became the ideological spark that ignited a hidden potential within the newly emerging phase of the Negro movement" (352). Cruse argues, however, that the Monroe model is a limited one, inapplicable to the realities of northern racism. More important, while the ex-marine may be a rebel, he is not a revolutionary; Williams's tactics may be controversial, but his objective remains identical to the NAACP's, integration. "The adoption of armed self-defense," Cruse maintains, "does not, in itself, transform what was a protest movement into a revolutionary movement" (353). To some extent, Cruse is correct. Williams's theory as described in *Negroes with Guns* remains essentially a defensive one: the use of armed defense is appropriate if *and only if* the rule of law breaks down and white Americans refuse the Negro's demands for integration. Despite his clashes with the civil rights establishment, Williams failed to see the ideological incompatibility underlying those disagreements. Williams, in Cruse's view, failed to recognize that "the NAACP was an inhospitable place for himself and his views . . . [or] he might have seen that his aims required a larger scope of organization, broader planning and a longer-range strategical vision" (353–54).

This criticism has a grain of truth in it, but it is ultimately unfair. As we have already seen, Williams did attempt to spark a black liberation movement. His publication of *The Crusader* and his alliances with Castro and Mao Tse-tung constituted attempts to not only disseminate Third World revolutionary theory but also to secure an independent power base for black Americans. That he did not succeed in engendering a revolution has more to do with the power of the U.S. police apparatus than it does with his inability to produce a new revolutionary theory. This, of course, is exactly Cruse's point. The position of black Americans as oppressed citizens of an industrialized superpower necessitates a unique set of strategies. Blind adherence to "force and violence" amounts to little more than a comforting, if irrational, faith. It may not lead to desegregation, let alone more radical societal change. On the contrary, it may instead provoke—as it did in Williams's case—greater state repression. "One can objectively shoot a Klansman 'defensively' or 'offensively,'" Cruse writes, "but to succeed in shooting one's way into voting rights, jobs and 'desegregated' public facilities calls for much deeper thought than certain revolutionaries seem to imagine" (354). Williams and his followers, in other words, are wielding a blunt tool to perform delicate surgery on the U.S. social and economic body.

However trenchant his attack, Cruse does not take Williams as his principle target. Instead, he scorns Jones and the group of northern intellectuals who have supported the use of arms without thoroughly analyzing their own relationship to such a movement. "What did Negro creative intellectuals have to do with Williams and armed self-defense? Was the Negro writers' role simply to support Robert Williams verbally or organizationally?" (358), Cruse demands. These questions require a reevaluation of the function of intellectuals, an analysis of how their skills can best serve the movement for black liberation. Their unwillingness (or inability) to perform such a reevaluation has led, in large part, to the current crisis in black intellectual life. Cruse also, of course, ignores Williams's own maneuvers on the cultural front, seeing them as merely support activities, overstating the case somewhat. Rather than being devotees of Williams, Cruse argues, third trend intellectuals should create their own political movements based on a thorough assessment of U.S. society. Cruse scoffs at the example of Jones and his peers: "Here was a spectacle of a group of young men, some of them college graduates, who dared to aspire to black revolution without even a glimmer of knowledge about the economics of social change" (366). Refusing to use their time and training to study the political, economic, and cultural aspects of U.S. society, black intellectuals were planning "protest actions," a fact that only revealed the depth of their "technical unpreparedness" (367). Ultimately Cruse describes a diverse group of intellectuals in incredibly broad and condescending strokes in order to establish the foundation for his own theory of black revolution.

Cruse's theory opposes the civil rights goal of integration. A comprehensive evaluation of the United States, according to Cruse, would reveal that segregation and employment discrimination are merely instances of a larger economic pattern, the "*ill-effects* of capitalist society" (367). In order to root them out, black revolutionary movements must oppose capitalist society itself. "Without an anti-capitalistic ideology," Cruse forecasts, "the Negro movement is doomed to be rolled back into submission" (367). That Cruse insists the black movement be anticapitalist appears striking, particularly given his critique of Western Marxists for viewing the civil rights movement as yet another front in the class struggle. This position, however, follows from his awareness that the state has an enormous capacity to incorporate resistance movements. Cruse astutely notes, "One of the keys to understanding the effectiveness of any tactic, idea, strategy or trend in the Negro movement, is to determine how well the American system can absorb it and, thus, negate its force . . . the American social system quite easily absorbs all foreign, and even native, radical doctrines and neutralizes them" (361). An anticapitalist ideology opposes the entire foundation on which the American system rests, thereby lessening, if not wholly eliminating, its chances of being incorporated. Opposition to capitalism, however, does not ensure a successful revolution; the black movement needs lasting institutions: "The *main* front tactics must always be organizational and institutional . . . revolutions occur only in those societies that resist new institutionalisms" (360). In essence, Cruse has an institutional theory of social change. Institutions, in his view, fundamentally structure societies and thus constitute the primary mode through which societies can be challenged and eventually overturned.

Calling for what he terms a "cultural revolution" that would transform U.S. institutions makes Cruse in the 1960s what historian Komozi Woodard has described as "the foremost theorist of cultural nationalism."[66] Black intellectuals must build autonomous cultural institutions otherwise the black movement would remain a domestic rebellion rather than a revolution with international impact. Like Jones, Cruse submitted that the United States had reached a cultural dead-end: "Western civilization is intellectually, spiritually and morally bankrupt."[67] Given this cultural crisis, America's racial strife is merely an "internal reflection of this contemporary world-wide problem of readjustment between ex-colonial masters and ex-colonial subjects" (105). As domestic colonials, African Americans could only spark revolution if they generated new ideas, infusing American culture with a new set of ideologies. In the case of the Cuban Revolution, the process had been reversed. Praxis, "force and violence" had forged a revolutionary theory, and by following it, the black movement thus far had "been a movement without any unique ideas" (109). In actuality, Cruse's assessment of Cuba was reductionist and inaccurate; he emphasized the country's belief in armed revolution without paying sufficient attention to the Castro support of cultural institutions before and after his victory.

Paradoxically, Cruse's prescription for a black cultural revolution involves many of the measures already undertaken in Cuba. He proposes that black radicals revolutionize "the administration, the organization, the functioning, and the social purpose of the entire American apparatus of cultural communication and [place] it under public ownership" (112). As we have seen, this was one of the earliest goals of the Castro regime. Cruse asserts that creating such a cultural revolution is the most effective means to swiftly and radically democratize U.S. society. Newly revitalized cultural institutions would finally reflect the multiracial reality of the society, toppling the "all-white ideal" currently propagated by "the American cultural arts" (113). These new cultural representations would in turn produce and reflect new more democratic and racially inclusive ideologies. Postulating an "organic connection in American capitalism between race, culture and economics," Cruse sees an attack on the culture industries as a simultaneous attack on the white supremacist cultural logic that sustains U.S. capitalism (113).

Cruse's theory of cultural revolution may have been inspired by a different understanding of Third World revolution than that of Jones, but both Jones and Cruse saw national liberation as inextricably linked to cultural regeneration, an idea indebted to the Cuban example. The Cuban revolutionaries, as Cruse very well knew, also saw themselves as overturning the Western cultural logic that held sway in Havana prior to the revolution. For Cruse, national autonomy was determined by the defining of anticolonial cultural priorities and the subsequent production of culture based on them. A coherent national identity constituted the primary component of any successful independence movement. Jones at least in the early 1960s inverted the causal chain, seeing force and violence as generative of a new culture and national identity. But by the middle of the 1960s, Jones had reversed himself, a shift that Cruse approvingly noted at the end of *The Crisis of the Negro Intellectual*.

Thus far, we have seen how the Cuban Revolution influenced Cruse and Jones's belief in the power of culture to effect political transformation. Cuba provided a concrete example of how revolution might actually occur within a social order deeply marked by Western cultural and political domination. Indeed, Cruse and Jones drew many of the same lessons from the FPCC trip, even though Cruse publicly criticized the young poet for his unreasonable faith in force and violence. Even if Jones saw armed revolution as a viable alternative for black Americans, his actions during the 1960s did not center on generating that outcome. Instead, the young Jones set out to fashion in Harlem, and later in Newark, precisely the sort of cultural revolution described by Cruse in *Rebellion or Revolution?* Not only did Jones attempt to create an autonomous black national culture but he also connected that culture to the formation of a black radical politics and an anticolonial front in the urban ghetto. A brief analysis of his efforts to do so concludes this chapter.

Black Cultural Revolution and the Anticolonial Front

Immediately on his return from Cuba, LeRoi Jones began acting on his new-found political and artistic convictions, defending the right of Third World countries and black Americans to choose their own destiny. Jones staunchly aligned himself with Robert Williams, working to raise money for Williams's legal defense and championing his right to practice armed self-defense in the name of integration. After Cuba, Jones also began drawing parallels between Third World colonies and black urban ghettos. In a 1961 essay, "Letter to Jules Feiffer," Jones argued the merits of self-determination by defending Williams and critiqued the condescension and moderation at the heart of white liberalism. Declaring himself opposed to any "Negro protest that does not distress the kind of ethical sterility" white liberalism represents,[68] Jones affirms Williams's right to bear arms in defense of his citizenship rights. He then connects that self-defense tactic to the larger context of Third World anticolonial struggles, saying, "I get the feeling that somehow liberals think that they are peculiarly qualified to tell American Negroes and other oppressed peoples of the world how to wage their struggles. No one wants to hear it" (66). Jones's sense that black and Third World independence necessitated an attack on white liberalism is not surprising given his former cultural and political location. However, his offensive is not only motivated by Feiffer's critique of armed protest but also fueled by this white liberal's objection to Negroes using the term *Afro-American* to describe themselves. Describing the term as both "historically and ethnically correct," Jones dismisses *Negro* as a vehicle for bland assimilation into a "cultureless, middle-headed AMERICAN" ideal (66–67). At this early stage, political independence was already bound up with cultural self-determination.

This dual agenda was expressed through a range of political and cultural activities Jones undertook during the 1960s. At the UN demonstrations organized by On Guard, Jones shouted along with other protestors the modified Cuban slogan "Congo, yes! Yankee, no!" and responded to the call "The word Negro has got to go!" with "We're Afro-Americans!" Defense of Congolese self-determination both expressed and reinforced a transnational black identity with local moorings. On Guard's leader and spokesman Daniel Watts best epitomized the sentiment at the UN, describing the demonstrators as "Afro-Americans fighting for African liberation."[69] The fact that the Lumumba protest occasioned the articulation of a new black identity demonstrates how 1960s anticolonialism and black cultural politics were mutually constitutive. A new black American identity was not forged in isolation; it did not emerge solely within the U.S. political context. Rather, it resulted from a transnational consciousness, one that drew on anticolonial critiques for its political analysis and international legitimacy.

In 1965 the assassination of another black liberation fighter, Malcolm X, propelled Jones to accelerate his efforts to foster black cultural independence. By then, Jones had published widely on the roots and meaning of black culture, most famously in the 1963 *Blues People*, which traces the formation of blues music to the history of slavery and sharecropping. He had also begun associating with black intellectuals, artists, and jazz musicians including Archie Shepp, Askia Touré, Ornette Coleman, Bob Thompson, and Barbara Teer.[70] After Malcolm's death, Jones (renamed Imamu Amiri Baraka) founded the Black

Arts Repertory Theater/School (BARTS) in Harlem as, in Woodard's words, a way of enacting Malcolm X's belief in "the priority of black cultural revolution, the centrality of the African Revolution, and the necessity of developing a black ideology of self-determination."[71] From all accounts, BARTS' opening ceremony was spectacular. Writers and artists armed with a black-and-gold flag paraded down 125th Street to the live music of Sun Ra. During the year of its existence, BARTS held a summer program for four hundred students in which Harold Cruse taught black history, Sonia Sanchez and Larry P. Neal read and wrote poetry, Baraka mounted theatrical productions, and Sun Ra, Albert Ayler, and Milford Graves held live jazz concerts (65–66). In many instances, speakers, actors, and writers performed in the street, harkening back to the heyday of Harlem's street speakers.

These activities eventually inspired Baraka to plan a black arts festival in Newark, at which Stokely Carmichael, Harold Cruse, and many others addressed the crowd. That Newark festival and Baraka's efforts more generally constituted critical catalysts for the national development of a black arts movement. In the festival's wake, numerous journals including *Black World*, *Freedomways*, and *Black Scholar* emerged, as did black arts institutions in Detroit, New Orleans, and Chicago (67). It is critical to see Baraka's cultural endeavors as central to his desire to build a black national culture that would eventually serve as the foundation for black liberation. As Baraka wrote during this period, "The Revolutionary Theatre must force change, it should be change."[72] In Black Arts veteran Larry Neal's words, Baraka was searching for a "unified identity, an identity . . . in tune with . . . the revolutionary tendencies in the social order, the Black community, the Third World and the necessity to bring aesthetics in line with ethics."[73] This sense that black aesthetics must produce and embody an ethics of black liberation was clearly articulated in Baraka's foreword to *Black Fire*, in which he described the contributions as "sources, and the constant striving (*jihad*) of a nation coming back into focus."[74] The *Black Fire* collection blends avant-garde literary, musical, and cultural forms in narrating everyday experiences in various African diaspora locations—Harlem, Tanganyika, and Georgia, for example. In doing so, the distance between geographic sites, cultural forms, and avant-garde art and popular audiences is productively engaged and metaphorically collapsed.[75]

In the years after BARTS dissolved, Baraka moved back to Newark and launched a number of initiatives combining new forms of cultural production and new ideas about political liberation. In the heart of Newark's Central Ward ghetto, he founded the United Brothers organization, the repertory company Spirit House Movers and Players, the African Free School, and eventually the

Committee for a Unified NewArk (CFUN). Convinced that political education must coincide with cultural entertainment, Baraka held events that were part political gathering, part community celebration. For instance, the United Brothers held weekly Soul Sessions, combining dance and song performances, speeches from Baraka, and a lively *Soul Train*–style dance line. In campaigning for black mayoral candidate Kenneth Gibson, CFUN enlisted James Brown and Bill Cosby, both of whom performed in fund-raisers for the "Community's Choice" slate. Such events exploited the mainstream cultural capital of Cosby and Brown to facilitate local community empowerment, shrinking the distance between mainstream culture and grassroots insurgency. The campaign effort by CFUN also directly emulated the Cuban mobile-media example as trucks drove through Newark's neighborhoods televising speeches by the candidates and telling residents how to register for the election.[76] During this period, Baraka, heavily influenced by Maulana Karenga's ideas about cultural revolution, even wrote an essay entitled "A Black Value System," which explained the seven principles known as Nguzo Saba, combining black unity, communal self-determination, and cooperative economics. This pamphlet circulated locally within Newark and nationally as black cultural nationalists in New York, Los Angeles, and Detroit studied Karenga's teachings.

After 1965, Baraka's identification with the Third World had shifted toward the decolonizing African countries, a move that eclipsed his interest in Cuba, though it was, in part, sparked by that very interest. Baraka explicitly credited African decolonization with inspiring him to found BARTS: "The emergence of the independent African states and the appearance of African freedom fighters, fighting guerrilla wars with white colonialism, had to produce young intellectuals (and older ones, too) who reveled in that spirit and sought to use that spirit to create art. An art that would reach the people, that would take them higher, ready them for war and victory."[77] We should not, however, take this statement as evidence that the Cuban Revolution was of anything but seminal importance for Baraka. Indeed, he owed his very understanding of the relation between culture and politics, his first experience of revolutionary change, to that Cuba trip during which his contact with Harold Cruse, Robert Williams, and Fidel Castro altered his political and cultural course forever. As he, Cruse, and other U.S. Third World Leftists struggled to define a radical, independent cultural and political identity, they based that identity on the emergent precedents of Third World anticolonialism. U.S. Third World Leftists in sometimes contradictory ways mobilized in global and local contexts at once. Informed by the global, an imagined black nation was produced in and through Third World identification and solidarity.

While Jones and Cruse were busy building the Black Arts Movement, other activists in New York City looked to the Third World as inspiration for their own local struggles. In the case of black and Puerto Rican hospital workers in Local 1199, it was the less theoretical and more immediate experience many workers had gained in anticolonial and civil rights movements that found articulation in their efforts to secure fair wages and decent working conditions in New York's hospitals. In fighting for these rights, these workers mobilized class, race, gender, and ethnic differences to build a powerful alliance that in the 1970s would be known by the slogan "Union Power, Soul Power."

2. Union Power, Soul Power

Class Struggle by Cultural Means

●

In the previous chapter, we saw Harold Cruse, LeRoi Jones, and Robert Williams chart new theoretical territory by analyzing the relationship of U.S. blacks to colonized peoples, debate effective revolutionary strategies, and assert culture's centrality in crafting oppositional identities. Their efforts helped articulate and shape a generation's cultural and political agenda. Yet however pivotal to the formation of a U.S. Third World Left they may have been, Williams, Jones, and Cruse do not fully define its scope. Other segments of this cultural formation did exist, segments that were less preoccupied with the architectonics of revolution and more concerned with the mechanics of grassroots political mobilization and institutional struggle. For this contingent of the U.S. Third World Left, theoretical questions proved secondary to strategic ones. How could one concretely alter the life chances and everyday living conditions of poor people of color? What organizational structure or political movement could best facilitate such a momentous shift in U.S. society? How could coalitions be built within and between various racial and ethnic groups without neglecting their potentially divergent interests? In the face of such questions, Cruse's distinction between rebellion and revolution was, if not meaningless, certainly less imperative than the insistent demands of grassroots organizing.

To understand the split between these two segments as simply that between intellectuals and activists is to miss the point. Williams, Jones, and Cruse were as much activists as they were intellectuals, and as this chapter will demonstrate, U.S. Third World Leftists, though primarily engaged in activism, did analyze and articulate the reasons for their particular organizing tactics. In fleshing out the discontinuities and continuities between these two segments of the U.S. Third World Left, this chapter considers a unique group of activist-intellectuals, the women and men of Local 1199, the Hospital Workers' Union. Though most 1199 members may not have heard of Harold Cruse, their struggle to build cultural institutions that would sustain the union's organizing efforts reflected his theoretical assessment of the relation between culture and politics. His assertion that political revolution in the First World depended on the building of cultural institutions serves as an intriguing blueprint for thinking about the role of culture in 1199's organizing campaigns.

In the 1960s, 1199 was one of the most successful and highly visible unions in the United States, truly an exceptional historical case. It consolidated a diverse workforce and wrung concessions from intransigent hospital administrations at a time when the House of Labor found its influence waning. Unlike other labor unions, 1199 crafted a highly effective coalition between Old Leftists and U.S. Third World Leftists. Leon Davis, Moe Foner, and Elliot Godoff, veterans of the Popular Front era, joined Ted Mitchell, Emerito Cruz, Doris Turner, Lillie Mae Booker, and Hilda Joquin, whose experiences in inner-city ghettos and U.S. colonies critically informed their identities as workers and union activists. Given the diversity of its membership, what allowed 1199 to prosper while other unions foundered? The answers are complicated and varied, as Leon Fink and Brian Greenberg's thorough history of the union demonstrates.[1] In part, 1199's emergence coincided with the postwar transformation of health care into big business, but historical opportunity never provides the full story, for as Fredric Jameson after Walter Benjamin reminds us, "History progresses by failure rather than by success."[2] If many factors led to the union's success, none is more intriguing and less examined than 1199's use of cultural production in its organizing campaigns.

The local's history provides us with an opportunity to consider the relationship between cultural production and political organizing, between cultural identification and economic empowerment. In its modes of cultural and political organizing, 1199 adhered to Cruse's dictum that political revolutions demand the building of autonomous cultural institutions. 1199 utilized theater, poetry, music, and film to organize and unify its African American, Caribbean, and Jewish constituents. The union paper *1199 News*, the Negro History/Salute to Freedom Celebration, Gallery 1199, and the films *Hospital Strike*, *Like a Beautiful Child*, and *I Am Somebody* all constituted attempts to advance a political and cultural agenda at once. The series of symbols, orchestrated celebrations, and strategic alliances 1199 deployed mobilized old members, recruited new ones, and inspired local communities. They also helped to forge a unique workers' culture. This culture—the product of a newly visible working class that was black, Puerto Rican, and largely female—mobilized antiracist and anti-imperialist critiques against the ills of inner-city life and workplace exploitation. It is this effort to craft an anti-imperialist, antiracist grassroots cultural politics that defines 1199 as a U.S. Third World Left institution.

Labor and the Left: An Old Debate Reexamined

Though this culture produced a set of ideologies to which I will pay close attention, it also produced a distinctly new way of waging the class struggle. "Zero work, unwork, the merging of the line of work and play," assert the editors of *The Sixties without Apology*, "signaled a new politics of labor."[3] This new politics of labor was founded on fresh, fluid, and contested understandings of what constituted a class or class struggle, what constituted work or play, and even what activities defined a union. In the story of 1199 lies a fundamental challenge to many long-held assumptions about the relationship between labor and the Left in the 1960s. It is by now collective common sense that the pact between the two disintegrated in the 1960s as New Leftists expressed their opposition to the Vietnam War and indulged in alternative lifestyles. Blue-collar workers found themselves increasingly alienated by the anti-establishment antics of white hippies and Black Panthers. According to this view, popularized by commentators such as Irwin Unger and Irving Howe, the collision occurred as much between two generations as it did between two classes; it was the inevitable clash of middle-class students and working-class parents.[4] This conflict spectacularly manifested itself in the 1970 hard-hat riots during which construction workers and longshoremen stormed Wall Street, mowing down antiwar protestors in their path.

Recently, however, critics have called this analysis into question, most significantly Peter Levy in *The New Left and Labor in the 1960s*. Levy argues that the two groups' relationship was dialectical, characterized by cooperation in the first half of the decade, confrontation in the latter half, and synthesis after 1970.[5] Emphasizing their commonalities, Levy cites instances of collaboration between New Leftists and labor unions including joint efforts during the Mississippi Freedom Summer and on behalf of the United Farm Workers

Movement. Even Levy admits, however, that in the late sixties organized labor clashed with the New Left as it became increasingly militant and enamored of identity politics. "Antagonisms fostered by the Vietnam War and Black Power," Levy writes, "intertwined with those generated by the counterculture to produce a deep rift between the two social movements" (107). After 1970, this rift was resolved as labor and the New Left recognized their need to band together in order to safeguard the reforms they had earlier secured. The rapprochement evident over the next two decades, then, was not so much an abrupt reversal in direction as it was the by-product of the previous decade's "contradictory legacy" (194). Though correct in his conclusion that the relationship was paradoxical rather than simply progressive, Levy does not sufficiently explore the exceptions to the rule he is so eager to discredit.

In essence, Levy remains indebted to the terms of debate established by earlier commentators. Though loath to indict the excesses of black radicals and counterculturalists, Levy nonetheless attributes the collapse of the Left/labor partnership to the emergence of those New Left tendencies. He admits, however, that the subsequent backlash was a necessary evil, enabling labor to grapple with issues that it had previously avoided. Though Levy does primarily fault white liberals for the breach, reiterating that it was their failure to align themselves with African Americans that led to the growth of the New Right, still more than a hint of historical inevitability haunts his analysis. For him, the New Left's evolution was as inescapable as labor's hostile response to it. Though this perhaps makes for an accurate assessment of much of the labor movement, 1199's history suggests an alternative trajectory, an example of the road not taken. Rather than opposing movements for racial and ethnic empowerment, 1199 wed its campaign for workplace justice to other antidiscrimination appeals. And it did so long before identity politics was seen as an ascendant political trend. What resulted was a thriving labor organization, a progressive force in electoral politics, and an active participant in movements for racial, ethnic, and gender equality. 1199's potent brand of cultural politics, encapsulated in the slogan, "Union Power, Soul Power," deployed racial and ethnic identification to create class-based group solidarity.

One might rightly rejoin that 1199 is an exceptional case, but in needlessly (and automatically) opposing labor and identity politics, Levy and his predecessors tacitly subscribe to two premises: first, that labor politics is not in itself an identity politic, one that hails individuals by their professional identity and their function in the economic structure; second, that to foreground one identity, for instance one's identity as a construction worker, necessarily negates or renders less primary one's identity as a black woman. These assumptions depend on a conception of identity as either static or additive, whereas it is more useful, and certainly more accurate, to imagine identity in Althusserian terms as the multiple and even conflicting ways in which institutions, organizations, and groups can and do hail individuals. Consequently, human beings hold multiple identities and allegiances simultaneously, choosing one or a range of identities as primary depending on the circumstances. Rather than assuming that the goals of movements based around racial, ethnic, and/or gender identities necessarily conflict with those of labor unions, what happens if we investigate the ways in which the vision, scope, and success of the U.S. labor movement has been severely hobbled by its incapacity to embrace these movements for individual and community empowerment?

The propensity to set labor and the New Left at odds with one another derives in large part from the myopic way in which the New Left has traditionally been defined. The young, middle-class, and mostly white students who emerged as its most media-friendly representatives are without exception seen by critics as the sum total of the New Left.[6] Terry Anderson's description in *The Movement and the Sixties* typifies this tendency: "They had been educated at liberal universities and colleges, as had most of their parents, who earned good incomes, had provided a secure and egalitarian home environment, and had raised democratic and questioning children. While a small percentage of parents were political leftists who raised 'red diaper babies,' most were liberals who voted Democratic."[7] The quintessential exemplar of this group is, of course, Tom Hayden, author of the Port Huron Statement and cofounder of Students for a Democratic Society (SDS). Seeking an escape from the conformity and consensus that according to Anderson defined the 1950s for white Americans, Hayden's generation gravitated toward activism as a means of rebelling against parental strictures (57).

Indeed, Hayden and his cohort were formative members of the sixties Left, but for too long their story has eclipsed many others. Working within and alongside of the New Left were members of a U.S. Third World Left that did not conform to the New Left profile. Cruse, Williams, and Baraka were born at least a decade before the baby boomers, were not middle class by typical measures, and all of them had begun their radical activities long before the New Left coalesced. Similarly, the women and men of 1199, many of whom were either African American migrants or Puerto Rican immigrants, were neither college educated nor middle class. Their dress, patterns of speech, and behavior were not countercultural in the historically specific sense of that term, but their politics were countercultural if by that we mean that they challenged the racist, classist, and colonialist foundations of the United States.

In essence, expanding the counterculture to include 1199 members requires one to redefine the counterculture beyond the markers—age, hair length, drug use, clothing—with which it is typically associated. By combining union, civil rights, and anticolonial politics, 1199ers helped define a U.S. Third World Left at once focused on domestic inequities and international ones.

By building a movement around their identities as low-paid hospital workers, bearing the full brunt of U.S. racism and economic exploitation, they simultaneously improved their own collective context and participated in a much larger, transnational movement for social change. Members of Local 1199 drew political experience and tactical inspiration from their firsthand knowledge of colonialism in the Caribbean and Puerto Rico and poverty and police brutality in U.S. ghettos. Although the influence of the Third World is less easily identifiable here than it is in the writings of Cruse, Williams, and Jones, it is nonetheless present in the range of issues articulated in the union's newspapers, in the kinds of speakers who regularly spoke to the union, and in an orientation that placed the local in its global context. 1199's predominantly female, often middle-aged members provide an important foil to my previous chapter's phallocentric focus. If Cruse, Williams, and Baraka envisioned radical social change in martial terms—the heroic guerrilla leader, the valiant cultural warrior—1199's members altered their economic and political plight by less romantic, though no less effective, means. The existence of these black, Puerto Rican, and white women and men complicates our often simplistic assessment of the radical politics of the 1960s, chiseling away at the hackneyed images of beret-clad, black-jacketed young militants who populate the nostalgic and critical fancy of most participants and observers alike.

1199's Old Left Origins

1199 began life in 1932 as the Retail Drug Employees Union, one of the Jewish and communist-led unions active in New York at the time. Its early leaders Leon Davis, Elliot Godoff, and Moe Foner played a decisive role in 1199's history until as recently as the 1970s. Products of what Michael Denning has dubbed the "Age of the CIO," Davis, Godoff, and Foner were committed to both interracial/interethnic solidarity and militant unionism.[8] Leon Davis, the son of well-to-do Russian émigrés, came to New York to embark on a career as a pharmacist. While working in Harlem drugstores, Davis began organizing pharmacists and drug clerks under the auspices of the Trade Union Unity League (TUUL), the labor-organizing wing of the Communist Party.[9] In 1929, his work with TUUL led Davis to the New York Drug Clerks Association, one of three fledgling pharmacists' unions, the others being the Pharmacists' Union of Greater New York and Local 1199, the Retail Drug Employees Union. When the three unions merged in 1932, Davis became the president of Local 1199, a post he would hold for much of the twentieth century.

The second of 1199's energetic early leaders, Moe Foner, was one of four sons born to Polish-Jewish immigrants. While a student at Brooklyn College, Foner became involved with the radical American Student Union. After graduation, he joined his brothers, Jack and Philip, at City College, where they taught in the history department and agitated for the inclusion of an African history course and the hiring of a black faculty member.[10] In 1941, all three were ousted in a statewide purge of leftists from institutions of higher education. Foner soon found work at District 65, the Wholesale and Warehouse Workers Union, where he stayed until 1954 when Davis offered him a job at 1199, editing the union's newspaper and organizing its various cultural activities.[11] It was Foner who masterminded the union's impressive array of cultural programming, the importance of which he had learned in his years with District 65.

Another son of immigrants, Elliot Godoff was born to Russian émigrés who encouraged him to pursue a pharmacist's degree at Columbia University. Through the influence of a wealthy uncle, Godoff became the head pharmacist at the Israel Zion Hospital in 1935, where, according to Fink and Greenberg, "he was dispensing not only drugs but the *Daily Worker*" (17). In 1945, Godoff left the pharmacy to become a full-time hospital organizer with Local 444 of the United Packing Workers Association and then with Teamsters Local 237 before joining Local 1199 in 1957 (18). It was Godoff who initially suggested organizing in health care, a thriving urban industry rife with exploited workers. With Godoff's arrival, this formidable triumvirate of Old Leftists began organizing workers in New York's nonprofit hospitals.

Because of their Old Left affiliations, Davis, Foner, and Godoff found themselves caught between the New Deal idealism of that era and the postwar red-baiting of the CIO's (Congress of Industrial Organizations) left wing (22). By 1948, many Popular Front ideals and the CPUSA that had won them mainstream status came under sharp attack. Consequently, all three men distanced themselves from their earlier engagement with the CPUSA; Davis fortuitously resigned from the party just weeks before the Hartley Committee called him to testify (23). On one hand, their actions and those of so many others accelerated the waning influence of the Communist Party in American politics. Although Davis, Foner, and Godoff never participated in the era's red-baiting, their disaffiliation certainly contributed to the marginalization of communists within the American Federation of Labor and the Congress of Industrial Organizations (AFL-CIO). Within 1199, it was tacitly assumed, though never explicitly mandated, that staff members would sever all ties with the CPUSA so as to avert the Hartley Committee's wrath. Fink and Greenberg contend that "union members were expected to give up political work before taking union staff positions" as Davis "insisted upon independence from all outside political directives" (24). As a result, the party's influence on 1199 had nearly evaporated by 1958. This explicit move away from party politics allowed the union to focus its energy on building a social movement, for the pervasive climate of right-wing backlash forced 1199 to strengthen its alliances with the city's black and Puerto Rican communities. "The siege years," Fink and Greenberg write, "bound the drugstore union more closely to its civil rights commitment and its black membership" (24). McCarthyism inadvertently facilitated a different kind of leftist organizing, forcing seasoned Old Leftists to encounter and interact with U.S. Third World Leftists Ted Mitchell, Emerito Cruz, Doris Turner, Lillie Mae Booker, Ossie Davis, and Ruby Dee.

However, the union's relationship with African Americans began during the Depression years. It was then that 1199 began organizing black pharmacists in Harlem, winning a successful fight in 1937 to secure jobs for black pharmacists and promotion for black porters to so-called soda men (21). The willingness of Jewish unionists to oppose employment discrimination in a trade dominated by Jews earned 1199 the loyalty and support of black pharmacists. A decade later, they repaid the union by striking at one hundred stores rather than allowing them to be certified by a rival union (24). 1199 further demonstrated its commitment to civil rights issues by inaugurating an annual Negro history celebration in February 1950. Inviting speakers such as Ralph Abernathy, the first vice president of the Montgomery Improvement Association, Thurgood Marshall, and T. R. Howard, the man responsible for gathering witnesses in the Emmett Till lynching, the union lent both public and financial support to the civil rights movement.[12] Based on his reputation as a civil rights advocate, 1199 president Davis received an invitation from black pharmacists to speak at the 1951 National Pharmaceutical Convention. In his typically outspoken fashion, Davis boldly denounced "discrimination, Jim Crow, segregation, and the whole vicious system of white supremacy."[13] Davis's antiracist views were far from typical among white unionists, nor were they confined to the African American community. 1199 also made significant overtures to New York's Puerto Rican population, becoming one of the earliest members of the Labor Advisory Committee on Puerto Rican Affairs.[14]

Until 1957, however, 1199's six thousand members were predominantly white, a reflection of the employment discrimination endemic to New York's drugstores.[15] Although the union was powerful within its particular economic niche, it had limited growth potential. All too aware of these realities, Godoff, Davis, and Foner turned their attention to a growing economic sector, the low-paid service and maintenance workers of New York's voluntary hospitals. Workers in the nursing, dietary, housekeeping, and building and maintenance departments provided vital support to patients, doctors, and staff, yet they stood on the lowest rung of the hospital hierarchy. Not only were they poorly paid but they were also isolated in separate and unequal dining and recreational facilities (3). Before World War II, many of these workers were white ethnics recruited from city welfare agencies and housed in hospital dormitories as virtual indentured servants. Their compensation was the measly sum of twenty-five dollars a month (6).[16] Supervisors ruled their departments as small fiefdoms where raises, pensions, and vacation time were all determined by personal preference and prejudice. By the early 1950s, migration patterns had substantially altered the composition of the hospital workforce, with Southern blacks and Puerto Ricans replacing the Irish, Italian, and Polish immigrants of earlier migrations. As a result, by 1970, 80 percent of the service and maintenance workers in hospitals were either black or Puerto Rican (6). These African American, Puerto Rican, and Caribbean workers brought varying experiences, languages, cultural lexicons, and work practices to their hospital jobs. To complicate matters even further, workers were segmented into various departments, in part a by-product of the hospitals' discriminatory hiring practices. Such segregation also resulted from established kinship and sociocultural networks: when job openings arose, workers told people in their family, on their block, and at their church, then vouched for them to their supervisors.

The Old Left Meets the U.S. Third World Left

This diverse workforce stood in striking contrast to 1199's drugstore membership, posing a series of challenges to the union's tried and true organizing strategies. In 1958 Foner, Davis, and Godoff began concentrating their organizing efforts at Montefiore, a large, nonprofit hospital in the Bronx. On entering the hospitals, they found a group of U.S. Third World Leftists who incorporated their experiences of Jim Crow segregation and U.S. colonialism into an understanding of their hospital context. In one of their shrewdest moves, the union organizers assigned Ted Mitchell, the union's vice president, to Montefiore as a full-time organizer. The grandson of a freed slave, Mitchell grew up in rural North Carolina before moving to New York where he found work as a drugstore porter. When 1199 entered the drugstores, Mitchell quickly rose through the ranks, becoming the shop steward for fifteen stores and eventually the union's first black official in 1949 (32). Presenting Mitchell as the union's most visible representative eased understandable tensions between white unionists and Montefiore's nonwhite workforce. "Mitchell's appointment," Fink and Greenberg note, "signaled a new adaptation to the racial realities of the hospital's service work force" (33). Rather than approaching workers as if their identities hinged solely (or even primarily) on their workplace function, 1199 devised an organizing strategy that addressed workers by their personal and professional identities. "Instead of ignoring existing divisions and stratifications among hospital workers," Fink and Greenberg assert, "the union turned an apparent obstacle to its advantage, seeking a kind of coalition of distinct social groupings" (33).

By utilizing a more flexible and nuanced approach to organizing, the 1199 staff quickly empowered a group of rank-and-file workers who already possessed a wealth of political experience gained in their local communities and in their countries of origin. For instance, Emerito Cruz, a cook at Montefiore, had previously served as a union officer in Puerto Rico in the 1940s, so he was well suited to organize 1199's Spanish-speaking workforce. The Caribbean immigrant Harold Harris had formerly been a radical political activist in Jamaica. A member of native son Marcus Garvey's Black Nationalist movement, Harris took part in the 1936 general strike in Kingston. Of the strike, Harris remembered, "I mean it was a strike, not a strike that you walk around with your hands in your pockets. This was a revolution" (34). Workplace organizing gave Harris an outlet for his organizing skills and political commitments, a way of relating his Black Nationalist activities to his fight against workplace injustice. Later, Harris would even compare the sense of community gained in the Garvey movement with "being in the union" (34). Even before 1199 began organizing at Montefiore, Harris had been a workplace activist. In fact, Harris and some of his fellow dietary workers precipitated the advent of the five-day workweek when they presented a set of grievances to their supervisor and threatened further action if their demands were ignored (34).

With the breadth of organizing experience and political enthusiasm present within Montefiore's rank and file, 1199 quickly signed up six hundred members, more than half of the hospital's eligible workforce.[17] Local newspapers, including the Spanish-language *El Diario* and the Harlem-based *Amsterdam News*, devoted considerable ink to the campaign's progress, adopting it as a noteworthy community issue.[18] Though these elements alone did not immediately compel Montefiore administrators to hold an election, on 6 December 1958, Montefiore finally agreed to recognize 1199's right to represent hospital workers. On 30 December 1958, just hours before Castro's assumption of power in Cuba, 1199 won its union election by a stunning 628 to 31.[19] In the resulting contract, workers won a thirty-dollar increase in pay per month, overtime pay, and a grievance procedure.

Although these constituted significant gains, the Montefiore victory did much more than improve the lives of hospital workers. It heralded a new day in labor relations: a predominantly Caribbean, Puerto Rican, and African American labor force had successfully challenged a health care industry thriving on the exploitation of its workers. Rather than subsuming their racial or ethnic identity to their workplace identity, workers drew from the range of experiences and identities they possessed. Fighting for union representation was both a blow against a white supremacist system that did not recognize black and Puerto Rican equality *and* a demand for better working conditions. Fink and Greenberg convey this sense when describing worker Henry Nicholas's motivation for supporting 1199: "The struggle at Mt. Sinai, he believed, was part of the same fight for survival faced by black farmers in Mississippi or black GIs—the threat of being run off the land, blacklisted by a dishonorable discharge or fired by the hospital reflected the same 'administration of things'" (69). The union, then, became a primary mode for symbolically and materially attacking the racism and labor exploitation facing people of color in New York City. "A growing sense of entitlement among racial minorities," Fink and Greenberg suggest, "had emerged as a potentially powerful force in urban industrial relations" (41). This was reflected in the tremendous support 1199 received from the larger civil rights community, without which the union might not have won its recognition battle. The hospital battles spectacularly united protest movements against Southern segregation with inner-city struggles for better pay and workplace respect. "The hospital strike," Fink and Greenberg propose, "was . . . one of the first Northern struggles to directly tap a growing civil rights constituency comprised of leading members of the minority community as well as white liberal and labor allies" (79). Though the support of prominent civil rights advocates—including black congressman Adam Clayton Powell, who walked the picket lines at Mount Sinai and Knickerbocker Hospital in Harlem—proved invaluable, the victories in 1959 resulted in large part from the tenacity of the hospital workers.[20] It was their self-organization and determination that produced a powerful force in industrial labor relations.

In each hospital 1199 organized, rank-and-file members demonstrated the same political will shown by Montefiore's workers. Foner, Davis, and Godoff did not so much ignite rank-and-file militancy as they supplemented it with their keen strategic sense and influence within New York's white liberal circles.

Even before Montefiore, hospital workers had successfully organized themselves. In May and June of 1956, three thousand workers at seven nonprofit hospitals had gone on strike. Although the resulting settlement did not recognize the union, they won substantial pay raises, a grievance procedure, and a forty-hour workweek.[21] The Montefiore campaign simply reignited the embers of worker self-organization that had sparked a few years earlier. Nonetheless, the Montefiore victory served as the foundation on which 1199 built in subsequent years. By November 1961, 1199 had ten thousand members in its various locals, an astonishing rate of growth due in large part to the rank-and-file leadership that emerged to complement that of Davis, Godoff, and Foner.

This new leadership force offers another window onto a U.S. Third World Left that combined antiracist, anticolonial, and pro-worker politics into a potent ideological and strategic blend. Differing in racial and ethnic composition from the white ethnic base of the Old Left, this group also consisted largely of women. For example, at Beth Abraham Hospital, women of color including Helen Mason, Mary Malcolm, Thelma Bennett, and Evelyn Jones comprised over half of the organizing committee.[22] Women's leading role in union organizing was also reflected in the fact that a majority of the graduates from a November 1959 leadership training class were women of color.[23] Just as women swelled the ranks of 1199's organizers, they also assumed high-profile positions during 1199's recognition fights.

Lillie Mae Booker, a migrant from rural South Carolina and a single mother of three, was a steward at Lenox Hill Hospital and a leader during their June 1959 strike. When the hospital administration retaliated by firing her, she took them to arbitration and won both her job and back pay. Puerto Rico–born Gloria Arana, a single mother of three, took an active role in Mount Sinai's recognition fight. She later recalled, "In 1959, when we went on strike, the boss told me if I went in everybody would go in. I stayed out."[24] For many years after that, Arana served as an elected union delegate. The firebrand Hilda Joquin left her home in Bermuda at the age of eighteen to study concert singing in New York. Once she arrived, she found her ambition quickly thwarted, and she eventually made her way to Beth Israel, where she subsequently became a leader in their organizing drive. "Getting on the picket line," she remembered, "was an important thing for us—it was recognition. We got out there to show that we had something inside us. They treated us as if we had no intelligence."[25] A proud and open supporter of the union, Joquin was even fired in May 1962 for collecting union dues while on the clock. When her firing sparked worker militancy rather than dampening it, the administration quickly moved to reinstate her.[26] It was Joquin who described the union's growth as "like a beautiful child," a phrase that later became the title of a 1967 film on the union.[27] Another union stalwart, Pauline Rigerman, fled with her family from czarist Russia and served as a steward in the Bakers' Union for twenty-nine years before becoming a nurses' aide at the Jewish Home and Hospital for the Aged.[28] In 1962, when 1199 organizers approached the workers there, she proved instrumental in successfully organizing the predominantly Spanish-speaking workforce.

Without question, the woman with the longest-lasting impact on 1199 was Doris Turner, who began as a rank-and-file organizer but in the 1970s ascended to become 1199's second president. Turner, the great-great-granddaughter of a slave midwife whose children, with the exception of one, were sold away from her, was raised jointly by her illiterate grandmother and her shoemaker father in Pensacola, Florida. She began working at Lenox Hill Hospital in 1956 as a dietary clerk. Striking up a friendship with an Italian woman in her department, Turner soon learned that she was in fact earning five dollars less than her white coworkers.[29] This blatant discrimination sowed the seeds of Turner's later union involvement; when 1199 organizers approached Turner and her coworkers at Lenox Hill, she and two hundred others signed cards within hours (51). Serving as the head of Lenox Hill's organizing committee, Turner emerged as a pivotal figure in the hospital's recognition strike.

After 1199's victory at the hospital, Turner continued to be a thorn in the administration's side and a champion of the union. In February 1960, when Turner demanded to know when the hospital intended to establish the new pay scale it had promised during the strike, her supervisors fired her. Petition drives and massive demonstrations ensued, and arbitrators eventually decided the case in Turner's favor. When she returned to Lenox Hill, workers laid their aprons on the ground, giving her a "red-carpet" welcome (100). In 1961, Turner became part of the union staff; three years later, she was elected a vice president of Local 1199, and in 1967 she became the vice president of District 1199's Hospital Division. Her appointment marked the first time an African American woman held such a high-ranking post in a union of 1199's size.[30] A longtime protégé of Elliot Godoff and Leon Davis, she succeeded Davis in 1982 to become president of the national union. By many accounts, Turner's presidency was less than successful. She battled with 1199's old guard, led the union into a disastrous strike, and allegedly tampered with ballot boxes to ensure her reelection in April 1984.[31] Eventually another black woman, Georgianna Johnson, unseated Turner, replacing her administration with the "Save Our Union" opposition slate. In fact, one of the members of that slate was Dennis Rivera, 1199's current president (228). Though Turner's tenure was severely flawed, marked by critical errors in judgment, and characterized by an autocratic streak, it is nonetheless significant that a black woman was able to achieve such unprecedented power within a labor organization. Indeed, according to one commentator, Turner had "more power than any woman in American labor history."[32]

Turner and other women of color proved extremely influential in ensuring 1199's success and shaping its future direction. But why would women with such demanding jobs and pressing family obligations devote countless hours and abundant energy to union work? The most obvious answer is of course that the union's success guaranteed them material benefits, higher wages, and better working conditions. Along with these tangible gains, however, anecdotal evidence suggests that women in 1199 also saw unionization as a means of achieving a measure of respect from callous and often racist supervisors. The nurses' aide Dorothy Johnson, a leader of the drive at Clara Mass Hospital, recalled: "People were pushed around pretty badly. . . . Since the union there's more respect for the people by management. It's an important part of what the union brings."[33] The presence of a union lessened the tendency of supervisors to act capriciously, and successful strikes no doubt impressed on them the value of workers they had previously considered expendable. As the worker Erving Teague reflected, "Our dignity has grown through the struggles of forming our union."

For women of color, however, union participation not only earned them management's respect but also the esteem of their male coworkers. Through organizing, female hospital workers became visible political actors in their units, recruiting new members, ensuring strike participation, and articulating members' grievances to management and higher-ranking union officials. Still women were not proportionately represented within the union's top leadership. Fink and Greenberg note that "gender inequality—particularly, the heavily male majority among the union staff and exclusively male coterie in policy-making circles—set up a difficult path both for aspiring leaders and those who sought to integrate them into the decision-making process."[34] Not only were most of 1199's leaders male but they were white men, notably Foner, Godoff, and Davis, a reality that curtailed opportunities for women and people of color generally. This may in part explain the quasi-paranoid atmosphere that seems to have surrounded Turner's presidency. The double impact of race and gender discrimination no doubt contributed to Turner's persistent belief that she and her administration were constantly under siege.

The concentration of women within the rank-and-file leadership may have made them less publicly visible, but it nonetheless provided them with a great deal of localized power. Since these women were usually the first and most sustained contact workers had with 1199, the quality and strength of the relationship between organizers and members quite literally determined 1199's strategies, and hence its success. Participation in union activities was significantly affected by the sense of allegiance and respect workers felt toward their organizers; political ideologies and praxis were molded by personal affiliations. Deciphering where one left off and the other began is nearly impossible. For the rank and file, Hilda Joquin, Gloria Arana, or Doris Turner literally embodied the union, manifesting its attributes as well as its flaws. The reason that Mount Sinai officials targeted Arana during the recognition strike was because her stature within the department was such that if she crossed the picket lines, then others would follow. These bonds of allegiance forge the connective tissue of unions (and other political organizations), yet they are often obscured by ceaseless attention to a group's "official" leaders. Rarely is it emphasized that these leaders would be ineffectual without the networks of individuals who disseminate their message and enact the group's strategies. Though imperfect, union organizing offered women of color one mechanism for honing and exercising their leadership skills. As a result of their efforts, 1199 won the right to represent all New York State hospital workers in 1965. By 1966, hospital workers' minimum wages had quadrupled, and by the end of the decade, so had its membership.[35]

Crafting a U.S. Third World Left Political Agenda

Obtaining material benefits and developing political leadership might have been sufficient impetus for union involvement, but these women had another primary motivation. The union was an important way for them to bring the civil rights movement into the so-called quiet zones of New York hospitals. Though less celebrated than the lunch-counter sit-ins or Freedom Rides, challenges to the inferior wages and dismal work conditions of black and Puerto Rican hospital workers made for a direct challenge to the U.S. racial order. If its very existence furthered the progress of the civil rights movement, 1199 also lent a great deal of financial and political support to the civil rights movement. In July 1960, hospital workers raised more than five hundred dollars to support the Southern sit-in protestors, and a year later they began another fund drive, pledging to raise three thousand to help the Freedom Riders.[36] Hospital workers also staged several protests in the summer of 1963 to demonstrate their solidarity with civil rights activists in Birmingham, Alabama. At one Harlem rally, Ted Mitchell roused an audience of six thousand people when he declared, "Segregation and exploitation must go, whether in Birmingham or

New York City."[37] The following year, 1199ers stepped up their support efforts, lobbying for a civil rights bill, marching to integrate New York's public schools, and joining a vigil outside the Federal Courthouse when civil rights workers James Earl Chaney, Andrew Goodman, and Michael Schwerner disappeared in Mississippi.[38] Through these various activities, 1199 demonstrated the integral relationship between labor and antiracist politics, a relationship already enacted through the partnership of white Old Leftists and black and Puerto Rican U.S. Third World Leftists.

The sense of common cause with those struggling for racial equality was not confined to the U.S. context, a fact that is not at all surprising given the union's member base and ideological origins. Since many hospital workers emigrated from countries that functioned as U.S. economic and political satellites, they brought with them the brutal experience of colonialism and a rich history of anticolonial struggle. This was something they shared with Foner, Davis, and Godoff whose Old Left political formation was steeped in an anti-imperial tradition. As a result, the union fostered concrete political connections between 1199 activists and anticolonial ones by sponsoring interns from Africa including Wentworth Kodjoe and Tom Mboya, whom *1199 Hospital News* described as a "young African freedom fighter."[39] The two students were summer organizers, participating in civil rights protests and hospital picketing. On one of those occasions, Mboya was walking the picket lines with labor veteran A. Philip Randolph when reporters asked him what prompted his involvement. In response, Mboya affirmed that the "hospital strikers were battling for the same goals of human dignity and freedom as are my brothers and sisters in Africa."[40] Mboya's words reflect his and the workers' own sense that 1199's union drives were symbolic enactments, if not actual replications of the anticolonial struggles occurring in Africa and the Caribbean.

In numerous articles, 1199 drew parallels between the civil rights struggle and anticolonial movements. Vehemently denouncing Jim Crow at home and imperialism abroad, Davis wrote in one column, "The exploitation and denial of jobs and freedom is the shame of our nation and might prove its ruination. Like colonialism, it must go."[41] Davis's words reflect an assumption that the workers whom 1199 represented would, as a matter of course, reject any notion of colonialism as a moral or political necessity. Appealing to members' own experience of discrimination, 1199 self-consciously accessed and invoked an anticolonial discourse: "There is a close similarity between the war against the poor and colored people here, and the war in Vietnam."[42] The comparison between Vietnam and U.S. ghettoes rendered visible the sustained policy of organized violence necessary to effect political marginalization and economic devastation. Months later, when inner-city rebellion swept the streets of Newark, New Jersey, the union took the offensive, blaming the Newark police, not black and Puerto Rican residents, for the widespread violence. Describing the city's police department as "an occupying power of a colony inhabited by Negroes," the union castigated city officials for unleashing organized police brutality to quell legitimate—if disorganized—social protest.[43]

Local 1199 further reinforced the comparison between black and Puerto Rican hospital workers and anticolonial activists through a series of forums the union hosted. In April 1967 Dennis Brutus, the exiled South African teacher and poet, told hospital workers that 13 million black workers were prevented from forming or belonging to South African trade unions. Detailing the "savagery of apartheid," Brutus also denounced U.S. corporations who aided and abetted the regime through large capital investments.[44] Ironically, 1199's credit union funds had been invested in one such corporation, a fact that led two Montefiore workers to write to *1199 News*, "urg[ing] the union to withdraw all funds presently at the First National City Bank." The two workers continued, "*It seems wrong to us that a union which is so strongly for the rights of man* should be helping to suppress 13,000,000 people in South Africa."[45] Soon after, 1199 did divest from the bank in a move initiated by its rank-and-file membership, not its leadership. In a more controversial episode, 1199 invited I. F. Stone, an outspoken critic of Israel and an advocate of Palestinian statehood, to address union staff, afterward printing excerpts from his speech in *1199 News*. Declaring, "We made the Palestinian Arabs homeless to make a home for our own people," Stone and the union drew both criticism and support from its members.[46] Julius Lampert wrote into the paper to decry the "nerve, or better, chutzpah, of this expert," while Rose Ann Libertelli judged Stone's comments to be "darn good."[47] Though it is fair to say that many Jewish members took umbrage at Stone's analysis, many other union members saw Israeli policy as another lamentable instance of settler colonialism.

These debates reflect the complicated ideological relationship 1199 members had with the Third World, but if this relationship was important in bolstering an antihegemonic, oppositional common sense, the union's activities had a similar impact on Third World activists. Not only did its African interns learn valuable strategies for political organizing but they also gained firsthand exposure to civil rights battles, which no doubt strengthened the interns' sense that a new day in global race relations had indeed dawned. As we have already seen, anticolonial activist Mboya's involvement with the hospital workers reinforced his own understanding that his anticolonial struggle and the union movement shared certain commonalties. In other instances of this transnational affiliation, Ghana, the first postcolonial nation in sub-Saharan Africa, sought information from 1199. In August 1960, the labor attaché in Accra requested brochures from the union to be used in organizing Ghana's health care sector.[48] Four years later, Ayoola Adeleke, vice president of Nigeria's United Labor Congress, chose to visit 1199 on his month-long tour of the United States. While meeting with Doris Turner, Ted Mitchell, and workers at Mount Sinai, Adeleke expressed his conviction that the U.S. government should follow Nigeria's example and subsidize hospitals in order to raise worker wages. In the face of state neglect, Adeleke declared himself impressed with the "job Local 1199 has done in improving wages, working conditions and securing other benefits for hospital workers."[49] Like the visit itself, the large article dominated by a photo of Adeleke alongside beaming 1199 workers bolstered members' sense that their struggles had relevance for newly independent African nations.

1199 News

Perhaps one of the most powerful means by which 1199 crafted and articulated a U.S. Third World Left political agenda was through its paper, *1199 News*. Drawing careful ideological and material connections between class oppression, racial discrimination, and opposition to colonialism, the paper utilized member profiles, coverage of current events, and interviews with prominent activists to create a series of shared ideologies. Within the pages of *1199 News*, civil rights activists of the mainstream and radical variety were celebrated, grassroots activism was encouraged, and U.S. imperialism was denounced.

Under Moe Foner's editorship, the paper provided a forum for political debate and artistic expression. Of course, the primary task of *1199 News* was to organize members and nonmembers alike. To that end, the paper updated members on the union's activities, the progress of strikes, the outcome of contract negotiations, and the frequent promotion of their peers within the organizing apparatus. The most salient and frequently articulated theme of *1199 News* was that opposition to worker exploitation necessitated opposition to racial discrimination, and conversely that support for labor meant endorsing racial equality. A typical example of this theme can be seen in the way the paper publicized a 1961 membership meeting, declaring, "This is a General Membership Meeting for all hospital workers, and it will be the occasion for launching Local 1199's all-out campaign to win decent wages and working conditions in the voluntary hospitals, and to mobilize hospital workers behind the great nation-wide fight to end segregation and discrimination in the

USA."[50] To underscore this connection, present at the meeting were none other than Harry Van Arsdale, the president of New York's Central Labor Council, and the Reverend Martin Luther King Jr., two clear symbols of 1199's commitment to both labor and civil rights. This dual focus was again foregrounded in a 1963 article describing a protest in front of New York's City Hall. "The struggle in Birmingham and our struggle in the hospitals," the article maintained, "are the same and far from over. They are both for a decent life and human dignity."[51] For union members, civil rights struggles outside of and within the hospital were more than simply rhetorically connected.

1199 News vigorously promoted active worker involvement in civil rights protests. In May 1960, the paper noted that hospital workers began picketing in front of Harlem's Woolworth store carrying signs that read "1199 Fights Segregation."[52] Inspired by their example, the predominantly white drug division planned to picket Woolworth's Midtown Manhattan store. In August 1963, mere weeks before the historic March on Washington, an editorial by President Davis urged all 1199ers to go to Washington, reasoning that the interests of African American and white workers were one and the same: "Full civil and political rights are being denied to the Negroes in the South to provide a base for the most reactionary, backward politicians in our nation. These Southern politicians serve the interests of big business. They prevent all of us from moving ahead. They hold back progress for all." Billing the march as the "most significant event of the decade," Davis directly condemned the AFL-CIO leadership, blaming the "dead hand of some of the conservative, segregationist elements within the labor movement" for the leadership's decision not to endorse the march.[53] In Davis's view, labor's fence-sitting would only further drive a wedge between it and African Americans, hampering the campaign for universal employment, a drive he likened to the CIO movement of the 1930s. Labor's lack of political courage would create long-term obstacles, hampering its ideological vision and ability to organize. Not surprisingly, such outspoken opposition drew 1199 further away from mainstream labor.

This was not the first time that 1199 would part ways with organized labor over the issue of race, nor would it be the last. *1199 News* publicized the instances when 1199 found itself decidedly to the left of the AFL-CIO, offering them as evidence that the union's first loyalty was to its predominantly black and Puerto Rican members. For example, when George Meany censured Negro American Labor Council (NALC) president A. Philip Randolph in 1961 for releasing a report exposing the widespread racial discrimination within the AFL-CIO's ranks, 1199 publicly condemned the action. That November, *1199 News* published a letter from Davis to "Brother Randolph" in which he described the NALC as a "necessary instrument in the struggle against all forms of discrimination, segregation and Jim Crow in every area of American life." "*Particularly*," Davis continued, it was necessary "*in those sections of the American labor movement where this indecent practice still exists.*" Arguing that in the U.S. the categories of race and class were inextricable from one another, Davis wrote, "The struggle of the thousands of hospital workers in the City of New York most of whom are Negro and Puerto Rican dramatized that exploitation and discrimination go hand in hand."[54] Such excerpts suggest that the union was reconceptualizing, rearticulating, and thus actively contesting the very definition of labor and labor politics produced by the AFL-CIO leadership. Opposing what appeared to be the AFL-CIO's single-minded focus on the workplace as the primary front of struggle, Davis insisted that racism was not only a union problem but also a problem within unions. In order to solve it, white unionists must welcome criticism particularly from within their own ranks and root out the racism they found there.

Although important, these episodes were mere skirmishes when compared with the union's decisive break with the AFL-CIO over its position on the war in Vietnam. Beginning as early as 1964, *1199 News* began publishing reports on the war that questioned whether President Johnson's policy was morally justified and strategically prudent. In November 1967, when the AFL-CIO issued a statement supporting the Johnson administration's Vietnam policy, *1199 News* published an account of a meeting in which 1199 leaders joined 150 other unionists in passing a resolution calling for the cessation of U.S. bombings, and a negotiated cease-fire followed by peace talks.[55] In other editions, the paper emphasized the human cost of Vietnam, commemorating the slain children of union members and exposing the widespread devastation wrought by U.S. troops and air raids. Urging opposition to the war and member participation in antiwar protests, an *1199 News* column declared, "Our members can neither ignore nor be unaffected by the war 10,000 miles away in Vietnam. . . . While we are spending 30 billion dollars a year on this tragic war, our cities are being turned into jungles of despair, crime and rebellion for lack of decent housing, decent education and job opportunities."[56] Emphasizing the domestic consequences of the war, the paper appealed to members' own self-interest, pointing out the devastating impact this diversion of U.S. funds had on the nation's inner cities. In doing so, the paper not only helped solidify opposition to the war but also drew members' attention to pressing domestic issues—housing, education, and employment. *1199 News* also exposed the role racism played in the execution of war policy. One exposé declared, "Black soldiers make up only 10 percent of U.S. troops in Vietnam, but they comprise 20 percent of troops on the line, and they are receiving more than 20 percent of the casualties." While African Americans were fodder for Johnson's war machine, their civil rights were routinely violated: "The oppression of black and brown minorities has been intensified . . . . At home blacks who speak out against racism find themselves prosecuted, persecuted and—in some cases—mowed down by the guns of police or national guardsmen."[57] The newsletter's insistence that racist ideology sanctioned military interference in Third World countries and violent repression of "black and brown minorities" reflects the kind of counterhegemonic ideology developing within the U.S. Third World Left.

For the rest of the war years, 1199 continued to oppose the Vietnam War, helping to found the group Labor for Peace in 1972, and thus remained at odds with the labor establishment.[58] Through these actions, 1199 gained recognition as an ally rather than an enemy of the New Left. Just as the AFL-CIO's support for U.S. foreign policy completely alienated it from the New Left, 1199's opposition had the contrary effect. Defying what Fink and Greenberg characterize as the "white male-dominated labor aristocracy grown conservative after years away from struggle," 1199 was seen as an anomaly by liberals and radicals alike.[59] For example, while AFL-CIO president Meany defended police brutality at the 1968 Chicago Democratic Convention, claiming that the police had not "overreacted with that dirty-necked, foul-mouthed group," 1199 News countered his historical amnesia with a brilliant article entitled "Chicago Massacre." Juxtaposing photos and newspaper accounts from Chicago 1968 with those of the 1937 Memorial Day Massacre in which Chicago police killed ten Republic Steel workers picketing for a union, the article countered, "Others remember that it wasn't very long ago (for hospital workers it was literally only yesterday) when workers on strike were regularly clubbed and even killed by the cops in the name of law and order."[60]

"Chicago Massacre" was an example of the newspaper's attempts to express solidarity with the New Left, the Old Left, and the Third World in whose name the Chicago demonstrations had been waged. "Here was a union," Fink and Greenberg contend, "that had finally made effective contact with the thirdworld constituency that lay at the heart of 1960s' radical political strategies."[61] Although Vietnam protest did draw 1199 closer to a generation of black and Puerto Rican activists considerably younger than its membership base, the union's antiwar stance did more than just cement 1199's fertile relationship to a so-called third-world constituency; rather, it indicates union members' central position within that very constituency. Though 1199's members may have been shaped by an earlier historical moment, they were nonetheless dissatisfied with the political, economic, and social order and attacked it from a strikingly similar perspective. Lillie Mae Booker or Julio Pagan may not conform to the conventional profile of the sixties radical, but their ideological commitments and political activities situate them firmly within the U.S. Third World Left to which Fink and Greenberg allude.

1199 News also considered New York's political context, featuring articles on 1199's involvement in local activism. Great care was taken to include stories that illustrated 1199's commitment to social justice in New York's communities of color. For example, an article in April 1963 told of a new drug division program for black and Puerto Rican teens. Training two hundred high school graduates to be drugstore clerks and cosmeticians, the program was described by President Davis as an attempt to "provide equal job opportunities for minority group workers and a concrete approach to dealing with the big increase in unemployment among Negro and Puerto Rican youth."[62] In December 1966, 1199 and the Columbia School of Social Work founded the Community Organizing Project in the southeast Bronx. Focusing on inadequate housing, poor city services, and consumer problems, the committee was described as a "union in the community" working to improve members' home lives, as well as their work lives.[63] Another article described workers' involvement in the Montefiore Neighborhood Health Center. Located in the Morrisania-Bathgate area of the Bronx, the center provided free health and dental care to thirteen thousand low-income residents.[64] Equipped with health care workers, staff lawyers, and community liaisons, the center was committed to fighting the range of conditions affecting area residents. Encouraging community empowerment, providing paid job training, and working to organize tenant councils, the center became a hub for political activism in this Bronx neighborhood.

These examples emphasize 1199's commitment to fostering black and Puerto Rican activism *outside* the workplace; they demonstrate a social vision well beyond the typical union-based one. Such activities demonstrate a desire to ameliorate—and eventually eradicate—the debilitating effects of structural poverty and political neglect. The union never lost sight of the fact that it was only the union's strength—its attention to bread-and-butter workplace issues—that enabled these larger ambitions; however, workers' own material progress was not seen as a substitute for group progress. The economic ascendancy of 1199's female, black, and Puerto Rican workers was viewed as the exception proving the general rule—that the American Dream was extremely circumscribed for these groups and only attainable when they were willing to unite and confront, not conciliate, the economic, political, and social order. Given this hard-nosed assessment of U.S. life, the union's agenda can hardly be seen as one of uplift; instead, community members were given access to educational and material resources so that they could determine their own destinies. In the end, individual or even group success was meaningful only because it represented a weakening—however slight—in the hegemonic forces; it was significant only in so far as it contributed to a wider movement for social justice.

It is in this context that one should understand the paper's frequent inclusion of member profiles. First and foremost, this device personalized the union, emphasizing the fact that individuals defined the union's philosophy and direction. Above all, these member profiles allowed *1199 News* yet another avenue to articulate the ideals for which the union was supposed to stand. Depicting individuals with whom readers could identify afforded the paper another opportunity to define the union's shared values. As one might expect, rank-and-file leaders such as Turner, Booker, and Mitchell were featured, but so were lesser-known figures identified as exemplary members of the union and their communities. Stock clerk Horace Hicks was featured in 1956 for his founding of the Jamaica Youth Organization designed to steer young boys away from "juvenile delinquency" and toward athletics. A Jamaican immigrant, Hicks worked with first- and second-generation immigrant youth whose introduction to U.S. life was primarily defined by potentially deadly police interactions and a too-early acquaintance with the criminal justice system.[65] Hicks's interest in youth organizing was one shared by the union. In fact, 1199 introduced a variety of programs for members' children including free summer camp and college scholarships. Importantly, the union did not interpret Hicks's involvement with Caribbean youth as evidence of either antiwhite sentiment or myopic racial pride. Instead, it praised Hicks for his timely intervention in an ethnic community to which he felt personally accountable.

1199 News also highlighted Local 1199 organizers Ramón Malavé and Lorenzo Santiago who helped found the Asociación Nacional Puertorriqueña por Derechos Civiles. Intended as a national group to address the housing, school, and employment discrimination facing U.S. Puerto Ricans, the group's founding convention in March 1965 brought together civic, religious, and union leaders.[66] In a Spanish-language article, a regular feature within the paper, Malavé's and Santiago's work was commended and meant to encourage further agitation in local, typically disempowered communities. As was the case with Hicks, Malavé's and Santiago's decision to organize individuals around their national identity did not preclude 1199's enthusiastic endorsement of the group's aims. The fight for U.S. Puerto Rican civil rights was seen to complement, rather than conflict with, 1199's agenda.

Another prominent example of this "profiles-in-courage" approach is the case of nurses' aide Lucy Merrill, featured in the 1964 article, "Slum Revolt

Spreads in Rat-Infested Tenement." Fed up with life among the ruins, Merrill helped organize a twenty-one–building rent strike in Harlem to protest the decaying, poorly heated, vermin-filled tenements in which she and other 1199ers lived. Merrill emphasized that she had previously tried official channels: "Recently, I've been down to the Board of Health and Dept. of Buildings to complain in person about housing conditions here. They write you later and tell you not to bother to call them, they will get in touch with you and that's the end of it." "Fed up" and unable to move, she vowed to "fight for services and repairs here and now." Union poet Marshall Dubin wrote an accompanying verse for the article, entitled "Rent Strike—A New 1199 Activity." The refrain declared, "Rent Strike, Rent Strike, that's the way. / To fight the Slumlord Rat today!"[67] Far from an auxiliary activity, the rent strike was depicted as an activity integral to the fight for better employment conditions. 1199's concern for workers' welfare did not end the moment they walked off the job. Indeed, Merrill's example was meant to inspire other union members, a fact underscored by an appeal to members to organize rent strikes in their own buildings.

Through these member profiles, as well as through the numerous articles denouncing governmental and AFL-CIO malfeasance and encouraging grassroots community organizing, 1199 News helped reflect and shape the union's antihegemonic ideology. As important as this function was, however, it was arguably not the paper's most significant contribution. The paper's signal role was to provide a forum where members could debate current events, the practicality or morality of union policy, and ultimately define the union's ideology. As one might expect, the union's opposition to the Vietnam War prompted members on both sides of the issue to write letters, but some of the most heated exchanges centered around the issue of racial politics. After 1199 News featured a series of articles on Black Power, significant numbers of union members weighed in on the subject. In October 1966, Alfred Simmons wrote, "Negro Americans must have a voice in and a real chance to share in government, industry, unions, housing, education and so on. White Americans shouldn't get excited because we want some power too. The call of civil rights leaders for black power is not a wild cry."[68] If Simmons defined Black Power as simply equal participation in all aspects of U.S. society, another member had a slightly less tempered view. Mount Sinai worker Margaret Carter went on the offensive, attacking white liberals for withdrawing their support from civil rights groups who endorsed Black Power. Decrying the fact that liberals refused to "recognize the new demands of blacks," Carter counseled whites to accept that "Negroes are no longer going to permit white liberals to direct or control, whether it is in jobs, schools, housing or anything else."[69] These members' differing definitions of Black Power reflect the instability inherent in the use of the term. Did it mean complete black autonomy, territorial segregation, or locally controlled institutions? The answer depended on the context and the speaker; in fact, its rhetorical appeal may have depended on this ambiguity. *Black Power* was a term that suggested an ideological commitment—for example, to black control—even as the route to that goal remained contested.

When the issue arose again, this time in the context of debate on the Black Panther Party, members once more expressed divergent views. Victor Weinberg wrote in to express his disapproval of the Black Panther Party, attacking them for "advocating separatism and anti-whitism." His letter provoked this defense from Brooklyn pharmacist Louis Dinnerstein: "[Weinberg] must read Panther leader Eldridge Cleaver's open letter to Stokely Carmichael in the September issue of *Ramparts* magazine. Mr. Cleaver definitely declares that the Black Panthers favor unity with whites who oppose capitalism, war, racism and discrimination."[70] Dinnerstein's words not only reflect his sympathy for the Panthers' agenda but also the implicit assumption that Weinberg might likely agree with much of their actual program.

Another debate was sparked by Bayard Rustin's article "The Negro and the Jew" in an October 1966 edition of *1199 News*, in which he identified the economic reasons for hostility between the two groups. Sophie Rosenfeld took exception to Rustin's statement that black people resent Jews because they "have made it." Asking, "What about the Jews without money?" Rosenfeld countered, "Union workers know that they are being exploited by the rich, Jew and non-Jew alike. Ford, General Electric, General Motors, U.S. Steel and many other powerful concerns rule our economic life. Whether they are owned by Jews or non-Jews matters very little."[71] Rosenfeld's belief that economic issues would more often make friends than foes of blacks and Jews was echoed by the black hospital worker Christina Johnson. She responded to Rustin's article by citing the successful partnership of Jewish pharmacists and black hospital workers within 1199. Though acknowledging that reasons for animosity existed, Johnson concluded, "We should recognize and treat a shyster like a shyster, a slumlord like a slumlord—be he Jew, white Christian or Negro. But also we must treat a friend as a friend and an ally as an ally."[72] Despite Johnson's assessment, the alliance between black hospital workers and Jewish pharmacists was not always an uncontroversial one.

Though black and Puerto Rican workers may have been heartened to see *1199 News* devote much of its coverage to race and class discrimination in New York, other members objected to the paper's increasing focus on social justice issues. Stanley L. Solomon criticized the paper for having "lost touch with reality and [becoming] a thinly disguised propaganda tool," saying, "certainly, it is not geared to the professional pharmacist's mentality."[73] Solomon's letter implies that more economically secure pharmacists have less reason to engage in oppositional politics since their lives and livelihoods are less likely to be immediately impacted by the Vietnam War, escalating police repression, or the lack of safe, affordable housing. Solomon's words are just one indication of the underlying class, race, and gender tensions between black and Puerto Rican service and maintenance workers and the professionally skilled members of the drug division. In another such letter, the wife of a union pharmacist wrote the paper in December 1967 to opine, "The pharmacist is a semi-professional man, not a hospital worker, and the two should be kept separate and apart. He should not be in the same category as a porter." The letter went on to attribute to the union the "type of thinking that contributes to race-riots, sit-ins and the other things that make equal opportunities equal for the Negro only." This example of white backlash replete with its attendant classicism and racism provoked porter Willie Staton to ask, "Does that mixed-up chick . . . live in a L.S.D. world?" before reminding her that pharmacists' wages and benefits had risen so quickly because of hospital workers' presence in the union.[74] If only the biases evident in the pharmacist's wife's letter could be dismissed as products of a drug-induced haze. Unfortunately, her sentiments reflected the deep and abiding divisions within 1199's membership.

Nonetheless, the strength of both the union and *1199 News* was the ability to provide members with the space to disagree politically without the union becoming so factionalized that unified action was no longer possible. During the 1960s and much of the 1970s, racial, ethnic, economic, political, gender, and generational differences did not hinder the union's ability to coalesce in the face of a common foe, whether it be hospital management, local government, the AFL-CIO leadership, or President Nixon. Though widespread diversity of opinion existed, 1199 members agreed on the common project of unionization and saw social justice as an integral part of that project. How one defined social justice was the central, often contentious issue animating much of 1199's strategic and ideological discussions. As members struggled with one another over the individual and institutional components of such a social justice commitment, they simultaneously gave the concept a range of complicated, at times contradictory meanings.

However varied their definition of social justice, though, one common thread did unite 1199 members. A broad consensus existed that unchecked state and police power proved antithetical to a truly democratic society. This opinion was not borne out of a naive belief in the virtues of U.S. democracy; after all, 1199ers had experienced firsthand the dangerous excesses of the latter. Witnesses to the purge of leftists from the AFL-CIO during the McCarthy era, members understood the varied and pernicious ways in which political dissent could be suppressed. Whether this was reflected in its opposition to police brutality, its resistance to U.S. colonialism, or the financial support for the communist Angela Davis's defense fund, the union fought for the rights of poor citizens and political dissenters. Believing that the state must safeguard its domestic minorities whether they be of the racial, ethnic, or political variety, 1199 not only advocated for their protection but also encouraged the state to be responsive to its grassroots critics. In doing so, 1199 presented its populist view of the state: democratic and representative government for all people was only accomplished through direct, often militant action against the conduct and policies of government and/or corporate entities. It is this theme that is most often underscored in the articles and commentaries of *1199 News*, and indeed it is the one that motivated the union's activities during this period.

Building U.S. Third World Left Cultural Institutions

Though *1199 News* may have been one effective way of crafting and disseminating the union's set of shared ideals, it was not the only, or even the most effective, means at the union's disposal. Instead, cultural production constituted an integral part of the union's organizing strategy, shaping both political beliefs and cultural values. Not content merely to hold cultural events in a piecemeal fashion, 1199 constructed an extensive and intricate network of cultural institutions. Through their annual Salute to Freedom celebrations, art exhibitions, soul and salsa dances, and theater and lecture series, 1199 built long-lasting alliances with activists, civil rights leaders, and members of New York's arts community. In the process, 1199 not only crafted a unique ideological blend of militant antiracism, anticolonialism, and labor unionism but also transformed union organizing into a community ritual and a cultural event.

One of the most potent elements in 1199's cultural arsenal was its annual black history celebration. An occasion for publicizing civil rights struggles and raising worker consciousness, along with much needed capital, the event featured a wide array of speakers and performers. Celebrated since 1950 in the drug division, the event flourished once Ossie Davis agreed to write and direct a musical play for the occasion. The 1954 Negro History Celebration marked the beginning of Davis's more than thirty-year involvement with the event. Recently, Davis recalled that Moe Foner had asked him to produce a Negro History Week show in order to "bring culture to the workers."[75] Davis promptly agreed, writing a play entitled *The People of Clarendon County*, which celebrated the South Carolina bus boycott of that year.[76] In 1959 and 1960, the hospital division held a parallel event also produced by Davis, but in 1961, the two events merged into a joint celebration that was eventually renamed the Salute to Freedom in 1964.[77] The name change signaled the union's increasing desire to use these events to stress its commitment to all freedom struggles, not just those in the United States or pertaining to black American rights.

On one level, these celebrations served a clear ideological purpose, but they were also entertaining. Davis and his wife, the actor Ruby Dee, wrote, directed, acted in, or emceed programs that combined prose, poetry, and song into a potent political and cultural amalgam. They were aided in this process by the Committee on Negro Affairs, which was established in 1958 to help plan the event and other cultural activities throughout the year. The event encompassed a vast array of individuals and activities, primarily because Dee and Davis helped draw other stage and screen stars to it including Ricardo Montalban, Godfrey Cambridge, Sidney Poitier, Dick Gregory, Diana Sands, Alice Childress, Beah Richards, and Will Geer. In addition to dramatic pieces, musical entertainment also formed an integral part of the celebration. Consequently, an eclectic group of performers including Miriam Makeba, Abby Lincoln, the Max Roach Quartet, and folk singers Leon Bibb and Pete Seeger appeared at the event.

The inclusion of such diverse performers as the Mark Twain interpreter Will Geer, the comic Godfrey Cambridge, Popular Front singer Pete Seeger, and South African vocalist Miriam Makeba represented a literal meshing of old and U.S. Third World Left cultural and political sensibilities. Audience members may have found Geer's folksy witticisms as entertaining as Cambridge's urban brand of humor, but distinct (though not unrelated) cultural traditions informed the two comics. While members may have found political—if not sonic—parallels in the music of Seeger, balladeer of the U.S. proletariat, and Makeba, voice of disenfranchised black South Africans, their music derived from autonomous cultural and political histories. Nonetheless, such diverse participation in the annual celebrations illustrated that difference need not preclude cooperation nor breed contempt. By participating, these performers demonstrated that they shared with 1199 members the belief that racial discrimination and economic exploitation must be eradicated.

If participation by this array of performers proved important for the forging of 1199's commonly held set of political values, it also aided a process of cultural education. Though black housekeepers may have attended the event to see Cambridge, they also encountered Makeba, Gill, and Seeger, perhaps for the first time. Likewise, Jewish drug clerks may have been drawn to the show because of Seeger, but they also heard Makeba's anti-Apartheid anthems and Cambridge's humor. While these experiences may not have produced total cultural understanding, they certainly served as a basis on which an already coherent political alliance could extend into the realm of cultural production. Mutual cultural consumption might eventually instill cross-cultural appreciation and perhaps greater political cooperation.

The shows fostered intercultural understanding among Jewish, African American, Caribbean, and Puerto Rican members, and they also exposed those members to cultures of the African diaspora. For example, the event often showcased facets of African culture including Davis's performance of an African folktale in 1958 and a performance by Olatunji and his African singers, dancers, and drummers in 1960 and 1961.[78] Whether Davis's skit was actually directly based on African oral or written texts or whether the Olatunji group itself hailed from or even studied in Africa is unclear. It is quite possible that both were North American interpretations of African-derived cultural rituals, a supposition that should not completely eradicate their meaning as signifiers of Africa. Their inclusion in the program demonstrates Davis's desire to connect such rituals to the identity of black Americans and the union of which they were such a significant part. Founded on a (perhaps naive) belief in cultural education as the road to racial tolerance, these acts contributed to a burgeoning internationalist perspective, moving 1199 members at least temporarily beyond the geographical bounds of their neighborhood, state, or even nation.

By highlighting areas of cultural overlap as well as dissonance, the Salute to Freedom celebrations reinforced the fact that culture was exchangeable and often mutually enjoyable, if not always wholly translatable. The audience might collectively laugh at Cambridge's jokes or sing along with Seeger's ballads, though they would not necessarily draw the same meanings or sets of associations from them. We should not assume, however, that members' associative streams were somehow structurally dependent on or reducible to their race, ethnicity, gender, or generation; cultural and political meaning was shaped by the intersection of all of these factors and many more, including individual idiosyncrasies. But these events did more than just promote intercultural exchange; they also facilitated interclass cultural exchange, temporarily ameliorating the economic barriers to cultural access. During these performances, working-class black and Puerto Rican members enjoyed acts that would otherwise have been financially prohibitive. Unable to afford frequent outings to Broadway, Carnegie Hall or the Blue Note where these performers routinely appeared, the Salute to Freedom enabled hospital workers to emulate the habits of their middle-class counterparts. The presence of Eartha Kitt or Sidney Poitier not only lent an aura of glamour to the union enterprise but also brought middle- and upper-class celebrities closer to a black and Puerto Rican working-class constituency. These events brought Forty-second Street to the union hall, where hospital workers could see Lorraine Hansberry's *Raisin in the Sun*, Langston Hughes's musical *Jerico—Jim Crow*, and *Jamaica*, the 1958 Broadway hit starring Davis and Lena Horne.[79] They symbolically leveled the playing field between upper- and middle-class performers and working-class audiences, forging temporary but important cross-class alliances. No doubt, the presence of stage and screen stars at the celebrations directly led to their various support activities, including walking the Montefiore picket lines in 1959.[80]

If Dee and Davis's involvement with 1199 helped forge a vital coalition with the New York arts community, it also cemented the union's long-standing relationship with the Harlem Left. Although ties to that Left formed during the Depression when 1199 helped organize black pharmacists, the couple proved stalwarts in Harlem's cultural organizations and thus represented a previously untapped black Left constituency. Early in their careers, the two were members of the American Negro Theatre (ANT), a popular front group with which Sidney Poitier was also associated. Although ANT scored a theatrical hit with *Strivers Row*, a parody of Harlem's famously elite neighborhood, the ensemble boasted little more than two hundred subscribers. After its dissolution, the couple then joined the Committee for the Negro in the Arts (CNA), an interracial coalition of communists, leftists, and liberals established in 1947 to encourage black integration in the cultural arts. The CNA operated its own theater where it staged several successful productions, despite widespread controversy over the involvement of white leftists. When four little girls in a Birmingham, Alabama, church were murdered by a bomb blast, Dee and Davis helped form yet another organization, the Association of Artists for Freedom.[81] Cofounded by Davis, Dee, Paule Marshall, LeRoi Jones, James Baldwin, John Killens, and Lorraine Hansberry, the association was overtly critical of white liberals, eschewed both separatism and integration, and called for a new dialogue on race.[82]

In addition to these activities, Davis also joined James Baldwin and Richard B. Moore on the editorial board of the black left journal *Liberator* whose masthead declared it the "voice of the Afro-American protest movement in the

United States and the liberation movement in Africa."[83] Though not directly involved in any of these organizations, both Paul Robeson and Harold Cruse moved in the same Harlem leftist circles as did Davis and Dee. A close friend of the pair, Robeson remained conspicuously absent from the roster of stage and screen stars appearing in Salute to Freedom celebrations. It is unclear whether Robeson was invited to participate and declined or whether the union failed to ask him, fearing red-baiting attacks. Cruse's lack of involvement in the annual celebrations is easier to explain since he saw himself as a countertendency to the one represented by Dee and Davis within Harlem's cultural Left. In *The Crisis of the Negro Intellectual*, Cruse devoted several unflattering chapters to a critique of Davis and Dee's Harlem circle. Accusing them of being opportunists, Cruse declared the couple's willingness to work with white leftists as sufficient evidence that they were not truly interested in or even capable of creating autonomous black cultural organizations. Cruse seems to have missed the larger significance of Dee and Davis's activity, for both did effectively use black cultural production to champion black, Puerto Rican, and white economic justice, an achievement Cruse would have found laudable. Narrowly focusing on whether or not white people participated in a given cultural institution blinded Cruse to the fact that race might be one—but not the only or the most important—criteria for establishing a shared cultural and political identity.

The earliest Negro History plays were, in Moe Foner's words, "living newspaper[s]," depicting the latest events in the civil rights struggle, including the Montgomery Bus Boycott, the Greensboro sit-ins, and the lynching of Emmet Till.[84] These performances helped breathe life into people and events at a geographical, if not ideological, remove from 1199 members. The Southern boycotters or the Greensboro students were no longer merely grainy newspaper photos; they became heroic protagonists, emblems of courageous, nonviolent resistance. The impact of these plays was twofold. For one, they provided another means for articulating and thus solidifying an antiracist ideology within the union. Facing a structure of entrenched white supremacy, black Americans were depicted as noble resisters who were unwilling to tolerate segregation, exploitation, and physical violence. By presenting the civil rights struggle in this light, the plays evoked empathy (even recognition) from the audience, prompting 1199ers to support the movement with their money and their activism.

However compelling, the national civil rights struggle was not Ossie Davis's only source of inspiration. In 1959, the annual play dramatized the strike at

Montefiore Hospital, giving hospital workers the opportunity to see their own recent deeds immortalized. Seeing themselves as active—even heroic—agents of history must have had an enormous impact on hospital workers for whom unionization was as much about attaining respect as it was about better pay and working conditions. In that moment, the Negro History play served as a surrogate for the union, publicly articulating (and thus restoring) the dignity and value inherent in the labor and lives of black and Puerto Rican low-waged workers. The mounting of the Montefiore strike as a play elevated it to the level of the Montgomery boycotts. In doing so, Davis, and by extension 1199, drew a clear parallel between Southern civil rights activists and northern union activists, suggesting that both were equally important milestones in the freedom struggle. As one might expect, every attempt was made to connect domestic struggles with those of freedom fighters in other parts of the world. The event constituted a frequent platform for anticolonial activists—African student leaders appeared in 1960—and generally served, in the words of one *1199 News* article, to highlight "the world-wide fight for equal rights."[85] The opportunity to symbolically forge the connection between geographically disparate sites of struggle was tremendously appealing to 1199 members, as evidenced by the large audiences the event attracted. By 1964, Salute to Freedom spectators numbered over one thousand; four years later, that figure had doubled to two thousand.[86]

As the 1960s advanced, the Salute to Freedom celebrations skillfully combined song, dance, drama, and star wattage to delight union audiences. Increasingly, the Salute to Freedom plays resembled less and less living newspapers and more and more variety shows. This did not, however, prevent the union from focusing on civil rights activities. In fact, a veritable who's who list of male civil rights leaders brought word from the front line. Each show always featured a well-known guest speaker: Ralph Abernathy in 1957, Thurgood Marshall in 1959, James Farmer in 1961, Bayard Rustin in 1964, Julian Bond in 1966, and Martin Luther King Jr. in 1968. Part informational, part inspirational, these guest speakers related the fight for black civil rights to the hospital workers struggle and to international events. In 1959, Marshall emphasized the need to fight discrimination both in the North and the South: "There is a lot of work to be done right here in New York but we don't intend to sit and wait. We demand that Negroes and all other minority groups be accorded their full rights in this country right now."[87] The Congress of Racial Equality (CORE) leader Farmer detailed the tactics and strategies of the Southern sit-in movement after an appearance by three North Carolina sit-in strikers recently released from a chain gang. In 1966, Bond stressed the immorality of U.S. foreign policy in Vietnam saying, "The United States should be less concerned with making the world safe for democracy and concentrate on making democracy safe for the world."[88] Addressing a crowd of well-wishers, speakers masterfully combined reasoned argumentation and fiery rhetoric into oratory equally influenced by the black church and the public school classroom.

Of all these speakers, though, none proved more important in consolidating the union behind a commitment to a democratic society devoid of racial or economic inequality than Martin Luther King Jr. Even before his appearance in March 1968, King was a close ally of the union, sending taped messages of encouragement and making frequent appearances during the 1960s. "More than any other national civil rights figure," Fink and Greenberg contend, "King publicly identified himself with the unionization of New York City's hospital workers."[89] His last visit to 1199 was arguably his most affecting and, in hindsight, most poignant, occurring less than a month before his assassination in Memphis. Speaking to a crowd of over two thousand, King began by describing himself as a "fellow 1199er," a comment that swiftly became part of union lore and helped solidify relations with the SCLC and Coretta Scott King after his death. There to promote the upcoming Poor People's March in Washington, King riffed on the theme of the event, "Two Americas." Chastising the government, King argued that a nation "overflowing with the milk of prosperity and the honey of equality" should not exist alongside a nation filled with people who "all too often find themselves living with wall-to-wall rats and roaches." King's words must have found enthusiastic support since he referred to conditions many hospital workers faced every day. Applauding the union's success, King described 1199 as the "authentic conscience of the labor movement," imploring labor to follow its example and organize poor workers. King spoke of the Poor People's March and the larger campaign, which would work to "demand more jobs and a guaranteed annual wage." In this endeavor, King hoped to incorporate "Negroes, Puerto Ricans, Indians and poor whites." Neglected by a government "more concerned with waging an unjust war in Vietnam than a just war on poverty," these groups, King argued, must unite if U.S. society was truly to be transformed. According to 1199 News, a "militant" King presented the march as the beginning of a massive, civil disobedience campaign against economic inequality.[90]

King's Salute to Freedom speech clearly outlined the future direction of his movement: championing the rights of the poor and opposing the Vietnam War. In delivering this speech just weeks before his assassination, King helped shape 1199's future agenda. Not only was King commemorated in the entire May issue of 1199 News but President Davis declared in that issue, "We will build our union in his image . . . Martin Luther King belonged to us, to our members, to the poor, to the ghetto-dweller, to the black man and to the poor white man. He walked our picket lines, carried our banners in our demos. He spoke to us, he encouraged us, he guided us."[91] Davis's suggestion that 1199 would take up the mantle worn by the slain King was meant to remind union members of the class and race agenda implied by his editorial. The issue's juxtaposition of photos of members enthusiastically applauding King's appearances and those of members weeping at the news of his death underscored the civil rights leader's powerful connection to 1199ers. King's death pushed the union to publicly commit to acting in his name, a commitment reaffirmed when 1199 christened its new Midtown Manhattan headquarters the Martin Luther King Labor Center.[92]

King's death created an even stronger working relationship between 1199, Coretta Scott King, and the SCLC. This connection led to close cooperation in two important union drives in Charleston, South Carolina, and Baltimore, Maryland. These were just two of the union's activities shaped by King's vision and that of his wife. After his death, Coretta Scott King became as important an 1199 collaborator as her husband had been. In support of her efforts to keep the Poor People's Campaign alive, six hundred 1199 members went to the rescheduled June March on Washington. Though the campaign soon stalled, 1199 lent it fervent support. If King's addresses to the union inspired union members, so did Scott King's appearances. In a speech delivered to the union two months after her husband's death, Scott King exhorted 1199 to begin organizing health care workers nationally. It was imperative, she argued, because a majority of the nation's hospital workers were economically disadvantaged black women.[93] While Davis's earlier commemorative words described King in gendered terms as the champion of the "black man," Scott King drew on her husband's memory to remind the union that its predominantly black, Puerto Rican, and female membership obliged it to take a leading role in organizing poor women of color nationally. Scott King's widening of the union's mission beyond its local context struck a chord. Spurred by its recent victories in New York, 1199 soon took its first step toward that goal, founding the National Organizing Committee of Hospital and Nursing Home Workers and naming Scott King its honorary chair.

In that capacity, Scott King was invited to be the featured speaker at the 1969 Salute to Freedom. Addressing a crowd of over 2,800, many of whom had seen her husband the year before, she enthused, "Your union is brotherhood. Your union is whites working side by side with blacks and Puerto Ricans. Your union is . . . my husband's dream come alive."[94] Though the last sentence was inflected with a hyperbolic flourish, Scott King's words underscored the degree to which union leaders and the rank and file alike understood themselves to be furthering King's unfulfilled mission. As we have already seen, 1199 loudly and consistently critiqued U.S. involvement in Vietnam, doing so several months before King took such a position. Of even greater ideological and political significance, however, was 1199's decision to organize health care workers nationally. In pursuing that goal, the union may have imagined itself acting in the name of the slain civil rights leader, but its actions were more closely tied to the pro-worker and pro-female agenda articulated by Coretta Scott King. When 1199 inaugurated its national union in November 1974, Scott King was again invited to address union members. Emphasizing the union's courageous stance in support of low-wage female workers Scott King explained, "I am particularly interested in your present campaign because so many hospital workers are women—black, Spanish-speaking and white—who are often the main supporters of their families."[95] While Scott King was specifically speaking of 1199's plan to organize hospital workers nationally, she was also articulating one of the union's central roles as a champion of poor black women's rights.

In addition to the powerful ideological and political work accomplished by the Salute to Freedom celebrations, they also served one eminently pragmatic function—fund-raising. Local 1199 contributed an enormous amount of money to various civil rights groups and individual activists. A portion of the Salute to Freedom celebrations was devoted to the ceremonial presentation of donations to various causes. During this period, the union's Brotherhood Fund gave an increasing amount of money to groups such as the NAACP, the SCLC, SNCC, CORE, the Negro American Labor Council, Cesar Chavez's United Farm Workers, the Puerto Rican group ASPIRA, the Black Congressional Caucus, the Black Panther Party Defense Fund, the Paul Robeson Archives, and both Daniel Ellsberg's and Angela Davis's legal defense funds. Individuals also benefited from 1199's largesse: Bronx borough president Herman Badillo, *New York Post* editor James Wechsler, Greek antifascist fighter Melina Mercouri, Coretta Scott King, and Clarence B. Jones, the publisher of the *Amsterdam News*, were all recipients of Brotherhood Fund awards. As this list demonstrates, 1199 was both generous and eclectic in its choice of beneficiaries, a policy President Davis defended at the 1968 Salute to Freedom. Alluding to the fact that SNCC and other groups had recently embraced Black Power, Davis acknowledged that some members had become disenchanted with certain organizations the union supported. In defense, Davis countered, "We support all of them because the road to freedom does not go along a single path."[96] This nonpartisan donation policy constituted part of the delicate balancing act the union performed during these years. By generously donating to a diversity of left-wing groups, 1199 expressed its solidarity with a number of causes yet did not alienate any one sector of its membership. People unenthusiastic about donations to Paul Robeson's archives or ASPIRA might be more impressed with 1199's donation to Daniel Ellsberg or Coretta Scott King. The union's policy of casting a wide net did not mean that 1199 expressed no bias; mainstream civil rights groups such as the NAACP and the SCLC received much more financial support over the years than did more militant groups such as the Black Panthers or SNCC. However, all of the recipients were politically left of center.

While the Salute to Freedom celebrations allowed 1199 to express solidarity with a wide array of left-wing causes, the union also sponsored smaller events spotlighting individual black political figures. On these occasions, 1199 was able to more explicitly declare its sympathy with particular political values, if not specific political ideologies. For example, in August 1970, 1199 raised $2,500 during its Night of Stars for the Angela Davis Legal Defense Fund. Performing to a capacity crowd of 750 were union regulars Dee and Davis, the comic Irwin Watson, and singers Mikki Grant and Irene Reid. After the cultural program, union members danced to the music of Mario Sprouse and his Orchestra.[97] Night of Stars, like 1199's other events, accomplished political ends via cultural means. Union members came to Angela Davis's political aid while enjoying an evening of music, comedy, and drama.

At the time of the event, Davis was awaiting trial on charges of murder, kidnapping, and conspiracy in connection with Jonathon Jackson's fatal attempt to free his brother George Jackson from Soledad Prison. Davis's forcefully articulated claims of innocence swiftly turned her into an international cause célèbre and eventually resulted in a not guilty verdict. The fact that 1199 held this fund-raising event cannot serve as evidence of its wholesale agreement with Davis's Communist Party affiliation or her support for other U.S. Third World Leftists such as the Black Panther Party or George Jackson. In fact, union members engaged in serious debate prior to the fund-raiser and afterward before passing a resolution demanding that Davis receive her full "constitutional rights as a citizen and a human being."[98] Violation of those rights compelled the union to defend Davis, whether or not all of its members endorsed her political beliefs. The union opposed the state's desire to railroad Davis through the legal system and into prison for her unpopular beliefs. Such tactics too closely resembled those of the McCarthy era, a time many 1199 members remembered too well to underestimate the danger to political, intellectual, and cultural freedom.

If the union's collective memory of McCarthy-era atrocities led it to defend

Angela Davis, it also prompted 1199 to resurrect a long-forgotten figure of the Popular Front era. The first cultural event in the union's new headquarters was a tribute to Paul Robeson. Conceived by Ossie Davis, the celebration was designed to "recall for older members of 1199 the varied and exceptional talents that brought Robeson world acclaim [and] to acquaint young members with his achievement." In essence, Robeson was meant to serve as a bridge between generations of union members. In publicity for the event, *1199 News* detailed Robeson's stage, screen, and political triumphs, defining him as a "man of profound social commitment" for which he paid a "terrible price" when the "repressive shadow of McCarthyism fell upon the nation."[99] Emceed by Ossie Davis and Mary Travers of Peter, Paul, and Mary fame, the star-studded cast included Melba Moore and Dizzy Gillespie and drew a crowd of nine hundred, including Cesar Chavez of the United Farm Workers Organizing Committee. Though Robeson was too ill to attend, his son Paul Robeson Jr. conveyed his "deepest appreciation to 1199" and remarked that Paul Sr. "would have enjoyed the fullness of this program."[100] In the following years, 1199 hosted other commemorating events including a second annual tribute and an art show at which Angela Davis spoke of Robeson's legacy.[101]

By hosting such events, 1199 once again broke ranks with an organized labor that took great pains to distance itself from Robeson during and even after his political persecution. As Pete Seeger remarked at one show, "A lot of unions that were helped by Paul Robeson have forgotten him. I'm glad to see 1199 hasn't forgotten."[102] However praiseworthy its actions in the 1970s, 1199, like the rest of organized labor, did not publicly support Robeson in the 1950s and 1960s, did not support him at the moment when its silence, its capitulation was most devastating. To have rallied behind Robeson might have crippled the union, placing it in a politically and perhaps organizationally precarious position; after all, it was during these years that the union quadrupled its membership and won impressive wage and benefit gains. But to have acquiesced under such red-baiting pressure ensured a stifling effect on public political discourse. Ironically, the union's failure to rally behind Robeson contributed to the very political climate opposed by 1199. Still its actions in the 1970s went some way toward redressing these actions. That the union would have paid tribute to Robeson seems only fitting since he fought for many of the same political and cultural values espoused by it. Tragically, such meaningful political gestures occurred shortly before and then after Robeson's death, long after they might have ameliorated the government's reprehensible treatment of him. Nonetheless, by staging these tributes, 1199 aided in the revival of Robeson, funding the preservation of his archives and actively contesting the web of innuendo and outright fabrication that surrounded his life. In doing so, the union provided a left-wing account, a counterhistory of Robeson's life, in the process making the actor and activist an accessible political model for its members.

Though they remained much smaller in scope, 1199 also held events to celebrate the culture and political achievements of its Jewish and Puerto Rican members. These events were organized with substantial input from the rank-and-file Jewish Affairs and Puerto Rican Affairs Committees. Beginning in 1958, these committees planned dances, group outings, the Salute to Israel, and the Latin America Fiesta. Information on the Salute to Israel is scarce, but it appears that the event was held at least twice, once in 1963 to celebrate Israel's twenty-fifth anniversary and again in 1967. The format followed that of the Salute to Freedom, varying only in the kinds of performers present and the groups and organizations to which the union donated.[103] The Jewish Affairs Committee was also responsible for organizing an exhibit of Holocaust photography entitled Never to Forget, Never to Forgive, which was displayed at the union's headquarters in April 1967 and sparked many impassioned letters from 1199 members.[104]

The Puerto Rican Affairs Committee was far larger and more active in organizing activities for Spanish-speaking members. In May 1958, the group held the first Latin America Fiesta featuring Ricardo Montalban, the nightclub singer Consuelo Moreno, and Emilio Medina and his orchestra.[105] The committee also organized dances, sponsored an annual Puerto Rican Day Parade float, and contributed articles to the newspaper's Spanish-language section. In 1971, the committee, renamed the Spanish Affairs Committee, held an evening of song and dance entitled, El Teatro 1199, a reference to the United Farm Worker's group El Teatro Campesino. Divided into two segments, the first included the songs and dances of Cuba, Mexico, the Dominican Republic, and Spain, while the latter part, "Puerto Rico Sings," featured Los Muchachos de San Juan and ended with the singing of La Borinqueña, Puerto Rico's national anthem.[106] As with most of the union's events, El Teatro 1199 exemplified the union's balancing of cultural and political elements. The cultural heritage of Cuba and Central America was respected, as was Europe's impact on that heritage. As a majority group within the union, however, Puerto Ricans and their culture not only dominated the program but a primary symbol of national independence was proudly and prominently showcased during it.

There were also several other committees that planned cultural activities. The Retirees Committee planned museum trips and discussion sessions for the union's seniors. The Affairs Committee served as a sounding board for various cultural projects and provided the logistical support to make them successful.[107] In addition to planning and executing Theater 1199 and Film Festival 1199, the committee also planned union-wide and area gatherings where members danced to Count Basie and His Orchestra, as well as lesser known acts including King Curtis and His Orchestra, Little Dave and His Soul Peppers, and Little Monty and the Unlimited Entertainers. Many family outings were also held, including picnics at Hecksher State Park, baseball games at Shea Stadium, and moonlight cruises around Manhattan. All of these activities contributed to the lively union culture of the 1960s and 1970s and even inspired imitation. In one instance, workers at Kingsbrook Jewish Medical Center founded their own Employees Art and Cultural Affairs Committee, which organized art classes, fashion shows, lunch-hour concerts, art exhibits, and evening lectures for enthusiastic employees.[108] For many, membership in 1199 meant art classes and salsa dances as much as it meant confronting one's supervisor and walking picket lines.

As important as the gala celebrations were, the logistical and monetary effort they required made them necessarily infrequent events. In an attempt to institute more systematic and sustained forms of cultural entertainment, the union launched two programs in January 1965. The first, Theater 1199, built on the relationships with stage and screen actors developed during the Salute to Freedom celebrations. Tickets for this series of theatrical events were sold by organizers within each unit and could be purchased at the modest price of $1.50 per performance. Consequently, union members had easy and affordable access to live theater. The first event, An Evening with Ossie Davis and Ruby Dee, featured the two actors reading poems by union poet Marshall Dubin, followed by an informal discussion with the audience about theater's ability to enrich people's lives. Other programs included Alan Alda and Rose Gregorio performing scenes from the Broadway hit, *The Owl and the Pussycat* and performances of excerpts from Shakespeare's *Hamlet, Twelfth Night*, and *Julius Caesar*. After each program, members mingled with the actors over coffee and dessert.[109]

Though an important means for making New York's vast cultural resources available to its residents, the program was partially underwritten by a patronizing ideology of cultural uplift. In a *New York Times* article on the popular program, Moe Foner was alleged to have said, "Most of the hospital workers, who are nearly 90 per cent Negro and Puerto Rican had never seen flesh-and-blood actors at work."[110] That comment reproduced in the headline, "Few Had Seen Live Actors," was first and foremost inaccurate since it overlooked the very cultural programming 1199 had provided throughout the preceding fifteen years. By 1965, stage and screen stars were familiar figures at the union hall. More disturbingly, that statement mistakenly assumes that if hospital workers had not been to Broadway they had never seen live acting, an assumption that denigrates the rich, multiple forms of community performance that flourish in oppressed communities and are often overlooked by majority communities. Lest we excuse Foner on the grounds that his sentiments were misrepresented in the *New York Times*, there is further evidence to suggest that Foner's attitude toward the hospital workers was not exactly free of condescension. In an article he wrote about the union's cultural programs, he concluded with praise from the comedian Sam Levenson: "As a former educator I am overwhelmed by the scope of the educational work of your union. Your respect for the cultural potential of the average man is an inspiration. More strength to you!"[111] Levenson's assessment reinforces the logic of Foner's earlier statement, namely, that it is 1199's job to tap the "cultural potential" of hospital workers, that it is the union's mission to bring culture to the unwashed hospital masses. What the article elides, of course, is the fact that from 1199's entry into the hospitals African American and Puerto Rican members incorporated elements of their cultural traditions into the union's style of political and cultural organizing. This dynamic process blurred—indeed, rendered obsolete—the distinction between high and low, mainstream and alternative culture this review implicitly reinscribes. If the union's Old Left contingent did in any way envision themselves as cultural ambassadors, they certainly understood the reciprocal nature of the union's cultural transmission.

Another series 1199 began in 1965 was a discussion-forum series organized around the theme "What's Ahead for America?" Designed as a political organizing tool for union delegates, the series featured one speaker a month between January and May. Michael Harrington spoke of the "war on poverty," the historian Philip Foner lectured on Frederick Douglass, and Bayard Rustin discussed the ongoing civil rights struggle. During Rustin's session, the civil rights crusader warned that "Negroes are facing what no other minority has faced in this country." Consequently, they must press the government to eradicate poverty and discrimination since "private enterprise will never do it because they are only interested in profits." According to Moe Foner, these sessions were characterized by "lively exchanges" in which members challenged the speakers and one another.[112] In promotional material for the series, President Davis assured members the topics were of "vital importance" and that each attendee would become a "better-informed trade unionist and a more effective leader of the members he or she represents."[113] That the union possessed the vision to connect contemporary political affairs with 1199's organizing campaigns is not surprising, but it is a no less remarkable example of the union's foresight. Recognizing that union participation was motivated by more than simply narrow economic self-interest, 1199 encouraged debate and discussion that would ultimately promote greater activism among its members.

In another unusual step, 1199 installed an art gallery in its new headquarters. Inaugurated in October 1971, Gallery 1199 became the first permanent union art gallery in the United States.[114] For several years, the gallery mounted six shows a year including an exhibit of political posters from around the world, painting and sculpture by Harlem artists curated by the Studio Museum of Harlem, and Earl Dotter's black-and-white photographs of coal mine and textile mill workers. These shows have simultaneously introduced members to different political contexts—state repression in Chile, worker conditions in Kentucky—exposed them to relatively unknown art and artists, and furthered member dialogue around these shared cultural experiences. Intended as an educational resource for members, students, teachers, and community groups, the gallery still stands as one of the union's longest-running cultural programs.[115] Significantly, the gallery periodically solicits and displays artwork from union members themselves, a practice that illustrates the seriousness with which the union has always taken members' labor and leisure lives and one that underscores 1199's implicit belief that cultural production is an important part of political organizing and everyday life.

Union Power, Soul Power

Of all 1199's efforts to create and support political art, none was more intriguing than the union's forays into film and filmmaking. After the Salute to Freedom, the union's film production was the single most important cultural institution 1199 built during this period. Even during its first hospital organizing drive, the union had a sense of the historic nature of its battle, producing under Moe Foner's leadership a film on the Montefiore campaign entitled *Hospital Strike* in 1958. Not only was the film meant to be an effective organizing tool, it also narrated the hospital workers' battle, largely ignored by the mainstream media. So successful was this enterprise that a decade later Foner produced another film, the 1967 *Like a Beautiful Child*. The title taken from member Hilda Joaquin's maternal description of the union showcased the tremendous strides the union and its members made during the 1960s. The film represented 1199 through the eyes of individual workers such as Ida Mae Cameron, whose profile did not present a rose-colored representation of urban life since the union. Juxtaposing scenes of Cameron on the job and at home, the film captured her admitting, "It's hard just living. You have to fight for hot water and steam in the winter. . . . But when you're together you're stronger and everything comes a little easier." Unionization was not depicted as a panacea for urban ills, but rather one step in the process to overturn the economic, political, and racial order. This order was represented in the film with images of white police wielding nightsticks against a multiracial group of picketers carrying signs reading "100,000 Negroes unemployed. Don't add more victims" and "Unemployment Insurance for Hospital Workers."[116] Those images encapsulated 1199's ideological commitments more saliently than any amount of *1199 News* columns or speeches by President Davis could ever have done.

Two years later, Foner decided to produce a film centered on the Charleston strike. This strike, known as the "Union Power, Soul Power" campaign was the first serious challenge to 1199's national organizing strategy. In March of 1969, 450 hospital workers at Charleston's Medical College Hospital went on strike after the hospital fired twelve union leaders. Almost immediately, 60 workers at the smaller Charleston County Hospital joined them, bringing the total to 510 strikers, 498 of which were black women. Ostensibly sparked by pitifully low wages and the high-handed and racist treatment meted out by white personnel, the strike soon became a protest over Charleston's entrenched white supremacist economic and political order. Evidence that blacks in the so-called New South would no longer tolerate the racism of the Old South, the strike struck a blow against the various institutionalized forms of racial and economic discrimination.

Led by Mary Moultrie, a practical nurse who had recently returned from working in New York City, the strike galvanized many segments of Charleston's black population. Moultrie and the other hospital workers were middle-aged, working-class women, mothers and grandmothers who decided to fight the racial status quo. Joining them were black students who boycotted the schools and flooded the city's prison. The Korean War veteran Williams Saunders and the Black Muslim Otis Robinson, the leaders of an armed self-defense unit in the city, lent the strikers tactical support in the form of so-called community militias present at meetings and demonstrations. Advocates of Black Power, Saunders and Robinson saw the strike as an opportunity to challenge the black middle class for political supremacy in the community. Saunders recalled, "I wanted [to involve] everybody in the community that had been in jail before, that had a record . . . the people that lived on the street."[117] With Saunders's help, the strike was able to tap into and direct the widespread anti-establishment sentiment present among the city's black underclass. Meanwhile, the SCLC (embroiled in a leadership battle between Ralph Abernathy and Coretta Scott King) and 1199 sought to involve the black middle class in the boycotts, night marches, and mass arrests underway. Ultimately, their efforts did not garner much middle-class support, but the pressure of civil disobedience, 15 million dollars in lost revenue, and national media attention quickly brought the city to a standstill (130–58).

At one strike rally, Abernathy spurred on the crowd by describing the strike as a combination of "union power and soul power."[118] This slogan quickly became the strikers' rallying cry. An obvious alternative to the then omnipresent "Black Power" slogan, "Union Power, Soul Power" was a mantra equally popular with middle-aged strikers, teenage students, Saunders's radicals, and Charleston's lumpen proletariat. The phrase *Soul Power* combined race and labor militancy into a potent amalgam. As one striker, Edrena Johnson, wrote in her jailhouse diary, "We're going to stand up for what is right because we're soul from our hearts, and soul power is where it's at."[119] To see the slogan as a compromise motto, more palatable than the controversial *Black Power* phrase, would be to miss the point altogether. The slogan did not render the strike any less threatening to Charleston's white supremacist, economically oppressive order. On the contrary, it provided a language to describe the coalition of white unionists, female strikers, black radicals, and civil rights advocates seeking to topple the city's power structure. In agreement that Charleston's racist, elitist economic order must end, each protestor chanting "Soul Power" inflected it with her or his own meaning. Its singularity lay in its ability to represent and articulate different political stances seemingly without contradiction.

After nearly four months, the strikers went back to work with better wages but without union recognition. Though only a qualified victory, the "Union Power, Soul Power" campaign had an extraordinary effect on the city. The hospital workers won raises of almost a dollar an hour, a grievance procedure, and the reinstatement of their union leaders. Black Charlestonians registered to vote in record numbers and a new sense of black pride and possibility pervaded the city. For 1199, the campaign boosted its national organizing drive. "Particularly for black urban workers," Fink and Greenberg suggest, "the 'union power, soul power' crusade broke down barriers separating labor organizing from the community-based black militancy of the era."[120] Mere weeks after the strike ended, 1199 organizers established bases in several urban cities including Pittsburgh, Philadelphia, and Baltimore where Madeline Anderson's 1970 film *I Am Somebody* was a regular part of their recruitment efforts.

I Am Somebody, directed by Anderson, a CBS filmmaker, was the first film created by a black American woman.[121] Anderson's inspiring depiction of black women shouting, "Soul power! I may be poor, but I am somebody. I may be black, but I am somebody," demonstrates that these demurely dressed, often

1. Charleston strikers walk the picket line. Still from Madeline Anderson's *I Am Somebody*.

2. Police arresting Charleston strikers. Still from Madeline Anderson's *I Am Somebody*.

bespectacled women were on the front lines of late 1960s militant racial struggle. As the striker narrating the film declares, "We proved to everybody that we could stand and fight together, that we were ready to sacrifice and that we would go to jail. And if I didn't learn but one thing, it was that if you are ready and willing to fight for yourself, other folks will be ready and willing to fight for you." The hospital workers' fight concretely reflected and impacted the daily lives of Charleston's vast black underclass. Importantly, the hospital workers inspired Charleston's black youth, not the other way around. As one young student in the film says, "We are here to help all the poor people in Charleston. . . . We feel as if we should come together now so we won't be in the same predicament as [the hospital workers] are now." Recognizing that their own self-interest depended on the outcome of the hospital strike, students organized support efforts, often defying their middle-class parents.

The "Union Power, Soul Power" crusade was arguably the quintessential example of 1199's vision during the 1960s and 1970s. The union saw absolutely no contradiction between black enfranchisement and worker empowerment. Since its earliest days, 1199 demonstrated the fact that a heterogeneous group of forces could form effective, strategic alliances. Old and U.S. Third World Leftists could struggle in good faith without being stymied by their ideological differences or dissolving those differences into the lowest political common denominator.

1199's interest in film extended beyond production and into the realm of exhibition. During the 1960s and 1970s, the union publicized and screened leftist films that would otherwise have received little media attention. In 1965, *1199 News* enthusiastically endorsed Michael Roemer's *Nothing But a Man* (1964), calling it a film "every 1199er should see." The film stars Ivan Dixon as Duff, a railroad worker whose marriage to the middle-class Josie (Abby Lincoln) precipitates a clash with the forces of segregation and anti-unionism. Though an unflinching indictment of Deep South poverty and discrimination, *Nothing But a Man*, 1199 argued, exposed "the problems of most of us no matter what our color."[122] 1199's attempt to place *Nothing But a Man* in the context of a larger anticapitalist perspective was apparent in its 1967 film festival which featured it along with Herbert Biberman's *Salt of the Earth* (1954), the story of U.S. Mexican miners fighting for a union, and Mario Monicelli's 1963 film *The Organizer*, starring Marcello Mastroianni as a unionist in an Italian textile factory in the 1880s. Combining "suspense, drama and humor" in order to highlight the "struggle of working people to live in dignity," the festival was yet another example of 1199's determination to both educate and entertain.[123] The 1967 film festival was followed up in 1974 with another film festival featuring *Salt of the Earth*, Cindy Firestone's *Attica* (1974), Guiliano Montaldo's *Sacco and Vanzetti* (1971), and *Battle of Algiers* (1965), Gillo Pontecorvo's semidocumentary on the Algerian guerrilla movement against French colonialism. Combining the various planks of its ideological commitments, the film festival, like all of 1199's cultural programs, offered multiple entry points for union members. A viewer's interest in Sacco and Vanzetti might lead her or him to watch *Battle of Algiers* or *Attica*, thus shoring up her or his nascent opposition to colonialism or police brutality.

Conclusion

So successful was 1199's variety of cultural programs that in 1976 the union made the following boast, "By the early 1970s, more than 12,000 members and their families participated annually in dances, picnics, moonlight sails, live theater programs with Broadway stars, film festivals, Christmas children's parties and displays at the union's own art gallery."[124] Rather than viewing the union's intense cultural activism as incidental to its tremendous organizing victories, it is clear that the two went hand in hand. As Moe Foner once remarked, "What the local and its members are doing is demonstrating that the fight for a living wage and decent working conditions is the start of the struggle for all the good things of life."[125] This effort was not simply a claim for inclusion in the U.S. political and economic status quo; instead, it was a militant, multiracial demand that workers attain not only access to but control over domestic resources. The strength and import of 1199's history during the 1960s and 1970s lies in the critical insight it lends into the radical, if often unfulfilled, potential of cultural politics. Through a diverse set of cultural and political activities, the U.S. Third World Leftists in 1199 crafted a flexible, multivalent, and above all rare counterhegemonic discourse.

In considering the visual and institutional manifestations of U.S. Third World Left identification, the next two chapters turn to Newsreel and Third World Newsreel, filmmaking collectives that combined the distribution of Third World films with the production of media chronicling the U.S. Third World Left. The issues debated among Williams, Jones, and Cruse—the value of armed defense, the parallel of communities of color and Third World colonies as metaphor and material reality, the relationship between class and race oppression—all found articulation in the impressive body of films produced and distributed by these two organizations.

3. Newsreel

Rethinking the Filmmaking Arm

of the New Left

●

Newsreel, for me, is the constant challenge of facing choices which are at once, and indissolubly film-making choices, political choices, activist choices, aesthetic choices.
—Norm Fruchter, "Newsreel"

When Melvin Margolies and Jonas Mekas called a meeting of filmmakers and activists in December of 1967, they had a fairly modest goal. Angry at mainstream's media depiction of the recent March on the Pentagon, these members of New York City's underground film movement called for filmmakers to pool their footage for a documentary. They envisioned a film that would be a counterhegemonic document, one sympathetically portraying antiwar demonstrators and exposing the state repression they faced. But they got more than they bargained for, inadvertently igniting an activist documentary movement that reverberated around the country. Over sixty people came to that 22 December meeting at the Filmmakers' Cinematheque, and a "radical film newsreel service" was born.[1] Drawing from statements he recorded at that December meeting, Mekas described the group in the pages of the *Village Voice*:

The Newsreel is a radical news service whose purpose is to provide an alternative to the limited and biased coverage of television news. The news that we feel is significant—any event that suggests the changes and redefinitions taking place in America today, or that underlines the necessity for such changes—has been consistently undermined and suppressed by the media. Therefore we have formed an organization to serve the needs of people who want to get hold of news that is relevant to their own activity and thought.[2]

Initially, the Newsreel—the preceding *the* was quickly dropped—was envisioned as a news source, one that would chronicle the events and people who might otherwise be elided from the historical record. Members understood themselves to be operating from a left-wing perspective, one defined by daily practice rather than written manifestos. Mekas described Newsreel's target audience in extremely broad terms: "All people working for change, students, organizations in ghettos and other depressed areas."[3] It might be argued that such an expansive definition could just as easily have defined the Young Americans for Freedom (YAF), a William F. Buckley inspired right-wing campus group, as it did Newsreel.[4] After all, YAF also worked for radical change, though not of the progressive kind. However, Newsreel's expansive political sense, its address to a purposefully broad constituency, facilitated the formation of chapters in several cities including Chicago, Boston, Detroit, Atlanta, Los Angeles, San Francisco, London, and Kingston, Ontario. In a few short months, Newsreel had become the filmmaking arm of the New Left.

The view of Newsreel as a New Left organization has dominated accounts of the group. Michael Renov and Bill Nichols have both described Newsreel as an important manifestation of New Left politics and culture.[5] For Nichols, Newsreel had a "barometric connection" to the "Movement" reflecting the views of a "large portion of the Movement."[6] Renov, rather than seeing Newsreel as simply a reflection of movement politics, emphasizes Newsreel's role in forging a "new language of contestation for the American New Left."[7] "Newsreel, taken as an ensemble of practices and effects," Renov argues, "occupied a crucial position in the largely unconscious construction of a political imaginary for the New Left."[8] Even as Newsreel films like *Columbia Revolt* and *Summer '68* tracked the unfolding of New Left history, the group's practices shaped the horizon of possibility for New Left audiences, visually representing in chaotic, nonlinear form the emergent identities, alliances, strategies, and utopian gestures that animated it.

It is the process and the vocabulary through which Newsreel represented this culture-in-formation that interest me in this chapter. Addressing this question, however, ultimately requires challenging Newsreel historiography, which has framed the group exclusively in New Left terms. That historical framing obscures as much as it reveals, erasing the Third Cinema techniques and anticolonial sensibility that profoundly impacted Newsreel film practice. Broadening the examination of Newsreel tendencies makes visible these influences and resituates the film collective as an integral part of an emerging U.S. Third World Left. It also works to unsettle sixties narratives that reduce this period to the sum of its New Left parts. To understand Newsreel as simply a product of the New Left or to see Newsreel and Third World Newsreel, its successor, as essentially distinct organizations, overlooks important continuities between the two. Rather than focusing on how these organizations differ in terms of mission and constituency, this chapter considers how Newsreel's theory and praxis led in part to Third World Newreel's emergence. To define Newsreel as solely a New Left product is to misapprehend the factors that have contributed to Third World Newsreel's nearly forty year history of producing and distributing media by and about peoples of color.

This chapter rethinks the political and cultural meaning of New York Newsreel, arguing that although it was a New Left organization, it was also from its earliest days one important to the U.S. Third World Left. If one takes seriously Renov's apt description of Newsreel as a "site of symbolic condensation, a kind of *tabula rasa* for projections of diverse character,"[9] then Newsreel need not be seen as either New Left or U.S. Third World Left. Rather, viewing the group in a dual sense lends new insight into this dense cultural formation, one that for a brief time enabled conflicting identities and competing interests to coexist. Even in its infancy, New York Newsreel reflected and participated in a larger domestic and international Third World community—for example, efforts to disseminate rarely seen Third World films dominated the group's distribution practices. By evaluating the distribution and production practices that structured Newsreel, I highlight the series of tensions that shaped the attempts by both the New and U.S. Third World Left to create an alternative, counter-hegemonic cultural and political space. The chapter's second focus rests on two early Newsreel films that depicted New York City's communities of color. I argue that these films can be fruitfully seen as representational and political laboratories in which a series of visual and narrative issues are worked through. These films grapple with a whole host of interrelated issues: what it means to be politically radical; the unequal relationship between white, middle-class, and often male filmmakers and their nonwhite, working-class, female subjects; and strategies for deconstructing the common sense that structures the traffic of bodies, things, ideas, and political histories between First and Third World sites. In short, many of the themes and anxieties evident in the U.S. Third World Left found their first tentative articulation in groups like Newsreel, helping to produce and reflect an emerging U.S. Third World Left consciousness.

Newsreel: The Early Days

Of Newsreel's thirty or so early members, most were white, male, and university educated. This does not suggest that women did not form an integral part of the organization: Roz Payne attended at the very first meeting, and Ellen Hirst, Lynn Phillips, Marcia Rizzi, Deborah Schaeffer, and Bev Grant were present either near or at the very beginning.[10] Some of the members were political and cultural activists with little filmmaking experience, others, including Melvin Fishman, Allan Siegel, and Shawn Walker, were part of New York's experimental film movement. A few—Norm Fruchter, Robert Kramer, and Robert Machover—straddled the ideological and experiential line between activists and filmmakers. This last group's ability to inhabit both worlds— borne out of their connections to the British and U.S. New Left—served as a critical model for Newsreel.

Early Newsreel's membership expanded for various reasons including the historical moment and informal networks. For instance, Fishman stopped Payne, a schoolteacher who had moved to New York City in 1967, as she was walking in the East Village with a camera and invited her to the founding meeting. She eagerly accepted and became a central member of Newsreel. It seems clear that Newsreel's eclectic membership and ideological expansiveness drew Payne to the group. Almost thirty years later, she recalled, "I think we were great because we came from various political backgrounds and had different interests. We never all agreed on one political line."[11] That diversity is certainly borne out in the individual biographies of other members. However, there are certain repeating tendencies that also emerge. For one, Newsreel's very practice troubled the line between culture and politics. Second, Newsreel's distribution and production networks included films made in the United States, as well as those created in decolonizing sectors of the Third World.

Fruchter lived in Britain in the early 1960s, writing film and theater reviews for several leftist journals and working as the assistant for *New Left Review* editor Stuart Hall from 1960 to 1962.[12] Covering postwar politics, media, and popular culture, *New Left Review* served as the theoretical sounding board for the British New Left, and Fruchter's involvement with it put him in an intellectual circle that included Hall, Paddy Whannel, and Peter Wollen, later the author of the groundbreaking *Signs and Meaning in the Cinema*.[13] Returning to the United States in 1962, Fruchter started doing political organizing in Newark with the Economic Research and Action Project (ERAP), SDS's attempt to spark a movement fighting inner-city poverty that would parallel the Southern civil rights movement.[14] The project later became the subject of a film Fruchter made with Machover entitled *Troublemakers*, which premiered at the Lincoln Center Film Festival in 1966. It was in the Newark ERAP that Fruchter met Kramer, another Newsreel founder. Having made two films, *In the Country* (1967) and *The Edge* (1978), Kramer already had extensive filmmaking experience prior to Newsreel.[15] Kramer, Machover, and Fruchter joined with filmmakers Peter Gessner and Alan Jacobs, the makers of a civil rights film in 1965 called *Alabama March*, to form two short-lived production companies, Blue Van Films and Alpha 60, both of which failed because they could not find distribution for their films.[16] These failed efforts led them to discuss forming a film organization, a plan that would eventually crystallize after the 22 December meeting.

The group that coalesced around SDS and other organizing projects formed one important sector within Newsreel, but a second cohort of activist filmmakers came to the organization via the underground film movement. Pivotal to this group was Newsreel founder and longtime member Allan Siegel. Born in Brooklyn, Siegel grew up in Levittown, the postwar suburb built for returning GIS on Long Island where both of his parents were community activists.[17] While his mother was involved in local electoral politics, his father engaged in what Siegel later described as "consciousness-raising": "He would go around and talk to different people, particularly in the Jewish community, about racism." As a result, Siegel was exposed to antiracist politics at an early age and became a member of CORE in high school. After briefly studying architecture and traveling around Europe, Siegel returned to the United States in the midsixties and made *The Grain* (1967), a black-and-white film depicting urban alienation via images of Baltimore's industrial landscape.

The film caught the attention of then underground filmmaker Ken Jacobs and critic Jonas Mekas, who showed *The Grain* at the Millennium Film Workshop and the New Yorker Theater—prime exhibition spaces for New York's underground filmmakers. Soon after, Jacobs suggested that Siegel teach a film workshop at the Free University of New York, an experiment in open education, modeled after a similar institution in Berkeley. Although most of Siegel's students had no filmmaking experience, the Free University workshop turned out to be a critical catalyst for Newsreel. Siegel and his workshop students, including Marvin Fishman, Melvin Margolies, and Shawn Walker, a black photographer living in Harlem, decided to film the antiwar March on the Pentagon.

On 21 October 1967, fifty thousand people gathered in front of the Lincoln Memorial for a day of street theater, folk singing, and speech making to protest the draft. In return, they met with naked brutality as military police, paratroopers, and U.S. Marshals attacked the predominantly white crowd: "Non-resisting girls were kicked and clubbed by U.S. marshals old enough to be their fathers . . . cracking heads, bashing skulls."[18] At the end of the day, almost seven hundred protestors had been arrested and scores of others were injured.[19] As Norman Mailer would later document, the Vietnam War had truly come home to roost.[20]

Though by 1967 U.S. audiences regularly viewed televised images of Southern black flesh violated by dogs and water hoses, they were unprepared for the type of spectacular violence being visited on large numbers of white protesters—though that, too, would change after the 1968 Chicago Democratic National Convention.[21] The March on the Pentagon presented mainstream media with a dilemma. If they televised the images of police brutality, they would expose the fact that violent coercion forms a constitutive element of the U.S. nation-state; but if they did not, then they would collude with the state in its effort to mask its coercive character. Predictably, the mainstream media refused to broadcast images that would challenge the state's official cover story, which blamed the violence on the protesters. Struck by the singular importance of the March on the Pentagon, many of Siegel's workshop students went to Newsreel's initial meeting, after which most of them joined the group, comprising another of the group's core segments.

Where Fruchter, Kramer, Machover, and others were primarily concerned with organizing, Siegel, Margolies, Walker, and the other workshop students saw their primary role as experimental filmmakers making art designed to mobilize audiences. As one early Newsreeler remarked, "[There were] those who felt Newsreel should pursue propaganda work, media work, and those who felt that wasn't as important as primary organizing." The member continued, "The people talking about primary organizing were thinking about staying with a constituency, living with those people and not having a separate identity."[22] For that group, Newsreel films should emerge from local organizing initiatives, just as *Troublemakers* had, rather than serve as substitutes for political activism. For the underground filmmakers, however, filmmaking was an end in itself, with the potential to spur viewers to political activity. In 1997, Siegel characterized the divide in Newsreel as one between those who "had a specific sense of a political direction, and those people who were involved in just making films."[23]

If Newsreel's films can serve as any measure, this assessment is unsatisfactory precisely because it restages the art-versus-politics divide that Newsreel's very existence sought to defy. Though activists and artists might have been unevenly incorporated into Newsreel, the films themselves are the product of politically engaged filmmakers. They present a political vantage point even as they challenge generic Hollywood codes that privilege linear narratives and the seamless integration of the camera into the narrative itself. Rather than seeing Siegel's assessment as proof that Newsreel never really forged a successful union of art and politics, one might take his words as evidence of the difficulty involved in escaping the binary altogether. One might also understand the group's collective way of working and refusal to credit individual filmmakers with specific films as one attempt to suture Newsreel's factions into a coherent whole.[24] If Newsreel did indeed possess distinct factions these cannot be neatly graphed onto the body of its films.

Given the centrality of cultural production to our contemporary understanding of the sixties, it is striking how often the binary logic of art versus politics creeps into histories of the period. Historians such as Terry Anderson rely on narratives that see political activists and cultural innovators as groups at cross-purposes. Anderson's *The Movement and the Sixties* poses a nearly unbridgeable divide between the counterculture and the New Left.[25] Hippies, as Anderson describes them, were more interested in opting out of the economic, political, and social arrangement than changing it. New Leftists, on the other hand, were serious intellectuals and politicos dismissive of—and largely unaffected by—the sixties cultural renaissance. To be sure, it is a long distance from Tom Hayden and SDS to Ken Kesey and the LSD-taking Merry Pranksters, but for every serious politico that dismissed the counterculture, there were individuals and groups who moved in the seams between political and cultural work, transforming definitions of both in their wake. Even if one agrees with Anderson's general argument, his privileging of the New Left and the overwhelmingly white counterculture skews his perspective, preventing closer attention to groups like Newsreel who presaged a U.S. Third World Left with much more fluid ideas about how culture and politics might be constructively intertwined in their daily activities.

In actuality, the culture-politics divide within Newsreel, as well as within much of the era's most innovative groups, proved far less rigid and far more permeable than has previously been acknowledged by sixties participants and observers alike. Newsreel members gave primacy to their identities as organizers or filmmakers depending on the political context and internal debate underway. While the intensity and seriousness of the debates over Newsreel's mission and methods should not be underestimated, Newsreelers often held both identities simultaneously. For example, Siegel himself left Newsreel briefly between 1970 and 1972 not to pursue a filmmaking career but to organize with the Black Panthers in New Haven.[26] Robert Kramer, although initially committed to primary organizing, later became a celebrated political filmmaker. What makes Newsreel a critical case study is the fact that it contended with and transformed culture-versus-politics debates, producing an important visual record—over twenty newsreels in 1968 alone—of left-wing activism that epitomized a singular brand of cultural politics.

It is within this context that I want to challenge Bill Nichols's assessment of Newsreel as a reactive rather than proactive social force. In his 1972 master's thesis, he argued that "the [Newsreel] filmmaking units were not vanguard units in theory or practice, politically or cinematically."[27] Nichols based this conclusion on a comparison of Newsreel to the Russian documentarian Dziga Vertov and the Workers Film and Photo League, whom he sees as having transformed newsreels into a tool for depicting the plight of the working class during the 1930s. Newsreel, in Nichols's view, could neither match the aesthetic innovation of Vertov nor the political sophistication of the league (7–15). Even more damning, according to Nichols, is the fact that Newsreel films did not provide a political analysis, did not, in other words, show where the movement could go, but only where it was at the time. This is due to the fact, Nichols argues, that "New York Newsreel's initial expectations and early accomplishments never solidified into an homogenous body of dogma" (90).

Here I would dispute Nichols's understanding of Newsreel. Though I agree with Nichols about Newsreel's ideological fluidity, what he sees as a flaw, I see as a significant strength. Newsreel's political hybridity ensured the rapid dissemination of the group's work and the development of alliances with a diverse range of New Left and U.S. Third World Left groups such as SDS, the Black Panthers, the Young Lords, Vietnam Veterans against the War, as well as activists fighting for women's liberation and affordable housing. Though these groups may have formed strategic alliances around issues including opposition to the Vietnam War, they did not necessarily see themselves as generally sharing a political or cultural project and would most certainly have been alienated by Newsreel's dogmatic adherence to a particular political doctrine. Departing from the New Left preoccupation with following the "correct" political line ensured Newsreel's continued existence and influence long after the rest of the movement dissolved.

Nichols's dismissal of Newsreel as insufficiently vanguard can also be disputed. After 1969, Newsreel films did not serve as mere reflections of the New Left; instead, films such as *El pueblo se levanta* (1971) and *Rompiendo puertas* (1970) depicted the Young Lords Party and a squatters' rights group, respectively, who were by no means at the center of a then disintegrating New Left. There is a very different political calculation and context involved in making a film like *Columbia Revolt* (1968), which documents an event that garnered national attention, and filming the reclamation efforts of Puerto Rican housing activists whose activities had gained little exposure outside of New York City.[28] Combining critiques of U.S. colonialism, domestic racism, and class exploitation, these U.S. Third World Leftists signified a political and cultural turn that the New Left simply did not take. In other words, these later Newsreel films attempted exactly what Nichols accuses them of failing to do. They visually represented the trajectory that the movement ought to take, a direction that joined anticolonial, antiwar, and antiracist critiques to understand both domestic race relations and international struggles for self-determination and autonomy. In addition, their choice of subject matter ironically commented on the very notion of a vanguard because the film's subjects—poor, middle-aged, and elderly black and Latina women—effectively mobilized themselves instead of waiting to be led by a New Left vanguard. In other words, a documentary like *Rompiendo puertas* contests vanguardist theories, exposing the condescension for working peoples inherent in such formulations. There is more than a little irony, then, involved in Nichols's evaluating Newsreel by the vanguard standard because the group's activities deliberately rubbed against that standard's antidemocratic grain. Newsreel by no means avoided all vanguardist tendencies, but the group's struggles to build an institutional structure and a film praxis that was both collective and democratic prove instructive because they reveal many of the tensions rife within both the New and U.S. Third World Left.

Filming Subjects, Building an Institutional Praxis

Soon after Newsreel's founding meeting, a small coordinating committee was established, but the group operated as a loosely defined participatory democracy.[29] This meant that a handful of people managed Newsreel's daily activities, but its upcoming projects and priorities were discussed at the group's infamous all-night meetings. Newsreel made these meetings public, and they usually drew around thirty participants.[30] Sometimes meetings did not focus on filmmaking at all. Robert Locativa, an early New York Newsreel member who formed San Francisco Newsreel with Robert Kramer and Robert Machover in 1969, remembered, "We did not see ourselves as filmmakers then. . . . We were political activists. We could talk about the current situation, what was happening and what needed to be done."[31] Attendees at weekly meetings soon broke down into interest-based caucuses. Along with the anti–Vietnam War, high school students, women, workers, Yippies, and sex, drugs, and party caucuses, there were also ones that focused on the Third World and anti-imperialism.[32] The decision-making process, however, was far more random and much less democratic than such a system might indicate. In Siegel's words, "It was sort of the illusion of democracy and the illusion of collectivity."[33] In principle, everyone had an equal say in Newsreel's direction, but in practice, it was the most knowledgeable, articulate, forceful, and financially well-connected members who determined Newsreel's course. Renov concurs, "The Fruchters, Kramers and Machovers of Newsreel were the bright and persuasive young men who could function within the world of capital, either by virtue of birthright or by acquired expertise."[34] Fruchter himself recalled: "Nobody was paid; so your participation depended on having another means to finance yourself. And there was a group of people who worked and therefore could never stay up all night because they had to go to work the next morning and couldn't shoot certain sequences. . . . All the income that was brought in and all the fund-raising that was done went right into the production of more films and that perpetuated the reign of the people who had self-sufficient resources or could somehow juggle their life or their job or whatever so that they could do that."[35] Since a small group of white men had the economic and cultural capital to control Newsreel's agenda, the women and few people of color involved were left to undertake the daily administrative tasks that kept the organization afloat. A gendered and raced hierarchy mirroring the larger society's quickly structured the Newsreel collective.

Though money proved a critical factor in Newsreel's film production, the group's ties to particular political issues or organizations and the rapid pace of current events ultimately determined which films Newsreel made. Through ERAP, Newsreel was intricately connected to SDS, an influence that was evident in early films like *No Game* (1967) and *America '68* (1968), but individual involvement in local protest movements also influenced Newsreel's choice of subject matter. Debates would erupt over certain issues—urban renewal, the health care crisis among the urban poor—and the member most intimately involved in these causes would convince the others to fund a film. In the case of

Columbia Revolt (originally entitled *The Columbia Revolt*), Marvin Fishman had begun filming a nascent protest movement in Harlem before Newsreel even existed.[36]

In the group's founding manifesto, Newsreel vowed to make three different types of films: short newsreels on movement activities, so-called tactical films or how-to films for community organizers, and longer analytical pieces.[37] The group also set itself the ambitious goal of making two films a month and distributing at least twelve prints of them across the country.[38] Lack of resources quickly forced a scaling back of that objective. With the exception of Norm Fruchter and John Douglas's *Summer '68*, filmmakers focused on producing two newsreel and tactical films, a fact that is significant because it reflects the group's belief that films were meant to inspire action, an outcome that could best be achieved by making short films featuring rapid-fire action and startling imagery. Befitting its New Left roots and historical moment, New York Newsreel's earliest films documented opposition to the Vietnam War. *Chomsky-Resist* (1968) featured an interview with Noam Chomsky, one of five draft-resistance spokespeople indicted by the U.S. government. In *Four Americans*, filmmakers interviewed four men who deserted the U.S. *Intrepid* and fled to Japan. For would-be protestors, *Riot-Control Weapons* told of the arms buildup underway in city police departments and how to protect oneself. The group also completed *No Game*, the film on the March on the Pentagon, and *Mill-In* (1968) in which antiwar protestors disrupt wealthy New Yorkers while Christmas shopping on Fifth Avenue.[39]

New York Newsreel also documented other protest activities in the New York City area. In *I.S. 201*, a community-controlled school in Harlem arouses the ire of city officials by holding a memorial service for Malcolm X. In the 1968 film *Garbage*, a radical anarchists group—Up against the Wall, Motherfucker—dumps garbage at Lincoln Center to express solidarity with striking sanitation workers. Reflecting the emergent feminist movement, *Up against the Wall, Miss America* (1968) depicts the 1968 Atlantic City protest during which demonstrators crown a sheep as the winner of a mock Miss America pageant. During New York Newsreel's first two years, its production primarily focused on the white student movement. One early Newsreel member described their films as "only [showing] the white movement and anti-war movement," defending that choice by saying, "At that point in the political history of the radical movement, that was where it was at—going to organized mass demonstrations."[40]

This assessment—that the white student movement "was where it was at"—conceals the fact that individual and collective filmmaking choices helped to construct and represent the movement as white, even in cases when it was not. Debates within the organization took place from Newsreel's founding as evidenced by the various caucuses, which represented different, sometimes competing interests. In the case of *Columbia Revolt*, for example, black and Latino/a activists are marginalized while white students take center stage, despite the fact that students of color and Harlem residents working together ignited the initial protests. Since 1961, black and Latino/a Harlemites, eventually joined by students of color from Columbia University, had been protesting the university's plans to raze Harlem's only public park to build a private gymnasium for its students. Reinforcing the de facto Jim Crow structure separating Harlem and the university, the architectural plans only allowed local residents to use 15 percent of the gym, all of which was located in the basement and could only be accessed by a separate backdoor entrance reserved for community members.[41] Though Fishman shot some of these early community protests, once a large, predominantly white group of Columbia students joined them, the nature of the protests changed and the number of filmmakers multiplied. When those students, some eight hundred strong, decided to take over Hamilton Hall on 23 April 1968, an action that would bring the campus to a virtual standstill for the rest of the semester, several Newsreelers began shooting the series of events that followed. When news crews remained outside the buildings throughout the initial seven-day strike, Newsreel was the only organization shooting from the inside.[42] When the strike was over, Lynn Philips, an experienced editor, edited the resulting footage and Newsreel members screened it repeatedly until they agreed on a print to distribute. "Speed was of the essence," Siegel later recalled.[43]

Columbia Revolt was truly a composite of various filmmakers' footage, a collective perspective on a watershed event in New Left history. There were five crews shooting from inside the five different buildings taken over by students. What those various views shared, however, was a concentration on white student protestors that visually obliterated the earlier alliance between Harlem residents and the students of color, some of whom were members of CORE, SNCC, the Black Panther Party and the Student Afro-American Society. Though we catch glimpses of black student protestors, we do not see the community residents most affected by Columbia's plans because the film hones in on the campus sit-in in order to capture the carnivalesque atmosphere inside the seized buildings. (Supporters crossing the police barricade to bring strikers supplies and an impromptu wedding ceremony are just two of the film's highlights.) Little attention is paid to the demands made by the protestors, of which there were initially six, and the gymnasium is never discussed in any detail. It is worth quoting Nichols in some detail: "The black students who act almost

3. Poster from the 1968 Columbia University strike. Still from
Newsreel's *Columbia Revolt* provided courtesy of Third World
Newsreel.

entirely off-camera, despite general agreement on their crucial role in the strike . . . had a more specific aim: to stop construction of the gym. The whites were inspired by the militancy of the blacks and credited them with being the vanguard of the strike. *They adopted the militancy, however, without its purpose: militancy itself became an end rather than stopping work on the gym or mustering community support.*"[44] *Columbia Revolt* appears to be a spontaneous record of events as they unfold, but a narrow focus on the white student movement obscures the complex race and class dynamics that culminated in the student strike, unintentionally mystifying the complicated steps that led to organized protest. Reframing the Columbia takeover as solely a student action conceals the cross-class, interracial coalition that had been forged in the Harlem community, replicating the exclusionary and dismissive dynamic that sparked the conflict with Columbia in the first place. Ironically, this visually unrepresented, nascent alliance has the potential to help bridge the multiple cultural and material gaps between those living in the shadow of Columbia and those reaping the benefits of its reflected glory. Once this larger context is evacuated, *Columbia Revolt* can only represent the takeover as a struggle against society writ larger, rather than a specific battle steeped in a long-standing history of institutional neglect and exploitation. In the most generous reading of the film, the largely white student protestors replace the absent black community but speak in its name; a more cynical reading might wonder whether the students feel the need to speak for or about the Harlemites at all.

The process that produced *Columbia Revolt* was an extreme example of

Newsreel's collective filmmaking approach. Ideas for films would be discussed among the entire group, and those without independent means had to convince a powerful bloc of members to allocate Newsreel funds for the project. Meanwhile those with access to money could make films without group approval. After production was nearly complete, films went through a final vetting process, and those that the group agreed on were distributed as Newsreel films. This final approval process largely determined a film's fate. For instance, *America '68* by Fruchter and Douglas was deemed "too cerebral" by a Newsreel majority, so very few prints were made and circulated.[45] In keeping with this collective process, production credits were replaced with a white Newsreel logo placed against a black background. Almost immediately after the logo's appearance, an unseen machine gun riddles it with bullets. The image is a somewhat ambiguous one: Is it meant to suggest that Newsreelers are members of a combat unit, metaphoric or actual? Or given the state's predilection for violent repression, was it meant to suggest that Newsreelers themselves faced attack, even obliteration, by these forces?

Despite its representational bias in favor of the white student movement, Newsreel did produce a few films on the situation of Third World and U.S. Third World communities. For one, the collective released the groundbreaking *People's War* (1969), the first U.S. film shot entirely in northern Vietnam; in fact, Fruchter, Kramer, and Douglas even had their footage seized by U.S. Customs on their reentry into the United States.[46] The film depicts the popular national liberation struggle in Vietnam focusing on the local organization of northern Vietnamese society and its role in sustaining people living in hazardous conditions. Once it emerged, *People's War* fueled the U.S. antiwar movement's already strong support for Ho Chi Minh's forces. Turning to local events, Newsreel's *The Case against Lincoln Center* (1968) lamented the fact that in order to build a monument to American and European high culture, the city planned to displace more than twenty thousand Latino families. *Community Control* (1969) detailed the clash between black and Latino parents and the United Federation of Teachers union over community-run education in the Ocean Hill-Brownsville section of Brooklyn. An interesting dichotomy exists in these early films. On the one hand, the group made films about the student movement defined as white; on the other, they made films depicting the community, defined as black and Latino. So, it is not so much that Newsreel began to film communities of color after the disintegration of the New Left as it is that those existing practices began to dominate the organization, effecting and reflecting a rapid turnover in membership.

A Crude Aesthetic, an Accessible Form?

Because of the collaborative production process, Newsreel films cannot be said to bear the imprint of one auteur. It is more appropriate to view these films as a product of a particular style and set of principles, despite the group's insistence that no one ideology guided their film practice. Reflecting the influence of the underground film movement, newsreels were shot with grainy, 16mm black-and-white film. An unsteady camera, inconsistent sound, and unusual editing also became hallmarks of Newsreel productions. Interestingly, films were often deliberately crude and amateurish despite the presence of experienced film-makers. This aesthetic rawness proved a source of repeated criticism and debate within the group, as Fruchter would later recall: "A lot of people inside Newsreel were very sophisticated artists and very sophisticated cineastes in terms of their film tastes. . . . So the gap between the really sophisticated film aesthetic that a lot of us had and the Newsreel films was severe—in some cases intentional and in some cases unintentional. I remember people who would come to Newsreel meetings . . . and there would be this three-hour, incredibly exciting discussion about this terrible film. And they'd say: 'I can't believe you people. If you talk like that, why can't you make better films?' "[47] If Newsreel's style was intentional, then what purpose did such a crude style serve? Who was Newsreel's intended audience, and did the group's films eschew complexity of analysis and form in order to reach that target audience?

Newsreel's choice of style betrayed its stereotypical view of working-class tastes. A supposedly crude style was meant to signify Newsreel's solidarity with the working classes and demonstrate for its largely middle-class viewers how one might talk to and about the working classes. As Nichols ironically suggests, "Revolutionary art was sloppy, inaudible art. This was presumably the vernacular of the people, of the working classes still enchained and of the student vanguard who would precipitate the revolution."[48] On the one hand, Newsreel's middle-class members were engaged in a self-deluding, thoroughly misguided exercise in condescension. Low production values were simply symbolic acts and ultimately inadequate substitutes for actively working to bridge the enormous material and ideological gaps between middle-class students and the "oppressed masses." Instead, they actually increased the distance between the middle and working classes, relying on an imagined working-class identity that bore little relation to reality. Each Newsreel film may have been designed to be people's art that countered the film industry's slick product, but they most often served to bolster the ranks of the student movement, reinforcing their own vision of themselves as vanguard revolutionaries. However, the ideological significance of such an aesthetic should not be dismissed altogether. Though it did not necessarily bring Newsreel closer to the so-called masses, such self-consciously low production values represented a direct affront to Hollywood aesthetics and a challenge to audiences accustomed to conventional narrative styles and easy visual pleasure.[49] In the end, Newsreel's crude aesthetic made for a compensatory strategy produced by and for the middle classes; consequently, it may have had an impact on the way in which middle class filmmakers and film viewers reimagined the purpose of film.

The stylistic imperative of Newsreel films was that they be akin to "battle-footage."[50] "Bullets kill, and some films get into people's heads," Fruchter declared, "to shock, stun, arrest, horrify, depress, sadden, probe, demand. We want that kind of engagement—films people can't walk away from."[51] By putting the audience on the front line of the turbulent protests of the era, individuals were forced to choose sides—an effective, albeit fleeting response. The collective's goal was not necessarily reasoned analysis, but rather an instinctive (even involuntary) response to an urgent threat. The militaristic tone evident in such metaphors as *battle footage* and *front line* betrays the extent to which Newsreel depended on a confrontational style.[52] In Robert Kramer's words, Newsreel strove to make "films that unnerve, that shake people's assumptions, that threaten, that do not soft-sell, but hopefully (an impossible ideal) explode like grenades in people's faces, or open minds like a good can opener."[53] Newsreel films were what might be called conflict propaganda, spurring the viewer from inaction into (political) activity of an often undefined kind by making the viewer uncomfortable, by making the viewer question her or his own complacency. "We want a form of propaganda that polarizes," Kramer wrote in 1968, "angers, excites, for the purpose of discussion—a way of getting at people, not by making concessions to where they are, but by showing them where you are and then forcing them to deal with that."[54] This emphasis expanded Newsreel's initial purpose somewhat; now films had to not only cover events ignored or distorted by the mainstream media but they also had to encode that disruption in the very form itself. As Nichols so eloquently puts it, "The concept of serving as an alternative moved from a differing notion of content . . . to a radically different notion of format itself."[55]

The effectiveness of this confrontation strategy was evident in a 1969 incident in which five hundred students at SUNY Buffalo burned down the campus ROTC building immediately after a screening of Newsreel films.[56] While this anarchic protest was not part of a clearly articulated political project, it did temporarily halt the military machinery on campus. Its impact, though, could only be fleeting because it was not connected to a larger political plan or linked to an organized protest movement. One student protester speaking in *Columbia Revolt* suggests what lay at the heart of the SUNY Buffalo act: "We didn't realize that we were much too timid, and that what we really had to do was show our moral strength and hold the building."[57] For this student, and presumably for others, the Columbia takeover became a symbolic action that demonstrated the morality of student protestors rather than any concrete political objectives. The ROTC action might also best be understood as a means of expressing individual and collective anger and outrage, a cathartic gesture that may have made the actors feel cleansed in some way but did little to stop the Vietnam War or the draft on which it depended. In other words, the SUNY Buffalo protest may have been dramatic, but whether or not Newsreel films facilitated the production of Herbert Marcuse's "new subjects" in that instance or any other remains an open question.

Clearly, Newsreel's style of reportage and its desire to show events and people in a way that mainstream television would not was designed to reconstruct its audience. Again, Dziga Vertov's example looms large. Working during the early Soviet era, Vertov envisioned newsreels as "fragments of actual energy" able, in the words of Bill Nichols, to "embody and perhaps forge the new man of Soviet Russia."[58] Though Marilyn Buck and Karen Ross of San Francisco Newsreel would have objected to Vertov's masculinist formulation, they echoed his general sentiments, seeing Newsreel films as a "way for filmmakers and radical organizer-agitators to break into the consciousness of the people."[59] Newsreel's self-proclaimed crude style was meant to encourage identification with the films' subjects as a first step in remaking consciousness, but not for the sake of creating a "new man." Central to remaking consciousness, in Buck and Ross's view, is a focus on the collective—"the people"—and on the transformation of community. Individual and communal remaking are not mutually exclusive, of course, but the focus on "the people" instead of "the man" reveals Newsreel's desire to affirm social change as the work of communities rather than the result of individual great men and their charismatic leadership. My argument here is not that Newsreel members uniformly held such a belief, but rather that the juxtaposition of Vertov's paradigm and that of Buck and Ross reveals ongoing debates about the individual's relation to the collective within Newsreel and the sixties Left more generally. These debates hinged on explicit or implicit theories of social change inevitably bound up in particular gender, class, and race positions and their resulting dynamics. Given the marginalized position of women in Newsreel, it hardly seems surprising that they emphasized the plural rather than the singular, the systemic rather than the personal.

If Newsreel films demonstrated successful mass actions, they did so by resisting in fundamental ways the emphasis on the narrowly personal that defined much of the sixties counterculture. Where mainstream media emphasized the power of the state to crush outright rebellion and peaceful protest, films like *Columbia Revolt* and *No Game* captured the sense of collective possibility that characterized the student movement.[60] When *Columbia Revolt* was screened at the University of California at Santa Cruz the day before a protest against the Board of Regents, it helped strengthen student resolve.[61] Another oft-cited example is the use of *Black Panther*, the 1968 film by San Francisco Newsreel, as a recruiting tool by the Black Panther Party who often screened the fifteen-minute film at their meetings. These examples bolster Renov's suggestion that Newsreel helped to "construct a political imaginary for the New Left,"[62] since in both cases the films work to document efforts at social change and to persuade others that these examples can be replicated elsewhere. If individual anecdotes do not necessarily prove the larger point, another way of assessing Newsreel's impact on the New Left is to examine the means by which Newsreel films reached audiences, in other words, their distribution practices and exhibition networks.

Distributing the Message, Building a Movement

Newsreel's distribution network, like its film production, was guided by the desire to disseminate counterhegemonic narratives. Since conventional media avenues, network or public access television, and commercial film distributors were barred to the group, Newsreel had to forge its own distribution network. As Allan Siegel later recalled, "The whole concept of an alternative form of distribution was central to Newsreel."[63] For much of 1968, Newsreel held a series of Saturday night screenings at the Filmmakers' Cinematheque, the New York underground's venue of choice.[64] However, such screenings only reached a limited audience, one that was already part of an alternative New York City art scene. The process of forging a national distribution network was accomplished thanks to the existence of Newsreel chapters in over sixteen large cities and college towns. For example, San Francisco Newsreel's *The Women's Film* (1971), Boston Newsreel's *Boston Draft Resistance Group* (1968), or New York Newsreel's *Columbia Revolt* became part of every chapter's film collection and thus reached a national audience. In this way, various organizations learned about protest activities across the country, and Newsreel films reached a much wider audience than they ordinarily would have. This national network continued to expand as various chapters developed ties with particular organizations. In Siegel's words: "The vehicle for distribution became all the different kind of nascent political organizations that existed throughout the country . . . which had to do with either the student movements, various forms of the student movement, whether it was SDS or a spin-off group from SDS [or] . . . the Black Panther network."[65] So Newsreel would circulate copies of new releases, often as many as thirty or forty at any one time, to all SDS branches and other organizations including the East and West Coast Black Panthers, and, according to Siegel, "ecological groups and the [*sic*] women's groups." In this way, Newsreel built both an audience and a reputation as the news service of the New Left. This process worked at the microlevel in the New York City area as well. When filmmakers shot a protest or focused on a community issue, they met local activists who then became an enthusiastic audience for the resulting film. These activists spread the word about Newsreel films, and people ordered titles directly from the collective for use in ongoing organizing efforts.

Newsreel also had a generous rental fee policy. Films were available to anyone who requested them at low rates, particularly if they were to be used for political organizing. The group's own films could be rented for between ten and twenty-five dollars, while imported films were usually more expensive, running between thirty and sixty. However, those fees worked on a sliding scale. Colleges and other institutions that could afford it were charged the full fee, but Newsreel often reduced or waived the fee altogether for groups or individuals unable to pay. This policy not only distinguished New York Newsreel from other left-wing film distributors but it also "made them invaluable to organizers and helped to forge," according to Nichols, "a concrete link with Third World and working class people."[66] Since Newsreel's distribution network primarily existed to disseminate information, spark debate, and possibly engender mass action, the organization required films to be presented in a context that connected the issues raised in the film to the local context. Consequently, filmmakers or relevant individuals accompanied the films and led discussions after the screenings. "The films were never looked at like self-contained entities," Siegel recalled, "but were always looked at in relationship to the issues that the films highlighted and organizing people in relationship to those issues."[67]

Newsreel's belief in film's power to organize people betrays the extent to which the Russian filmmaker Vertov influenced the group. During the 1920s, Vertov traveled the Russian countryside showing newsreels to the peasants in support of Russian troops. Important as Vertov's example may have been, Siegel recalls, for the United States, "that model didn't quite work."[68] As a concession to pragmatism, Newsreel assigned people to travel with the film, whether it was screened in churches, union halls, campus dorms, or public parks. In the process, Newsreel created political organizers, people adept at talking about the multiple issues raised in the films and equipped to organize a response to them. This exhibition context also shaped the newsreels themselves since each film had to be constructed so that it facilitated discussion on a wide range of issues depending on the context.

Although the antiwar movement initially sparked Newsreel's Third World orientation, their distribution practices widened that orientation beyond Vietnam. In fact, Newsreel quickly became a virtual clearinghouse for Third World anticolonial film. To be sure, the Vietnam conflict made for a continuing focus. Peter Gessner's *Time of the Locust* (1966), a film that showed both sides of the Vietnam War debate, joined *People's War* (1970) and *Hanoi, martes 13* (1967) in the group's collection. However, Newsreel also distributed *Fueras Yanquis*, a film exposing U.S. interference in putatively free elections in the Dominican Republic. If that film offered a somewhat bleak assessment of U.S. power to thwart Central and South American autonomy, other films emphasized Third World defiance of U.S. domination. The Cuban filmmaker Santiago Álvarez emerged as a particular favorite of Newsreel; the group distributed his *Golpeandos en la selva* (1967), *Cerro pelado* (1966), *Seventy-nine Spring Times of Ho Chi Minh* (1969), and *Hasta la victoria siempre* (1967), among others. The latter film is a moving tribute to Che Guevara produced after his death. With characteristic economy, Álvarez uses excerpts from Guevara's own speeches to illustrate his belief that his doomed Bolivia campaign fit into a tradition of Third World struggle that included the efforts of Patrice Lumumba in the Congo and Ho Chi Minh in Vietnam.[69] Other films distributed by Newsreel included *F.A.L.N.*, on Venezuela's Fuerzas Armadas de Liberación Nacional, and *Medina boe*, on the armed struggle of the PAIGC (the African Party for Independence in Guinea and Cape Verde), cofounded by Amílcar Cabral, to end four hundred years of Portuguese colonialism.[70] Nichols confirms Newsreel's singular status when he describes the group as "virtually the only source of Cuban and other Third World films" in the late 1960s.[71] At times, these films idealized Third World nations and their liberation struggles. Nonetheless, the distribution of this impressive film archive presented an important challenge to Western imperialism, affirming the right of Third World peoples to determine their own fate. Newsreel's distribution network served as a critical pipeline ferrying the strategies, philosophies, events, and people that helped build a Third World anticolonial common sense.

A New Direction Emerges

Just as New York Newsreel established effective production, distribution, and exhibition methods, the group itself underwent an extended period of reorganization between 1969 and 1972. Though accounts differ widely on what occurred in the period of transition to Third World Newsreel, the following is relatively clear: Just as the ranks of the New Left had been significantly depleted by the end of 1969, so, too, had New York Newsreel's membership. Debates over inequities within Newsreel coupled with the collapse of the New Left sparked this transformation. For one, many Newsreel members began to look toward organizing within a community, including Fruchter in Newark, Kramer in Vermont, Siegel in New Haven, and Machover in Saint Louis.[72] At the same time, the remaining members who were influenced by the U.S. Left's turn to Marxist-Leninist-Maoist philosophy engaged in lengthy criticism–self criticism sessions out of which several issues arose, including the uneven distribution of filmmaking skills, the group's overwhelmingly middle-class composition, and the unequal status of women. All of these issues had bedeviled Newsreel since its inception, but an even greater consciousness of the Third World and the women's rights movement lent marginalized members new ammunition in their fight for full participation.

In terms of women's participation, Fruchter admitted, the issue had been there from the very beginning: "The organization was dominated by men and by particular types of men. I don't think that we were at all conscious of the disparity or worried about that at all, and I think that the women were conscious of it from the beginning and sort of took it for a while and then got increasingly frustrated and angry about it. And it boiled over in a variety of different ways."[73] One manifestation of that "boiling over" was the demand by female members and others that Newsreel reevaluate its structure and institutional practices, which had left the power and control of resources in the hands of educated white men. For the first time, Newsreel's internal structure and the inequities inherent in it came under intense scrutiny by the group. In response, Newsreel created several caucuses, including ones for Third World people, working-class members, and high school students; the recruitment of people of color, what the group referred to as "Third World people," also assumed top priority. As one member described it, "People began to talk about the importance of how [our] work got done, how people worked together and relate[d] together."[74] As a result, those members unwilling to share their power departed, and some left to pursue other projects, most often community organizing.

By the spring of 1970, most of Newsreel's core membership had left.[75] Six months later, the remaining members began actively recruiting Third World members, a move that reflected developments in the larger New Left movement. As early as 1967, the focus of U.S. protest had begun shifting toward Third World issues. The Third World student strikes at San Francisco State and the University of California, Berkeley, the emergence of the Black Panther Party, the Young Lords Party, the Brown Berets, and the American Indian movement, and the increased momentum of the Chicano movement were all indications of a seismic shift in the U.S. political landscape. By the early 1970s, the organizing of local Third World communities had become the single most important issue in U.S. leftist politics.[76] In some sense, this shift married the antiracist critiques initiated by the civil rights movement with the anticolonial and anti-imperial critiques gaining renewed U.S. prominence in the wake of Third World decolonization. U.S. activists became increasingly influenced by such critiques as the war in Vietnam dragged on and the civil rights movement for equal rights metamorphosed into a northern movement for autonomy and freedom. Analyzing structurally embedded forms of racism and discrimination and linking those forms to the Third World–inspired focus on Western, and specifically U.S., imperial adventures spurred the consolidation of a U.S. Third World Left. Though Newsreel had long distributed films critiquing U.S. and Western imperialism, for the first time the anticolonial critiques expressed in these films now extended to Newsreel's own internal structure, leading eventually to the reformation of Newsreel as Third World Newsreel. The common sense emerging in leftist circles undermined the group's bifurcation of its films into representations of the white student movement and those of communities of color. This is evident in the fact that Newsreel's film practice had moved toward a concern with New York's communities of color. This shifting lens developed just as the newer Third World members demanded greater access to filmmaking skills and an expansion of Newsreel's fluid politics beyond Marx, Engels, and Mao to include black American and other Third World writers.[77]

This was by no means coincidental; in fact, the seeds of a U.S. Third World Left consciousness were already sown long before Newsreel formally declared itself Third World Newsreel. This is most evident in the films produced during the transitional period, including *El pueblo se levanta* on the Young Lords Party and *Rompiendo puertas* on a squatters' rights movement composed largely of middle-aged and elderly Puerto Rican and black women. Though the films were produced by white filmmakers, they began to depict U.S. Third World communities rather than student groups, defining them as public actors—independent and militant.

Although little has been written on either *El pueblo se levanta* or *Rompiendo puertas*, the films' existence complicates the view of Newsreel as solely a New Left organ rather than one that incorporated various tendencies including a Third World Left one. These two films reflect a burgeoning consciousness in both the white filmmakers and their black and Latino subjects. Both are defined by their insistence that the roots of Puerto Rican oppression in the United States stem from the colonial status of Puerto Rico itself. Rather than collapsing all Third World struggles into a blur of nameless warriors and long-suffering women, the films clearly delineate the specific conditions unique to Puerto Rico. Despite this level of specificity, these films still vacillate between an idealization of their subjects and a concrete analysis of the social conditions and ideologies that have shaped these grassroots political movements. Though this chapter will conclude with a close examination of *Rompiendo puertas*, I want to consider *El pueblo se levanta*'s depiction of the Young Lords Party first because I am interested in the way that the film works to distinguish these young activists from both the older, middle-class Puerto Ricans with which they find themselves in conflict and the Black Panther Party after which they initially modeled themselves.

El pueblo se levanta: We're Here Because You Were There

Newsreel began filming *El pueblo se levanta* in 1969, but the film was not released until 1971.[78] As in all Newsreel films, no individual receives credit, though Bev Grant, Tammy Gold, and Robert Lacativa were central to its production, aided by Allan Siegel in the beginning.[79] Fifty minutes in length, the film constitutes a significant departure for Newsreel, both in terms of style and theme. The film has comparatively high production values; it is well shot and edited with alternating segments of voice-over narration and Latin soul excerpts. Production took a great deal longer than it did with earlier Newsreels, allowing the filmmakers to develop an in-depth portrait of the Young Lords' activities rather than just cobble together a hurried focus on a spectacular event.

Featuring footage of several protests along with lengthy interviews with party leaders and rank-and-file members, *El pueblo se levanta* presents a complicated portrait of the Young Lords Party (YLP). Not only do we see their protest activities but the Young Lords are also allowed to articulate the reasons for each protest and its connection to their thirteen-point program. If one compares this to San Francisco Newsreel's fifteen-minute *Black Panther*, the contrast is striking. Because of its abbreviated length, the Panther film only captures a few spectacular protests and features monologues from two of the Panther's most charismatic leaders, Huey Newton and Bobby Seale. *Black Panther* fails to convey a full sense of the group's ideology and its translation into everyday practice. In sum, *Black Panther* stands as an ideal recruitment film, long on black-jacketed paraders and radical icons, but short on critical analysis. The iconic status of Seale and particularly Newton is reinforced, but only at the representational sacrifice of everyday Panther members.

El pueblo se levanta was the first and until recently the only film depiction of the Young Lords Party.[80] Although the New York branch only existed between 1969 and 1973, after which it became the Puerto Rican Revolutionary Workers Organization (PRRWO), the Young Lords became well-known defenders of East Harlem's poor, criticizing both the white and Puerto Rican establishment. Like the Black Panthers, they ran several programs providing vital services for the community that the city's bureaucracy did not. They also invested in alternative cultural forms, founding an alternative radio program and a bilingual newspaper, *Palante*.[81]

The Young Lords formed part of what has become known as the *Nuevo Despertar* (New Awakening), the late 1960s spike in Puerto Rican radicalism that was fueled in part by the New Left and civil rights and in part by developments in Puerto Rico, where pressure for independence was mounting. Another critical factor in their emergence, however, was demographic in nature; by 1970, nearly half of the baby-boomer or second generation of Puerto Ricans were U.S. born.[82] Former Young Lord Iris Morales argues that the second generation was radicalized precisely because of its intermediary position between the first generation of Puerto Rican immigrants and the English-speaking world. Acting as a go-between for her Spanish-speaking parents and elders with the English-only welfare bureaucracies, Morales "got to feel . . . the disdain and injustices with which people, bureaucrats, and institutions responded to Puerto Ricans."[83]

The sociopolitical context in which the Young Lords claimed to represent New York's Puerto Ricans and linked the situation of U.S.-born Puerto Ricans to those on the island was an extremely complicated one. Typically, New York's Puerto Rican community of the 1950s and 1960s is depicted as uniformly working class, but what this elides is the multiple fissures—differences in regional background, racial formation, political formation, immediate self-interest—within each class segment. Each class was itself "stratified" as Roberto Rodríguez-Morazzani asserts: "Among workers there existed differences of skill, industry, education, etc. The same can be said of other social classes (e.g., professionals, merchants, the petty bourgeoisie, and so on). With the influx of tens of thousands of migrants from the island [during the 1950s] this internal stratification would increase."[84] In this context, one class fragment might support political stances vehemently opposed by another fragment, making it difficult to speak in the name of an entire group. One concrete example of this is the Young Lords' campaign to rid El Barrio of heroin dealers seen by many residents as a menace. Although it exposed the state's complicity in the Spanish Harlem drug trade, it sparked a conflict between those with interests in the drug trade and those without.[85]

Tensions also existed between Puerto Ricans born in the United States and those born on the island. For example, many of the leaders of the Partido Socialista Puertorriqueña (PSP), a socialist group that emerged at the end of the 1960s, were upper-class white Puerto Ricans who "looked down their noses at poor and working-class darker-skinned Puerto Ricans born in the United States." It did not help that the PSP privileged Spanish as a marker of Puerto Rican nationality, when many U.S.-born Puerto Ricans were not fluent Spanish speakers. Tensions between Puerto Ricans from the island and those in the diaspora made it difficult for the YLP and its offshoot to work with the PSP and, in the view of Rodríguez-Morazzani, meant that the Lords gravitated toward the examples of revolution presented by China and Cuba.[86] This raises an interesting proposition, namely, that attempts to link the situation of Puerto Ricans in the United States and that of those on the island may have been buoyed in large part by other Third World revolutionary examples even as they were thwarted by race and class conflicts within the group itself. The Young Lords continued advocating Puerto Rican independence even though nationalists did not necessarily affirm their diasporic identities. This no doubt contributed to the YLP's insistence on forging an intersectional approach linking critiques of racism, class exploitation, and colonialism.[87]

It also fueled the group's early adoption of the divided-nation thesis, which claimed that the island was divided with two-thirds of its citizens living there and one-third living in the United States. At its core was the definition of Puerto Ricans in the United States as a national minority whose first priority must be Puerto Rican independence. This thesis constituted a version of the internal-colony thesis, an attempt to balance concerns of class and nation that would ultimately fail. It did, however, focus attention on prisons and schools as sites for ideological indoctrination and rampant brutality. In 1971, the divided-nation thesis was abandoned because it was perceived to take the Young Lords too far away from their organizing base in New York.[88] This clash between the romanticized ideal of Puerto Rican unity and the everyday reality of entrenched hierarchies lends a certain poignancy to the Young Lords' slogan:

"Tengo Puerto Rico en Mi Corazón" ("I Have Puerto Rico in My Heart"), a grammatically incorrect slogan, notes former Young Lord Pablo Guzmán, that reflects the "bad Spanish" spoken by "Ricans raised in the states."[89]

The New York Young Lords Organization (YLO) began in June 1969. José Martinez, a member of SDS in Florida, attended SDS's annual convention where he met members of the recently formed Rainbow Coalition consisting of Black Panthers, Young Lords from Chicago, and a group called the Young Patriots, a white gang/political organization. After the convention, Martinez decided to form a YLO in New York and with that goal in mind began working with youth on the Lower East Side. He also decided to merge his fledgling group with another, the Sociedad de Albizu Campos. The Young Lords would later describe this as a "merger representing the uniting of the street people with the students of the working-class background."[90]

In October 1969, the Young Lords opened an office in El Barrio, the New York City community between First Avenue and Fifth Avenue running from East 96th Street to East 125th Street whose population was primarily Puerto Rican and African American. Its members were an amalgam of inexperienced students, working-class activists, Vietnam veterans, former New Left activists, recovering addicts, and factory and hospital workers. About 25 percent of the membership, according to Morales, was African American, and other Latinos also joined the group.[91] Like Martinez, Juan González was active in the New Left; in fact he had been jailed for his part in the 1968 Columbia strike. David Perez, a recent migrant from Chicago, and Denise Oliver were students at SUNY Old Westbury, as was Pablo Guzmán (aka Yorúba), who had recently returned from Cuernavaca, Mexico. Three months before Guzmán's arrival in Mexico, student uprisings had led to the October 1968 police massacre at Tlatelolco Plaza in Mexico City that killed thirty-five students and saw thousands more disappeared.[92] Exceeding the violent outcomes in Prague and Paris, this massacre left an indelible mark on young Mexican activists. Finally, some members of the new organization were also born in Puerto Rico, including Gloria Gonzalez, a staunch supporter of the Nationalist Party and a cofounder of the Health Revolutionary Union.[93]

Initially, YLO's emphasis was on high-profile street protests, but the group soon began to focus on providing programs to black and Puerto Rican residents of Spanish Harlem. Modeling themselves after the Black Panther Party, the Young Lords devised a thirteen-point program calling for self-determination for all Puerto Ricans, all Latinos, and Third World peoples generally. The only internal challenge to the program was one undertaken by female Young Lords to replace point 10, which read, "Machismo must be revolutionary and not oppressive," to, "We want equality for women. Down with machismo and male chauvinism."[94] Demanding community-controlled institutions, the group saw itself building "a society where the needs of the people come first, and where we give solidarity and aid to the people of the world, not oppression and racism." In achieving that society, the Lords did not rule out the use of self-defense and armed struggle.[95] During their brief existence, the Lords organized clean-up patrols in what they termed the "garbage offensive," confiscated a city-run x-ray truck to perform mobile tuberculosis testing, and took over the Lexington Avenue Methodist Church for their free breakfast program. These activities provided desperately needed community services, exposing the corruption and bureaucratic neglect behind the uneven distribution of resources.

By the end of 1970, the Lords had over one thousand members working in El Barrio, the South Bronx, and the Lower East Side. This community base helped the Young Lords mobilize impressive displays of strength including a conference entitled "Free Puerto Rico Now" attended by one thousand students and, in October 1970, a ten thousand–person march to the UN to demand Puerto Rican independence. Two other demands that no doubt galvanized support were that the United States stop drafting Puerto Ricans and end its genocide of them and all "third world peoples."[96] Official branches existed in at least four other states and on the island, with supporters in at least a dozen states and within many of New York's prisons.[97]

El pueblo se levanta itself begins with the incantatory words of the Nuyorican poet Pedro Pietri performing his "Puerto Rican Obituary."[98] It begins:

> They worked
> They were always on time
> They were never late
> They never spoke back
> When they were insulted
> They worked
> They never went on strike
> Without permission
> They never took days off
> that were not on the calendar
> They worked
> Ten days a week
> And were only paid for five
> They worked
> They worked

They worked
And they died
They died broke
They died owing
They died never knowing
What the front entrance
Of the First National City Bank
looks like

A moving requiem for the generations of Puerto Ricans who never knew "the geography of their complexion," Pietri's poem honors those elders who have "died waiting dreaming / and hating." Murdered by life on the "nervous break-down streets," this first immigrant generation has seen their American dream turn into one long nightmare. One might expect such a bleak poem to inspire a certain amount of pathos in the audience. And it does. What is surprising, however, is the air of joy commingled with anger that Pietri's words also evoke. Although the setting offers few clues as to the whereabouts of this performance, "Puerto Rican Obituary" feels paradoxically like a vital part of a communal celebration. The audience is locked in a call-and-response rhythm with the young poet, but we as film viewers cannot fully make sense of the context. *El pueblo se levanta*, in characteristic Newsreel fashion, throws us into the middle of the action, but in this case, we can only be spectators, rather than participants. This temporary withholding of access—an acknowledgment of our distance from the on-screen action rather than an attempt to eradicate that distance—serves as a reminder that the stakes have changed significantly; entry into the world of the Young Lords is neither easy nor assured.

The film is divided into three sections. The first section, to which "Puerto Rican Obituary" serves as prelude, features the Young Lords eleven-day occupation of the First Spanish Methodist Church. The takeover footage explicitly reveals the multiple fissures within the Puerto Rican community; the Young Lords' main adversaries in this struggle are not the police or even whites, but rather the Puerto Rican members of the church, many of whom are upwardly mobile residents of the suburbs.[99] In October 1969, the Young Lords approached the pastor at the church about using space for a free breakfast program. When he repeatedly refused to discuss the request, the Young Lords appealed to the congregation during Sunday services, a move that prompted the reverend to call the police. In the ensuing melee, police and congregation members attacked several Young Lords.[100]

A few weeks later, on 28 December, the Young Lords decided to address the congregation again; this time, however, they intended to stay. In a press conference filmed by Newsreel, Juan Gonzalez describes the groups' motives for the occupation: "The main thing that we're clear on is that it's a simple thing to give us space. And now that we've gotten into this church and eaten here and been here for hours, we know what a big place it is. It's incredible, the space in the church. All unused, you know, never open to the community." While the request may seem entirely fair to the Young Lords, the middle class and largely middle-aged Puerto Rican congregation members oppose the plan. Footage intercut with Gonzalez's interview shows parishioners in front of the barrio church singing "We Shall Overcome" in protest. The spectacle of these demonstrators mobilizing well-worn civil rights tactics to keep poor residents out of their church is made all the more ironic by Gonzalez's commentary. "These people can claim to be Christians," he says, "but they've forgotten that it was Jesus who said that it's easier for a camel to pass through the eye of a needle than for a rich man to enter the kingdom of Heaven." Gonzalez continues, "We're after following the tenets and the spirit of Christianity and not the letter and the Bibles that have perverted Jesus' real revolutionary and social consciousness." Appropriating the language of liberation theology, Gonzalez resituates the Young Lords as the true Christians, but his commentary cannot erase the fact that the film has captured an intense moment of intergenerational and interclass conflict, one that cannot be resolved by appeals to an overarching rubric of Puerto Rican nationalism.

Renaming the building the People's Church, the Young Lords began running the free breakfast program, clothing drives, a daycare center, a liberation school, and free health programs where El Barrio residents could obtain routine preventative care. *El pueblo* shows the popularity of these programs as scores of residents file in and out of the church entrance. In the process, they talk with each other and with the Young Lords, taking copies of the YLO newspaper, *Palante*. Agustin Lao estimates that approximately three thousand people attended the People's Church during its brief existence. Not only did these programs satisfy obvious material needs but they also strengthened the political fabric in El Barrio, radicalizing individuals and building coherent social networks. In one hilarious scene, for example, young boys in the liberation school perform a play during which they dramatize the rifts in the Puerto Rican community, interspersing dialogue—"Our people are poor, and you know damn well nobody wants to be poor!"—with impromptu wrestling matches. The play's finale consists of the children singing a raucous version of "Power to the People." Here an appeal to nationalism, "the people," masks advocacy on behalf of a particular class of Puerto Ricans, the urban poor.

An attention to representational politics was a conscious part of the Young Lords' radical strategy, allowing them to use by-then familiar visual symbols to locate themselves vis-à-vis other radical groups of the period. In a filmed interview, Guzmán acknowledges that the Young Lords utilize the media in order to get their message out to community residents. After the first seizure of the People's Church, he watched the first day's press conference on television. "I didn't like myself," Guzmán recalls, "I came across as this stereotyped image of what a militant was supposed to be—the Afro and the shades and all this. I was up there talkin' all kinds of shit about this, that, and the other. And it was so routine and blasé."[101] The routine image to which Guzmán refers is, of course, the image propagated by the Black Panther Party, a style insistently circulated by both it and the media.[102] I am inclined to agree with Nikhil Singh's understanding of the Panther style as a "repertoire of styles, gestures, and rhetorical equations," a form of "insurgent visibility" revealing "Black visibility as the defining antithesis of national subjectivity in the United States."[103] Read in this light, what then to make of Guzmán's rejection (or at least softening) of that style? For one, I am not entirely sure that the Young Lords Party's adoption of the Panther style signified in the same way—at least not entirely. Blackness as both a phenotypic and symbolic phenomenon stands in a differential relationship to African Americans and Puerto Ricans regardless of skin hue because of the differing historical conditions under which the two forms of exclusion have been forged. The link to a "real" homeland and the more recent experience of diaspora undergirding Puerto Rican calls for liberation altered the ways in which this "insurgent visibility" registered to a (white) North American audience.

Second, the Panthers identified the lumpen as their primary constituency, as did the Young Lords, but the Lords seemed to possess a more complicated understanding of the lumpen as a variegated group that might include elderly grandfathers and unemployed churchgoers who might be organized if the Young Lords' style did not intimidate or infuriate them. That is to say, Guzmán's recognition of the multiple ways in which his style might resonate takes into account the uneven interpellation of the lumpen and the working class into the U.S. nation-state. Possessing an investment in particular forms of behavior and appearance might not necessarily disqualify one from agreeing with the Young Lords' radical agenda, just as the adoption of radical chic did not automatically denote a radical actor. If organizing is a process involving both confrontation and strategic compromise, then Guzmán's style of public performance may have been intended to reach a more variegated audience. During subsequent press conferences, Guzmán consciously styled himself in contradistinction to the famous militants, wearing clear glasses, sitting behind a table, and refraining from cursing so that his "radical" representational style—black leather jacket, sunglasses, beret, rifle—did not needlessly alienate Puerto Ricans who might otherwise support his position. On the question of his style change, Guzmán later described himself as having "reject[ed] the bad Panther imitation."[104] In another conscious manipulation of the press, the Lords "gave the media something" every day of the church siege, imagining that they were "talking to 300 of the most assorted kind of Puerto Ricans in the world in one room."[105] This strategy no doubt extended to the Newsreel camera that was capturing the siege from the inside. Though the Young Lords do not completely control the image that emerges in the *El pueblo se levanta*, they certainly have significant sway over it. In addition, they benefit tremendously from the previous media coverage of student protesters and militants, tailoring their image to gain community acceptance and packaging their brand of socialism for the mass media.

All too suddenly, however, police interrupt this version of utopian socialism by breaking into the church and hustling out the bedraggled but smiling church occupants. Here Newsreel's editing of the section proves critical. Just before the mass arrests, a Young Lord reminds the protesters: "It ain't just ya'll in this church. It ain't just East Harlem. Remember we relate to an international struggle. So it may sound ridiculous but this all links up to what's happening in Vietnam, Puerto Rico, Watts. Don't ever forget that." Just as he finishes the speech, the film cuts to the police raiding the People's Church. In effect, *El pueblo se levanta*'s editing elevates the Lords to the level of national liberators. They, like other Third World peoples, are simply fighting for independence; the people are rising. In a predictable turn of events, however, they are forcibly prohibited from remaining on top. Framed by this stark footage, the second segment of the film, in which Young Lords describe their party's program, assumes the character of a national liberation platform. Demands for education, adequate housing, and health care coexist side by side with assertions for the right to self-determination: "The Latin, Black, Indian and Asian people inside the U.S. are colonies fighting for liberation." In underlining this point, *El pueblo se levanta* combines military iconography—the machine gun silhouette characteristic of Newsreel films—with the thirteen-point program. The result is the equation of the Young Lords' demands with that of anticolonialists defining the terms of their own independence. It is important to note here that the film's insistence on framing the Lords in pseudo-military terms becomes one of the main visual techniques for linking them to Third World anticolonial struggles, even as it risks distancing the Lords from their primary constituency.

In the first sequence of the platform segment, the word *education* is emblazoned across a gun silhouette. In subsequent footage, several Young Lords hold a discussion in the group's office. The viewer watches as the group comes to define education as the awakening to the realization that racism and economic exploitation characterize U.S. relations with Puerto Rico and its immigrants. "In Chicago, I went to school where I could see the racism and how Puerto Ricans was treated. We lived in the worst places. They treated us like animals," one Lord contends; "then I came to notice the suffering that my people were going through. I understood how in the U.S. and in the world there was a conflict that existed between the rich and the poor. The rich had the power and the poor didn't have anything." This awareness of the interrelation between racism, economic exploitation, and imperialism, in turn, leads to a reevaluation of Puerto Rican culture and identity. Young Lord Morales remembers that rather than thinking that "Puerto Ricans had no culture, that Puerto Ricans had no history and that Puerto Ricans had nothing," she began reading histories of the Puerto Rican Left and the Tainos, Puerto Rico's first inhabitants. For her, this led to a growing radical consciousness about both what it means to be Puerto Rican in the United States and what it means to be female in a patriarchal society.

Morales's feminist consciousness is an attribute the film takes pains to extend to the Young Lords Party itself. In another conscious revision of the conventional Black Panther Party media image, more than half of the testimonials come from female Young Lords. Even male Young Lords reiterate the party's commitment to gender equality. Decrying what one Lord refers to as that "king of the castle shit," Morales asserts, "In the party, you don't deal with females and males. You're just comrades." As if to underline this evaluation, *El pueblo* then features an extended segment during which female Young Lords represent the party on street corners, in rallies, and at the Puerto Rican Day parade. The interview with Morales does significant ideological work, redefining Puerto Rican culture as explicitly antisexist, leftist, and seamlessly linked with activists on the island in the face of evidence to the contrary. This position is reinforced by the soundtrack's privileging of female voices, another significant departure from earlier Newsreel films.[106]

As the other three rifle silhouettes appear—one each for health, food, and housing—they are paired with testimony and live-action footage underscoring their relation to the development of the Puerto Rican nation. For the health segment, we see the Lords picketing the South Bronx's Lincoln Hospital, demanding reforms that would significantly improve its treatment of workers and its care of patients. In the section on food, a breakfast program cook explains why the Young Lords feed children nutritious meals every school day. Just as he proudly announces, "I wake them up every day," a school boy interrupts with "Hey, you didn't wake me up yesterday." The chef chuckles and replies, "Yea, I know, but yesterday was Sunday." In a relatively short period, *El pueblo* seems to suggest that this program has become an accepted and necessary part of Puerto Ricans' daily life. In an appalling sequence, another Young Lord takes the viewer through a typical El Barrio apartment, pointing out the rat infestation, exposed plumbing, and broken-down structures typical of the housing in this neighborhood. In one of the film's most effective segues, footage of New York tenements ushers in extensive footage of Puerto Rico, where barefoot children live in ragged shacks and play amid garbage. American tourists, meanwhile, repose in luxury, high-rise hotels. A narrator intones:

> Our people on the island are forced to buy from the United States whose companies control 85 percent of the Puerto Rican industries and economies. . . . For the people on the island, the results are 35 percent of the population living on welfare or charity, four hundred thousand illiterates, 40 percent of the housing classified as unsuitable for human habitation, 20 percent of the workforce unemployed and another 15 percent underemployed, a 25 percent higher cost of living than the United States.

This tangle of statistics is made explicable—though no less comprehensible— by the telling evidence confronting the viewer. Economic exploitation has simultaneously created the desperate circumstances of Puerto Ricans and the conditions under which the Young Lords emerged as effective radical actors.

It is the Young Lords' ability to articulate, to both vocalize and bring together, the contradictions of life in the United States and Puerto Rico that make them such an impressive group of activists. For instance, the exploitation of Puerto Rican garment workers is integrally related to their inability to purchase adequate clothing, hence the need for the Young Lords clothing drive. The refusal of Lincoln Hospital to allow community input contributes to the unnecessary death of Puerto Rican men, women, and children. The military presence within Puerto Rico echoes the wanton police brutality plaguing U.S. Third World communities. "Why do we have pigs in the community," a Young Lord asks; "they're not there to serve and protect the people. They're there to make sure that the natives, the Third World people, or poor people keep in line, rather than begin to deal with the poverty by getting better housing, better education, and all these things." The Young Lords crafted what Láo

4. The Young Lords Party on the march. Still from *El pueblo se levanta* provided courtesy of Third World Newsreel.

describes as a "social equation that integrate[d] the community with the workplace, the employed with the underemployed and unemployed, the low stratum workers with the economically marginalized, the people as direct producers and as consumers [and] began to draw the contours of a politics grounded on the lifeworlds of the Puerto Rican subaltern."[107]

In the film's concluding section, over two hundred Young Lords and community residents retake the People's Church. This time, however, the occupation is a mass event accomplished with the aid of arms. Outraged when prison authorities rule the suspicious death of Young Lord Julio Roldan a suicide, hundreds of Puerto Ricans marched to the church, holding banners that read "fight police repression," "smash corrupt union leadership," and "blacks and Latinos unite." They also requested that the church be used as a clearinghouse for legal aid information for any Puerto Ricans and other Third World people who wanted it. This time the pastor agreed to this, telling one reporter, "These young men represent a legitimate voice of the community."[108] Whether his words are motivated by the presence of the reporters or an abrupt change of mind is impossible to tell. Interestingly, his cooperation with the Young Lords Party is not depicted in the film. Is this because it might weaken the film's narrative of intergenerational and interclass strife or diminish YLP's radical image premised on the threat they pose to the dominant society? If indeed the pastor's conscience has been piqued it would seem to suggest that the Young Lords represent critical interests of this Puerto Rican community, ones even their former opponent can support.

El pueblo se levanta never shows us the outcome of this second seizure; the protestors will eventually be forced to leave the church or face arrest or outright violence. The missing conclusion is replaced with a voice-over: "For that revolution that's within the United States, we see ourselves hooking up with black people, with Native Americans, with Asians and with other Latinos to form a united front of oppressed people to wage against the real enemies," and the film ends on an upbeat note (characteristic of Newsreel films of the period). An effective coalition of U.S. Third World peoples is prophesized, if not accomplished, by the film's conclusion.

El pueblo se levanta constitutes a significant departure for Newsreel. Besides providing a more in-depth analysis of the group by balancing one-on-one interviews with protest footage, Newsreel also presents a fairly complicated portrait of the Puerto Rican community. Though the Young Lords are central to that portrait, the filmmakers did not avoid highlighting the class and generational tensions that led to the takeover of the First Spanish Methodist Church. This enables an idealized yet more nuanced depiction of the group to emerge, one that shows the Young Lords as the young dreamers and fallible human beings they ultimately were. The film's conscious deconstruction of the idealizing impulse makes for a running theme in the film, rubbing explicitly against the representational grain embodied most prominently by the Oakland Black Panther Party. This is not to say that the film remains completely free of any such impulse; yet it at least stands as an attempt to build a more variegated representational vocabulary.

At several points, the film draws attention to the fact that any claim to represent the "people" can only refer to a certain segment of the community rather than the totality of it. The juxtaposition of the militant Young Lords and the suburban Puerto Ricans singing "We Shall Overcome" reveals the significant political and ideological schisms present within the decade itself. The use of the song by congregation members determined to hold their church empty rather than allow poor people to use it also foreshadows the appropriation of Martin Luther King Jr.'s radical antiracist, antipoverty politics for neoconservative ends that is to become a veritable cottage industry in the decades ahead. Though the film does present the Young Lords' endorsement of gender equality as if it occurred without significant turmoil, this response serves as a corrective, explicitly refuting sixties iconography that endlessly recycled the myth of the young, male revolutionary dressed in leather. The film also attempts to deconstruct any definition of the Young Lords as a vanguard group; rather, their actions are placed in a larger history of collective struggle sustained by the old as well as the young. Juxtaposed to the representation of the Young Lords are images of elderly Puerto Ricans, some of them members of the squatters' rights group that is the subject of *Rompiendo puertas*. Breaking down the generational binaries reinforced by the earlier images of congregants, this juxtaposition locates the impetus for struggle in one's class position, which, as the conflict over the church shows, is not reducible to one's Puerto Rican identity.

While *El pueblo se levanta* details the exploits of young Puerto Rican activists, *Rompiendo puertas* depicts the courageous efforts of female-headed Puerto Rican families to obtain safe, affordable housing. Whereas the Young Lords film emphasizes the differing political views and economic positions of the first and second generation of Puerto Ricans, *Rompiendo puertas* profiles a squatters' rights movement organized and executed by middle-aged and elderly women.

Rompiendo puertas: We're Here to Stay

Taking its name from police speak for house burglary, the 1970 film *Rompiendo puertas* focuses on one of the crucial political issues of the era, the dearth of safe and affordable housing. Though often overlooked in histories of the sixties, the problem proved particularly acute for urban communities of color and consequently sparked intense political activism, especially in the latter part of the decade.[109] Like *El pueblo se levanta*, *Rompiendo puertas* was a transitional film, created as Newsreel evolved into Third World Newsreel. Roughly the length of *El pueblo*, the film juxtaposes analysis of the causes of New York's housing shortage with the group's now familiar battle footage in which demonstrators and police clash. *Rompiendo puertas* also extends the group's focus on communities of color, portraying an embattled segment of the U.S. Latino/a working class. Unlike *El pueblo se levanta*, however, the film does not depict young militants; instead, the film blends the voices of young girls, single mothers, and elderly women, all members of Operation Move-In, a squatters' rights group that occupied and repaired a series of abandoned buildings on the Upper West Side in the spring and summer of 1970. In capturing these compelling voices, *Rompiendo puertas* emerges as one of Newsreel's most powerful films, highlighting radical political actors overlooked in both mainstream and alternative accounts of the sixties.

From the film's initial moments, it is clear that Newsreel's technical method is in transition. Rather than with frenetic bursts of energy or ceaseless, rapid-fire action, *Rompiendo puertas* begins in relative calm. The first shot features a young girl perched on the steps of a brownstone. Her voice captured in mid-sentence, she argues that the city should make larger apartments so "bigger families can live in it. But they just want to break it down to fit more of them in smaller apartments."[110] The "them" to which she refers are rich whites who can afford the luxury apartments that will eventually stand on the man-made ruins of her neighborhood. As a visual punctuation mark, ensuing footage reveals a bulldozer wrecking low-income housing followed by shots of luxury high-rise apartment buildings. Those images are scored by the translation of a Spanish-speaking elderly woman who anxiously muses, "I don't know what they're going to do with us. . . . The people next door were kicked out five or six years ago. . . . The rich are grabbing everything. They push the poor to the side." She continues, her face a picture of despair and anger, "I've been looking for another place for five years already. . . . For twenty years I've been waiting to get into public housing." Though it seems amazing that one would have to wait two decades for public housing, the woman's experience is typical rather than exceptional. By 1970, New York City's housing crisis had entered a critical phase, but the crisis had been a long time in coming. Public officials had begun to note the increasingly dire housing crunch at least twenty-five years earlier at the end of World War II. Having won the war for democracy, the United States found itself unable to provide its citizens with a basic democratic right.

Even before the United States entered into the Second World War, immigrants and black migrants had begun relocating to New York in large numbers searching for jobs and relief from religious, ethnic, and racial persecution. Between 1930 and 1940, the city's population grew from 6.8 to 7.5 million. During the economic boom of the 1940s, new arrivals quickly found work in New York's manufacturing plants, but housing construction and rehabilitation failed to keep pace with the boom and a housing shortage quickly ensued. After the war, as the city's white population fled to the developing suburbs, they left behind decaying buildings and blighted neighborhoods inhabited by black and Puerto Rican workers.[111] This situation did not go unnoticed by New York City public officials. When Mayor Fiorello La Guardia came to power in 1934, he selected Robert Moses, a conservative Republican and former park commissioner, to direct the city's infrastructure expenditures. This decision transformed New York redevelopment from what Joel Schwartz describes as a "neighborhood movement" in the 1930s to a "large-scale operation" overseen by Moses.[112] With President Harry Truman's signing of the 1949 Housing Act (better known as Title I), Moses accelerated the razing of slums and the selling of public land to private developers who built housing for the upper and middle classes in prime areas of New York.

In order to make room for such ambitious projects, massive so-called slum-clearance projects were sanctioned, and the poor and lower middle-class people of color living there were resettled in belts of public housing in East Harlem, on the Lower East Side, and near Brooklyn's Navy Yard. These attempts to reserve prime real estate for whites while ghettoizing blacks, U.S. Latino/as, and Puerto Ricans were dubbed "Negro removal" projects, a term coined after the infamous Manhattantown project, which rendered approximately five thousand families homeless. By 1954, "Negro removal" had already deracinated a total of twenty-seven thousand families and threatened to push out forty-five thousand more, 60 percent of them black and Puerto Rican.[113] An Operation Move-In activist sums it up best: "You see the master plan is for all the poor people to be moved out of this city, Manhattan per se and to be moved into the outer boroughs such as Brooklyn, Queens and the Bronx. Why should these people move? Why should I move? I was born here. I was raised here. Why should I have to move into a neighborhood or a borough that I know nothing about." In the face of such widespread devastation and dislocation, the public housing system utterly collapsed, prompting fifty-five of New York's fifty-seven senators to introduce a resolution to classify New York's slums as "disaster areas" qualified for "immediate emergency federal aid."[114]

If by the mid-1960s it was clear that New York's redevelopment policy was an abysmal failure, a new series of pressures emerged. With the 1965 reform of restrictive and racist immigration policies, a new flow of immigrants began arriving in New York. Census data indicates that between 1966 and 1979, over 1 million legally recognized immigrants settled in the city.[115] This same period saw the severe downturn in New York's economic fortunes with employment declining 2.1 percent per year as the private sector followed whites to the suburbs.[116] These factors exacerbated an already critical situation. In 1965, the newly elected mayor John Lindsay called a housing state of emergency when the vacancy rate dipped to 3.19 percent; by 1968, that rate had plunged to 1.23 percent. In 1961, there were only 1,000 deserted buildings in the city; by 1968, that number had skyrocketed to 7,100 as an average of 2,500 buildings a year were abandoned. This served as only one indication of the widespread land-owner divestment happening all over New York. Between 1968 and 1976, private landlords found it financially profitable to abandon housing because of the urban uprisings and the local and national recessions that followed them. Consequently, this divestment was concentrated in inner-city neighborhoods on the Lower East Side, in the South Bronx, in Bedford-Stuyvesant, Harlem, and East New York.[117] A 1969 *New York Times* article estimated that the entire population of Arizona could fit into New York's decayed housing, with 8 million New Yorkers currently living in inadequate or unsafe housing. Though middle-class New Yorkers were adversely affected, low-income families were by far the hardest hit. The demand for subsidized public housing was so extreme that a family ranked 103 on a public housing waiting list of 800 would have to wait fifty-one years for a housing unit.[118]

These developments represented the beginning of a fundamental shift in the conception of the role and function of the urban city. Where Mayor La Guardia celebrated New York's diversity, citing its multiracial, multiethnic history and its activist unions as the backbone of the city, postwar mayors Robert Wagner and Lindsay enacted policies that undermined these ideological affiliations. In fact, after 1953, as New York became a postindustrial city, it began catering to the needs, whims, and desires of the moneyed classes. In 1970, Albert A. Walsh, the city's newly appointed housing and development administrator, openly celebrated this agenda. Vowing that no community group would veto any housing program, Walsh declared that his policy was "aimed at attracting substantial numbers of middle-class residents—white and black—to the slums."[119] Though expressing his desire to encourage heterogeneous neighborhoods populated by all races and income brackets, Walsh ultimately catered to the interests of middle-class and elite citizens, subsidizing their housing and effectively pushing out poor residents. As Harloe, Marcuse, and Smith sum up: "These trends are really parts of a single process of spatial and social restructuring in which housing provision is becoming increasingly oriented towards the needs of an upper middle class of professional and managerial elites. Lower-middle-income groups and manual workers find increasing difficulty in gaining access to affordable housing, while the unemployed and more marginal sectors of the labor force are left trapped in poor housing and deteriorated neighborhoods with little or no prospect of a better housing future."[120] As the city's manufacturing base was replaced by service-sector employment, city officials and corporate CEOs alike saw New York as a workplace and playground for the wealthy and upwardly mobile classes. Thus the parallel coexistence of Third World and First World cities was unerringly planned and executed in New York, a result exemplified in the parasitic placement of neighborhoods such as the posh Upper East Side and the devastated El Barrio. In that case, investment bankers, insurance brokers, entertainment moguls, and physicians literally worked and lived a few blocks from the chronically unemployed or underemployed people who aspired to jobs cleaning their toilets and tending to their overprivileged children.

Such pervasive inequity and dislocation understandably created a great deal of resistance, much of it during the spring and summer of 1970. Columbia University's SDS chapter organized a one-day strike to protest the university practice of holding as many as five hundred Columbia apartments vacant rather than renting them out to community members.[121] Small and large groups of squatters organized all over Manhattan, arguably none more successfully than Operation Move-In. *Rompiendo puertas* portrays the struggles of 150 U.S. Latino/a and Puerto Rican families occupying buildings in the Upper West Side Renewal Area, struggles that involve battling city officials, private developers, and the armed police protecting their interests. The film skillfully explores the ways in which Operation Move-In's activities represented a multi-fronted challenge to the hoarding of property and resources facilitated by urban renewal policies. By defining the city as a space built by and thus in a fundamental sense for poor people, by asserting that the seizure of abandoned apartments is a morally justifiable and politically legitimate form of activism, by ideologically linking urban renewal and U.S. imperialism, and by showcasing elderly, middle-aged, and young mothers undertaking militant and effective political struggle, *Rompiendo puertas* depicts a radical politics of place that challenges the economic and political forces shaping the postwar urban city.

One of the earliest and most salient points articulated by *Rompiendo puertas* is the fact that working-class (often native) New Yorkers whose labor built the city are unjustly removed from their homes. As we watch people moving their belongings out in sacks and paper bags, a voice-over intones, "Hundreds of working people like us are being evicted and forced into the streets." As with *El pueblo se levanta*, an activist or an individual performing the role of activist reads the voice-over narration, perhaps to emphasize the fact that Operation Move-In controls the film's content. This is, of course, a misleading implication since the filmmakers, three of whom—Bev Grant, Tammy Gold, and Robert Lacativa—also worked on the Young Lords film, ultimately determined the shape of the film. Once the original residents have been removed, many landlords refuse to rent to families with children or to those receiving welfare, setting the rents prohibitively high. The forced removals are not only evidence of widespread discrimination but they also reflect the devaluation of poor people's labor. Between scenes of men pushing clothing carts and women sewing in factories, a speaker asserts, "We are the people who built this city. We work here. We work in factories, in hospitals, supermarkets, subways, banks. So we are the city." Through sweat equity, the film argues, Puerto Ricans and U.S. Latino/as have earned the right to safe and affordable housing. Unfortunately, capitalism's profit-maximizing imperative translates their abundant labor into pitiful wages. An older woman tells an interviewer:

> In order to bring forty dollars to my house, I had to bring them at least two hundred dollars profit. . . . And it's hell. You know they're making more than you or I . . . but they are not giving us a fair salary. It's no more than survival

that they give us for pay. Because of the wages and discrimination of black and Spanish people in this country, that's why there are so many single women, so many children without a family. It's because the men can see that they don't bring home enough and they get disgusted and disappear.

Producing a trenchant analysis of the cycle contributing to her community's plight—discriminatory wages lead to worsening poverty and family dissolution—the activist inverts the racist, dehumanizing logic that blames capitalism's poor for their predicament.

The film contests the very definition of the city as a space for white elites built on their highly specialized labor. "Wherever the city sets up urban renewal programs," a woman's voice suggests, "it removes working people and poor people and removes them from their homes and replaces them with rich people and big business." The woman's indignant words are then contrasted with the comical image of a middle-aged, effete businessman walking a tiny poodle down the street. Demanding to know why the city is prioritizing the interests of the man (and, by extension, of his poodle) over the needs of poor families, *Rompiendo puertas* proclaims urban spaces to be equally the domain of working-class communities whose labor entitles them to suitable housing. As one woman demands, "Housing is a necessity. Why should we pay for a necessity?" This quasi-socialist assertion forms the ideological foundation on which the squatters build their movement. Rather than as the result of fractious and ideologically driven meetings, the film presents this position as an achieved one, the result of the housing authority's numerous and systemic betrayals of working people.

This betrayal is emphasized in the film's first section as inner-city residents catalogue their repeated attempts to wrest minimum concessions from an indifferent bureaucracy. *Rompiendo puertas* goes to great lengths to reiterate the fact that the squatters have exhausted every other avenue to attain affordable, safe housing. Officials promise some residents housing that never materializes; one man recalls, "Sure we went to the city, many times. What did we get? Lies, false promises, threats." In other cases, people wait interminably for scarce public housing. Meanwhile the processes of removal and demolition continue. "The city says they will continue with urban renewal. They will continue with luxury housing," one activist declares; "we say, 'It will not.'" Her words implicitly critique liberalism's reliance on legal channels for redress since the housing authority and the state that stands behind it are not structurally incapable of addressing poor people's needs, but rather politically intransigent.

However frustrating this institutionalized neglect is, the precipitating factor for the squatters' mobilization is not the callous treatment by city agencies. Instead, the death of a neighborhood teen serves as the catalyst for Operation Move-In's emergence. Fifteen-year-old Jimmy Santos died of asphyxiation because his landlady refused to fix a faulty boiler. Outraged, community activists organized a funeral march through the streets of the Upper West Side. At the end of the march, they seized their first building, because in the words of one participant, "The Santos family needed a safe place to live and so did we." Jimmy's death appears to give the filmmakers a narrative hook, a political alibi for the seemingly extreme action undertaken by the group. However, the film then takes great pains to frame the building takeover in larger structural terms, rather than as a vengeful response to an individual tragedy. The testimonials go to great lengths to emphasize that this protest is not aimed solely at the landlord's negligence. Instead it is a studied assault against the city's deeply flawed housing priorities. One participant explains, "We don't always blame the landlady. We blame the city because this family had already been asking for better housing and they had been denied." Astutely pinpointing the systemic factors sanctioning property-owner indifference, the activists appear to have created a movement more significant than any single act of retribution could have been. Asserting the group's right to "live where they want and how they want," the activists explicitly describe their actions as "liberating" neighborhoods and instituting "community control." "What you do with the money instead of paying to a landlord, a slumlord? You invest that money in your apartment," one activist insists. "You do your own thing 'cause it's yours. It's not for the landlord. It's not going in anybody's pocket."

Rather than a form of private income, individual investment yields group benefit. The film depicts the collective that squatters formed to undertake building repairs and parcel out responsibility for them. Organizing themselves into a grassroots socialist collective, residents pool their money and labor power to repair dilapidated buildings and develop a highly organized structure with "house captains" who assess the number of vacant apartments in a building, collect money to repair them, and then organize the cleanup effort. *Rompiendo puertas* also depicts Operation Move-In's other cooperative enterprises including a day care and a communal kitchen. Operation Move-In built this network of social and cultural services by canvassing for support door-to-door in an attempt to build a mass movement.

Filling the gap left by city bureaucrats, the group established an apartment registry in order to equitably distribute newly repaired apartments and avoid cronyism. In this way, Operation Move-In expanded its base of support, becoming what Manuel Castells has described in the Latin American context as an expression of "urban populism," the "process of establishing political legitimacy on the basis of popular mobilization . . . aimed at the delivery of land, housing, and public services."[122] This urban populist movement was led by people truly at the bottom of the economic and political ladder. Most of the squatters were first- or second-generation immigrants from Spanish-speaking countries in the Caribbean and Central America who encountered discrimination on their arrival in the United States. Though the Young Lords did initially help to organize the squatters, Bill Nichols asserts that the filmmakers worked to elide their impact, choosing instead to focus on the middle-aged and elderly activists. He rightly sees this as a shift away from any investment in the vanguard theory of revolution, but perhaps it also illustrates the fact that the vanguard theory does not fit this movement. By their very nature, squatters' movements cannot work without the initiative of tenants themselves; no amount of outside organizing can effectively sustain such efforts.[123] Given that, it seems perfectly appropriate that the Young Lords recede into roles as supporting players.

The film's willingness to foreground the middle-aged and elderly Puerto Rican women as the leaders of this movement contests the sixties mythology that routinely centers white students and black civil rights workers. It affirms the fact that out of people's everyday lived experiences can evolve a sophisticated political analysis perhaps informed but not overdetermined by an investment in Western philosophically driven models of revolution. Bringing to the United States enduring memories of life under and in the aftermath of colonialism, a woman explains, "They're from Majorca, the people we have and Santo Domingo and my people from Puerto Rico." According to her, new immigrants' fears and timidity were lessened by the confrontational attitude of Puerto Ricans, by which she presumably means the Young Lords, as well as widespread opposition to the Vietnam War. The squatters' movement, then, combines homegrown critiques of U.S. colonialism with the momentum supplied by the decade of turmoil that was subsiding.

As marginalized immigrants, expecting but failing to find a better life, they were uniquely situated to launch a thorough critique of U.S. policies and practices, one that draws on the liberal rhetoric enshrined as a constitutive part of U.S. democracy. For instance, in one scene an elderly woman holds forth, angrily declaring:

> When you're tired, you have to stand up even in your last years of life. They only want tax . . . the longer you work the more tax they want. . . . You know where the tax goes? To Vietnam and to rockets to the moon where they can't

go. Take that money and put it in housing for us, the poor people. What are they doing in Vietnam? They didn't lose anything there. What are they going to do in Santo Domingo? That's why we killed so many of them so they stop fucking over us."

To peals of laughter and applause, the elder concludes by saying that the United States "wants to put their nose in everything. And they are losing. . . . The U.S. has colonies too, Alaska. It has Puerto Rico. It bought St. Thomas for two cents." Her belief that U.S. colonialism has created the conditions against which she and her fellow activists now struggle makes the woman's speech compelling and, in part, explains the source of the determination displayed by these activists. Operation Move-In participants saw themselves engaged in a local war with international repercussions. The squatters' struggle is concretely linked to—is understood as a mimetic replay of—the unequal relations between the First and Third Worlds. Furthermore, the woman's fiery words are imbued with hope, reflecting the sense that U.S. imperialism is vulnerable to attack, waning rather than waxing. Another woman echoes the elderly woman's words, listing a roll call of nations whose growth has been stunted by U.S. imperialism: "We're all poor, one Puerto Rican, one Dominican, one Cuban. . . . We have to stick together." Another activist in the group expresses the belief that colonialism has created the conditions for its overthrow: "From Saigon to Hanoi we have to move. From San Juan to Santiago, we have to move." Richly significant, these lines simultaneously bear witness to the forced dislocation wrought by Western imperialism and call for a mobilization against that very dislocation.

Like *El pueblo se levanta*, *Rompiendo puertas* represents a significant shift in Newsreel's film practice, as well as a significant challenge to a sixties historiography that ignores such movements and the set of historically specific conditions that enabled them. If the past twenty years of cultural theory have taught us to be wary of essentialism in its many guises, it is still the case that the film's depiction of working-class Puerto Rican women represents an important political shift, one that contests any vanguard theory of political activism. The inspiring efforts of Operation Move-In activists directly refute the implicit politics represented by films such as *Columbia Revolt* where audiences are meant to be carried away by the pat belief that white students are center stage in any radical change to come. The fact that we do not see the inevitable compromise or defeat that may eventually come makes the film all the more effective an inspiration to radical action. In the process, the film lends teeth to C. L. R. James's passionate insistence that "every cook can govern."[124]

Newsreel should not be viewed as solely a reflection of the New Left. From its inception, the film collective brought together warring political affiliations and ideological orientations, in short, men and women with variegated personal and political lives that found contradictory rather than coherent form in their early films. Through an analysis of Newsreel's production, exhibition, and distribution practices, I have tried to tease out the elements of the collective's practice that make it, if not a full-fledged U.S. Third World institution, then certainly one with a significant U.S. Third World Left component. In the next chapter, I extend this discussion to a consideration of Newsreel after it renamed itself Third World Newsreel, outlining more fully the central preoccupations and influences evident in this U.S. Third World Leftist organization.

4. Third World Newsreel Visualizes the Internal Colony

•

The transition from Newsreel to Third World Newsreel represents a transformation rather than a radical break with the group's past. As I have argued, Newsreel's history reflects an investment in anticolonial struggles, even if largely at the representational level. Nonetheless, this work proved critical because it disseminated a range of images and voices hidden from the U.S. public's view. Early Newsreel films relied on a montage effect to suggest a general Third World political landscape rather than analyzing specific struggles in depth. Still, many of the Third World films the group distributed subtly responded to this generalizing tendency by narrowing their focus to one site— Cuba, Vietnam, Venezuela—and situating it within a larger context of struggle. The founding of Third World Newsreel signaled a more subtle shift in Newsreel's practices; though the group continued to distribute many of the same films Newsreel had to generate income, Third World Newsreel also forged a new institutional practice, one that sought to concretely connect local struggles in urban communities of color to larger Third World dynamics. This was achieved by creating artistic networks, running production workshops for local community members, and integrating Third Cinema techniques more thoroughly into Third World Newsreel's filmmaking practice.

Though this process began while the group was in transition, Third World Newsreel developed a sharply honed political sense and a different visual vocabulary from that of its predecessor. That vocabulary enabled U.S. Third World Leftists to articulate and describe the similarities between U.S. minorities and Third World majorities in new ways. It also helped them articulate themselves, in the sense developed by Stuart Hall, to Third World anticolonialism. In one interview, Hall summarizes articulation's meaning this way: "An articulation is thus the form of the connection that *can* make a unity of two different elements, under certain conditions. It is a linkage which is not necessary, determined, absolute and essential for all time. . . . The 'unity' which matters is a linkage between that articulated discourse and the social forces with which it can, under certain historical conditions, but need not necessarily, be connected." When Hall clarifies his point by saying "the theory of articulation asks how an ideology discovers its subjects," I understand him to mean that it helps us understand how a particular ideology disrupts common sense and speaks to a subject in a new, historically specific way.[1] Louis Althusser's theory of interpellation captures some aspects of this process, except that articulation allows for more dialecticism, acknowledging that groups and individuals speak back to a particular ideology, that they transform it and can discard it altogether.[2] Hall's term is useful in thinking about Third World Newsreel and other U.S. Third World Leftists because it requires one to account for the historical factors that lead to an ideological shift, but it also provides a way of exploring why and how a given political project, site of contestation, or discourse becomes prominent, assumes a palpable urgency.

In light of this, I wish to make three interrelated claims about Third World Newsreel's practice in the 1970s. First, the group's adaptation of Third Cinema practices, particularly in its first film, enacts and reflects on modes of transnational cultural exchange. This hybrid style allows Third World Newsreel to blend elements of Marxism, feminism, and anticolonialism. The result is a depiction of a community of struggle defined by its opposition to oppression based on multiple identity categories—class, race, ethnicity, and national identity. Rather than seeing this representation as a true and accurate portrait of the subjects and their context, I recognize in it Third World Newreel's attempt to construct and visualize a radical Third World public. That public takes as its object of focus, is constituted by, its resistance to state violence as it manifests itself in prisons, policing practices, and the parallel structure of poverty maintenance—welfare, substandard housing, low wages, etc.—the "modes of oppression" that articulate U.S. people of color to Third World colonized subjects.[3] Central to this ideological and political work is the question of whether this enterprise fixes the Third World as simply "a screen for [U.S. Third World Leftist] desire," one that is held together by multiple suturings of place, position, and power.[4]

In some senses, Third World Newsreel stands as the quintessential U.S. Third World Left organization. Urban-based, the group used its filmmaking and distribution to build cultural alliances and political networks across racial, ethnic, and national lines. This chapter begins with the dissolution of Newsreel and its reformation as Third World Newsreel, identifying the reasons the group incorporated *Third World* into its new name. Next, I turn to the group's film *Teach Our Children* (1971), which uses the internal colony paradigm and Third Cinema aesthetics to compare urban U.S. ghettos and Third World colonies. I conclude by considering the group's institutional efforts—the founding of a community theater, the offering of production workshops, and the organizing of the Association of Afro-American and Third World Filmmakers in the USA—to realize a radical U.S. Third World public culture. A brief coda looks at how Third World Newsreel adapted its rhetoric and tactics, focusing more on cultural resistance, as a conservative pall settled over the United States.

Third World Newsreel Builds a Cultural and Political Community

El pueblo se levanta and *Rompiendo puertas* represent an intermediate step in Newsreel's transition, emerging amid the group's intensifying efforts to recruit so-called Third World people. This new recruitment priority stemmed from fractious debates about whether or not white members were equipped to make films about people of color, debates that reflected larger conflicts about race, class, and gender inequality. Members saw such recruitment as a way of shifting the leadership base, "[carrying] within it a self-destruct mechanism against Newsreel's previous mode of organization." At the time, a Newsreel member told Bill Nichols, "the change from middle-class leadership was necessary because few middle-class people grew up in the neighborhoods or near the places about which Newsreel films are needed."[5] Equating *Third World* with nonwhite and working class oversimplifies the race, class, and power inequities at play in the Third World—and in the United States, for that matter. It ignores the fact that anticolonial does not automatically mean class or race struggle. Though the three forms of oppression intersect, they do so in unpredictable, contradictory ways that do not dictate a clear and coherent plan of attack. One might even interpret this member's statement as a disguising of class struggle in the trappings of Third World rhetoric. Newsreel's inability to adequately distinguish between the two soon became evident as people of color entered the organization. As the pace of events slowed, Newsreel instituted what it called "political education" for all new members. When new members of color entered these sessions, they critiqued the sessions for privileging Marxism and virtually ignoring the history of struggle and body of thought developed by U.S. people of color and Third World peoples. Outnumbered, they finally called a national meeting of all Third World Newsreel members in 1970, which brought together either four or five people, depending on the account.[6]

Shortly thereafter, the twelve remaining members of New York Newsreel effectively split into caucuses, though accounts of their actual composition vary. "New York Newsreel members split themselves into 'haves' and 'have-nots,'" argues Michael Renov, "with the distinctions among ethnicity, class background, and functional class position somewhat blurred."[7] This blurring, according to Nichols, resulted in endless debates about which category a particular individual might inhabit. If a member of color held a master's degree, was she or he a have or a have-not?[8] The political chaos of such a process further eroded the membership. Third World Newsreel cofounder Susan Robeson's recollections are more pointed. She recalls that the organization explicitly divided along racial and ethnic lines into a white and a Third World caucus.[9] It was the white caucus, according to another cofounder, Christine Choy, who then divided along class lines into the haves and have-nots, though eventually the haves departed, leaving an organization of working-class whites and people of color.[10] Nichols agrees with Robeson and Choy, implying that this was the first time a Third World caucus existed, but Newsreel cofounder Roz Payne suggests that such a caucus existed almost from the beginning, though admittedly with few if any members of color.[11] Discerning the lines along which Newsreel split is not merely a matter of historical accuracy. If Newsreel did, in fact, divide itself into race-, ethnicity-, and nation-based caucuses rather than class-based ones, it suggests that the group had begun to see class through the lens of race and empire rather than the other way around. It was not an either-or choice between class, race, and nation; the group's 1970s films focused on class oppression as it intersected with particular racial formations and national contexts.

By the winter of 1971–72, whites and nonwhites had officially divided themselves into two caucuses, though it is likely that this merely constituted the formal sign of the collective's established practice. During this period, Newsreel essentially consisted of two parallel organizations: the white and the Third World caucuses were each responsible for their own distribution, production, and finances. While the white caucus engaged in self-criticism and debate, the Third World caucus, now consisting of twelve members, argued for a major reorientation of the group, calling for the production of films by and about Third World peoples in the United States. In an attempt to rid New York Newsreel of what were felt to be its voyeuristic tendencies, control of production on films about Third World peoples was to be put in the hands of Third World peoples. White members of Newsreel could no longer use footage of New York's communities of color to politicize white, middle-class students. Instead, the goal was to foster media activism within those communities by "help[ing] the people involved in [local] struggles create their own propaganda."[12] This was a highly charged debate since the white caucus consisted of middle-class people with filmmaking skills, while the Third World caucus had neither the skills nor the class background to ease their transition into filmmaking. Not content to solely transform New York Newsreel, the latter caucus even issued an edict to all of the other extant Newsreels demanding that they recruit and train U.S. Third World peoples.[13]

The Third World caucus had set itself a clear political agenda, one that left the white caucus rudderless and unable to define its purpose. According to Choy, the have-nots began to debate "working class issues, working class filmmaking, definitions of and strategies for cultural work, filmmaking, and organizing work."[14] For the first time, white Newsreel members explicitly and extensively addressed the issue of a white, working-class film praxis. If they were to no longer make films about the white middle-class student movement or radical groups of color, then who were the new subjects of their films to be? Unable to articulate a response to this question, the white caucus disbanded in either late 1971 or early 1972, leaving the organization to the Third World caucus, which soon thereafter renamed the organization Third World Newsreel.[15]

A series of events precipitated the name change. After the white members departed, all of Newsreel's filmmaking equipment was mysteriously stolen. This loss of equipment coupled with the loss of those individuals financially able to sustain the organization's work seriously impaired the group. Without filmmaking skills or money, Third World Newsreel turned to the recently departed members for equipment and skills training, but most of them refused. In a 1982 interview, Choy recalled, "Only one or two [former members] were sincere enough to teach us how to use the camera. The rest wouldn't have anything to do with us. So it was out of anger that we called ourselves 'Third World Newsreel.' "[16] The new name was meant to underscore the material imbalance between the white and the Third World caucus, a relationship in which the raw, manual labor was often supplied by the members of color without the economic resources and skills training possessed by the white members. The use of the term *Third World* stood as an angry commentary on the racist paternalism evident in Newsreel. Choy defined the group's use of the term *Third World* in this way: "[It is] more applicable to an underdeveloped country, and domestically speaking, it applies to a national minority struggling for equality. When we use the term Third World, we use it superficially, since we distribute films from Latin America, Africa and Asia. But the production we do does not relate to Third World issues but to conditions in the United States, especially among minorities and working-class people as a whole."[17]

The historical record troubles Choy's observation that the group used the term *Third World* "superficially." If one only considers the literal meaning of the term, then of course Choy is correct: the group's members were not living in the Third World nor were their films (exclusively) about the Third World. But if one probes deeper, thinks of the term as shorthand for complex material structures, then Third World Newsreel's adoption of the term recontextualizes it to describe a condition rather than a geographic location. In the case of U.S. national minorities, this condition included segregation, cultural denigration, racial discrimination, and labor exploitation. The term *Third World* helped provide a language for national minorities not juridically colonized but who saw themselves as facing many of the selfsame structures underpinning colonialism. It leant them access to a perspective that would prove critical in challenging their own particular forms of oppression. Affiliating with anticolonial struggles, connecting economic exploitation and cultural supremacy in the First and Third Worlds constituted an important political move precisely because it depended on and helped solidify a global analysis, one that forged transnational forms of solidarity and support. Choy's reduction of Third World Newsreel's complicated history may in part reflect her position as an Asian immigrant mindful of the tremendous differences between the United States and the Third World. Her focus in those years was clearly on the social and political inequities in the United States, but that focus was always related to global power dynamics. For instance, her 1976 film *From Spikes to Spindles* connects conditions in New York City's Chinatown to the trade inequities between Hong Kong and the United States; Choy parallels sweatshop labor in Hong Kong to the low-wage or unpaid restaurant work performed by illegal immigrants in Chinatown.

Choy's comments about Third World Newsreel's name may also be explained by the interview's conditions of production. The published interview resulted from two different interview sessions with Choy in December 1978 and two years later in January 1980. Another two years after that, the interview was spliced together from the earlier sessions and published in *Jump Cut*. Consequently, it is difficult to determine whether Choy's comments were refashioned and taken out of their original context. By 1982, if Choy had input into the interview's final form, she must have been mindful of repositioning Third World Newsreel for a Reagan-era audience hostile to leftist rhetoric of any kind, let alone of the sixties variety.

Whether her distancing of the organization from its name was intentional or unwitting, Choy's comments uneasily coexist with the collective's cultural reorientation, a process in which she herself participated. By the time the white caucus left, the Third World caucus had declined from twelve to only three members: Robert Zelner, Christine Choy, and Susan Robeson, the latter two of whom were the most active. Choy had been recruited by Newsreel cofounder Norm Fruchter in 1970 and was the first nonwhite woman in the group. A Chinese-Korean immigrant, Choy was born in Shanghai, where she grew up on a steady diet of Chinese, Russian, Polish, and Czechoslovakian films. She spent her teen years in Korea before immigrating alone to New York. Once there, she attended Manhattanville College for one semester and then transferred to Columbia University to study architecture. Her mentor Buckminster Fuller left Columbia for Washington University in St. Louis, and Choy enrolled there for two years between 1969 and 1971. Choy eventually earned a scholarship to Princeton University where she, in her words, "met a bunch of radical philosophers, activists, Marxists."[18] When the bombing of Cambodia came to public light, she joined protests demanding the establishment of a Third World Center. Fed up with Princeton, Choy began working for the Urban Institute in Newark, where she met Tom Hayden, Steve Friedman, and Norm Fruchter. While completing her architecture degree at Columbia University, she became increasingly drawn to Newsreel, attending a screening at the suggestion of Fruchter. While Choy was excited by Newsreel's political commitment, she was struck by its lack of nonwhite members. Despite her misgivings, however, she became an indispensable member, serving as the head of distribution and film maintenance and eventually founding the Third World caucus.[19]

When Susan Robeson joined Newsreel in the summer of 1971, she was an eighteen-year-old student fresh from a summer filmmaking course at New York University. Robeson, the granddaughter of the acclaimed actor, singer, and political activist Paul Robeson, was born in West Harlem in 1953. The child of a white mother and black father, she spent much of her early childhood in the Manhattanville Projects until her family moved with Paul Robeson Sr. to the Upper West Side of Manhattan in 1965. Because of the Robesons' involvement in leftist circles—her parents were both members of the Harlem youth branch of the Communist Party until 1960—Robeson grew up in what she describes as a "politically charged atmosphere."[20] By the time she joined Newsreel, Robeson was a fledgling photographer and had completed her first year at Antioch College in Ohio. Although she had little filmmaking experience, she seems to have possessed a precocious political vision and tireless energy. The self-described "scribe" for early Third World Newsreel, Robeson's desire to forge links between Third World communities and U.S. communities of color critically informed the group's direction.[21] Because it was female-headed for the first time in its history, the contribution of women of color to the struggles within black, Asian, and Latino communities was consistently highlighted, a focus explicitly at odds with the phallocentric perspective on sixties and seventies activism to which we have since grown accustomed.[22] Choy and Robeson's early work challenged the exclusive focus on male-gendered modes of resistance—armed revolt, public demonstrations—that came to eclipse other effective forms of protest.

In October of 1972, Third World Newsreel released a statement entitled "Act First, Then Speak" presenting its members' perspective on the mass exodus from Newsreel. They emphasized the inability of the white caucus to define a film praxis based on their political beliefs and then outlined their own vision for the organization. Stressing the fact that Third World Newsreel did not solely want to make films about Third World people, they insisted that they wanted to "build a working relationship with Third World organizations and community people." This approach would enable them to produce artifacts integrally related to local disenfranchised communities, films that possessed intrinsic use value. As they described it, they wanted to "pass on [their] knowledge and produce what [their] people need[ed]."[23] In these statements, one sees the attempt to balance the fact of their cultural capital with an approach to the local community that did not simply locate Third World Newsreel as its vanguard leadership. The attempt to further specify the composition of "their people" and their needs motivated the writing of other organizational papers in an attempt, in keeping with the era, to solidify the "correct line" on these matters.

Shortly after the "Act First, Then Speak" statement, Third World Newsreel released another manifesto entitled "Organizational Principles of Third World Newsreel." Here, the group more clearly defined its mission and its audience, articulating the philosophy that seems to have guided the organization for much of the decade. Defining the collective as a "propaganda organ for the progressive forces in general and the proletarian forces in particular," Third World Newsreel, as had its predecessor, positioned itself as a conscious alternative to the mass media, which it deemed an "instrument of social control." However, the collective did not define its constituency, the "proletarian forces" in specifically race- or ethnicity-based terms. Instead, Third World Newsreel emphasized its structural position in the U.S. economy. The "proletarian forces" were the "working people" and "the most exploited sectors of this country." Asserting Marxism-Leninism as its guiding political theory, Third World Newsreel declared itself willing to work with "all progressive, Communist, and labor groups which [sic] have the interests of the masses at heart."[24] Explicitly rejecting the prevalent left-wing sectarianism of the period, the manifesto also moved beyond narrowly defined identity politics, stressing solidarity along economic, not race, ethnicity, or gender lines. This entailed, however, an attention to how those categories structured economic relations. Maintaining a constructive tension between analyses that centered class and those that centered race proved admittedly difficult given the group's determination to maintain its newfound independence from white control. Choy recalls that the group sometimes found itself welcoming members of color with little interest in class-based politics.[25] It is easy to see how this would result from an implicit conflation of Third World and working class, a conflation that worked as long as members of whatever class were committed to overturning class exploitation but broke down quickly if members were not. Though this understanding may have faded as the organization developed, at its founding it is accurate to say that it held significant sway over the organization. Group members may not have possessed the sophisticated language available to contemporary race theorists, but they seem to have grasped the fact that, paraphrasing Stuart Hall's much-quoted maxim, race (and other identity categories) are all modalities through which class is lived.

As Hall reminds us in the seminal essay "Race, Articulation, and Societies Structured in Dominance," "Race is thus, also, the modality in which class is 'lived,' the medium through which class relations are experienced." He continues, "This has consequences for the whole class, not specifically for its 'racially defined' segment."[26] Third World Newsreel's understanding of race, one that privileged the structural position of groups rather than their biological inheritances, depended on recognizing that racism derived in no small part from economic exploitation and from the global web of colonialism Third World Newsreel's name underscored. Colonialism was understood by the group to be first and foremost a system of economic exploitation, but also one that spawned racial hierarchies. By attacking racist common sense, the group was attacking racialized hierarchies that buttressed exploitative social relations. The reverse, of course, also held true. The film collective hoped that its films would forge a political commonality based on a counterhegemonic understanding of history that reinforced an oppositional common sense. Its films sought to produce a viable imagined community based on identification with those still living under colonialism and those plagued by its aftereffects. This meant an acknowledgment of colonialism's devastations and, most critically, recognition of the fact that the United States benefited from those devastations almost as much as it did from its imperial projects. Nikhil Pal Singh's understanding of Henry Luce's essay "The American Century" astutely describes the postwar era in which the United States thrived: "'The American Century' was a conscious rationalization for containing the reformist impulse of the New Deal at home, while re-orienting the expanded power of the U.S. state according to the prior cartographies of empire."[27] Given this reality, Third World Newsreelers found themselves complexly situated, at once subject to the racist and exploitative common sense that animated Western colonialism and imperialism and unevenly benefiting from U.S. world supremacy.

What is also apparent in Third World Newsreel's early formulations is the belief that the primary goal of cultural production is not technical perfection but rather the making of a contribution to a group's sense of shared political purpose. The collective's first priority was to produce revolutionary propaganda, defined as much by the conditions of its production as its content. In this, I hear the echoes of Frantz Fanon's reflections on culture in *The Wretched of the Earth*, a central text for U.S. Third World Leftists. Fanon insists that the formation of a national culture ought not to be a reflexive enterprise, concerned with meeting or exceeding standards set by the colonizer; nor should it be a return to a fictive, reified precolonial past. Rather, it must be joined in some fundamental sense with national struggles for liberation. Fanon's reflections proved absolutely critical to the ways in which U.S. Third World Leftists defined themselves as artists and intellectuals. In *The Wretched of the Earth*, Fanon insists: "A national culture is the whole body of efforts made by a people in the sphere of thought to describe, justify and praise the action through which that people has created itself and keeps itself in existence. A national culture in underdeveloped countries should therefore take its place at the very heart of the struggle for freedom which these countries are carrying on."[28] The translation of this theory to the United States, of course, meant several substitutions. For "national," U.S. Third World Leftists had to make do with local communities of color. "Underdeveloped countries" became U.S. national minorities, and specific incidents had to be read as events in a national liberation struggle. Third World Newsreel's manifesto declared, "Revolutionary propaganda involves the conscious class elements integrating themselves wholly with the masses in order to . . . serve the masses, and depict realistically the struggle of the masses in order to show the common links of the various levels of the mass struggle."[29] Repetitive jargon aside, this passage suggests that the group would not only portray instances of local political struggle but that it would put those struggles in a context emphasizing their structural parallels to national and international events. This was a radical departure from Newsreel's earlier film praxis in which analysis was secondary to reportage. Newsreel films were records of events, not necessarily analytical pieces meant to articulate, in the sense outlined by Hall, disparate phenomena. Third World Newsreel's avowed purpose implicitly defines its films as acts of solidarity, rather than as proof that members were either supposedly authentic members of the working class or its designated leaders. With this redefined role, the collective consciously rejected much of the vanguardism that animated Newsreel and other New Left organizations during the 1960s. It eschewed membership in what philosopher Herbert Marcuse termed the "young middle-class intelligentsia" that was supposed to inspire the masses to revolt by its radical example.[30] Further, Third World Newsreelers rejected the role of "intellectuals or isolated individuals producing works . . . to distribute to the people."[31]

Instead, they hoped that the subjects as much as the filmmakers themselves would guide film production. This perspective made for yet another departure from Newsreel's earlier cultural and political practices. By insisting that the group's production be concretely tied to oppositional groups or movements, Third World Newsreel sought to avoid the voyeurism and romanticism that had characterized its predecessor. Although the group's films were in part designed to educate communities of color, Third World Newsreel openly acknowledged that it had as much to learn from U.S. Third World communities as those communities did from them. This perspective redefined the role and function of cultural producers, positioning them as organic intellectuals in the Gramscian sense, rather than cultural or political missionaries.[32] Third World Newsreel films were intended to be group articulations, a collective call to arms. Accomplishing this lofty goal was not always easy since Third World Newsreel filmmakers' educational and cultural capital distinguished them from the communities they represented. Nonetheless, their efforts marked important steps in that direction, enacting a significant collaboration between middle- and working-class people of color.

During the transition from Newsreel to Third World Newsreel, Choy and Robeson began shooting *Teach Our Children* with a larger crew consisting of white Newsreel members. Slowly these other participants fell away, leaving Choy and Robeson, the only ones without any filmmaking skills, to complete the film. I read this film as a visual representation of the cultural and ideological vision the group articulated in its initial public pronouncements. Released in 1972 shortly before Third World Newsreel's official founding, the film serves as the group's visual manifesto.

Teach Our Children and the Discourse of Internal Colonization

Many of the tendencies and tensions within Third World Newsreel's early history are apparent in its first film, *Teach Our Children*. It is no accident that the film focuses on the Attica prison rebellion. An event involving hundreds of prisoners of color, primarily African American and Puerto Rican, Attica became a seminal political event for U.S. Third World activists, seeming to demonstrate the similarities between Third World colonies and U.S. communities of color. The film was only the first of four films on prisons and their social control function, making Third World Newsreel a primary source of prison films and a valuable resource for community groups agitating for prisoners' rights.[33] These film projects developed out of an extant internal-colony discourse equating U.S. black, Latino, Native American, and Asian communities with Third World colonies. The use of prison as a metaphor for Third World oppression was a standard device in the decade between 1965 and 1975. Reflecting a commonsense investment in this paradigm's utility, Nichols remarked in 1980, "The degree to which prison represents a vivid and often all-too-real symbol of Third World oppression by a capitalist system is beyond doubt."[34] By emphasizing the social-control function of U.S. prisons and their parallels to other state disciplining procedures, Third World Newsreel added material substance to the analogy of inner cities to internal colonies.

The likening of black communities to internal colonies has a long history in communist and black Left politics. As early as 1916, Lenin suggested that Southern blacks should be considered an "oppressed nation" because their freedoms had been increasingly curtailed in the aftermath of Reconstruction.[35] In 1928, the Sixth World Congress of the Communist International affirmed this position, declaring black Southerners' right to control their political and economic destiny, their right to complete self-determination and territorial secession. This so-called Black Belt nation thesis signified a break with both Marx and Engels who had distinguished between nations and nationalities, the latter of which were incapable of economic independence. Cedric Robinson has argued that a sufficient understanding of this distinction would lead to the designation of African Americans as a nationality, not a nation. Though Lenin was the original architect of the Black Belt nation thesis, it was Joseph Stalin who refined the concept, arguing that the black South qualified as a nation because it was "a historically established, stable community of people, coming into existence on the basis of a community of language, territory, economic life, and psychological constitution, which manifest themselves in a community of culture."[36] As Robin D. G. Kelley has demonstrated in *Hammer and Hoe*, the Black Belt nation thesis proved extremely influential, igniting an organizing drive during the 1930s among sharecroppers and tenant farmers in Alabama and fostering a generation of black communists including Harry Haywood, Hosea Hudson, and Angelo Herndon.[37] Yet the definitional and ideological tension involved in considering black American or other nonwhite groups in the United States as either a nation or a nationality persisted, particularly among U.S. Third World Leftists. As I argued in the previous chapter, this tension found expression in the Young Lords Party's adoption of the divided-nation thesis, which was eventually discarded as inconsistent and unworkable.

That thesis, however, formed part of a resurgence of the internal-colony discourse with the appearance of Stokely Carmichael and Charles Hamilton's *Black Power* (1967), Cruse's *The Crisis of the Negro Intellectual* (1967), Robert L. Allen's *Black Awakening in Capitalist America* (1969), Amiri Baraka's formulations, particularly in his journal *Black Nation*, in Mario Barrera, Carlos Muñoz, and Charles Ornelas's "The Barrio as Internal Colony" (1972), and Nelson Peery's *The Negro National Colonial Question* (1972). Cornel West has dismissed much of this work as lacking in critical sophistication. The "internal colony," he once wrote, "remains a mere metaphor without serious analytical content."[38] It is easy enough to conclude this, but I think there is something worth examining. If the theory itself is incoherent in places, it nonetheless constitutes an attempt to resolve at the ideological level the situation of U.S. national minorities that are at once residents of the United States without being fully enfranchised citizens of the nation. During this period the thesis became a compelling framework for U.S. Third World Leftists to explore, even as they recognized the ways in which it failed to fully capture the complexities of their situation.

One intriguing and largely unexamined text that articulates the internal-colony thesis in some depth is Peery's. By the time he published *The Negro National Colonial Question* in 1972, Peery had been active in leftist circles for much of the preceding thirty years. Descended on one side from a Cherokee survivor of the Trail of Tears and on the other from enslaved Africans in Kentucky, Peery was born in 1923 to Ben and Carrie Peery. His father was a World War I veteran who supported his wife and eight children as a postal clerk—a rare achievement for a black man of his generation—first in rural Wabasha, Minnesota, and eventually in Minneapolis. It was in Minneapolis that the adolescent Peery became politically active, spearheading an effort to desegregate the local YMCA and attending meetings of the Young Communist League.[39] Though never an official member of the league, Peery was profoundly shaped by the Popular Front era, associating Russia and the Communist Party, as did so many black leftists, with the fight for the Scottsboro Boys and racial equality (83). On hearing news of the Nazis' invasion of Russia, Peery began to seriously consider joining the war effort and immediately enlisted in the army once the United States officially entered World War II (128).

Like LeRoi Jones, Robert F. Williams, and Harold Cruse, it was Peery's experience in the Jim Crow armed forces that solidified his commitment to the Left. A member of the Ninety-third division, at eight thousand members the largest unit of black soldiers, Peery soon became one of the division's de facto leaders (188). In 1943, with reports of Southern lynchings and urban race riots frequently headlining newspapers, the regiment learned it would be stationed in Louisiana. As a preemptive measure, Peery helped organize the stockpiling of weapons and ammunition in case of attacks by white Southerners, a move that earned the Ninety-third a reputation for militancy and Peery a place on the army's G-2 list, a register of soldiers suspected of communist activity (173). Peery later recalled, "Every country, even states within the United States, feared the effect our militancy and aggressiveness would have on their own second-class subjects. Black soldiers had become engaged in street fighting on the side of the people in Trinidad, British Guiana, Panama, the Bahamas, St. Lucia, and Jamaica" (207). Soon after this incident, the Ninety-third was shipped off to the Pacific Islands, where Peery spent the remaining war years.

Days after U.S. victory was declared in 1945, Peery's regiment was deployed to the Philippines, where it took part in "crush[ing] the new Philippine revolution" (274). Instead of following orders, Peery and other communists in the army subverted that effort by working with members of the Philippine Communist Party and the underground resistance movement. Connecting the racism he experienced in the armed forces with the naked imperialism evident in the Philippines, Peery soon defined his own commitment to communism and antifascism as a commitment to "anti-imperialist war. Freedom, national freedom, the self-determination of nations, the unity of the colored colonial peoples—this was the new war" (297–98). His dedication to an international anti-imperialist war never wavered, eventually leading him to the Communist League (CL), what he refers to as the Communist Labor Party of the United States of North America (USNA) on the title page of *The Negro National Colonial Question*. Formed by former SDS members and Los Angeles activists, the CL consisted primarily of African Americans whose ideology was shaped more by pre-1956 Stalin than either Third World Leninism or the post-1968 Maoism persuasive among U.S. Third World Leftists. Seeing itself as the heir to an uncontaminated Marxist-Leninist tradition, the CL nonetheless felt it necessary to utilize the internal-colony paradigm to fuse the African American and the working-class causes.[40]

In his lengthy pamphlet, Peery argues that the United States is a "multinational" state holding Puerto Rico, the Philippines, the Black Belt, and the Southwest United States as "direct colonies" and exercising "dictatorship" over several national minorities including African Americans, Asians, Chicanos, Inuit, and Native Americans.[41] In asserting the Black Belt region's colonial status, Peery surveys U.S. history, identifying the factors he thinks have made the Black Belt a cohesive nation-state and have led to the consolidation of U.S. imperial power. Following Lenin's *Imperialism: The Highest State of Capitalism*, Peery defines imperialism as the concentration of production and capital into monopolies, the development of finance capital into "financial oligarchies," and the increasing export of capital rather than commodities. These three elements facilitate the formation of "international monopolists," and eventually of the territorial division of the world among the "biggest capitalist powers" (5). In the post–World War II period, Peery argues, the "United States of North America, has converted its military dominance into economic and political hegemony: The camp of world imperialism has been regrouped, fully dominated and headed by USNA imperialism" (6).

This imperialism, asserts Peery, has its economic foundation in slave labor. Culling from Marx and Engels's writings on the U.S. Civil War, Peery opposes what he calls the "revisionist" position of the CPUSA, which in his view sees slavery as a precapitalist form, reframing its policies after the death of Stalin and the revelation of his crimes. Peery, an antirevisionist, argues that the slave economy was a form of latifundist capitalism controlled by large plantations and producing surplus value. This profit was the basis for capitalism's growth and consolidation in the United States and worldwide. Peery relies on Marx's *The Poverty of Philosophy* to strengthen his argument, particularly this passage: "It is slavery that has given the colonies their values; it is the colonies that have created world trade, and it is world-trade that is the pre-condition of large-scale industry."[42] Having established slavery's formative impact on global capitalism,

Perry then links slavery to the creation of a black national minority. Negroes are a "historically evolved people, socially and culturally developed from the framework of slavery," their identity forged by white supremacist ideology, political disenfranchisement, and economic exploitation.[43] Peery is careful, however, not to conflate the Negro people and the Negro national movement, a failure for which he condemns the CPUSA. Instead, he dates the origin of the black nation at the end of the nineteenth century, in other words, after the demise of Reconstruction and the rise of U.S. imperialism. Echoing Stalin's formulation, Peery defines the Negro nation as "a stable community of people formed on the basis of a common language, territory, economic life and psychological make-up manifested in a common culture" (11). Northern finance capital has exploited the Black Belt and the South generally since Reconstruction. It is this colonial relation, according to Peery, coupled with the USNA's imperial ambitions abroad that have precipitated the formation of the Negro nation.

In substantiating his contention that the Negro nation constitutes an economically and culturally coherent entity, Peery has to account for several theoretical and practical impediments. Most obviously, what are the Negro nation's geographical boundaries? What is the citizenship status of Anglo-Americans within its borders? Are African Americans born and/or living outside this nation still citizens? Relying on demographic information, agricultural surveys, economic indicators, and Civil War and Reconstruction histories, though curiously not on W. E. B. Du Bois's *Black Reconstruction*, Peery argues with an obvious sleight of hand that the Negro nation encompasses not only the sixteen hundred miles of the "Black Belt and surrounding areas" but also the "peripheral areas that are economically dependent on them" (68). Disputing the claims by U.S. Marxists that migration has diluted the density of the Southern black population, Peery insists that despite migration, "52% of all Negro people live in the South, roughly 15 million" (62). Not only does this population share a common linguistic and cultural heritage but Black Belt members also possess the means for economic self-sufficiency. The Negro bourgeoisie control half a billion dollars in assets, and Negro financial institutions have assets equaling another billion dollars (71). Most important for Peery, the Negro national proletariat, a segment of black Southerners that has increased by 75 percent between 1945 and 1966, controls much of the USNA's cotton, sugar, tobacco, and rice production (74). As such, Peery defines them as potentially radical agents of history.

Interestingly, Peery does admit that Anglo-Americans are a substantial presence within the Negro nation; nonetheless, they are merely a national minority whose proletarian members are subsumed, by Peery, within the ranks of the Negro proletariat. On the status of the 11 million African Americans residing outside the Negro nation Peery remains equally cagey. He maintains that they cannot be successfully integrated into Anglo-America and thus constitute "extensions of the Negro Nation": "We must stress the point, however, that we are obliged in each instance to examine the particular, concrete relationship and the extent of the common ties that each 'removed' community of the Negroes has to the national base" (113).[44] Presumably, a removed community might have little relationship to the Negro nation, but Peery never considers whether this rogue community would thus claim citizenship of Anglo-America. He does assert, however, that this is not the case, generally speaking, for black migrants to the North. In their case, economic parity and social integration have eluded them, and so they remain a vital link between the white working classes and the Negro nation. The fact that northern Negroes share some common conditions of oppression produces a sufficiently concrete relationship between them and the Negro nation.

It is easy to see the theoretical gaps in *The Negro National Colonial Question*. Some of them I have already identified, but there are others. Peery relies too heavily on statistical data to prove that the Black Belt is a U.S. colony with the potential to become an economically viable nation-state. His treatise never seriously addresses the logistical questions attendant to any secession from the United States. Peery thus too easily collapses economic vitality and total independence. Too often he relies on argumentation by analogy, concluding that economic exploitation and white chauvinism, characteristics of some forms of colonialism, signify that the Negro nation indeed constitutes a colony. While his data does persuasively demonstrate the economic centrality of the Black Belt and the oppressive conditions under which most African Americans live, Peery blithely assumes that a common economic and political plight will produce a shared, revolutionary ideology. In doing so, Peery lapses into an unjustified, quasi-mystical faith in the black working classes. In the process, he badly underestimates the power of the state and its apparatuses to win consent and forcibly impose its agenda. Peery's privileging of the economic base also leads him to reduce race, culture, and class into a neat base-superstructure relation. He writes, "The development of music, literature, poetry and all of the aspects of a national character which become manifested in a distinctive culture bear the imprint of the oppression of the Negro people and their struggle against the slavers' whip. *To take a specific example, the present day 'soul music' of the Negro people can be traced back to slave times*" (82). The first part of

Peery's statement is so vague as to be uncontroversial, but his insistence on a straight line between 1970s soul and the economic conditions of the antebellum South effectively writes out two hundred years of intervening cultural history. He continues, " 'Soul,' this elusive substance, is nothing more than the national characteristic of the Negro people" (83).[45] Peery's insistence on viewing culture as a pure, authentic realm wherein race and class categories can be neatly delineated leads him to ignore the tremendous influence of white Southerners and northern producers on soul's development as both a musical and cultural style.

It is this one-dimensional reading of African American history, one that privileges the economic without sufficient attention to the other elements—for example, culture, region, ethnicity, and religion shaping it—that enables Peery to compare black Americans with colonized peoples. Peery asserts, "The Negro question is not a race question or a question of a national minority, but a national question and an integral part of the world colonial revolution. Basing ourselves on the teachings of Marx, Engels, Lenin, Stalin and Mao Tsetung, 'we must inevitably reach the conclusion that the self determination of nations means the political separation of these nations from alien national bodies, and the formation of an independent national state' " (59), A nation, for Peery's purposes, is a "historical category belonging to . . . the epoch of rising capitalism" (58). Therefore, Peery argues, after Stalin, that the proletariat must oppose capitalism and imperialism; in short, it must participate in both anticapital and anticolonial movements. The concept of the Negro nation draws both of these strands together, surpassing calls for racial integration and agitating instead for complete national independence. The Negro nation, in a very real sense, stands as the intermediary between the white working class and the Third World masses. As Stalin declared in his *Foundations of Leninism*, "The interests of the proletarian movement in the developed countries and of the national liberation movement in the colonies call for the union of these two forms of the revolutionary movement into a common front against the common enemy, against imperialism."[46] Though Peery's ideas reflect U.S. Third World Leftist thinking during a brief period, roughly 1967–75, his insistence that class oppression and imperialism subsume racial oppression was repudiated by many who tried to wage these various struggles simultaneously without sacrificing the antiracist platform. Max Elbaum's comprehensive history of the new communist movement, *Revolution in the Air*, sums this position up by saying, "Freedom movements among peoples of color were simultaneously integral components of the working class movement and cross-class liberation struggles have a revolutionary thrust in their own right."[47] This does not disqualify Peery for membership in this group of leftists; rather, it illustrates the pervasiveness of the internal-colony discourse, even if it was deployed and defined in multiple ways.

Peery and the Communist Labor Party in whose name he speaks form part of a U.S. Third World Left struggling to craft a hybrid alternative informed by mainstream civil rights and the Old (and New) Left but emphasizing elements that speak to the contemporary importance of anticolonial, transnational solidarity. Like the Alabama sharecroppers and tenant farmers of the 1930s, Peery sought to adapt Lenin's anti-imperialist theory for a U.S. context and in the process build the theoretical basis for an alliance with the white working class. Read in this context, Third World Newsreel's *Teach Our Children* takes on a more complex significance, though this film clearly deviates from Peery's privileging of the Black Belt South. In illustrating the structural conditions that circumscribe inner-city black and Latino/a life and emphasizing the causal relation between that context and urban rebellion, Choy and Robeson created a visual rebuttal to Peery's *The Negro National Colonial Question*. In an interview, Choy argued that there seemed to be a conflation of national identity and nationhood with which she disagreed, a position that flies in the face of Peery's theoretical construct.[48]

At the time, the distinction between nation and national minority seemed less a theoretical problematic than a pragmatic one for Third World Newsreel. The comparison of U.S. national minorities to anticolonial fighters was one critical narrative available to them, but they refused to fall prey to the New or old Left preoccupation with ideological correctness that preceded them. As one Third World Newsreel member only identified by Nichols as Ernie explained: "It seems to me the national question shall be whether we will continue to be oppressed by Chrysler, General Motors, Nixon, and the rest of them. . . . They'll resolve the national question and the actual conditions will remain the same."[49] While Peery argued for the building of a political opposition to the "imperialists of the USNA,"[50] Third World Newsreel, according to Nichols, made a conscious decision to abstain from debates raging among "largely white political organizations about the formation of a new communist party in the U.S." Instead, Third World Newsreel became "less concerned with leaders and flashy rhetoric than with the common people and the forms of expression that come out of everyday experience,"[51] choosing instead to mobilize the visual symbols connecting U.S. Third World communities to their Third World counterparts.

Teach Our Children: Revolt in the Prison and the Ghetto

Teach Our Children is a collage of news footage and personal interviews set to a soul- and gospel-inflected soundtrack that retells the tragic events of the Attica prison rebellion. On 9 September 1971, thirteen hundred black, Puerto Rican, and white inmates, almost half the prison population, captured more than three dozen guards and employees at Attica Correctional Facility in upstate New York. The mostly black and Latino inmates were protesting the intolerable living conditions and vicious brutality of the prison guards. They were subjected to severe overcrowding, rationing of toilet paper (one roll a month), up to sixteen hours a day in solitary confinement, severely restricted medical aid, and rectal searches before and after they received visitors, despite the fact that a wire-mesh barrier separated them from their callers. In addition, the authorities arbitrarily withheld inmates' correspondence, denied them access to newspapers and magazines, curtailed the religious freedom of Muslim inmates, and separated politicized inmates from the rest of the prison population.[52]

Before the September takeover, Attica inmates had twice sought peaceful resolution of their grievances. In May, a group of inmates mailed a list of thirty demands to police commissioner Russell Oswald, an administrator known as a "liberal reformer." Receiving no response, a five-man negotiating committee mailed Oswald a similar list in July, asking most notably to be "granted the right to join or form labor unions."[53] During the Attica rebellion, Oswald agreed to thirteen of the prisoners' demands, but, when he refused to concede to the lawful prosecution of prison guards for cruel and unusual punishment, negotiations broke down. Refusing to meet with the rebels, Governor Nelson Rockefeller ordered a police attack—what independent investigator Malcolm Bell later described as a "turkey shoot"—during which ten hostages and twenty-nine inmates were killed and eighty-nine others seriously wounded.[54] In the aftermath of the massacre, state police engaged in rampant torture, indiscriminately beating inmates suspected of inciting the rebellion. In the fallout after Attica, conservative and liberal media alike criticized police authorities for attempting to cover up instances of abuse. Years later vice-presidential nominee Rockefeller was even dropped from Gerald Ford's 1976 presidential ticket over the controversy.

As one might expect, *Teach Our Children* does not solely focus on the events of the rebellion. Instead, the film links the conditions at Attica—overcrowding, police brutality, labor exploitation—with the conditions in poor black and Latino communities. The result is an angry, humorous, and ultimately powerful indictment of both prison and urban community life.

The film opens with a voice reading from a statement delivered by the rebels at a press conference during the siege: "To segregation of prisoners from the mainline population because of their political beliefs, we demand an immediate end."[55] While we as viewers struggle to decipher the phrase's context and meaning, this brief sound bite is immediately juxtaposed with the voice of Malcolm X declaring, "Don't be shocked when I say I was in prison. You're still in prison. That's what America means, prison." The film then moves from Malcolm X to black-and-white footage of an inner-city community in which kids play in abandoned lots, women idly stare through the bars of their tenement windows, and unemployed men congregate on the city streets. From *Teach Our Children*'s initial seconds, the rebelling inmates are defined as freedom fighters whose existence can be explained by the state of their communities. They are not solitary heroes, but rather ones inextricably bound up in a larger Third World public. This near deification of the Attica rebels can be seen as problematic. Choy and Robeson risk obscuring precisely what it is that makes these inmates such compelling and ultimately recognizable figures: namely, that their demands are reasonable and their methods ordinary. The rebels have simply used the limited means available to them to wring concessions from the state. However prone to mythmaking such a comparison may be, it does invert the state's dehumanizing logic, which treats the inmates as expendable, and it challenges the mainstream media's construction of the inmates as hapless victims of police brutality.

The film represents the inmates primarily through the use of excerpts from their own speeches. In one segment from the Attica press conference, a speaker shouts:

WE ARE MEN. We are not beasts, and we do not intend to be beaten or driven as such. The entire prison populace (and that means each and every one of us here) has set forth to change forever the ruthless brutalization and disregard of human lives of the prisoners here and throughout the United States. What has happened here is but the sound before the fury of those who are oppressed. . . . We call upon all the conscientious citizens of America to assist us in putting an end to this situation that threatens the lives of not only us but of each and every one of you as well.

Attica, the prisoners insist with a Shakespearean flourish, is but one scrimmage in a much larger battle. The upheaval in Attica and other U.S. prisons is only the latest symptom of an ailing body politic. The film reinforces this point by flashing the names of nine other correctional facilities that have been the site of recent protests. Clearly these uprisings constitute a response to deteriorating conditions, but they are also a response to a widespread pattern of police corruption and state violence. For example, Attica inmates were angry over the 1969 murder of Fred Hampton who was ambushed by an FBI-orchestrated police raid while he lay sleeping in Chicago's Black Panther Party headquarters. And just one month before the Attica uprising, George Jackson, a radical writer and prison organizer, was shot to death by San Quentin guards during an escape attempt because they claimed to believe he was hiding a gun in his Afro. In his honor, Attica inmates held a one-day hunger strike and wore black armbands.[56]

While black radicals made for a spectacularly visible target of state violence during the 1960s and 1970s, *Teach Our Children* demonstrates that unchecked police power affects far more people than just individual black rebels. In lengthy footage from the 1967 Newark rebellion, during which National Guard troops wounded twelve hundred Newark residents, we see police roaming the streets, harassing pedestrians, conducting arbitrary searches, and violently subduing anyone deemed to be resisting their absolute authority. As we watch this graphic footage, we cannot help but compare urban communities of color with their Third World counterparts. Newark, and by inference U.S. Third World communities generally, quite literally constitute occupied territories, figurative extensions of Attica prison.

This assertion is strengthened by interviews with inner-city residents. Their poignant testimony links squalid prison conditions and desolate inner-city life, illustrating that communities of color are economically and politically disenfranchised in much the same way Third World countries have been under colonialism. We meet Carlos, a middle-aged Puerto Rican man, who sits in a crumbling New York apartment, surrounded by his wife and several children. An ex-convict, he contends that Third World peoples' civil rights are routinely violated once they are arrested:

> Over here real justice for the Puerto Ricans and blacks and other minorities that find themselves in prison does not exist. . . . For example, we are poor and we don't have the money to pay for a lawyer, a good lawyer. We have to take those lawyers that are paid for by the city. . . . We have to take this defense and this is no defense . . . because those people are paid for by the state. Those people are going to work for the state.

Carlos not only questions the legitimacy of the legal system but he also indirectly raises the question of whether Attica inmates are criminals or economic and political prisoners as he describes the structural conditions that plague the people in his neighborhood:

In Brooklyn, you have that part in the south where mostly all blacks and Puerto Ricans live. They're condemned to live in those places which are slums. . . . At the jobs we have the worst jobs, the worst paying jobs, jobs that no white would want to do, salaries are the lowest, and you either have to take it or leave it. . . . We don't have sufficient money to pay the rent which is high for decent apartments where only upper middle-class people with good salaries are able to live in. But we can only afford to live in apartments that are infested with rats and roaches.

Carlos concludes his trenchant critique saying, "There's really no difference in the places we live in and the way we live and the life in prison. There's no difference. The only difference may be that in our communities the walls are invisible and we don't see them and in the prisons we do." As he concludes, the camera pans from the faces of his children to a view of the gated fences that enclose his apartment complex. By focusing on Carlos, a middle-aged family man, *Teach Our Children* complicates the film's thus far romantic view of black and Latino men. Men are not only valiant war heroes; they are also dedicated family men frustrated by their circumstances. Unlike the Attica inmates, Carlos is neither slim, particularly attractive, nor garbed in the early 1970s style we have come to associate with militant youth—bell-bottoms, army fatigue jackets, perfectly manicured Afros. Nonetheless, his words illustrate that he is acutely aware of and dissatisfied with his circumscribed life and is anxious to change it. The leap from Carlos to the Attica inmates, the filmmakers assert, is a small but significant one.

If the depiction of Carlos counters the predominant view of sixties-era radicals, so does the presence of angry, articulate women, many of them mothers who present the too often invisible aspect of male incarceration. Although she is not nearly as prominent as Carlos is in the film, his wife angrily describes the ways in which she was harassed after his arrest: "The system tries to force a lot of things on me, but I cannot give in like they would like me to. . . . When Carlos was first arrested, they tried to throw me out of where I was living. They tried a lot of things. The police would be around where I lived." Although brief, her comments impart political significance to the domestic space and her critical role there. *Teach Our Children* implies that her fight to keep her family intact is every bit as revolutionary as the actions of the Attica rebels. The very fact that she and her several children have resisted bureaucratic attempts to evict them and break up their family attests to her persistence in the face of state interference. Her actions may not be as spectacularly visible as the Attica rebellion, but they contribute to the community's ultimate survival, undermining male-centered definitions of political action and revolt.

The film further emphasizes women's centrality in the domestic and public sphere by featuring another vocal woman: a young black mother. A moving counterpart to Carlos and his family, she speaks in detail about the perils of raising children alone in the ghetto. In one excerpt, she describes the area in which her children play: "I have five children, and I can speak about genocide in every aspect that you can look at it in. I live in a housing project. We have no facilities here for children to play. We have a lot out there, a concrete lot about twenty by forty feet. We have here in this one building about seventy children. Can you see little kids out there playing in a concrete lot with glass and everything?" Because the children are forbidden to play on the grass, they play in the project's busy parking lot. A car, the woman explains, recently hit a boy who was riding his bike on this makeshift playground. Genocide, according to this woman, literally truncates the lives of poor black people, but it also robs them of the ability to lead meaningful lives—in her words, "keep[ing] people from knowing who they are and what they are and what they should be about doing." A local community activist, this woman has organized protests against the callous and inhumane treatment that plagues her community. She, like Carlos and his wife, has maintained the ability to both critique the state forces that restrict her existence and imagine an alternative existence outside of them. By demonstrating the persistence of this collective, oppositional imaginary, *Teach Our Children* situates U.S. Third World communities squarely at the center of their own destinies.

As a narrative bridge between this community testimony and eyewitness accounts of Attica survivors, the film includes a long cartoon interlude skewering U.S. imperialism. A grotesque Uncle Sam clutching a U.S. flag shaped like a hatchet morphs into the head of Richard Nixon and then the head of Russell Oswald. These images are then superimposed onto a sketch of Africa, Southeast Asia, and South America, the men's grimacing countenances completely obscuring the landscape they have invaded. The sketch concludes with a series of scales being gleefully manipulated by Uncle Sam on which various people(s) are balanced. A menacing U.S. soldier outweighs three young children, three white politicians a black factory worker, a flag-waving white woman a Vietnamese mother and son. Here, these scales might be read as the mythical scales of justice, or as scales that measure a given commodity's "value." Their use here exposes the fact that justice is far from blind, or alternately that "the logic of economic exchange" measures racial inequality and exploitation not human worth.[57] The imagery might also remind one of slave trade auctions, which reduced human beings to their composite parts and labor potential.

Admittedly, the crude politics espoused in the sketch is not nearly complicated enough to hold together the various elements the film embraces—Attica, anticolonial struggles, inner-city devastation. Russell Oswald is not Nixon, nor are African Americans the North Vietnamese. However, as the film amply demonstrates, certain power inequities and structural similarities hold true in the United States and in North Vietnam. What proves wonderful about this interlude are its elements of comic play. The humorous parodying of white hegemony allows the film a utopian moment of inversion during which black men, women, and children trapped behind prison bars are replaced by the "real" criminals, Nixon, Rockefeller, and Oswald. As the film is well aware, that inversion would involve a dramatic shift in U.S. ideology, economic policy, and political perspective, but such playful whimsy forms a memorable part of the oppositional imaginary constructed and articulated by the film.

The section on the Attica inmates begins with the footage of their press conference. A bespectacled, young prisoner reads: "To all people of color worldwide, so many times and so often the black man in the federal penal institution and concentration camps throughout America read about you on the other side of Babylon calling for what you label as 'nation time.' All I want to say is please, those people on the other side of Babylon, let our actions here in Attica concentration camp be a prime example to you." It is the Attica inmates who most directly link the perilous situation of people of color in the United States and in the developing world. As this excerpt from the press conference illustrates, the prisoners were speaking to and acting in solidarity with a real and imagined international constituency, those people calling for "nation time." Just as the film depicts a community of politicized urban residents, it also presents the Attica inmates as articulate and committed political prisoners who have been energized by a larger Third World community. Through interviews with the surviving rebels, Choy and Robeson detail the variety of incidents that preceded the rebellion. We hear one inmate tell of a truncated visit with his two sisters, one of whom he had not seen for many years. When he challenged the guards' refusal to extend the visit or even allow him to say good-bye, they attacked him. He recalls, "They bit me, punched me, threw me on the ground, put the shackles on my legs, put chains around my waist with a padlock, put the handcuffs on, and you know commenced to beating me . . . they maced me, blinded me, kicked me in the cell." Once in solitary confinement, he was sprayed with "nausea gas" for seventeen hours by the guards. This gas, he notes, has been banned from use in Vietnam. Whether or not this last assertion is strictly true matters less than the inmate's belief that Attica prisoners receive the same treatment as their Vietnamese counterparts. For him, this incident has its quite literal parallel in Southeast Asia.

Another prisoner describes the dangerous working conditions that inmates face in Attica's metal shop, where fingers, arms, and legs are frequent fodder for obsolete machinery. Such dangerous work is the only way to secure even small amenities such as soap and cigarettes, and solitary confinement comes swiftly to those who refuse to do such work. Placed in this context, the inmates' demands for the right to organize a union assume greater significance. Unionization, a seemingly mainstream demand, would at least allow the inmates to negotiate the conditions of and compensation for their labor. In this instance, the ability to form unions challenges the prison's dehumanizing logic, which seems determined to banish inmates from the very realm of civil society with its attendant protections.[58] *Teach Our Children* also links the situation at Attica to other instances of economic exploitation, contrasting images of prisoners working in the metal shop with sketches of black slaves toiling in the fields of colonial America. Admittedly, such juxtapositions flatten the very real and quite different structures of slave and prison labor economies. Nonetheless, as a cinematic strategy, the comparison serves to highlight the justice of the inmates' list of demands: working conditions that meet New York State standards, minimum wage pay, adequate visiting conditions, and the lawful prosecution of correctional officers. These reforms are radical in a U.S. context that does not guarantee Attica inmates the benefits of a liberal democracy.

Once the inmates refuse to compromise on these demands, though, they become a threat that must be violently repudiated. The vicious response that the inmates meet serves to strengthen the comparison between them and the Third World guerrilla forces they self-consciously emulate. Despite the fact that officials knew the men to be armed only with sticks and homemade knives, the state troopers armed themselves for combat. One inmate describes the attack:

> They came in there with bazookas, AK-47s. They came in there with machine guns, they came in there with flamethrowers . . . they came in and shot us down like animals. They seen [sic] one brother that was holding a black liberation flag (red, black and green flag). They shot him off the balcony, and they continued to shoot him while he was on the ground. The brother was still clenching onto the flagpole. They stomped him in his head, they stomped him and continued to shoot him.

5. Attica prisoners corralled by police. Still from *Teach Our Children* provided courtesy of Third World Newsreel.

Even a wholly symbolic statement of political or cultural independence—such as the flag held by the slain inmate—must be swiftly and violently eradicated. The surviving inmates tell of troopers who murdered or brutally punished inmates as they surrendered, accounts that are supported by mainstream media accounts of the incident. Unlike those reports, though, the prisoner's testimony crackles with righteous indignation and anger. As one of the leaders recalls, he and fifty-nine other inmates were stripped, marked with an *X*, and made to crawl around the muddy perimeter during a downpour. As he describes this episode, the film juxtaposes footage of the Attica aftermath with still photography of World War II concentration camp victims and drawings of enslaved Africans on Southern plantations.

With this extreme juxtaposition, Attica is elevated to the level of a historic tragedy comparable, in the filmmakers' discourse, to Hitler's crusade against the Jews and every bit as central to a community's collective memory. Claiming Attica's parity with the Holocaust is both politically loaded and audacious considering white Americans have historically resisted any attempt to compare their treatment of enslaved Africans and the Nazi's treatment of the Jews. Though it is clearly inaccurate to compare Attica and the Jewish Holocaust— on the level of scale and sheer horror the Jewish Holocaust far surpasses Attica—the comparison highlights the insufficient value placed on black American life. It also labels enslavement a genocidal practice. In addition, the film asks the viewer to consider how valuable prisoner lives are, and if they are indeed valuable, then what is civil society's responsibility in preventing future

Atticas. The comparison forces the viewer to confront the everyday forms of racist state violence that go unmarked and unresisted by its beneficiaries and raises the hope that future generations may view Attica in terms no less harshly than they do the Jewish Holocaust. This is, of course, wishful thinking as race and class oppression militate against the memorializing of the black and Latino victims of Attica.

However bloody the suppression of the Attica rebellion was, *Teach Our Children* refuses to dwell on the rebellion's defeat. Instead, the film alludes to the militant action Attica may ultimately inspire in urban communities around the United States. To the upbeat, soul-inflected gospel anthem "Let Us Sing This Simple Song for Freedom," *Teach Our Children* argues that the spirit of Attica thrives in individual and collective memory. Shots of inmates pumping iron in U.S. jails alternate with shots of massing guerrilla armies in Southeast Asia, Latin America, and Africa. The voices of women and children intone, "We the people here don't want no more," while Malcolm X's voice excoriates U.S. imperialism: "They are violent when their interests are at stake, all that violence that they display at the international level. When you and I want a little bit of freedom, we're supposed to be nonviolent. They're violent in Korea. They're violent in Germany, in the South Pacific. They're violent in Cuba. They're violent wherever they go." As his words and the images of Third World armies fade, we are left with a view of black and Latino/a children playing amid broken bottles and the hostile eyes of the police. Rather than remain passive victims or become murdered inmates, the film asserts, these children will eventually mobilize to liberate their communities by any means necessary.

Teach Our Children marked a clear departure from earlier Newsreel films. It was the first production made exclusively by filmmakers of color about communities of color. Choy and Robeson present a sympathetic yet fairly complicated portrait of New York's marginalized communities. In telling the story of Attica, *Teach Our Children* does not focus solely on the sensational aspects of the rebellion, as early Newsreel would have done in order to jolt the viewer into unthinking sympathy. Instead, the film places Attica in a context that stresses its relation to a larger anticolonial struggle. The viewer is given an analytical framework in which to understand a sensational event. Rather than treating the inmates as if they had emerged fully formed from the revolutionary womb, *Teach Our Children* traces the roots of their dissatisfaction within the correctional system itself and in the communities in which they live. In doing so, *Teach Our Children* makes women's perspectives central at the level of production and representation, recontextualizing an event that on its surface appeared to be a collective male expression of outrage.

If Third World struggles powerfully shape *Teach Our Children*'s thematics, the film's style is also indebted to the Third World, particularly the Third Cinema techniques perfected by the renowned Cuban documentarian Santiago Álvarez who cofounded ICAIC and directed its Newsreel Division. A tireless supporter of Castro's revolution and a fierce opponent of Western imperialism, Álvarez traveled throughout Latin America, Africa, the Caribbean, and Asia filming anticolonial struggles. Álvarez's eclectic mix of original and found footage, cartoons and still images, the strategic alternation of color and black-and-white images, and the judicious selection of music characterized a style shaped to meet the dictates of the documented event. For Álvarez, newsreels did not simply provide information; rather, he argued, they could "join things up in such a way that they pass before the spectator as a complete entity, with a single line of argument."[59] Álvarez's new conception of newsreel revolutionized the genre, transforming it into a documentary form that could at once provide information and analysis while capturing a particular mood, whether of exuberant excitement or devastating loss.

Teach Our Children relies on Álvarez's towering example. The film mixes found footage of the 1967 Newark rebellion, Oswald's official statements, and the Attica inmates' press conference with original interview footage of the Attica survivors and community residents. Most of the film is shot in grainy black-and-white film, and some segments feel as if they have been put together in haste as if to stress the urgency of this report. The cartoon interlude awash in color mimics similar techniques used by Álvarez in films such as *LBJ* (1968) and *Hanoi, martes 13* (1967), in which he lampoons a club and gun–wielding president Lyndon B. Johnson figured as a grotesque Texas cowboy riding a bronco. Choy and Robeson's use of the soul anthem "Let Us Sing This Simple Song for Freedom" echoes Álvarez's use of Lena Horne's riff on "Hava Nagila" to comment on U.S. racism in the 1965 film *Now*. Álvarez, in the critic Michael Chanan's words, "uses the cultural associations of his chosen music (its iconography) to orient the viewer's frame of reference."[60] Above all, *Teach Our Children* unabashedly bolsters its moral and political point of view through the juxtaposition of perspectives—the Attica inmates and the inner-city residents —the framing device of Malcolm X speeches and footage of anticolonial fighters, and the use of realist techniques such as on-the-spot reportage and personal interviews. Connecting the fight against U.S. and Western imperialism in the Third World with the fight for justice in U.S. prisons provides the kind of uncompromising global framework to which Álvarez dedicated his career.

By presenting a multigenerational, multiethnic group of men and women, *Teach Our Children* also challenges the very notion of radicalism that dominated the decade of the 1960s and is still memorialized today. Radicalism was not only armed revolt but also intellectual critique and communal survival. Rebels were not only bright-eyed, camera-ready soul brothers but also world-weary middle-aged women demanding that playgrounds be built and rogue police be prosecuted. Third World Newsreel's first film successfully incorporated the domestic and international planks of earlier Newsreel filmmaking. The result was a scathing critique of the forces that placed Third World communities in the United States and abroad under siege. This emphasis, one that foregrounds ordinary people of color in all too typical circumstances, may well explain why Newsreel's activities have so often eclipsed those of Third World Newsreel. In many ways, Newsreel's films confirm the conventional narrative of sixties activism, one that foregrounds white student and black civil rights activists. Third World Newsreel's work during this era challenged that familiar story, worked in the seams between various racial and ethnic groups, between various local, national, and international spaces, documenting the daily struggles that at times united and at times divided different urban populations and members of the First and Third World.

The use of Third Cinema strategies in the context of the United States makes *Teach Our Children* a rare and noteworthy example. Nonetheless, its content raises the important question of how the empowerment of U.S. communities of color trades on a particular depiction of Third World radicals. For one, none of the Third World people depicted in the film is given voice; instead, they are shown as massing armies or individual fighters in the jungle. In the absence of their voices, Malcolm X, whose words bookend the film and frame it in internationalist terms, becomes their mouthpiece. In some sense, like the Newsreel members before them, Choy and Robeson end up reducing Third World anticolonial struggle to mere background constructed through decontextualized montages. Audiences of the early 1970s would have recognized the North Vietnamese footage, but little else is visually familiar. This decontextualization flattens specific colonial contexts and the varying strategies used in them. It also borrows the hard-won legitimacy or, in some cases, outlaw status that has accrued around a given struggle in service to urban communities in the United States. This strategy, no doubt, reflects the exigencies of Third World Newsreel's situation. The group had neither the money nor the time to film footage in Guinea-Bissau, Algeria, or Vietnam; it did, however, have footage from various Third World films from which to cull. No matter the explanation, the evacuation of the political context and specific anticolonial meaning performed by this montage strategy enacts a silencing of Third World voices and an emptying out of meaning that replicates, albeit unintentionally, the flattening of difference among colonized peoples characteristic of colonial discourse. In this case, however, *Teach Our Children* reduces difference not to "other" Third World peoples but to build commonality with them. Though this is a distinction with a difference, this flattening leaves a troubling trace that should not go unmarked.

Building U.S. Third World Institutional Practices

After the film's completion, Third World Newsreel continued to reinvent itself, seeking to further break down the distinction between itself and New York's communities of color. First, its ranks expanded as African Americans Larry Bullard and Maxine Williams joined the group. Williams came to Third World Newsreel from the New York City Socialist Alliance and the Third World Women's Alliance, which she defined in a 1970 article as a "revolutionary Black women's movement," and Bullard went on to complete at least one film, *A Dream Is What You Wake Up From* (1979).[61] Allan Siegel also returned to Third World Newsreel in 1972, bringing with him the film *We Demand Freedom* (1974). Siegel's return created some friction within the group since he was its first and only white member. However, he was accepted because he possessed valuable filmmaking and fund-raising skills and because ultimately his political and aesthetic vision coalesced with that of the other members.[62] Throughout the 1970s, as Third World Newsreel consolidated, the group initiated several programs designed to integrate film into the local and international struggles occurring among U.S. Third World peoples. During those years, the group established a distribution network, an exhibition site, and a film production workshop, helping to create networks for filmmakers of color. Simultaneously, Third World Newsreel produced several films, including *From Spikes to Spindles* (1976) on New York's Chinatown community and *Percussion, Impressions, and Reality* (1978), produced in collaboration with Hunter College's Center for Puerto Rican Studies. These two films constituted efforts to connect localized racial, gender, and economic inequality to the persistence of colonialism in Hong Kong and Puerto Rico, respectively. They also helped Third World Newsreel situate itself as a community film collective dedicated to an anticolonial and anti-imperialist politics. The size of Third World Newsreel's membership during these years is hard to estimate and no doubt fluctuated greatly, partly because the group tended to function as a loose alliance of artists and activists who at times lent their expertise to Third World Newsreel and at other times borrowed the group's resources. Choy, Siegel, Robeson, Williams, and Bullard may have formed the group's core, but others came in and out of the organization, making a mark that is undeniable yet hard to quantify. Of course, the film production workshop facilitated this flow; for instance, Ada Gay Griffin, who led Third World Newsreel throughout the late eighties and into the nineties, joined the group after taking the workshop.

By 1973, Third World Newsreel's institutional structure had stabilized largely due to the storehouse of films the group had in its archive. Despite the less than amicable dissolution of early Newsreel, Third World Newsreel maintained prints of many of Newsreel's early films, and they now distributed titles such as *America* (1969), *People's War* (1969), *Los siete de la raza* (1969), *Lincoln Hospital* (1970), *Rompiendo puertas* (1971), and *The Earth Belongs to the People* (1971). Fortunately, the popularity of these films meant they were a much-needed source of revenue. Just as Newsreel had been, Third World Newsreel was less concerned with profit margin than accessibility, so they made their films available to community groups and individuals on a sliding-scale fee. However, the former distribution network had depended on the existence of a larger social movement through which Newsreel films could be advertised and circulated. Newsreel's connection to SDS and other student groups ensured their films a certain political currency and a ready-made audience. But as the New Left waned, so, too, did this informal distribution network. As a result, Third World Newsreel had to devise strategies for reaching New York's communities of color. Annual catalogues advertised the incredible variety of films available for distribution, many of them Newsreel films or other leftist media. The group distributed Hollywood 10 director Herbert Biberman's classic *Salt of the Earth* (1954), Howard Alk's *The Murder of Fred Hampton* (1971), and *Finally Got the News* (1970), a documentary on the *League of Revolutionary Black Workers* produced in collaboration with two former Detroit Newsreel members, Peter Gessner and Stuart Bird.

Third World Newsreel also expanded Newsreel's distribution of films on Third World liberation struggles. Films such as *Nigeria: Nigeria One* (1973), *We, the Palestinian People* (1973), *Laos: The Forgotten War* (n.d.), and *Proclamation of the Nation of Guinea-Bissau* (1973) supplied scarce information about anticolonial struggles unfolding around the globe.[63] Though many countries were represented in the catalogs from this period, films on Cuba and North Vietnam dominated the collection. Robeson later recalled: "Cuban cinema was way ahead of everybody else. It was the first revolution that wanted to deal with art. That's how it came across to everybody. . . . As a political motivated filmmaker, it was like the Mecca. It was the only place in the world where that was happening, and those were the films that Newsreel distributed." Even before Robeson joined Third World Newsreel, she had heard about Cuba's national film institute, ICAIC, and hoped to study there one day: "I was really affected by what was happening in Cuba in terms of cinema and the whole role that art and culture was playing in revolution."[64] After founding Third World Newsreel, Robeson found that Choy, Siegel, and others in the group shared her appreciation for Cuban cinema. Cuba had so completely captured the imagination of Third World Newsreel that the group distributed many films by the Cuban filmmaker Álvarez, including *Hanoi, Tuesday the Thirteenth* (1967), a tribute to Vietnamese peasants, and *Golpeanda en la selva* (1967), a depiction of Colombian guerrillas massing in the mountains. Third World Newsreel also distributed *Cerro pelado* (1966), which documents the U.S. government's attempt to bar Cuban athletes from the 1967 Pan-American Games, and *Por primera vez* (1967), which depicts the successful efforts of ICAIC to reach remote villages and screen films where none had been seen before. Another film, *Children of the Revolution,* uses film footage of infant day care centers, nurseries, schools, and workplaces to illustrate how Cuban young people were being shaped by a socialist society.

Despite the predominance of Cuban and North Vietnamese films, Third World Newsreel also distributed a selection of rare films on Africa, Latin America, and other parts of Southeast Asia. The group rereleased a film Newsreel had edited from a Dutch television documentary entitled *Viva Frelimo* (1971) on the anticolonial struggle in Mozambique. The collective also became the first distributor for *Nossa terra* (1971), which depicted the war of independence being fought by Amílcar Cabral and the liberation army of Guinea-Bissau against the Portuguese. Another film, *Mi patria ocupada*, focused on the difficult life of Oaxaca de Mejia, a Guatemalan woman who joined a guerrilla movement after many years of working for the United Fruit Company. Third World Newsreel even distributed a feature film from the Democratic People's Republic of Korea entitled *The Steelmakers*, which followed one factory's troubled attempts to implement a new assembly-line process. The sheer diversity and number of films collected by Third World Newsreel quickly drew the attention of film festival organizers and political groups around the country.[65] By the mid-1970s, the group was becoming an important distributor of radical film and filmmakers from around the world.

In 1975, Third World Newsreel also created its own exhibition space, a theater in a loft on West Twentieth Street called the Higher Ground Cinema. Founded to "bring the audience into active participation in the selection of films and the development of follow up discussions," Higher Ground Cinema was designed as a film club in which individuals became members, helping to determine which films were shown and in what context.[66] Meant to shatter barriers between the audience and exhibitors, Higher Ground was clearly inspired by Cuba's history of film clubs. Just as Cuban film clubs were spaces where critiques of imperialism and an interest in artistic innovation coincided, Third World Newsreel saw Higher Ground Cinema as a vehicle to spark political debate and collective struggle.[67] The theater's mission statement declared that it would "operate as an extended resource of the community," screening films intended to be "a summons for action which will aid our audience in developing new concepts of why we must struggle, and how to struggle."[68] Culling material from Third World Newsreel's expanding distribution network, Higher Ground Cinema held a series of screenings every year, incorporating films from the United States, Cuba, Vietnam, South Africa, and elsewhere in the developing world. "We knew that there were lots of films that were being produced in Latin America, Africa, Asia," Siegel later recalled, "and there wasn't a venue for those films. That's how Higher Ground Cinema came about. We created this theater so that people could see films that they couldn't see in this city."[69] The common theme of these films was local, national, and transnational resistance to Western cultural and economic imperialism. The theater showed everything from *Broken Treaty at Battle Mountain* (1975) depicting Shoshone Indians struggling to retain their land and indigenous culture to *Last Grave at Dimbaza* (1975), a film smuggled out of South Africa, and *Sambizanga* (1972), celebrating the Angolan freedom fight as told from the perspective of a black woman searching for her husband. Other films memorialized grassroots struggles against a variety of ills.

Third World Newsreel's distribution and exhibition efforts clearly provided an alternative to mainstream media, but they did not dramatically affect U.S. media at the point of production. That was a more difficult and arduous task, which the collective tried to undertake by founding the Association of Afro-American and Third World Filmmakers in the USA. As early as 1971, Susan Robeson began to develop the idea for what she then termed a "Third World Media Center." Situated within the black community, the center was to "serve as a means of distributing and making films in the community" in order to create the "revolutionary, that is—human—consciousness of Black and Third World people." The distribution and exhibition process was again modeled after Cuban cinema; "mobile film and sound units" would "show films in the streets to the people." In Cuba, these units were predominantly a rural phenomena designed to reach an illiterate and isolated populace; Robeson's urban units, however, were to serve as a "means for organizing and mobilizing people already involved in struggle," thereby giving them the "theoretical and practical bases for remaking themselves and their environment." Envisioning the center as an "activist-oriented organization" that was "international in scope," Robeson planned to include Cuban and Vietnamese films, as well as leftist classics such as *Battle of Algiers* (1965).[70] On the production end, the Third World Media Center was intended as "a vehicle through which the grassroots [could] define and make themselves heard." Not only would the Third World Media Center involve community people in the technical aspects of filmmaking but communities would also determine the subject matter based on their own needs. If the community faced a particularly pressing issue or was embroiled in a difficult, ongoing battle, then that would become subject matter for a film. Planned as a flexible and eminently useful entity, Robeson even imagined the group making short newsreels providing practical organizing and educational information such as "The Street Fighter's Guide to Survival" and "How to Handle Your Welfare Hassles," a goal that the group shared with early Newsreel.

Taken together, the distribution and production aspects of the Third World Media Center would make it a "revolutionary communications network of, by and for Black and Third World people of America." A means of breaking mass media's stranglehold, the center would produce short films that could be distributed weekly to a national constituency. Robeson expected these activities to bring the center into direct conflict with conglomerates such as ABC News and Loews Theater. In her musings on the subject, Robeson envisioned the center usurping traditional media by, for example, broadcasting on ABC each night at 7 p.m. in order to foreground issues and people absent from the mainstream media apparatus. Robeson also imagined pressuring Loews and other theater chains to donate an evening's proceeds in order to fund the Third World Media Center's operations. Robeson's ideas never came to full fruition, although some of them were incorporated into Third World Newsreel's activities. For instance, the group established a filmmaking workshop for people of color directed by Siegel, whose wealth of experience teaching film at the Free University of New York and elsewhere made him the logical choice. This workshop, renamed the "Advanced Film and Video Production Workshop," still runs today and is one of the most well-known aspects of Third World Newsreel, having trained hundreds of media-makers.

In 1974, Robeson and other Third World Newsreel members began looking for ways to extend their activities into the national arena. By then Third World Newsreel had already participated in several international film conferences during which group members met filmmakers in Europe, the United States, Africa, and Latin America. In December 1973, Robeson attended a Third World Filmmakers Meeting in Algiers. Convened by a host of international filmmakers including Senegal's Ousmane Sembene, Cuba's Manuel Pérez, Colombia's Jorge Silva, and Mauritania's Med Hondo, the meeting was called to discuss the role of Third World film in the fight against imperialism and neocolonialism. Divided into several commissions including one on people's cinema, the meeting produced several statements. In the manifesto issued from the People's Cinema Commission, the role of media within national liberation movements was defined. The "militant film-maker," the authors wrote, must produce a "dialectic analysis of the socio-historic phenomenon of colonization" in order to effect the "disalienation of the colonized peoples." This could only occur if films were considered to be a "social act" enabling filmmakers to extend themselves into other "fields of action such as: articulating, fostering and making the new films understandable to the masses of people by associating himself with the promoters of people's cinemas, clubs and itinerant film groups." In the manifesto released by the Production-Coproduction Commission chaired by Sembene, the group declared that Third World productions must be a "manifestation of anti-imperialist solidarity." Filmmakers must build autonomous media infrastructures, collaborate across national borders, and seek new aesthetic forms stemming from the "economic means and possibilities of the Third World countries."[71] As we have seen, these formulations greatly influenced and were reflected in the diversity of Third World Newsreel's activities.

Members of Third World Newsreel also attended the Pan African Federation of Film Producers meeting held in Senegal in the fall of 1974 and the International Meeting for a New Cinema in Montreal in June 1974. Organized under the title "On the African Film Maker and His People," the Dakar conference was convened in order to define the role and function of the African filmmaker in society. Fostering discussion on what constituted cinema, a filmmaker, an African filmmaker, African cinema, and its audience, each attending association had to furnish the other attendees with a report on one of the conference topics.[72] The Montreal conference, on the other hand, was not confined to discussion of African cinema; rather, participants gathered to discuss the creation of a new cinema. Speakers included Fernando Solanas, director of *La hora de los hornos* (1968), Argentinean filmmaker Edgardo Pallero, and Newsreel cofounder Robert Zellner speaking on the evolution of Newsreel. Discussion focused on the ways filmmakers could make themselves and their work available to liberation movements. There was even talk of creating a Bureau of Third World Cinema that could coordinate filmmaker collaboration and help create alternative distribution networks.[73]

So influential were these opportunities to discuss and debate the aesthetic and political imperatives of radical cinema, Robeson later recalled, that she, Choy, and other Third World Newsreel members talked about creating an organization that would serve as a counterpart to the Pan African Federation of Film Producers. The Association of Afro-American and Third World Film-makers in the U.S. was to provide an institutional base through which U.S. Third World filmmakers could network with one another.[74] In the fall of 1974, Third World Newsreel, the Philadelphia Filmmakers Workshop, and the Film Workshop of the National Black Media Conference organized several regional meetings to discuss an upcoming conference of African American and Third World filmmakers in the United States at which the new organization would be founded. The meetings drew several renowned (but then unknown) film-makers and critics including Madeline Anderson, Pearl Bowser, Ed Guerrero, Jacqui Jones, and Michelle Parkerson. The Los Angeles filmmakers Larry Clark and Haile Gerima sent a message of solidarity apologizing for their absence. Over several months, debate was structured around many of the topics discussed at the various international conferences in which Third World Newsreel had participated, and eventually the group renamed itself the Association of Third World Filmworkers and produced a statement of its principles of unity. Citing imperialism and monopoly capitalism as the "main enemy of Afro-American and Third World peoples," the statement identified the mass media as the "communications (propaganda) instrument of the U.S. ruling class." In order to combat it, U.S. Third World people must use films to "clarify, educate, organize, and mobilize the masses for the struggle against imperialism."[75] In a much-abbreviated form, the principles of unity echoed many of the ideas Robeson had expressed back in 1971. Though it began impressively, the organization never coalesced. The regional planning meetings, however, did create a network of filmmakers that resulted in the 1974 Independent Film Arts Festival held in Philadelphia.

Taken together, Third World Newsreel's distribution, exhibition, and production practices in the 1970s began building the context and level of specificity needed to flesh out a parallel between black, Latino, and Asian U.S. communities and Third World peoples.[76] Members tried to counter the sedimented generalizations and stereotypes that had previously been mobilized by early Newsreel. This does not mean that one tendency elides the other; rather, we might understand the two as counterparts, expressing the contradictory elements at work in sustaining U.S. Third World Left discourse and politics. Nichols wrote in 1980:

> At this point it is not possible to do more than suggest the possibility that a study of the American left in the sixties will find its main line of development in the movement from the Civil Rights demonstrations through SNCC and the Black Panthers to the Black Workers Congress and the Congress of Afrikan People. If this is the case, however, it may also mean that recording the history of Newsreel since 1971 is not the writing of an epitaph but the recognition of the Third World people's struggle to gain mastery of forms of communication previously denied them.[77]

As true as Nichols's statement is, it is equally true that the "main line of development" he describes has not shifted the terms of sixties historiography. If anything, current scholarship continues to privilege a certain set of actors and organizations despite the increasing number of recent studies that call that myopic view into question. Even more disturbing is the fact that Third World Newsreel has largely been ignored outside of cinema studies circles and even there, with the notable exceptions of Nichols and Renov, remains continually overshadowed by a focus on Newsreel. And this although Third World Newsreel has existed more than thirty years longer than its predecessor.

This chapter has tried to address that lack and shift sixties historiography by showing how the group's early work transformed Newsreel's practice and in the process articulated a U.S. Third World Left discourse with its own sets of images and political preoccupations to which we must attend. Third World Newsreel's desire to use film to empower U.S. communities of color was far from a locally bound enterprise. Poverty, police violence, discrimination, and unemployment were depicted as local manifestations of a worldwide dynamic of exploitation between First and Third World nations. The filmmaker's role was to expose and critique the extant ideological and cultural forms of domination while simultaneously foregrounding the elements of an emergent consciousness that might contest it. Film, in this formulation, had a central role in decolonizing culture and presenting new cultural and political possibilities.

If the debates between Jones, Cruse, and Williams served as a lens through which to refract and reflect back on the work of Newsreel and Third World Newsreel, I now turn to the work of Angela Y. Davis as a bridge between those Newsreel filmmakers and the ones active at UCLA in the 1970s. Davis brought an internationalist framework informed by a deep immersion in Western Marxism, rethinking the internal-colony thesis in ways that might help us differently understand the link between Newsreel documentaries and the narrative films on the Los Angeles community of Watts. Her intersectional approach proves useful for grasping more complexly the ways that oppressions are interlinked, even if they are not reducible to one another. It also helps us complicate the view of political organizing we have thus far considered, raising the question of how state violence and the state's delimiting of the internal colony might foreclose or delay political action and sustained transnational analysis.

5. Angela Y. Davis and U.S. Third World Left Theory and Praxis

●

No one in the media has dealt with the fact that there exists a tradition behind Angela. They have, instead, described her as if she just popped from the sea, black and beautiful from nowhere.

—Haywood Burns, *Who Is Angela Davis?*

Haywood Burns, one of Angela Y. Davis's lawyers during her now infamous trial on murder, conspiracy, and kidnapping charges, could not have known how true his words from the early 1970s would still ring today. Davis has become a literal icon for the 1960s, most often described as a figure that emerged from the U.S. civil rights movement. Strangely, even the academic community has maintained a certain critical distance. More than thirty years later, with the notable exception of Joy James, few people have examined the particular intellectual and political formation out of which Davis emerged.[1] Though several published interviews have done important contextual and critical work, to date, few full-length critical essays on Davis have been published.[2] This critical silence obscures the complicated political and intellectual tradition in which her early writings and activism must be understood.

This chapter takes up that tradition, situating Davis as a unique U.S. Third World Leftist. Before the twenty-six-year-old Davis found herself on the FBI's "Ten Most Wanted List," she had been a student of Frankfurt School philosophers Herbert Marcuse and Theodor Adorno and had met Algerian, Vietnamese, and Cuban anticolonialists while living and traveling in Frankfurt, Paris, London, and Havana. In fact, Davis spent much of her time between 1960 and 1967 far removed from the modern civil rights movement, living in the northern United States and traveling and studying in Europe. When she did return, she was active in Communist Party circles rather than immersed in civil rights or Black Power circles. Davis's early internationalist orientation impacted her domestic racial politics, rather than the other way around. I want to suggest that it is precisely Davis's complex history, one that does not fit into the neat, conventional narratives of the 1960s, that explains this critical silence. Her identity and her forms of analysis challenge the customary boundaries between political movements, philosophies, and nations, demonstrating that forms of analysis and oppression are always mutually imbricated, even as they seem to depart quite dramatically from one another.

In his essay "On National Culture," Frantz Fanon argued against what he termed "facile internationalism," concluding, "It is at the heart of national consciousness that international consciousness lives and grows."[3] In one sense, his elusive formulation recognizes that Western colonialism and imperialism bequeathed to the "wretched of the earth" the modular form(s) of the nation-state as the global lingua franca. In Fanon's estimation, it was only once a radical national project was successfully embarked on that emerging postcolonial nations could vigorously support and defend other emergent nations in their quest to overthrow colonial domination. In his view, the history of colonialism and imperialism had left former colonies with little choice but to emulate First World nation-states, despite all their apparent flaws.

If Fanon's ideal anticolonial subject was supposed to move from the local to the global, from the national to the international, Davis's path troubled that prescription. She moved from the local to the global and then back to the local. She moved outside U.S. borders in order to assess its national forms of order and ways of spreading disorder. This is clearly a consequence of Davis's position as an oppressed national minority living at the very heart of U.S. imperialism. Davis's First World position required certain forms of translation. The anticolonial project could not be transplanted whole into the economic and political body of the United States, as Harold Cruse warned in *The Crisis of the*

Negro Intellectual. Davis did not achieve international consciousness by moving through a nationalist project as others of her generation; instead, Davis's burgeoning international consciousness propelled her deconstruction of the political, social, and economic forms of the U.S. nation-state. Rather than enshrining new, more radical forms of "national consciousness"—to pick up another phrase of Fanon's—Davis began a radically deconstructive project, unraveling U.S. imperialism at its point of origin. She began interrogating the forms that state-sponsored race and class oppression takes in the United States, producing a new theoretical viewpoint from which to fight the oppression she witnessed in the United States and abroad. This involved a critique of the nation-state as the global building block. Instead, her political vision assumed a loose alliance among Third World peoples and oppressed peoples in the First World, assumed a certain geographic and ideological fluidity that cohered into a revolutionary internationalism.

Combining elements of Marxism, feminism, antiracism, and anticolonialism, this revolutionary internationalism was characterized by two critical elements: an intersectional theoretical approach that consistently foregrounds the ways in which class, gender, race, and national oppression produce and reproduce one another; and a focus on state violence and incarceration as tools for consolidating racial oppression in the First World. Davis was deeply marked by the ways in which diverse, seemingly divergent influences—Western Marxism, U.S. antiracism, and Third World anticolonialism—coalesced. Davis's cultural and political formation embodies, if in an extreme form, the complicated ideological and political currents at work among a generation of U.S. Third World Leftists. The first sections of this chapter look at Davis's complex genealogy by analyzing how her 1974 autobiography positions her as an activist-intellectual. In that autobiography, she highlights her childhood in the Jim Crow South, her training with Frankfurt School philosophers, and her encounters with anticolonialists as the keys to her later political and intellectual direction. The final section of the chapter turns to Davis's early essay "Political Prisoners, Prisons, and Black Liberation" to explore how her revolutionary internationalism found articulation in this seminal early piece. Ultimately, I am concerned here with considering how her autobiography and essay articulate a forceful critique of the U.S. nation-state, helping us understand its forms of domestic racism and global imperialism.

State Violence and Alienated Citizenship

Davis begins her autobiography on the run in the days before the FBI captured and charged her with murder and kidnapping. Her decision to begin there, on the run, literally hunted, cannot help but echo slave narratives. In both cases, the goal is physical freedom, escape from impending captivity. This framing device marks all that follows. Once Davis details her imprisonment, highlighting the kinship networks and modes of solidarity that female prisoners forge, she quickly moves to describe her childhood in Birmingham, Alabama, a city mockingly known as "Bombingham." As she describes it, Davis's early life was indelibly shaped by racial apartheid. The routine indignities of Jim Crow segregation and economic discrimination were underlined by brutal terrorism. As a preschooler, she moved with her family into the neighborhood nicknamed "Dynamite Hill" because of the Ku Klux Klan's frequent bombings of black families within the previously all-white enclave. Under the reign of Eugene "Bull" Connor, the commissioner of public safety from 1937 to 1954, and again from 1957 to 1963, these bombings—if not directly orchestrated by the state—were sanctioned by state and city political inaction. Consequently, Davis learned early on the violent lengths to which many white citizens would go to maintain a system of white supremacy premised on black disfranchisement. "The eyes heavy with hatred on Dynamite Hill; the roar of explosives, the fear, the hidden guns, the weeping Black women at our door," Davis later recalled, shaped her childhood and adolescence.[4] Like many black Southerners, Davis learned to live with state-sanctioned terrorism, literally held captive by it. She reflects, "Every night now . . . I'll hear white crackers planting bombs around the house. We are supposed to be next anyway."[5] Though Davis's family was relatively privileged within Birmingham's black community—her mother and father were schoolteachers before her father opened a gas station—her parents were both politically active. They were members of the local NAACP chapter and Sallye B. Davis was also a national officer in the Southern Negro Youth Congress, a CPUSA-affiliated organization that in the 1930s lobbied on behalf of the Scottsboro Nine. Though they themselves did not join the Communist Party, many of their friends did and were subsequently forced underground during the McCarthy era.[6] The Davises' political involvement no doubt resulted from black Birmingham's long-standing engagement in civil rights and labor activism stretching back to the 1930s. As Robin D. G. Kelley has shown, black sharecroppers' attempts to unionize in the early twentieth century left a deep mark on the city's political landscape.[7]

In addition to encouraging political activism, Davis's parents prized education. Here again is yet another echo of slave narratives, in which the path to freedom leads through literacy.[8] In fact, Sallye Davis commuted back and forth during summers to earn a master's degree at New York University. During her childhood, Angela and her sister Fania accompanied their mother on these trips, where they got a glimpse of Northern life, which had a contradictory impact on Davis. On the one hand, it only made her "more keenly sensitive to the segregation [she] had to face at home."[9] But on the other hand, Davis reflected that she "felt her blackness more than she ever had in the South—not in the customary racist ways, but because people made such effusive overtures to her and because of their awkward attempts to ignore that she was black."[10] In short, the difference between Northern and Southern racism seemed one of degree rather than kind. The North did not display its racism and race consciousness in the same ways as the Jim Crow South, but it was far from a racial utopia.

Like white middle-class children of the time, Davis was schooled in Western "high" culture, taking ballet and music lessons from a young age. But if her mother expected her to become a debutante, plans that eventually collapsed, she also expected Davis to be a critic of her social environment. "Our parents," Davis reflected in an interview, "encouraged us to look beyond appearances and to think about possibilities, to think about ways in which we could, with our own agency, intervene and transform the world."[11] While political struggles engulfed Birmingham in the mid-1950s, the adolescent Davis spent much of her time at the public library reading Booker T. Washington's *Up from Slavery* and Victor Hugo's *Les misérables*, among other titles. Seeking what she described in her autobiography as an "avenue of escape," Davis applied for and won a Quaker scholarship for Southern students to attend Northern schools.[12] Landing at a progressive high school in Greenwich Village and living with the Melishes, a family of white activists, Davis found herself far removed from the Southern civil rights movement by the fall of 1959.

It was at the Elizabeth Irwin High School, an outgrowth of the Little Red School House, that the young Davis first encountered Marxist theory. The school was a haven for blacklisted schoolteachers expelled from the New York City public school system. In her history classes, she learned about socialism and read Marx and Engels's *Communist Manifesto*. In her autobiography, Davis stresses that she read Marx's text repeatedly, focusing on one passage in particular: "All previous historical movements were movements of minorities, or in the interests of minorities. The proletarian movement is the self-conscious independent movement of the immense majority." From this passage, Davis glimpsed what she described as "a vision of a new society, without exploiters and exploited," one in which the proletarian majority liberated the oppressed minority (109). Linking the progress of human history to a mass movement of the proletariat must have seemed appealing precisely because it foretold a future in which the proletariat willingly emancipated oppressed minorities, a far cry from the reality she observed in the South and the North. Davis's attraction to this passage enabled her to begin coupling the situation of black Americans with the global struggle to end economic exploitation: "What struck me so emphatically was the idea that once the emancipation of the proletariat became a reality, the foundation was laid for the emancipation of all groups in the society" (110). However, Marx and Engels's prediction that the proletarian majority would lead the socialist revolution was not borne out by events in the 1960s and 1970s; instead, a vocal, militant minority sought to transform the structures supported by the immense majority. This reversal occasioned a rethinking of revolutionary theory among Western Marxists, particularly the Frankfurt School and the New Leftists and U.S. Third World Leftists they later influenced.

While in New York, the fifteen-year-old Davis also joined Advance, a CPUSA-affiliated youth organization to which Bettina Aptheker, Eugene Davis, Margaret Burnham, and Mary Lou Patterson, the daughter of the black communist attorney William Patterson, also belonged. Davis's Advance activities included protesting in front of the local Woolworth's store to express solidarity with the Southern sit-in movement she had left behind. Like other Elizabeth Irwin students, Davis also joined SANE (the Committee for a Sane Nuclear Policy), as well as the local NAACP chapter, and she worked with Inside Pharaoh and Outside Pharaoh gang members and their girlfriends at the Brooklyn Heights Youth Center. These activities had their intellectual counterpart in a series of lectures given by the radical historian Herbert Aptheker at the American Institute for Marxist Studies, where Davis "absorbed," according to biographer Reggie Nadelson, "social theory and economic history."[13] Before she even went to college, Davis had the beginnings of a strong Marxist intellectual foundation.

Once she arrived at Brandeis University in 1961, that foundation was further solidified. Davis, one of ten black students in a college of fifteen hundred, found herself immersed in an environment where "intellectualism was the brain of Brandeis, its political radicalism the guts."[14] Indeed, Davis was not the only sixties radical produced at the college; Abbie Hoffman and several Weathermen were also graduates. While at Brandeis, Davis met James Baldwin and studied with Herbert Marcuse, the Frankfurt School philosopher and media-anointed "New Left theorist" with whom she developed a lasting personal and intellectual relationship.[15] Though cloistered in Waltham, Massachusetts, at quite a cultural, political, and geographic distance from Birmingham, Davis did not remain immune to the shock waves emanating from the national civil rights struggle. In the fall of 1963, while studying at the Sorbonne, Davis learned that four teenaged girls—Carole Robertson, Cynthia Wesley, Addie Mae Collins, and Denise McNair—had been killed in the Sixteenth Street Baptist Church bombing in Birmingham. It is clear that this event struck a deeply personal chord, in part because the girls were friends of the Davis family. In the intervening years, Davis has since written and spoken about this incident repeatedly, acknowledging that it prompted her to consider her own responsibility to and distance from the civil rights fray. Her sense of horror and outrage was inexplicable to those around her, causing a political dissonance that shaped her future direction. She writes in her autobiography, "No matter how much I talked, the people around me were simply incapable of grasping it. They could not understand why the whole society was guilty of this murder— why their beloved Kennedy was also to blame, why the whole ruling stratum in their country, by being guilty of racism, was also guilty of this murder."[16] The failure of Europeans and white Americans in Paris to acknowledge their own complicity in such brutal white supremacy pushed Davis to further reexamine her relationship to the U.S. nation-state more generally.

Davis's analysis may have been inimical to white Americans' conceptions of themselves, but it was by no means inimical to black Americans' conceptions of them. In fact, her analysis reflects the very different assumptions on which black U.S. citizenship has always been premised. Black Americans have historically had—and still have—a fundamentally different relationship to the United States than do their white counterparts. Given that black citizenry possess a contradictory relationship to the nation-state, one defined by hypocrisy and betrayal, black citizenship can only be described as an uneasy, even alienated form of national belonging. It is a belonging unachieved, built on the *long durée* of brutal exclusion from and halting steps toward a marginalizing inclusion within the body politic. One has only to survey U.S. black history to identify multiple manifestations of and responses to this alienation ranging from prolonged exile to armed rebellion. During the modern civil rights movement, these civil contradictions and their attendant forms of alienation intensified. Black citizens could not help but recognize their alien and alienated status, could not help but understand that their citizenship was premised on the denial of rights and privileges, vicious disfranchisement rather than enfranchisement. In fact, mass-media technology disseminated and mediated this knowledge as images on the nightly news and stories in the daily papers repeatedly underscored the antagonistic relation between black people and the U.S. nation-state.

Davis's alienated citizenship provoked her to question, and eventually theorize, the place of black Americans in the United States and to question the fictions that undergird all First World nation-states. At a remove from the U.S. nation-state, her physically exiled body paralleled the experience of alienated black citizenship. Geographic distance from the United States mimicked and further encouraged an intellectual and political distance from it. In Paris when news of John F. Kennedy's assassination broke, Davis gathered with other citizens at the U.S. embassy, but she felt estranged from the collective expression of mourning. She later reflected: "I felt out of place at the Embassy, surrounded by crowds of 'Americans in Paris' and it was difficult to identify with their weeping. I wondered how many of them had shed tears—or had truly felt saddened—when they read the *Herald Tribune* story about the murders of Carole, Cynthia, Addie Mae and Denise."[17] White and black U.S. citizens could never experience a so-called national tragedy in the same way, particularly while black lives were so casually devalued by everyday racist practice and institutionalized white supremacy. As happened with other black American activists and intellectuals, Davis's alienated subjectivity served as a model for new forms of international affiliation and solidarity, an impetus for rethinking and transforming the U.S. social order. In a recent article, Robin D. G. Kelley asserts, "The particular transnational, global perspective developed by African American intellectuals . . . was a product of a state refusing to grant black people citizenship . . . and a political refusal on the part of many black intellectuals to prop up American nationalism and its national myths."[18] Davis's belief that the Birmingham bombing formed part and parcel of the structure of exploitation and white supremacy undergirding white citizenship eventually led Davis to think more complexly about how such structures were replicated around the globe.

Viewing the national from the vantage point of the global produced an analysis of the interrelation between the two. The social, cultural, political, and even physical death of black Americans depended on, recirculated, and helped reify a global structure of oppression and exploitation. In other words, the logic of U.S. citizenship and imperialism relied on the fostering and exportation of modes of oppression,[19] the pitting of the white citizen against the black noncitizen.[20] At moments of profound national crisis—Kennedy's assassination, the Birmingham bombing—Davis's inchoate divestment from U.S. national mythologies only intensified. This remove from U.S. nationalism laid the groundwork for a more systematic critique of the social, political, and economic world order that her training with Frankfurt School philosophers and encounters with anticolonial activists and artists would develop.

Critical Theory: Constructing a Utopian Imaginary

As a French and then a philosophy major, Davis found herself immersed in Frankfurt School philosophy, an interest that only fueled her radical social practice. During her senior year, Davis sought Marcuse's advice on a course of philosophical study, and their initial meeting turned into weekly one-on-one tutoring sessions. Those sessions were largely responsible for Davis's decision to pursue a Ph.D. at the Institute for Social Research at Goethe University in Frankfurt, Germany. While there, Davis wrote a thesis under Adorno, but decided to return to the United States in the summer of 1967 rather than complete her degree in Frankfurt. To a large extent, this decision reflected her desire to participate in U.S. racial struggles, but the move also indicated Davis's preference for Marcuse's philosophical orientation. She immediately enrolled in the philosophy program at the University of California at San Diego, where she began work on her doctorate with Marcuse. Though colleagues and close friends for many years, by the late 1960s, Adorno and Marcuse found themselves increasingly on different philosophical and political paths, particularly after Adorno returned to postwar Germany. Marcuse, with the publication of *An Essay on Liberation* in 1969, became known as a champion for the New Left, while Adorno expressed serious reservations about the New Left's goals and tactics, wondering if they might replicate the same kind of fascism they claimed to oppose.[21] Adorno also became more and more invested in theory as the highest form of praxis, while Marcuse increasingly came to believe that praxis, even flawed praxis, needed to stand at the core of critical theory.

Marcuse grew up in a suburb outside of Berlin as a member of an affluent, assimilated Jewish family in the textile business. The Marcuses' trajectory, argues Barry Katz, closely paralleled the social history of the ascending industrial bourgeoisie of the late empire.[22] Educated in a Wilhelmine German educational system premised on the rigid maintenance of social classes, Marcuse studied the German classics, as well as the French avant-garde literary tradition. Had he not been drafted into World War I, he might have continued along the road to a settled bourgeois life. But Marcuse was drafted in 1916 and because of his bad eyesight was stationed in Potsdam where resistance to the war was brewing within the military ranks. In Potsdam, he began reading Marx, eventually joining the Social Democratic Party (SPD) in 1917, one of three warring factions within Germany's working-class movement. While serving as an elected delegate to the soldier's council in Berlin, Marcuse's active membership in political parties ended abruptly in January 1919 when the SPD helped orchestrate the murder of Rosa Luxemburg, a member of the German Communist Party.[23] That incident precipitated Marcuse's return to academia. He matriculated at the University of Freiburg in 1920, beginning nearly a decade of work with Martin Heidegger and Edmund Husserl during which he studied Marx and Hegel extensively. That collaboration ended when Heidegger's collaboration with the Nazis strained Marcuse's relationship with both men. Husserl did, however, help garner Marcuse an introduction to Max Horkheimer, the newly appointed director of the Institute for Social Research.[24]

In 1932, Marcuse published his first book *Hegel's Ontology and the Founding of a Theory of Historicity*, a work heavily indebted to phenomenology and Heideggerian philosophy. After that, though, he became increasingly drawn into Horkheimer's inner circle where critical theory was being generated. With the consolidation of the National Socialist Party, the institute's members—Horkheimer, Adorno, and Marcuse among them—went into exile in 1933 until after World War II, spending the bulk of their time in the United States at Columbia University and in Santa Monica, where they joined other exiles including Bertolt Brecht and Heinrich Mann.[25] When Adorno and Horkheimer returned to Frankfurt at the war's end, Marcuse chose to stay in the United States, serving between 1942 and 1951 as a low-level intelligence analyst along with over ninety other academics. He was charged with assessing the mentality of German citizens under the Nazi regime. After his stint in U.S. government service, Marcuse taught at universities, first Columbia University and Harvard University, and between 1958 and 1965 at Brandeis, until the administration refused to renew his contract. Eventually he moved to UC San Diego, where he taught until he retired in 1976.

Between 1955 and 1972, Marcuse published three works that proved particularly influential for the New Left, *Eros and Civilization* (1955), *One-Dimensional Man* (1964), and *An Essay on Liberation* (1969). It is clear that Marcuse's work loomed large in Davis's own intellectual formation. Of Marcuse, Davis once reflected, "I never cease to stand in awe of his ability to relate ideas, ostensibly buried under the sands of time, to the current situation we have to deal with in our social and political lives."[26] There are several elements of Marcuse's thought that Davis found useful for her intellectual and political development. They include the conceptualizing of a critical theory; a rethinking of the relationship between theory and praxis; a reinvestment in utopia as an achievable political project; and a belief in the power of students and U.S. peoples of color to help ignite—if not sustain—a socialist revolution.

According to Martin Jay, a historian of the Frankfurt School, critical theory's progenitors extend back to the 1840s as leftist Hegelians began to apply Hegel's theories to contemporaneous social and political life in Germany. Their most well-known member, Karl Marx, developed an enormously influential revolutionary theory that held sway for much of the nineteenth and early twentieth century. By the end of World War I, however, Marx's theory had become a kind of metaphysics, an undialectical paradigm that violated many of the core ideas held by Marx himself. In the early 1920s, Karl Korsch's *Marxism and Philosophy* and Georg Lukács's *History and Class Consciousness* ushered in a period of critical rethinking during which Marx's debt to Hegel was examined anew and many of the core epistemological and methodological questions of classical Marxism were investigated. Building on this work, Frankfurt School members reasserted the role of consciousness within Marxist theory. Turning Marxists' dialectical method in a more materialist direction, they began to focus on the question of how to fuse philosophy and social analysis and transform the world through human praxis or practical activity.[27] At its core, Frankfurt School philosophers rejected all metaphysical truths, dismissing any notion of absolute truth, instead stressing the individual's role in society and exploring how social psychology might help bridge the gap between the individual and society. In his writing, Horkheimer stressed the following three points that illustrate more fully the early concerns of critical theory: For one, he suggested that philosophers had gone too far in emphasizing subjectivity and inwardness; second, he argued that they neglected the material dimension of reality; and third, he cautioned that philosophers "overstated their case and seemed to be rejecting reason itself" (51).

Proposing a materialist theory of society, Horkheimer, Adorno, Marcuse, and other Western Marxists argued that the economic base and the cultural, political, and ideological superstructure constantly interacted; thus civil society and politics had begun to assume a primacy unimagined in Marx's time (53). Frankfurt School philosophers took as their mission a closer analysis of the individual's interaction with the state and civil society, a deeper critique of bourgeois society and its ideological and social conventions. In the 1937 essay "Traditional and Critical Theory," Horkheimer systematically articulated the theoretical orientation that would guide the work of the Frankfurt School.[28] Contrasting traditional theory with critical theory, Horkheimer argues that the historical moment demands a break with Enlightenment modes of inquiry. In traditional theory, Horkheimer contends, scientists and social scientists base their models on what they see as transparent, objectively known facts. The explanatory value and validity of traditional theory depends on one's accurate observation and interpretation of phenomena. In explaining historical events, traditional theory posits a cause-and-effect chain in which specific objective conditions lead to certain events; the range of historical outcomes is thus limited by the conditions themselves. Consequently, for Horkheimer, traditional theory's social function was the "critical examination of data with the aid of an inherited apparatus of concepts and judgments."[29] Absent from this type of theory is an awareness that facts and their interpretation are indeed human made, products of a particular social arrangement.

Critical theorists, on the other hand, take society itself as their object of study, seeking to understand the "individual in his real relation to other individuals and groups, in his conflict with a particular class, and finally, in the resultant web of relationships with the social totality and with nature" (211). Unlike traditional theory, critical theory does not assume that the social totality is unified or coherent; nor does it assume that it can be known and understood purely through the exercise of reason. Instead, critical theory begins by recognizing the "two-sided character of the social totality" (207), which entails a dialectical opposition between social life and the natural world. This opposition propels the critical thinker to at once apprehend the rules that govern social life, even as she or he recognizes them to be powerful conventions that obscure the chaos lurking below (34). The theory, in this paradigm, can never be separated from its social context. Its purpose is to rigorously historicize reason and its relation to current social conditions, to ask how facts come to be facts and impact the world in which they exist. In Thomas McCarthy's estimation, "Critical Theory is concerned precisely with the historical and social genesis of the facts it examines and with the social contexts in which its results will have their effects."[30] In this way, critical theorists depart from leftist Hegelians in believing that a "determinant negation" can restore a sense of the rational self. Deconstruction is not the endpoint but rather part of the process in restoring an authentically rational self no longer tied completely to the market.[31] In Jay's words, "Reason . . . was the 'critical tribunal' on which Critical Theory was primarily based." He continues, "The irrationality of the current society was always challenged by the 'negative' possibility of a truly rational alternative."[32] Such an analysis necessitates an engagement with the principles animating society, a questioning of what democratic principles mean in a social order premised on dominance and exploitation. For Horkheimer, critical theory was a form of "philosophically oriented social inquiry" whose aim was to reveal the ways in which concepts such as *truth*, *justice*, and *freedom* have been distorted by the hegemonic order.[33]

If in Horkheimer's view a ruling-class faction was responsible for the hegemonic order, for black Americans the hegemonic order was also inevitably a racial order. Given her historical experiences, Davis had to incorporate race into critical theory's frame of reference. For her, it was not difficult to believe that truth, justice, and freedom had been unmoored from their egalitarian meanings by a white supremacist order. Developing a useable critical theory required Davis to account for how both race and class structured the current social order. This is not to argue that Davis was any less convinced than Horkheimer that market forces and capitalism ultimately lay at the very core of social injustice; however, for her those market forces were always shaped through and by a white racial order with both local and global dimensions. In a 1971 interview, she remarked, "The only true path of liberation for Black people is the one that leads towards a complete and total overthrow of the capitalist class in this country and all its manifold institutional appendages which ensure its ability to exploit the masses and enslave Black people."[34] Like other black radicals, she saw race and class as complementary not contradictory categories of social analysis; one could not fully describe the dimensions of black oppression without recourse to both of them.

In "Philosophy and Critical Theory," Marcuse defined critical theory's primary purpose as social analysis that looks at the cultural supports for unfreedom, injustice, and unhappiness.[35] Central to this type of social analysis was the understanding of how ideologies function within societies. Marx defined ideology as an "entire superstructure of distinct and peculiarly formed sentiments, illusions, modes of thought and views of life" that rises under a particular mode of production.[36] In a world buffeted by war and mass extermination, it is not surprising that ideology and cultural production assumed a new primacy. The question of how populations acquiesce to and actively support evil and irrational regimes such as National Socialism in Germany or Jim Crow in the Southern United States involves at its core the question of how ideologies deform one's perspective on the world. For Western Marxists in the postwar period, then, understanding contemporary systems of thought and cultural institutions assumed a new importance. Historically contextualizing existing ideologies was a way of rethinking how such ideologies might be rethought, repositioned, redeployed. According to Barry Katz, in critical theory "the dominant concepts of modern thought and ideology [are] dismantled, traced back to the material circumstances in which they originated . . . and then systematically reconstructed so as to reveal their changed political functions in new circumstances. The truth as well as the falsehood of the concepts that guide philosophy, science, and social *praxis* is thus exposed, and their ideological hold is loosened."[37] If for Western Marxists ideology's placement within the economic superstructure and thus its implications for class domination constituted primary preoccupations, black Marxists analyzed ideology's function in securing both class and racial domination. A focus on ideology, in this case, allowed black radicals to understand white supremacy's enduring hold on the U.S. nation-state. Racism and class oppression were both constitutive elements of the nation-state; an attack on white supremacy, then, must fundamentally transform the cultural and ideological structures of the United States, if not completely eradicate class oppression.

Just as critical theory formed the centerpiece of Frankfurt School philosophy, utopia was one of its guiding principles. Indeed, Marcuse's work, particularly that of the 1950s, relied on the revivification of utopia as a goal and a basis for praxis.[38] In his recent *Freedom Dreams*, Robin D. G. Kelley defines utopia as the "idea that we [can] possibly go somewhere that exists only in our imaginations."[39] In Marcuse's view, utopia was far from unattainable; it was simply a condition that was being "blocked from coming about by the power of the established societies."[40] A vision of a classless society free of exploitation and racial oppression, then, should not be dismissed as an impossibility; rather, the current state of affairs might be aberrant, the inevitable outcome of a class- and race-based society vulnerable to attack and overthrow. In defense of this idea, Marcuse argued that "the utopian element [has] long [been] the only progressive element in philosophy."[41] Utopian thinking, far from otherworldly, enables us to identify the potential social elements on which to construct a radically different future. In a 1956 lecture, Marcuse contended, "It may be less irresponsible today to depict a utopia that has a real basis than to defame as utopia conditions and potentials that have long become realizable possibilities."[42] Pragmatic social movement building needs acts of radical imagination. It is this type of radical dreaming, Kelley argues, that has motivated black feminists, Pan-Africanists, and other black radicals to conceive of a better, more egalitarian world. Historically, utopia has given black Americans, however paradoxically, a starting point, a place for which to aim. In our dreams, we have long fashioned our future. As Kelley reminds us, effective social movements "transport us to another place, compel us to relieve horrors, and most importantly, enable us to imagine a new society."[43] Amid the grim determination and hopeful optimism of global decolonization and U.S. civil rights, a call for a return to utopian thinking proved uniquely attractive to young antiracist activists. This perhaps holds all the more true in the case of activists outside of mainstream civil rights organizations such as the SCLC or CORE, which were conceived within and sustained by black church traditions. Marcuse's brand of utopian thinking was not tied to any religious tradition, did not even depend on a belief in God or an afterlife; rather, it may have served as a kind of secular spirituality that propelled radicals such as Angela Davis to organize against extraordinary odds.

Central to the idea of critical theory was the insistence that theory always implies praxis, even if that praxis does not directly follow from the theory. Jay argues that "*praxis* and reason were in fact the two poles of Critical Theory."[44] The importance of human practical activity was consistently emphasized as one way of refuting Hegel's identity theory with its belief that subject and object were in fact identical. The space for human transformation of the social, economic, and political landscape depends on "the irreducible mediations between subject and object, particular and universal."[45] It is on the relative import of theory versus praxis that Adorno and Marcuse began to differ, particularly by the mid-1960s. For Adorno, theory could never be seen as prescriptive, as a way of forecasting or designing strategy; to collapse theory and praxis was to commit a grand error. In his view, theory was seen as the highest form of praxis, the most important transformative act.[46] As such, correct theory might quite reasonably be seen as critical theory's end goal. Marcuse certainly agreed that there was and should not be any crude, causal link between theory and praxis; however, he insisted that theory must always be tied to an activity in the world, even if the theory did not lead directly to any form of praxis. In a sense, critical theory might be seen as an alienating practice, one designed to defamiliarize or decenter one's perspective on the world in order to realign it. For Marcuse, the messy business of praxis was ultimately necessary if true social change was to occur.

This belief explains in part Marcuse's investment in the New Left as an agent of profound social change. In Morton Schoolman's view, "The New Left came to occupy a definite place in Marcuse's theory as a practical force for sweeping change."[47] With its emphasis on both political and cultural revolution, Marcuse believed that the New Left "gave expression to new conceptions of human need, happiness, and freedom, to goals transcending the established form of life."[48] For Marcuse, "the radical political practice involves a cultural subversion. . . . Political radicalism thus implies moral radicalism: the emergence of a morality which might precondition man for freedom."[49] Ushering in a new moral and political era, Marcuse predicted in *An Essay on Liberation* that the "young middle class intelligentsia" and the "ghetto populations [might] well become the first base of popular mass revolt (though not of revolution)."[50] Though Marcuse's formulation did not encompass Davis's identity, one which straddled and ultimately defied his categorization—she was part of a new intelligentsia and part of a black (though not urban ghetto) population—his prediction that the seeds of revolutionary change might not necessarily be sown by the white working class certainly fueled her own revolutionary vision. Echoing prominent anticolonial theorists such as Frantz Fanon, Mao Tse-tung, C. L. R. James, and Mohatma Gandhi, Marcuse's positioning of African Americans and other peoples of color as world historical actors represented a serious revision of Marxist theory, the impact of which cannot be overestimated. At a moment in history when black Americans were fighting for full enfranchisement, this theoretical move placed their struggle within the global struggle for freedom, justice, and equality. Placing "ghetto populations" within a Marxist frame of analysis once again placed class analysis in relationship to race analysis. The question of how the eradication of racial oppression might impact class oppression would inevitably arise, even if the reverse question need not. Marcuse's celebration of new social movements undoubtedly drew Davis closer to his radical philosophy and away from Adorno's seemingly more abstract investment in theory. For Davis, Marcuse served as a critical bridge between Western Marxism and her identity as a young black woman.

If, as I have argued, Davis saw herself as an alienated U.S. citizen, one unmoored from any national affiliation, a philosophical theory designed to reexamine and act to change human hierarchies and oppressive relations must have proven uniquely appealing to her. Marcuse conjectures that this is the case in an open letter he wrote to Davis while she was being held in jail without bail. He writes, "The world in which you grew up, *your* world (which is not mine) was one of cruelty, misery and persecution. To recognize these facts did not require much intelligence and sophistication, but to realize that they could be changed and must be changed required thinking, critical thinking: knowledge of how these conditions came about, which forces perpetuated them, and of the possibilities of freedom and justice. This, I believe, you learned in your years of study."[51] Critical theory, then, was a mode through which Davis could question and act to change her social context. In the face of historical precedent and social custom, it was a means for producing constructive alienation: careful, clear-eyed analysis with the aim of radical social transformation. Davis's interest in Frankfurt School philosophy was not motivated by an investment in European philosophy for its own sake; rather, it provided a tool for rethinking the position of all black Americans in a global field of relations.

Anticolonials in the Metropole

As Davis immersed herself in Frankfurt School theory, she also began encountering anticolonial activists in the metropoles of Europe and the outposts of the colonial world. In 1962, just after her first year at Brandeis, Davis visited Paris on her way to the Eighth World Festival for Youth in Helsinki. Her desire to, in her own words, get "a better perspective on things" was satisfied by her encounters with (ex-)colonials living in the French metropole. Witnessing the hard-scrabble struggle of Martinicans searching for work and the racist attacks on Algerians, Davis began to forge an anticolonial perspective. In her autobiography, Davis wrote, "To be an Algerian living in Paris in 1962 was to be a hunted human being . . . paramilitary terrorist groups were falling indiscriminately upon men and women in the colonialist capital because they were, or looked like, Algerians." At a protest for Algerian independence at the Sorbonne, Davis saw state-sponsored terrorism firsthand as police used high-power water hoses against the anticolonial protestors. Such incidents increased her sense that the struggle of French colonials and African Americans shared certain commonalities. "[The French police] were as vicious as the red-neck cops in Birmingham who met the Freedom Riders with their dogs and hoses," Davis reflected. "The new places, the new experiences I had expected to discover through travel turned out to be the same old places, the same old experiences with a common message of struggle."[52] Distance from the United States allowed Davis to link disparate geographic locations, enabling an understanding of the features shared by colonialism and U.S. white supremacy.

The Algerian struggle was not the only one with which Davis closely identified while abroad. Critique of French and more frequently U.S. imperial domination also confronted her via the intense culture of resistance forged by Vietnamese immigrants living in Paris. During a Vietnamese Tet celebration, Davis saw thousands of Vietnamese cheering performances parodying the U.S. government for its military intervention in Vietnam. While studying in Frankfurt, Davis also took part in civil disobedience, mass demonstrations, and teach-ins against U.S. intervention in Vietnam. For Davis, the domestic civil rights movement was beginning to fit into an anticolonial framework in which Third World peoples and African Americans might find a common basis for struggle. It is no doubt quite significant that distance from the United States robbed Davis of some of the privilege and willful ignorance enjoyed by most Americans. Critique of the United States was not obscured by biased news reports; instead her identity as an American implicated her in the forms of oppression being exported across the globe.

The example set by the Cuban Revolution also focused Davis's anticolonial consciousness on the United States, impressing on her the fact that it was an imperial power to be opposed. At the Helsinki conference, it was the Cuban delegation that most impressed her. In her autobiography, Davis recalled that the young Cuban militants (many of them women) conveyed "a fiercely compelling spirit of revolution" as they satirized the way "wealthy American capitalists had invaded their country and robbed them of all traces of sovereignty" (130). Just as the Vietnamese performers had reduced the United States to an object of ridicule, so, too, had the Cuban delegation—only their triumph had occurred just ninety miles shy of U.S. shores. Davis's interest in Cuba culminated in a month-long trip in July 1969, which she characterized in her autobiography as "a great climax in my life" that left a "permanent mark on my existence" (215). If her view of the Cuban delegation in Helsinki had been romanticized, her reflections about the month-long trip differed considerably. "It was then that I began to realize the true meaning of underdevelopment: it is nothing to be Utopianized," Davis writes; "romanticizing the plight of oppressed people is dangerous and misleading" (208). If Davis's autobiography had until this point stressed the possibilities inherent in Third World solidarity, here she sounds the first cautionary note, beginning to transcend the "facile internationalism" against which Fanon warned. An insistent materiality belies any easy identification with the plight of the Cuban—or any other—masses. Davis does not make the mistake of collapsing her situation into the Cubans, but knowledge of her relative privilege does not produce political paralysis. It is not an excuse for inaction, but rather an impetus for greater nuance and sophistication in crafting a transnational political analysis.

In the summer of 1967, Davis returned from Europe, deciding to pursue her Ph.D. with Marcuse at UC San Diego instead of with Adorno in Frankfurt. On her return to the United States she immersed herself in graduate training and political organizing. Her biographer Nadelson writes, "She saw the task of the intellectual and of the organizer in the streets as basically the same: to make changes, to make revolution."[53] Briefly an ally—though never an actual member—of the Black Panther Party, Davis was also active in the campaign to establish a Third World College at UC San Diego. After much debate and research—Marcuse opposed her decision—she formally joined the CPUSA in the summer of 1968, becoming an active member of the Che-Lumumba Club, a party branch consisting solely of people of color whose main international focus was revolution in the Third World, not the Soviet Union. Before long, one of the Che-Lumumba Club's central campaigns was waged on behalf of the Soledad Brothers, three black inmates—George Jackson, Fleeta Drumgo, and

John Cluchette—accused of murdering a white guard at Soledad Prison. The three men, widely believed to have been framed because of their political organizing in prison, were held incommunicado for almost a month without access to lawyers or family members. The case quickly helped ignite a nascent prisoners' rights movement, the reverberations of which California still feels. Like so many others, Davis took a keen interest in the case and in Jackson himself, becoming the L.A. cochair of the Defense Committee for the Soledad Brothers, which hired lawyers, devised legal strategies, raised funds, and organized protests on behalf of the men. A passionate advocate for Jackson and his comrades, Davis also grew close to the Jackson family, serving as a mentor to Jackson's teenaged brother Jonathan who had only been five years old when George was first incarcerated.[54]

While organizing on behalf of the Soledad Brothers, Davis was simultaneously writing a dissertation on Immanuel Kant's analysis of the use of force during the French Revolution. In the spring of 1969, she applied for and won teaching jobs at Yale University and Swarthmore College, though she declined them both to join UCLA's faculty so that she could continue organizing in a large, black community. Davis's tenure at UCLA turned out to be an embattled one. Before she even began teaching, the University of California regents, under pressure from Governor Ronald Reagan, fired Davis on the basis of a Cold War statute prohibiting the employment of known communists. Their decision sparked a pitched battle: on one side, leftists and others supporting the principle of academic freedom; and on the other, staunch anticommunists and conservatives concerned about Davis's increasing visibility as a communist and an advocate for black liberation. During the ordeal, Davis took the University of California regents to court and won, though they ultimately succeeded in firing her by choosing not to renew her contract.

In the midst of Davis's fight to keep her job, the Soledad case took an unexpected turn. During the trial of James McClain, a black prisoner accused of assaulting a prison guard who sustained no injuries, the seventeen-year-old Jonathan Jackson staged a doomed prison-break attempt. An armed Jackson spontaneously enlisted inmates McClain, William Christmas, and Ruchell Magee, who took hostages (including a judge and a prosecutor) and hurriedly exited the courthouse, entering a waiting van. Minutes later, shots were fired by San Quentin guards and the captured prosecutor, killing Jackson and Judge Harold Haley. Days later, it was learned that three of the weapons used by Jackson were registered to Davis, a revelation that prompted the FBI to issue a warrant for Davis's arrest on kidnapping, murder, and conspiracy charges. Davis immediately went underground, evading capture for two months until she was eventually arrested in New York. In a bitter parallel to the Paris police dragnets she had witnessed, Davis's warrant served as the excuse for massive police dragnets that eventually rounded up hundreds of light-skinned, Afro-wearing women around the country. Over the next two years, Davis became the most well-known political prisoner in the nation and possibly the world. The struggle to secure her freedom sparked an international movement; activists in Oakland, New York, Accra, and Havana signed petitions, raised money, and lobbied local and California state officials, all of which helped create the political climate for Davis's eventual acquittal.[55]

The Praxis Becomes Theory

While in prison awaiting trial, Davis wrote "Political Prisoners, Prison, and Black Liberation." Though its immediate inspiration was her own impending trial and imprisonment, it was also spurred by the political work she had been doing in defense of the Soledad Brothers and her own observations of state violence against colonized peoples. The essay's intersectional approach to race, class, and national oppression depends on Davis's analysis of U.S. prisons and prisoners as opposed entities in a structure of relations that bears striking resemblance to colonialism. For Davis, revealing the oppression that permeates U.S. prison policies enables a two-pronged attack on U.S. racism and First World colonialism and imperialism.

By asserting that the penal system has been "transform[ed] into a prominent terrain of struggle, both for the captives inside and the masses outside,"[56] Davis really sets out to produce it as such through an analysis of prison's social-control function. Seeking to undermine the ideological support for U.S. laws and their attendant practices of criminalization, the essay illustrates the prison's role in maintaining race and class inequality and fortifying a repressive U.S. state. Using historical examples, Davis understandably begins with enslavement. The injustice of chattel slavery, she argues, compelled black people "to openly violate those laws which directly or indirectly buttress[ed] our oppression" (20). Thwarting slave catchers, harboring fugitive slaves, and in the spectacular instances of Nat Turner and John Brown organizing slave rebellions, black people and their white allies have repeatedly questioned the validity of unjust laws through direct extralegal action. Surveying postbellum American history, Davis compares this principled opposition to that of Southern blacks resisting the Black Codes, Ku Klux Klan violence, and Jim Crow segregation. Davis's historical examples appear to be aimed at the choir of black American readers—she repeatedly uses the personal pronouns "we" and "our"—but she is also chiding white liberals for whom "redress through electoral channels is . . . a panacea" for U.S. racial woes (19). Recourse to courts and legislation, she asserts, represents a fundamentally flawed strategy. If, as I have argued, it is more accurate to consider black people in this period as alienated (non)citizens, then they were not endowed with rights respected by courts and legislators. Pushing this logic further, if this marginalized position was not only endemic to the U.S. nation-state but also critical to its maintenance of power, then appeals to the democratic rhetoric of equality and social justice would never prove successful. Davis's argument implicitly undercuts the very sense that black people are indeed (North) Americans with inalienable rights, and so she understandably categorizes them, as well as Puerto Ricans and Chicanos, as "nationally oppressed people" (20). These groups are quite literally citizens of nations distinct from and oppressed by the United States. Placing people of color in a structurally different position than white Americans and distancing them from the label of *U.S. minority* allows Davis to reference and hail international anticolonial and Marxist constituencies to whom black and Chicano people may look for support. It exposes the alienated position inhabited by people of color and thus reveals the structurally racist foundation on which U.S. laws rest.

Davis then takes her argument a step further, arguing that the United States uses its legal system to both identify and neutralize political threats to its stability. It seeks to isolate, disempower, and further alienate those at the margins, in reality beyond the structural limits of its national identity, whose exclusion enables the maintenance of state power. The essay fills out this line of reasoning in two steps. First, Davis distinguishes between an individual breaking the law "in the interests of a class or a people" or for her or his own "individual self-interest" (21). Where "at stake has been the collective welfare and survival of a people," the imprisoned reformer or revolutionary might be identified as a "political prisoner," while in the other instance the self-interested lawbreaker is simply labeled a criminal. Neither case is as straightforward as it might seem, however. In the first instance, the very category *political prisoner* stands on shaky, ever-disappearing ground, for how can a liberal democracy, indeed the premier liberal democracy reigning during what *Time* publisher Henry Luce described as the "American Century," produce political prisoners? A hallmark of U.S. democracy is the belief that well-established, constitutionally protected channels exist to protect political dissenters. Davis demonstrates, however, that U.S. structures of law and order render invisible the existence of political prisoners by labeling them criminals rather than political threats to the stability of the state. She lists several examples: International

Workers of the World (iww) organizer Joe Hill was framed for murder; Nicola Sacco and Bartolomeo Vanzetti were convicted of robbery and murder; armed self-defense advocate Robert Williams was falsely accused of kidnapping and forced into exile; and even the elderly W. E. B. Du Bois was indicted by the federal government. Davis concludes, "The offense of the political prisoner is political boldness, the persistent challenging—legally or extra-legally—of fundamental social wrongs fostered and reinforced by the state" (25). Though she neglects to mention her own case, Davis's writing of the essay from prison and its placement in *If They Come in the Morning*, a volume designed to aid in her defense, underscores the point that the fighter for black liberation is imprisoned for contesting the very conditions that oppress her. She writes, "The political act is defined as criminal in order to discredit radical and revolutionary movements. A political event is reduced to a criminal event in order to affirm the absolute invulnerability of the existing order" (25). It does more than that, though, serving the ideological function of resolidifying the state's democratic edifice, confirming the belief that fundamental political opposition does not exist because it *need* not exist. To admit the existence of political prisoners, then, calls into question the state's legitimacy. Political prisoners pose a challenge to the U.S. nation-state, testing its status as just, benign, and stable, while criminals presumably do not.

But Davis undercuts even this distinction when she returns to the figure of the supposedly self-interested criminal. In familiar Marxist fashion, she asserts that "the majority of criminal offenses bear a direct relationship to property" and thus the prison functions as an "instrument of class domination" (27). Theft, from this perspective, is "at once a protest against society and a desire to partake of its exploitative content," while imprisonment constitutes a "means of prohibiting the have-nots from encroaching upon the haves" (27). Though this line of argumentation seems fully in line with traditional class analysis, Davis pushes further, challenging the frequent Marxian dismissal of the "criminal class" as part of a lumpen proletariat inherently untrustworthy and immaterial to the coming revolution. Acknowledging her debt to the Black Panther Party, which saw great organizing potential in the lumpen class,[57] Davis advocates on the lumpen's behalf, noting that many black, Chicano, and Puerto Rican men and women are unemployed at a rate twice that of their white counterparts and thus structurally positioned within the lumpen proletariat because of racial oppression. Davis then reminds readers that Marx himself described the lumpen proletariat as "capable of the most heroic deeds and the most exalted sacrifices," *before* following with the clause "as of the basest banditry and the dirtiest corruption."[58] From the vantage point of a race-based analysis, criminality—"banditry and the dirtiest corruption"—is revealed as a structurally derived fiction useful for the perpetuation of class inequality and white supremacy, rather than a viable basis on which to construct Marxist theories of revolution.

Returning to the issue of criminality by way of the lumpenproletariat allows Davis to make her second critical point: that the penal and judicial systems—police officers, judges, prison guards, parole boards—merely reinforce the line between white citizens and alienated black and brown noncitizens that has already been demarcated by ghetto life. Unemployment, squalid housing, police surveillance, and the everyday realities of the inner city mirror the codes of disfranchisement that define colonial societies. For black people in the United States, colonial domination means both relative isolation and extreme brutality: "In Black communities, wherever they are located, there exists an ever-present reminder that our universe must remain stable in its drabness, its poverty, its brutality. From Birmingham to Harlem to Watts, Black ghettos are occupied, patrolled and often attacked by massive deployments of police. The police, domestic caretakers of violence, are the oppressor's emissaries, charged with the task of containing us within the boundaries of our oppression" (32). Davis, like other U.S. Third World Leftists, viewed the ghetto as an internal colony, a miniature manifestation of colonial dynamics. For Davis, the black and brown ghetto dwellers and inner-city police had their colonial counterparts in the Third World. "Fanon's analysis of the role of colonial police," Davis insists, "is an appropriate description of the function of the police in America's ghettos" (32). Ghettos are primary manifestations of the deepening social contradictions produced under capitalism and imperialism. Geographically isolated, economically exploited, and brutally policed, they warehouse a black and brown reserve labor army. If the penal and judicial systems, particularly in moments of heightened cultural and political crisis, work within a system of "preventive fascism" to stifle opposition to the state's practices and policies, they also unevenly target people of color. "The disproportionate representation of the Black and Brown communities," Davis writes, "the manifest racism of parole boards, the intense brutality inherent in the relationship between prison guards and Black and Brown inmates— all this and more cause the prisoner to be confronted daily, hourly, with the concentrated, systematic existence of racism" (29). But one could go further: The (white) U.S. nation-state treats its black and brown populations as if they constitute a continuous and palpable threat to its very survival, as if their very presence—let alone demands for justice and equality—creates an ongoing political crisis that must be managed with the harshest tools at the state's disposal. Given this reality, even the self-interested criminal can be viewed as a political prisoner. If indeed the state manages a perceived threat from ghetto populations by surveying more acutely, punishing more severely all crimes, even petty ones, then it is all the more crucial that inmates of color be reimagined, resituated within an antiracist and anticapitalist political context. Inmates of color are on the political front lines, their predicament a critical site at which state violence, racist repression, and economic exploitation visibly articulate (to) one another. It is not that black inmates are a priori revolutionaries or even political activists; rather, it is that their structural position within the U.S. nation-state may propel them to "swiftly becom[e] conscious of the causes underlying their victimization" (29). Davis is careful here not to essentialize black people as revolutionaries, framing her appeals in optimistic tones designed to spur black political organizing rather than forecast its imminent success.

As is the case with Third World Newsreel, the analogy of ghettos to internal colonies allows Davis to place massive black and brown incarceration within an anticolonial context that connects U.S. peoples of color to Third World populations. It allows her to bridge local, national, and international levels of analysis and struggle. Beginning with a distinction between political prisoners and "ordinary" criminals, Davis proceeds to deconstruct this binary, indirectly revealing how her own status as a political prisoner mimics the commonplace situation of poor black Americans. Placing both the ghetto and the prison at the center of her analysis reveals the blind spots of both orthodox Marxist and antiracist struggle, demonstrating that class struggle mandates antiracist struggle, just as antiracist struggle mandates anticolonial and antiimperial struggle.

In its historical moment, "Political Prisoners, Prisons, and Black Liberation" constituted an important political intervention on many different levels. Not only did it attempt to stretch the retracted boundaries of Marxist organizing in the United States but it also troubled the middle-class moorings of mainstream civil rights activism. If integration's political appeal required an affirmation that black people were indeed citizens faithful to the ideals of the nation-state, Davis implicitly reframed civil rights disobedience as an act of resistance to the nation-state that went beyond the challenging of Jim Crow segregation. She was not alone here, of course. Much of the Black Power phase of the civil rights movement in the late sixties and early seventies challenged the belief that black equality meant black assimilation. In this instance, though,

Davis gives political shape to black rebellion by relying on the forging of an imagined anticolonial community made up of black Americans and their counterparts across the Third World.

This chapter has taken up the political and intellectual formation of Angela Davis as a way of engaging questions of black radicalism, transnational identification, and their various intersections with the project of disarticulating and dismembering the body of U.S. imperialism. Without attention to the complicated ways in which Davis's experience of alienated citizenship, her training with Frankfurt School philosophers, and her encounters with Third World anticolonialists shaped her, one cannot fully make sense of Davis's political and intellectual trajectory. If today Davis has been reinscribed as a product of U.S. civil rights, she was just as clearly impacted by Third World decolonization and developments in Western Marxism. I do not intend here to compare Davis's internationalism to the alleged parochialism of U.S. civil rights; rather, I wish to resituate U.S. civil rights, revealing the movement's ongoing dialogues with anticolonial and Marxist theory and praxis. Such a project also punctures the pervasive American exceptionalism that clearly perceives the impact of U.S. culture and politics on the rest of the world but rarely the reverse. For at the same time that Davis and other U.S. Third World Leftists agitated for full empowerment and social justice, they contributed to a global vision of Third World liberation. They participated in a very particular anticolonial and Western Marxist moment in which radicals in the United States and the Third World recognized and targeted the United States as a producer and disseminator of a new imperialism premised on the fiction of free markets and the triumph of (state-protected) capitalism.[59]

If Davis used her sense of alienation as a way of forging international affiliations, the UCLA filmmakers examined in the next chapter explored what happens when one's alienation is so acute, one's existence so bounded, that affiliation, productive political activity, appears foreclosed. They visualized the internal-colony's effect on the body and the mind. This appears fitting as the era shifted to a more conservative time, one with fewer avenues and productive channels through which to exercise a certain kind of transnational analysis. In response, narrative filmmakers in the 1970s turned inward, exploring the psychic internal colony.

6. Shot in Watts

Film and State Violence in the 1970s

●

Hey baby, what you know, girl?

I'm just getting back but you knew I would.

War is hell.

When will it end?

When will people start getting together again?

What else is new my friend,

besides what I read?

Can't find no work, can't find no job, my friend.

Money is tighter than it's ever been.

Say man, I just don't understand what's going on
    across this land.

Ah, what's happening, brother?

Yeah, what's happening?

—Marvin Gaye, "What's Happening, Brother?"

Marvin Gaye's "What's Happening, Brother?" offers a fitting frame for this final chapter. The song follows the 1971 album's title track "What's Going On," repeating and then riffing on the question asked in the spoken introduction to Gaye's better-known song. One flows out of the other, so much so that "What's Happening, Brother?" feels like a remix, one with a drastically different mood and tone.

If Gaye intended his album's title track to encapsulate the conflicting impulses and sensibilities that characterized the sixties and early seventies, he succeeded brilliantly. "What's Going On" bears witness to the era's turbulence with the unforgettable lines: "Mother, mother, there's too many of you crying. Brother, brother, brother, there's far too many of you dying." These opening lines announce Gaye's intention to transform the title's meaning from an interrogative into a declarative, from "What's Going On?" to "[Here's] what's going on." A colloquial greeting becomes the means for narrating current events in a way that connects local conditions to national ones, personal relationships to political ones. The fact that the song emerges out of party noise, out of the casual "What's happening?" heightens these linkages and at the same time blurs the distance between Gaye as singer and as narrator.

It is impossible not to confuse Marvin Gaye the singer with the narrators he inhabits in the album's nine songs. With *What's Going On*, Gaye departed from the Fordist mode of production that epitomized Motown in the 1960s. It was a concept album over which Gaye had complete creative control, and it was intended to work as a cohesive unit chronicling the impact of war, racism, poverty, and environmental destruction. Where Motown efficiently produced and promoted its deliberately apolitical hits via a musical assembly line of songwriters, studio musicians, etiquette coaches, and choreographers, Gaye experimented and improvised with musicians, writers, and producers over several years in a mode that Gaye later described as akin to the way an "artist paints a picture."[1] The result was a highly personal album that reflected the chaotic world around him.

This conflation of narrator and singer haunts the album; *What's Going On* seems to be both an unarticulated stream of consciousness and a call and response between the singer and his audience. Party noise, layered repetitions of "What's going on?" and "What's happening?" frame the narrator's public or private musings, adding texture to what would otherwise be a more conventional protest song. "What's Going On" might be a performance, interrupting or accompanying the party—party noise interjected at the bridge suggests that it is—or it might be an internal monologue: how Gaye would respond to the greeting in another context? Whether the narrator's intended audience hears him or whether there is an intended external audience hardly matters. In Gaye's world, the semiprivate space of the party and the dancing, drinking, and laughing that go along with it are shadowed by the grim realities of the outside world. Whether private thoughts or public declarations, the lyrics insert the partygoer into history; he—and it is a male-dominated environment—is both witness to and participant in these turbulent times. The ambient noise of black men greeting one another sets the song in a black American community. It inserts Gaye into an inner city marred by poverty and "trigger-happy policin'" described in "Inner City Blues (Make Me Wanna Holler)." These forms of black male address encode the historical experiences, linguistic styles, and musical practices intentionally stripped from Motown songs in order to make integration palatable and nonthreatening to white audiences.[2]

The up-tempo, insistently percussive "What's Happening, Brother?" uses much of the harmonic structure established in "What's Going On" to produce its obverse. Where the latter song confidently asserted, "Only love can conquer hate," "What's Happening, Brother?" confronts the listener with a vulnerable narrator, one struggling to get his bearings. Told from the perspective of a returning Vietnam vet, the lyrics detail the narrator's attempts to reintegrate himself into a community that has changed in his absence. He knows the neighborhood and the people, but he is just "slightly behind the times." His long-awaited homecoming has turned into a search for answers; rather than safety and certainty, he finds disorientation. Behind the casual questions he poses—"Are they still getting down where we used to go and dance?"; "Will our ball club win the pennant? Do you think they have a chance?"—are more urgent ones about the state of the world, about the gap between the media's representation of life and the reality he sees around him. The narrator's questions fill out the second verse—"Are things really getting better like the newspapers say?"—but his quest for answers, for a semblance of order, only meets with further insecurity—"Money is tighter than it's ever been." The confident "Talk to me so you can see what's going on" has been replaced with "Say man, I just don't understand what's going on across this land. What's happening, Brother? I want to know now. What's happening, Brother?"

The alienation expressed by the narrator suggests that the Vietnam War has infiltrated his consciousness just as domestic unrest has infiltrated his old neighborhood. He and other veterans are returning to inner cities that have been transformed by urban rebellions, welfare bureaucracies, and draft policies that disproportionately target working-class men of color. At the same time, the Vietnam War reverberates in the neighborhood bars and clubs these vets frequent as they narrate the war for family and friends. In fact, Gaye personally experienced this process when his brother Frankie returned from Vietnam in 1966. Frankie's difficult transition to civilian life so moved Gaye that he wrote "What's Happening, Brother?" as a tribute to him.[3] The "Brother" queried by the narrator is both an unnamed male community member and Gaye himself. The narrator's description of himself in the song's last line as "slightly behind the times" might be understood, then, to describe the international's interruption of domestic, kinship, and community relations as Vietnam's casualties—in both the psychic and physical sense—are transposed into U.S. inner cities.

It is, however, too simple to understand the narrator's dislocation as solely a repercussion of war. Though his sense of alienation echoes the alienation spawned by the Vietnam War, it does not necessarily originate there; instead, the narrator's alienation seems to reflect the instability palpable in the inner city more generally. Seeing "What's Happening, Brother?" as the counterpart to "What's Going On" suggests this possibility. In the most transparent reading, the two songs call and respond to one another, the second song posing questions that the first song addresses. However, if this is the case, then why does Gaye position "What's Going On" after "What's Happening, Brother?" on the album? It is as if the former song cannot quell the chaos and insecurity about which it speaks. "What's Happening, Brother?" seems to be the remainder, the fear and uncertainty that cannot be assuaged.

At least one other possibility can be suggested. If, as I have argued, the formal structure and lyrical content of "What's Going On" leave interpretive room to view the song as either the narrator's internal monologue or a communal call and response, then the uncertain, interrogatory "What's Happening, Brother?" might be understood as the lurking unconscious of "What's Going On." It might form the anxiety-ridden ground out of which Gaye's salient critique develops. The reverse also holds true. The uncertainty, fear, and doubt revealed in "What's Happening, Brother?" might be the result of that earlier conviction, one that has now vanished. Both songs clearly represent a narrator embedded within the same community, and may have the same narrator, only in "What's Happening, Brother?" his vulnerability and confusion have stripped away all claims to certainty, leaving behind questions rather than declarations. This dissonance is suggested in the contrast between Gaye's somber lyrics and the female background vocalists who parrot the Motown sound's warm, soothing tones. The oscillation between certainty and confusion, between community and isolation, between familiarity and foreignness underscores the fragility of human connection, the indecipherability of the once familiar world. These conditions can be ameliorated but not eradicated by the forms of familiar address, the warm informality of the party audible in the background.

It is this ambiguity about whether *What's Going On* is ultimately despairing or hopeful, or, more precisely, the evidence that it is both at the same time, that makes the album so powerful and poignant. Gaye's own ambivalence, his insistence that pessimism and optimism constantly vie for supremacy, his investment in forms of culture and collectivity as a way of transcending, if only temporarily, the forces of war and destruction are central to this chapter. They form the framework within which I want to read the work of the UCLA filmmakers.

Known variously as the L.A. School or the L.A. Rebellion, a group of African and African American filmmakers including Haile Gerima, Charles Burnett, Larry Clark, Ben Caldwell, Pamela Jones, Abdosh Abdulhafiz, Jama Fanaka, John Reir, Majied Mahdi, Julie Dash, Billie Woodberry, Barbara Mc-Cullough, Alile Sharon Larkin, and Bernard Nichols transformed independent black cinema in the early 1970s. The L.A. Rebellion's individual and collective activities reveal certain political and aesthetic problems with which they grappled. It is those tensions that I wish to uncover not only because they enrich our understanding of the U.S. Third World Left but also because they reflect the impact of more conservative times on that group's output. Though their films of the 1970s reflect the hope and optimism of the sixties and early seventies, they were also shadowed by the encroaching recession, white backlash, and the so-called law-and-order ethos that followed it. Films like *Four Women* (1975), *Killer of Sheep* (1977), *Bush Mama* (1976), *Ashes and Embers* (1982), and *Passing Through* (1977) addressed many of the dilemmas posed by the sixties: the cultural roots of identity, the possibility of black freedom despite political alienation, and the similarities between the ways that the U.S. nation-state secured local and global domination of nonwhite peoples.

L.A. Rebellion films deployed many of the themes and techniques common to U.S. Third World Leftists, but the group also significantly transformed them. As with Third World Newsreel, one can discern the influence of Third Cinema, but that influence primarily manifests itself in the production of narrative rather than documentary film. This formal difference enables an exploration of the ongoing aesthetic debates between fiction and nonfiction filmmakers. Such debates profoundly shaped the forms of address, cinematic techniques, and political perspectives articulated in their films. Filmmakers who participated in the L.A. Rebellion circled back to Jones, Williams, and Cruse's ideas on the relation between culture and politics and the viability of armed revolt, but they ultimately presented a more nuanced, even pessimistic view on the possibility for inner-city revolt. In particular, Charles Burnett's *Killer of Sheep* and Haile Gerima's *Bush Mama* represent state violence within communities of color by depicting it as a routine strategy of containment and control peppered with instances of physical violence but not necessarily dominated by them. The perniciousness of U.S. state violence consists in its everydayness, its slow eroding of individuals until they can no longer imagine alternatives, until their very existence represents a powerful, if limited, form of resistance. State violence, then, in order to be successful, must regulate and demarcate a community's psychic as well as physical terrain. This reformulation of state violence and its impact expands the definition of the internally colonized to entail a process of psychic domination. The examination of the internal aspects of domination differentiates these UCLA filmmakers from the other U.S. Third World Leftists I have discussed. Often the subjects in L.A. Rebellion films are ordinary residents of Watts facing typically oppressive circumstances without extraordinary means to challenge them. Earlier U.S. Third World Leftists highlighted instances in which people—Attica inmates, Operation Move-In squatters, armed self-defense advocates—directly confronted and sought to change their circumstances. Such instances emphasized the heroism of those willing to fight and potentially die for their beliefs and disrupted the representation of poor people of color as passive victims of circumstance. In L.A. Rebellion films, this heroism often remains absent or at least severely compromised; rather than providing strategies for survival or resistance, these films are less action oriented, meditatively turning inward in an effort to redefine survival as heroism and state violence as a force that significantly diminishes one's humanity. The turn represented by these films provides an opportunity for considering how the analysis produced by U.S. Third World Leftists began to crack and mutate by the middle of the 1970s.

If black cultural nationalism, Third World Marxism, and Third Cinema informed the L.A. Rebellion's theory and praxis, these influences also threatened to divide the group both by national identity (U.S.-born versus Third World–born) and ideology (cultural nationalism versus Third World Marxism). These tensions had always existed within the U.S. Third World Left, but the decline in domestic and international protest cast such tensions in a radically different light. A turn toward introspection and a focus on the local supplanted entirely or at least coexisted with earlier efforts to connect the global to the local, the individual to a larger community. The UCLA filmmakers' use of narrative rather than documentary filmmaking in the production of radical social analysis troubles the boundaries of fiction and reality in ways that nonfiction essays or documentary films do not. This is not to suggest that the latter two forms do not reflect a circumscribed, sometimes fictionalized, perspective; rather it is to underscore narrative's field of ambiguity, its space for imaginative play, multiple readings, and interpretations that the other two forms seek (albeit unsuccessfully) to foreclose.

Examining the group as a cultural formation, this chapter defines its trajectory as one marked by Third World anticolonialism, Pan-Africanism, black cultural nationalism, and Third Cinema practices, but also one ambivalent about whether revolutionary or even significant social change can be achieved. In the contrasts between Burnett's *Killer of Sheep* and Gerima's *Bush Mama* I see evidence of a vexed dialogue on U.S. Third World Left discourse and purpose. Though both filmmakers utilize similar discursive elements—including the depiction of urban communities as internal colonies, a belief in collective rather than vanguard leadership, and the powerful deconstruction of state violence—neither film reaches a point in which liberation or even collective organizing is achieved. If such a discourse effectively exposes the U.S. nation-state's imperial and racist underpinnings, it provides a less convincing response to the question of how U.S. communities of color might situate themselves within a larger Third World public. Instead, both filmmakers present numerous obstacles—social, political, economic—that prevent their characters from awareness of or membership in that larger counterpublic. Class, gender, and generational tensions abound in both films, and the retreat into any uncomplicated form of community is often frustrated rather than facilitated. Compelling in their depictions of the black working class as neither heroic nor craven, neither omniscient nor ignorant, Burnett and Gerima's different choices about how to situate their characters within a larger U.S. Third World context has much to tell us about the decline of U.S. Third World Left discourse and praxis in the 1970s.

In this chapter's first section, I examine the ideological and aesthetic roots of the L.A. Rebellion, describing the ways in which the work of Frantz Fanon and Ngugi Wa Thiong'o shaped the group's ideas while Third Cinema shaped its aesthetics. The second section analyzes *Killer of Sheep* and *Bush Mama*, contrasting the ways in which Burnett and Gerima define Watts as an internal colony and the political prescriptions that arise from those differing viewpoints. I am primarily interested in teasing out some of the cultural and political tensions between these differently situated members of the African diaspora as a way of thinking through their attempts to fashion a cultural expression capable of exposing, if not closing, some of the gaps between subjects in the United States and elsewhere. Charting the ways in which various transnational influences mark the work of Burnett and Gerima enables us to see the ways in which their seemingly Watts-specific films spoke to larger debates and conflicts within the U.S. Third World Left.

L.A.'s Rebellion Begins

A number of factors came together to produce the L.A. Rebellion. Kenyan-born Ntongela Masilela, an undergraduate member of the group, has argued that the 1965 Watts Rebellion, the assassinations of Malcolm X and Martin Luther King Jr., the Tet Offensive, as well as movements for national liberation in Africa all served as precipitating events for the group's formation.[4] At UCLA, two other developments catalyzed the group. In 1969, student activists and the assistant professor Eliseo Taylor established the Ethnocommunications Program, a unique affirmative action project that brought the first group of Third World film students to UCLA. Functioning outside the control of the film department, ethnocommunications recruited undergraduates and graduates from other departments who wanted to learn filmmaking. In fact, Burnett taught those undergraduates as a graduate assistant for Taylor's class. Though it lasted only four years, ethnocommunications recruited several African American, Asian American, Native American, and Chicano students during that time, including Haile Gerima, Larry Clark, Robert Nakamura, and Betty Chin. The second spark was the formation of a multiracial group called the Media Urban Crisis Committee (MUCCERS) that held a series of protests and sit-ins until the film department agreed to reverse its racially exclusionary admission practices by reserving 25 percent of the undergraduate and graduate admission slots for racial minorities. These two initiatives helped to attract and train dozens of filmmakers, including those in the Asian American group Visual Communications (VC), and the founders of two public broadcasting consortia for minority filmmakers, the Latino Consortium and the National Asian American Telecommunications Association.[5]

The most intense period of the L.A. Rebellion lasted roughly between 1970 and 1978, though some critics push forward its year of dissolution to 1982.[6] Composed of African Americans and Africans, key early figures include Burnett and Gerima, both of whom arrived at UCLA in 1968, as well as Larry Clark, Ben Caldwell, John Reir, Pamela Jones, Abdosh Abdulhafiz, and Jama Fanaka. Billie Woodberry, Alile Sharon Larkin, Bernard Nichols, and Julie Dash made up what Masilela describes as the group's second generation.[7] Though it is tempting to restrict membership to those who directed films, that approach does not provide a full sense of the L.A. Rebellion's vitality and scope. The group constituted a hub of diasporic activity at UCLA. In fact, the late Toni Cade Bambara cites the formation of off-campus study groups as pivotal to helping the group develop "a film language to respectfully express cultural particularity and Black thought."[8] In addition to the more well-known filmmakers, Masilela, Teshome Gabriel, Bambara, and Barbara O. Jones were also active participants, and there were numerous others who flowed in and out of the L.A. Rebellion, providing organizational support and informing the group's ideological and aesthetic debates. The retrospective grouping of these filmmakers into a school poses certain problems because they themselves did not explicitly define themselves as such by writing manifestos, publishing an organizational newspaper, or holding regular meetings. They did, however, crew on each other's films, offer critique of each other's rough cuts, work together in study groups, organize film exhibitions and lectures, and attend international conferences as representatives of the group.

Linguistic simplicity aside, instead of thinking about these filmmakers as a school, it seems more accurate to think of them as a group that forged an eclectic filmmaking tendency, though I disagree with Clyde Taylor's description of that tendency as a "black film aesthetic."[9] L.A. Rebellion films do not necessarily represent a singular black film aesthetic, so it is perhaps more useful to describe this tendency through its aesthetic and ideological commitments instead of its shared aesthetic characteristics. A focus on ideology and politics is perhaps the most critical link to Third Cinema, which includes styles that are "as varied as the social processes it inhabits."[10] In other words, style was defined both by historical imperative and material context rather than abstract principles.

Defining a Third Cinema Aesthetics

Rather than offering a single aesthetic blueprint, Third Cinema offered a mode of critique. Historically responsive, Third Cinema fashioned tools for analysis and action that could not be formalized in advance. Paul Willeman offers a useful contrast between Third Cinema and European countercinema that is worth quoting: "Whatever the explanation . . . and regardless of the political intentions involved, the notion of counter-cinema tends to conjure up a prescriptive aesthetics: to do the opposite of what dominant cinema does. Hence the descriptive definition of dominant cinema will dictate the prescriptive definition of counter-cinema. The proponents of Third Cinema were just as hostile to dominant cinemas but refused to let industrially and ideological dominant cinemas dictate the terms in which they were opposed."[11] This distinction is important because it enables a more fluid, historically specific understanding of Third Cinema and its relation to L.A. Rebellion films. Third Cinema did not lend these filmmakers a particular aesthetic as much as it helped them develop an orientation to the mainstream medium that was critical without being simply reactive. It modeled a cinematic critical theory that could neither be predicted in advance nor replicated wholesale.

Most seductive of Third Cinema's tenets was the insistence that a film's political and ideological content always trumps the aesthetic content. The seminal articulation of this viewpoint appears in the 1970 manifesto "For an Imperfect Cinema," in which the Cuban filmmaker Julio García Espinosa argued that revolutionary cinema, cinema emerging from the Third World, must value ideology over aesthetics since the beautiful image had been used to lull audiences into passivity. Instead, García Espinosa suggested that film must be interested, must assert a viewpoint, must move the audience to action. As the film critic Michael Chanan writes in *The Cuban Image*, "[This] authentically modern cinema . . . seeks to engage with its audience by imaginatively reinserting itself and them into social reality, to film the world around it without make-up, to make the kind of film which [*sic*] remains incomplete without an actively responsive audience taking it up. This sense of incompleteness without the audience is part of what García Espinosa means by imperfection."[12] If imperfection meant inserting social reality at the very core of film practice, then it also meant compelling the audience to intervene in the social reality rather than passively accept it. Self-critique as well as critical analysis was not only a goal of imperfect cinema but also its express purpose. Because imperfect cinema shifted to accommodate the perceived needs of the surrounding social struggle, it prized aesthetic experimentation as much for its deliberate departure from Western cinematic standards as for its ability to unsettle and estrange the viewer.

Favored Third Cinema models included those developed by Cuban documentary and Brazilian Cinema Novo. Both offered UCLA filmmakers a conceptual paradigm for centering film within a counterhegemonic, international culture. As in the case of Third World Newsreel, Cuban documentary influenced the form and content of L.A. Rebellion films. Like Third World Newsreel, the L.A. Rebellion saw Cuban cinema as the "preeminent film movement of the Third World." Its members admired it for clarifying the "relationship between film and national culture," for providing a model that they could emulate in one way or another. In assessing the school's overall body of work, Masilela once remarked: "The influence of the Cuban revolutionary cinema on the cinema of the Los Angeles School was profound, immediate, and undeniable: note the parallels between Solas's *Lucia* (1968) and [Dash's] *Daughters of the Dust*, between Guttiérez Alea's *Memories of Underdevelopment* (1967) and Gerima's *Harvest: 3,000 years* and *Sankofa,* between Solas's *Simparele* (1974) and [Dash's] *Praise House*."[13]

Even though Burnett's early films were primarily fictional, he, too, describes Cuban documentarians as critical to his work because they created "images that were representative" but "weren't manipulative."[14] Though Burnett's suggestion that documentary offers an unfiltered lens on reality is debatable, what proves intriguing is the sense that narrative film might resemble documentary, that it might be a truth-telling rather than a fantasy-making device. Regardless of whether one agrees with this perspective, it lends important insight into Burnett's use of narrative film as a certain kind of window onto reality. If Hollywood film reflected myth, fantasy, and pure imagery arguably without substance, then these filmmakers looked to documentary as an alternative form that might help shift the terms of narrative cinema.

Gerima also refers to the blurring of the line between documentary and narrative film, seeing it as a necessary technique in conveying the reality of black American life. In an interview, he admitted that he wanted *Bush Mama* to have "the texture of documentary" so that the audience would "believe" it.[15] Standard cinematic techniques were inadequate for the task of depicting Watts' violent reality. Given the film's grim events—police murder an unarmed man, a police officer rapes a young girl, a welfare bureaucrat pressures a pregnant woman to abort her baby, a desperate mother nearly jumps from a roof with a crying baby in her arms—*Bush Mama* could almost be dismissed as melodrama. So unrelentingly violent is the reality of urban black life that realist cinema cannot represent it. Conventional cinematic language meets its limit when it confronts a surrealistic social world in which the rules of law and order do not hold, an upside-down moral universe in which the bad find reward in punishing the good. In such circumstances, a hybrid cinematic form, one that blended narrative and documentary, realism and surrealism, rendered the realities of black urban life for viewers, some of which were altogether unfamiliar with it and others who were so familiar that they had ceased to be moved by its horrors.

In addition to Cuban cinema, Brazilian Cinema Novo also had a profound influence on the UCLA filmmakers because it "revealed a dynamic relationship among regionalism, national culture, history and class struggle."[16] Cinema Novo formed in 1962 in explicit opposition to the Hollywood films flooding the Brazilian market. Filmmaker Carlos Diegues's essay simply entitled "Cinema Novo" declared that this new movement's goal was "to study in depth the social relations of each city and region as a way of critically exposing, as if in miniature, the socio-cultural structure of the country as a whole."[17] Mise-en-scène rather than plot proved central to Cinema Novo, with a particular emphasis on the auteur. As Glauber Rocha, another Cinema Novo filmmaker insisted, the role of these films was to portray a hero living the crisis of Brazilian society. "Our hero," Rocha writes, "must be the *multiplex Brazilian man* who is living every crisis. . . . Our filmmaker takes part in the discovery of the consciousness of what is Brazilian, through his wish to discuss in the light of what he knows (or thinks he knows) of man, ourselves and others."[18] Rocha's formulation clearly borrows a certain ideological energy from Che Guevara's conception of the "new man" under socialism in order to redefine the prototypical everyman of cinema and literature.[19] The UCLA filmmakers took up Rocha's challenge, though they consciously incorporated both men and women "living every crisis" as an antidote to Rocha's masculinist conception and the Third World discourse underpinning it.[20]

If Third Cinema opposed Western, and specifically Hollywood, film as an agent of cultural imperialism, UCLA filmmakers saw it in much the same terms. In their context, however, Hollywood's brand of cultural imperialism and racial ethnocentrism not only centered Europe and the United States but it also neglected and distorted the experiences of U.S. peoples of color. Consequently, the L.A. Rebellion, like Third World Newsreel, understood separate production, distribution, and exhibition as absolute necessities for maintaining independence from Hollywood.[21] As a result, Watts became an alternative site of cinematic production, a move that necessitated involving the Watts community in the group's filmmaking, as both subjects and producers.

Geographically located in Los Angeles yet isolated from its postwar prosperity, Watts became a dynamic tableau—both a specific geographic location and a representational field—enabling L.A. Rebellion filmmakers to explore the forms of black disfranchisement particular to the community. In Watts, residents experienced the kind of extreme poverty, discrimination, and violent policing that provoked comparison with Third World colonized peoples. For L.A. Rebellion filmmakers, Watts provided an important backdrop for exploring the various contradictions at the heart of U.S. democracy. As two commentators wryly note, "The fantasy of equality and integration was being destroyed no further away from Hollywood than the streets of Watts."[22] During World War II, accelerating production pushed thousands of Southern black migrants to Los Angeles where they soon found themselves in conflict with the existing middle-class black community. The postwar loss of industrial jobs did not prevent further migrants from coming to Los Angeles, and increasing suburbanization and deindustrialization, exclusionary zoning, restrictive covenants, and employment discrimination meant that, in Gerald Horne's words, "the overall quality of black life fell precipitously during this period."[23] The Los Angeles Police Department's (LAPD) long history of brutality toward and disregard for South Los Angeles residents only added fuel to the fire of black discontent, which eventually exploded in August 1965 after a police officer stopped a driver for suspected drunk driving. That incident sparked a six-day riot in which forty thousand rioters and the sixteen thousand National Guard and other law enforcement officers who fought them caused 200 million dollars in property damage. By the time the smoke had cleared, thirty-four people were dead, over one thousand people were injured, and four thousand had been arrested.[24] Lyndon B. Johnson expressed his shock and sorrow in a nationally televised address, but the ensuing white backlash against Watts and the scores of other riots that followed it began slowly starving his Great Society programs. The Watts riot proved such a seminal event that it replaced Vietnam as the issue of greatest concern among those polled by Gallup in the fall of that year.[25] Converging at UCLA in the early 1970s, the L.A. Rebellion confronted a Watts community that had been economically devastated and politically forgotten, a community that gave the lie to a post–civil rights common sense that said equality had been achieved, social justice had been attained, and racism no longer dominated U.S. life.

L.A. Rebellion filmmakers sought to include Watts in their films in various ways. In the case of Burnett, who grew up in Watts, that meant hiring Watts residents as crew members and actors. When they suddenly failed to show up for shoots, crew members impatiently suggested that Burnett continue shooting, but he insisted on waiting for them, sometimes bailing them out of jail or halting shoots until they resurfaced.[26] Scott MacDonald reads this community-based commitment as one indication that Italian neorealism influenced Burnett, though the filmmaker himself denies this, saying that he only became familiar with Italian neorealist film after *Killer of Sheep* was completed. That influence, however, certainly reached Burnett indirectly via Third Cinema, which was informed by Italian neorealism.[27] A more direct motivation for Burnett's community-oriented film praxis may instead have been his desire to reaffirm a connection to Watts that felt imperiled at UCLA. Though he still lived in Watts, on campus Burnett was confronted with a twilight zone in which, for instance, students flaunted their drug use without fear of police harassment. For him, this represented a form of white privilege—the privilege to act without fear of punishment—in stark contrast with the brutal forms of surveillance endemic to Watts. "I come from a community," Burnett once remarked, "where if you walk down the street the police would stop you, search your pockets, go all in the seams of your pants, looking for any evidence."[28] The glaring differences between UCLA and Watts made Burnett realize that "even though you're from the community, once you go to the university, your whole outlook changes, and you wonder if you can still say that you speak for the community you came from."[29] Ironically, while L.A. Rebellion members saw Burnett as an "authentic" representative of Watts, he questioned his suitability for that role. His Watts affiliation, then, was resecured through the inclusion of community residents in his films.

Other L.A. Rebellion members also found ways to include Watts in their productions. Larry Clark possessed an extensive knowledge of Central Avenue's jazz tradition, which helped him build and sustain cultural connections to Watts musicians and artists. In fact, the local musician Horace Tapscott composed music for Clark's *Passing Through* and *Saw Above, Saw Below* (1975).[30] In *Passing Through*, the cinematography echoed Tapscott's soundtrack representing in Clyde Taylor's estimation the "most ambitious effort to structure a film according to the rhythms and movement patterns of that musical tradition."[31] Clark's Watts affiliations literally determined the very structure and substance of *Passing Through*. Along with Gerima, Clark was also involved with local black theater, another important avenue for building artistic networks within Watts.

As an African immigrant, Gerima had a relationship to Watts that was more complex than either Clark's or Burnett's. He, like the other two men, included members of Watts both in front and behind the camera, but unlike them, Gerima also had to learn the geographic and cultural contours of Watts, a project he single-mindedly pursued, in Masilela's view, more than any other African member of the group.[32] "Independent African American cinema is without foundation," Gerima once wrote, "if organized outside of the African American community."[33]

Julie Dash, on the other hand, used professional performers in her early films, but she underscored the disparity between Hollywood and Watts through the use of absence and intentional camouflage. In *Illusions* (1982), the wholesale exploitation and dismissal of Watts reverberates through the representation of two black women, both of whom must pass in order to work in Hollywood. A black studio executive passes as white, while a black singer sees her voice appropriated for use by a white woman.

These various efforts to integrate Watts into black film praxis underline the L.A. Rebellion's explicit rejection of Hollywood, which it condemned for its circulation of racist and distorted stereotypes. Ed Guerrero argues, "If there is one common aim among black film-makers expressed in a divergent trajectory of works . . . it has been the wish to portray black humanity honestly in contrast with Hollywood's dehumanizing stereotypes, box-office dictates and the sovereign optic of the industry-constructed white spectator/consumer."[34] While whites could look to the silver screen and find multiple identities and numerous narrative possibilities, nonwhites could not. Hollywood relegated nonwhite performers to playing maids, butlers, dancers, singers, or generic exotics who filled out the scenery or provided comic relief. On the rare occasions when Hollywood did tackle race, it was depicted as a problem to be overcome, an individual quirk rather than a societal flaw. The interracial love story and the interracial buddy film, several of which starred the distinguished Sidney Poitier, became the vehicles of choice for depicting race for a predominantly white audience. Rather than reflecting an appreciation for Hollywood's efforts, articles and reader letters in *Ebony* and *Jet* complained about one-dimensional, integrationist fantasy films such as *The Defiant Ones* (1958) and *Guess Who's Coming to Dinner* (1967).[35] The L.A. Rebellion countered these depictions by emphasizing the enormous distance between the privilege of Hollywood and the poverty of Watts. The geographic and institutional context in which Hollywood produced its images was brought back into a cinematic frame from which it had been painstakingly elided. *Illusions'* depiction of racial discrimination in casting or Burnett and Gerima's portraits of Watts as a neighborhood completely isolated from the rest of L.A. constitute attempts to reveal the structure of inequality that enables Hollywood's industrial practice and fuels its image production.

If these filmmakers disdained Hollywood films, they viewed blaxploitation films in little better terms. Though promoted by many at the time as the site for new representations, ones in stark contrast to Hollywood's slate of butlers, maids, and mammies, L.A. Rebellion filmmakers viewed these films as white-controlled, poorly made imitations of standard Hollywood fare. To add insult to injury, as the UCLA filmmakers struggled to find their voices, "minutes away, Hollywood was reviving itself economically through a glut of mercenary black exploitation movies."[36] The hypervisibility of black bodies and the narrative reversals allowing black men and women to triumph over whites could not change the fact that such films remained within the limits imposed by Hollywood. In particular, many members objected to the frequently demeaning and misogynistic treatment of black women, a topic of significant concern within the group.[37] At the ideological level, the L.A. Rebellion must have rejected the blaxploitation formula in part because it reduced black protest to black criminality, black success to the maintenance of law and order, and black identity to Afros, soul music, and pimp walks. "In the sixties," Burnett once remarked, "we were all influenced by the idea that either you're part of the problem, or you're part of the solution. And to us it was quite obvious that exploitation films were part of the problem."[38] At the cinematic level, the school wanted to break new aesthetic ground, a goal largely ignored by a genre that rarely delved into new aesthetic territory other than to imitate cinematic techniques used by Melvin Van Peebles in his boundary-breaking *Sweet, Sweetback's Baadasssss Song* (1971). By contrast, James Snead argues, the UCLA filmmakers' "chief ambition was to rewrite the standard cinematic language of cuts, fades, frame composition, and camera movement in order to represent their own 'nonstandard' vision of black people and black culture."[39] Rather than concentrating solely on blaxploitation's thematic content, L.A. Rebellion filmmakers linked that content to a cinematic vocabulary so tainted that it could not be recuperated. In "Healing Imperialized Eyes," Ann Kaplan suggests that any challenge to Eurocentric discourse must "seek to intervene in the imaginary— to change how images are produced—rather than to present minorities 'as they really are.'"[40] Her assessment helps situate the L.A. Rebellion's remaking of cinematic imagery as primarily an intervention in representational and institutional politics rather than in avant-garde aesthetics. Instead of understanding their images as inherently more honest, I see the L.A. Rebellion's disruption of the dominant imaginary as an ideological and aesthetic interruption, one that seeks to contest dominant racial representations and articulates in sometimes explicit, sometimes inchoate ways a counterhegemonic politic.

I am not, however, arguing that the group's (or any filmmaker's) antiracist intent guarantees a static antiracist outcome. The importance of the L.A. Rebellion's deviation from Hollywood film's conventional camera angles, fades, cuts, and shot composition lies in the fact that they drew attention to the ways in which cinematic production and consumption occurred within overlapping economic, political, and cultural contexts that shape a film's meaning and reception. This is an obvious point and yet it is one that Hollywood seeks to render invisible by rarely attending to the industry's formal conventions. Just as whiteness derives its cultural power from being the unseen universal, so, too, do conventional cinematic techniques reinforce race, class, and gender hierarchies by seeming to depict life as it is or as it ought to be. Paradoxically, the supposed realism of conventional Hollywood film is most often used to construct a racist, sexist, and classist ideal. The irreality of Hollywood film is simultaneously affirmed and denied through the use of realist cinematic techniques. Dash's *Illusions* beautifully illustrates this point through the depiction of a black singer who is asked to record a soundtrack that will be dubbed over the screen image of a white female singer. Technological innovation enables a white actor to pass as a black singer and a black singer to pass as a white actor. The L.A. Rebellion's remaking of film imagery indicated an understanding of representation as an active, ever-shifting process, rather than an achieved end. In a conversation with Clyde Taylor, Teshome Gabriel described the group as wanting to make films "that project onto a social space" rather than onto the "privatistic, individualistic space of Hollywood's film theater."[41] Gabriel's words frame that social space as one that is already formed: a collective arena that has been ignored by Hollywood film. But his description downplays L.A. Rebellion films' active role in creating a social space—in hailing members and participants—in other words, in producing a space as social rather than solitary. In that space, Watts was central rather than marginalized, black people were valued rather than disregarded, and the First and Third World were linked rather than disparate realms.

The exhibition of Third Cinema films helped the UCLA filmmakers position themselves both in terms of Watts and the Third World. Like Third World Newsreel, the L.A. Rebellion built transnational cultural networks by screening little-known Third World films and participating in international film conferences. In the fall of 1970, UCLA's African Studies Center organized the first documented African film festival in North America. Not only did this unprecedented event showcase several Ousmane Sembene films but it also brought Sembene, arguably the most well-known figure in postindependence African cinema, the Nigerian Stephane Allisante, and the Cameroonian Oumarou Ganda to Los Angeles. Masilela would later remember this event as an amazing opportunity for the L.A. Rebellion to enter into a dialogue with African filmmakers. For instance, Gabriel and Ganda debated issues ranging from independent financing for black film to the impact of "European cultural imperialism." Soon thereafter, the UCLA filmmakers also sponsored longer visits by Sembene and the Cuban documentarian Santiago Álvarez.[42] In turn, these events helped the L.A. Rebellion take a more active role in Third Cinema circles. For instance, Haile Gerima led the first black American delegation to FESPACO (the Festival of Pan African Film and Television) held in Burkina Faso. Then in 1974, Burnett, Gerima, Masilela, and others organized the Third World Film Club, which continued to screen films, primarily those from Latin America, over the following two years. As was the case with Third World Newsreel, a majority of the films shown by the Third World Film Club were Cuban films that had rarely been screened in the United States, let alone on the West Coast. This focus helps explain why the group also actively fought the ban on U.S. cultural exchange with Cuba (110). The L.A. Rebellion's activities ebbed after a series of 1978 discussions between then UCLA professor Gabriel and Brazilian film director Glauber Rocha (111, 107). Filmmakers left UCLA, moving on to other projects, though the creative networks they forged persist to this day. Those discussions eventually informed Gabriel's theoretical inquiries into Third World film in his 1982 *Third Cinema in the Third World: The Aesthetics of Liberation* and the 1985 "Towards a Critical Theory of Third World Films."[43] The combined efforts of Gabriel, Burnett, Gerima and others in the L.A. Rebellion helped transform UCLA into a diasporic site circulating a range of cultural texts and Third World filmmakers. Though the opportunity to "exchang[e] viewpoints with like-minded filmmakers throughout the diaspora, most especially in Britain and on the Continent,"[44] shaped the group's filmmaking commitments, so, too, did the reading and discussion of anticolonial theory.

Defining the Revolutionary Intellectual's Role

In addition to activities centered on Third Cinema, the L.A. Rebellion also read and discussed Third World anticolonial theory in an off-campus political study group it formed. Though the members read many authors, including Ian Watt and Georg Lukács,[45] Masilela identifies Frantz Fanon's 1963 *The Wretched of the Earth* and Ngugi Wa Thiong'o's 1972 *Homecoming: Essays on African and Caribbean Literature, Culture, and Politics* as particularly important for the group. *The Wretched of the Earth* had a profound influence on much of the U.S. Third World Left; for members of the L.A. Rebellion, however, its significance lay in its ability to, in Masilela's words, "clarify the historical moment in which these filmmakers found themselves," though there was no single "canonical reading" of it.[46] If Masilela's explanation seems a bit abstract, it is clear after reading and viewing the work of the UCLA filmmakers that three aspects of Fanon's work informed their films: a defense of violence and a dismissal of nonviolence as a pacifying tactic of the national bourgeoisie; an analysis of the dangers of the national bourgeoisie who use nationalism as a way of securing class power and economic resources; and the importance of building a national culture rooted in the struggle for liberation rather than in a return to a fictive precolonial past. I have discussed Fanon's *The Wretched of the Earth* earlier, but now I would like to return to it, locating the UCLA filmmakers in relationship to Fanon's ideas.

On the question of violence, Fanon insists that colonialism depends on various prohibitions or disciplining strategies—rules about where to live, which jobs to hold, what language to speak and learn in school, and so on—and overt violence—aggressive policing, torture, and detainment. "Agents of the government," Fanon insists, "speak the language of pure force," but the subtler machinations of power are equally destructive.[47] Colonial bureaucracies—school systems, cultural institutions, and the like—domesticate the colonized by impressing on her or him the superiority of Western civilization in order to produce a submissive and passive "native." Nigel Gibson understands Fanon's view of ideology as a structure of thought that reinforces physical coercion rather than masking or replacing it: "Colonial violence is not hidden by ideology, in fact colonial ideology simply mirrors it, drumming into the native the idea that all indigenous culture, customs, and traditions are the products of 'constitutional depravity.' "[48]

On the face of it, Fanon's description of colonial ideology does not quite fit Gramsci's or Althusser's sense that ideology functions to win the consent of those who are dominated. In the colonial context, ideology need not accede to the rules of polite civil society; no such civil pretense is necessary. However, this assertion is not quite right either. If colonialism works, in part, by stratifying and dividing the indigenous population, as Fanon is well aware, then that strategy requires consent from at least some of the colonized. Without that consent, colonial bureaucracies cannot function. Indeed, colonial societies themselves cannot function without a group serving as buffer between the colonizer and the most colonized. The myriad forms through which colonialism forges its domination over the colonial subject surely include the use of ideology to win (some, though not the vast majority of) the indigenous population's consent. I would like to focus, however, on another aspect of Fanon's expansive sense of colonial violence. If colonial bureaucracies quite literally represent another form of violence, one that assaults the mind as well as the body, then the comparison by U.S. Third World Leftists of urban communities and colonies cracks the shell of U.S. civil society, exposing its innards—the schools, welfare offices, churches, hospitals, courts—as a manifestation of brute force. This is a provocative idea, one that helps close the gap between Third World colonialism and First World civil society and depends on taking seriously, deadly seriously, the everyday forms of oppression visited on communities like Watts. It also, of course, depends on the same liberation strategy often necessary in the colonial context: violent struggle that literally transforms the colonized into a "new subject," the "product of a constant movement and principled criticism."[49] Like Gibson, I am inclined to see this movement and ongoing critique as a way of moving beyond the Manichaean perspective for which Fanon is quite often criticized.

Evidence of a movement beyond binary categories is implicit in Fanon's discussion of the national bourgeoisie, a class fully complicit in the colonial enterprise that seeks to consolidate its own power and domination in the transition to independence by appealing to nationalism. Nationalism, in this instance, obscures real class, race, and "tribal" divisions, anointing a national bourgeoisie that seeks to exploit the masses just as thoroughly as have the former colonizers. As Fanon reminds us in the essay "The Pitfalls of National Consciousness," the "national middle class" sees independence as a means for "the transfer into native hands of those unfair advantages which are a legacy of the colonial period."[50] In fact, the "national bourgeoisie," Fanon continues, sees itself as the "transmission line between the nation and a capitalism, rampant though camouflaged, which today puts on the mask of neo-colonialism" (152). Cautioning against nationalisms that are "crude and fragile travest[ies] of what they might have been," Fanon advocates a "national consciousness" that rigorously expresses the entire society's interests rather than one class's interests, a consciousness that draws the "battle line against ignorance, against poverty, and against unawareness" (203). Privileging national consciousness over nationalism does seem to support Edward Said's contention that for Fanon nationalism is "a necessary but not sufficient condition for liberation," that it is a stage through which nations or peoples move before alighting at an expansive, internationally resonant state of liberation.[51] Fanon asserts that the way to avoid the consolidation of power in the hands of this "useless and harmful middle class" is the "combined effort of the masses led by a party and of intellectuals who are highly conscious and armed with revolutionary principles."[52] Here, he reserves a vanguard role for the revolutionary intellectual, even if he says little about how that class has attained a consciousness defined by revolutionary principles.

Clearly, one can critique Fanon for suggesting that the colonized exist as passive victims of colonialism until the moment of decolonization. From Fanon's perspective, not only is colonialism able to produce the view of the colonized as backward but it also produces them as such.[53] In overcoming this backwardness, the colonized must disidentify with the colonizer and begin struggling against the forms of violence and oppression that define her or his life. But how precisely does that process of disidentification begin? A focus on the leap from passivity to action ignores the transitional stage. If for Fanon, as Benita Parry suggests, "it was only when the movement for decolonization was set in motion that there occurred a qualitative leap from stagnation to modernity, from passivity to insurgency,"[54] then what sets the decolonization in motion? What precipitates that Hegelian act of violence, the decisive struggle between slave and master, that will produce a historical subject? How does this historical break from stagnation to modernity set the stage for the emerging postcolonial nation? Fanon's new historical subject is neither citizen nor slave, is fully human but not enfranchised. Ultimately, the forging of a new historical subject is the work of the revolutionary intellectual, who working hand in hand with the masses' party must shape the nation and its citizens. Again, we find silence in *The Wretched of the Earth* about how exactly the revolutionary intellectual comes into existence. To appropriate James Baldwin's famous quip about Aimé Césaire, what is left out in Fanon's condemnation of colonialism is "precisely that it ha[s] produced men like himself."[55] If Fanon's description of a revolutionary intellectual class directly interpellated the L.A. Rebellion, it gave them little insight into their own cultural and political formation, little description of how that formation might help mobilize themselves and the masses in the period that might be termed prerevolutionary. Consequently, this prerevolutionary in-between period and its accompanying state of mind constitutes a central preoccupation of the L.A. Rebellion's work. The desire to reconcile the privilege and responsibility of their middle-class location at UCLA with the poverty and despair of Watts propelled an exploration into the intermediary role of the revolutionary intellectual in transitional times. Films like *Bush Mama* and *Killer of Sheep* were both efforts to fill in certain gaps left in Fanon's seminal text.

For Fanon, one central task of the revolutionary intellectual's identity was to shape the emerging nation's national culture. In fact, he explicitly charged the artist with creating new national cultures that would draw on the ongoing struggles for liberation. "The struggle itself," Fanon wrote in the essay "On National Culture," "in its development and in its internal progression sends culture along different paths and traces out entirely new ones for it."[56] Attention to the paths traced by anticolonial struggle again assumes that the struggle has already begun, that the transitional period has passed, that the lines are clearly demarcated. In Fanon's view, a truly national culture is a corollary to and a result of political revolution. If Fanon helped UCLA filmmakers understand their own historical moment, was that moment defined by an ongoing anticolonial struggle or the latent period before struggle begins? Was Watts a site of struggle or a site in need of struggle? This question of how to frame Watts and any cultural production centered there directly relates to the question of how one might understand the cultural forms that existed prior to overt revolutionary activity.

Fanon's view of national culture under colonialism parallels his view of the colonized prior to decolonization. Like the "native," indigenous culture has been decimated: "By the time a century or two of exploitation has passed there comes about a veritable emaciation of the stock of national culture. It becomes a set of automatic habits, some traditions of dress, and a few broken-down institutions."[57] For Fanon, there is no return to the source. There is no unmediated access to a culture untainted by colonialism. Understanding the full weight of colonialism necessitates a break with prerevolutionary forms. Fanon gives little credit to these forms for sustaining oppositional identities or building the revolutionary consciousness that has led to overt anticolonial struggle. To him, they are at worst tools of colonial collaboration or at best opponents of the modernity that he sees heralding a new postcolonial day. If one takes this reading seriously, then how might we understand the UCLA filmmakers' project of cultural excavation, their use of music, dance, and spiritual traditions to anchor a black oppositional identity? Can one access a precolonial cultural heritage, and even if one could—an outcome Fanon flatly dismisses—then what relevance would it have to ongoing social struggle, particularly since the struggle itself transforms the very contours of individual and national identity? Here again, the L.A. Rebellion found itself in a precarious position, for what really differentiated their activities from those of Fanon's national bourgeoisie, which latched onto originary cultural practices as a prop for their self-interested nationalism and a bulwark against revolutionary change? The linking of culture and colonialism was central to Fanon, and yet the connective tissue between anticolonial intellectual activity and mass political struggle remains missing in *The Wretched of the Earth*. That absence left a vacuum, one inhabited, in part, by Ngugi's *Homecoming*.

Deeply influenced by Fanon, Ngugi's 1972 collection opens with the essay "Towards a National Culture," a title that self-consciously echoes Fanon's earlier essay. Advocating a national culture that will reflect an emancipated society, Ngugi contrasts Kenyan cultural traditions in the precolonial and colonial eras, concluding that the formation of a socialist state is necessary because "political and economic liberation are the essential condition for cultural liberation, for the true release of a people's creative spirit and imagination."[58] Like Fanon, Ngugi insists that Africans cannot return to traditions rooted in a precolonial past as the source for national culture and nor, by implication, can those in the African diaspora. To do so would be to invest in an ossified cultural heritage that bears little relation to the present historical conditions. Written in a neocolonial era, after independence in most of the colonial world had been won, Ngugi's essay, like Fanon's, attempts to retrieve those elements of nationalism that are useful, without ignoring the fact that nationalism often serves as an alibi for the national bourgeoisie. As Ngugi bluntly states in another essay, "Nationalism is not an ideology. Too often it falsely appeals to the camaraderie of the skin" (56). Like Fanon, Ngugi sees the job of the artist, specifically the writer, as lying in highlighting societal flaws, "seek[ing] out the sources, the causes and the trends of a revolutionary struggle which has already destroyed the traditional power-map drawn up by the colonialist nations" (66). If the writer is to aid in the decolonizing of culture, she or he cannot do so by relying on the past; rather, the writer must seek inspiration in the history being made around her or him.

What is new in *Homecoming* is not so much the broad outlines of Ngugi's argument; rather, it is his critical attention to the emerging cultures and conditions in newly postcolonial nations. His essays offer paths by which postcolonial cultural producers might build emancipated national cultures. For example, he analyzes the ways in which African and Caribbean writers George Lamming, V. S. Naipaul, Chinua Achebe, Wole Soyinka, Okot p'Bitek, and David Rubadiri both adapt and challenge the European literary tradition. In "Wole Soyinka, T. M. Aluko, and the Satiric Voice," for instance, Ngugi praises Soyinka for his use of satire in *One Man, One Matchet* to skewer the colonizer's use of benevolent paternalism to cover his tyrannical acts (56–66). Though decentering Europe is one of Ngugi's primary objectives—see, for instance, his extensive comments on the Kenyan university education system's slavish worship of English literature and neglect of African literatures and languages—of equal importance to building an emergent national culture is the writer's ability to expose the remnants of inequality not justified with new nationalist ideology. Echoing Fanon's caution against equating independence and equality, Ngugi applauds those writers who unveil corruption among the national bourgeoise, those who are willing to turn against their own class to realize a new social order that truly represents the majority's needs and interests. This process depends on the Third World writer recognizing and then overcoming his or her own alienation from the masses. For Ngugi, the reclamation of African languages and literatures constitutes a mode through which the revolutionary intellectual can simultaneously overcome her or his alienation and build a national culture that represents the reconciling of different class interests in its name. In doing so, Ngugi manages to break out of Fanon's all-or-nothing logjam; he advocates a revival of African languages and literature even though colonialism enables only impure access to them. Ngugi recognizes the dynamic exchange between indigenous cultural traditions and colonialism without altogether dismissing the import of cultural recovery and excavation.

The search for an oppositional cinematic language capable of holding various tensions together—those between cultural producers at UCLA and community residents in Watts, between Africans and African Americans, between cultural nationalists and Marxists—parallels Ngugi's call to found a national culture on African languages and literatures. The fact that the L.A. Rebellion used cinematic debates to work through ideas about a useable past, culture's relationship to politics, or the intellectual's role in forging a national culture should not distract us from those debates' relevance beyond the realm of cinema. Fanon and Ngugi's ideas catalyzed simmering divisions between the African Americans and the Africans in the group, for example. Heavily indebted to the ideas of Malcolm X and the Black Panther Party, the African Americans in the group tended to be cultural nationalists who believed that the source of culture derived from African diasporic history and experience.[59] By contrast, Masilela, Gerima, and Gabriel tended toward Marxist revolutionary internationalism, insisting on the interrelation of race and class domination.

Even this binary description, however, tends to obscure the tensions within the two tendencies. Cultural nationalists placed emphasis on different aspects of African diasporic experience depending on their orientation or subject matter. Marxists debated whether the peasantry or the urban working class would be the central agents of Third World liberation. Both positions were, of course, open to vigorous critique. If cultural nationalists could be accused of using nationalism to mask class divisions under the banner of race or national identity, Marxists were vulnerable to the charge that class analysis neglected the specific inequities wrought by racism. In addition to these internal schisms, there was also a great deal of instability across the two tendencies. L.A. Rebellion members moved back and forth across them, refusing to become distracted by unproductive sectarian debates. Masilela recalls that many members of the group switched positions frequently or tried to reconcile the two theories by constructing a hybrid and malleable field of analysis that encompassed both nationalism and Marxism.[60] Rather than seeing this as a sign of ideological inexactitude or incorrectness, I think this fluidity reflects the difficulties inherent in analyzing one's historical moment, let alone producing cultural texts that reflect that moment. While from one perspective it may reflect the weaknesses of both positions, it also suggests that both types of analysis must ultimately be brought to bear.

This ideological fluidity represents the L.A. Rebellion's efforts to move beyond the either-or dilemma that had hamstrung earlier leftists. In Masilela's view, the Africans came to understand the "indissolvability of Pan-Africanism and Marxism."[61] The same can be said, however, of the African Americans in the group. They, too, learned to think through the ways in which race and class analysis cohere. In a sense, this hybrid, syncretic space encouraged a focus on U.S. Third Worldism because it could encompass both race and class analysis, signaling both specific newly independent nations and a loose network of international affiliations. It helped skirt certain concrete ideological and aesthetic tensions by appealing to a sense of shared oppression and shared possibility just as it created an optic through which both modes of analysis could operate, if not without significant tension.

This hybridity and syncretism is ultimately what makes a comparison of *Killer of Sheep* and *Bush Mama* so resonant. It allows us to make sense of the fact that these two very different films share certain ideological preoccupations, even if they do so in less than overt ways. The line between cultural nationalism and Marxism splinters and reconfigures in both films, producing something unexpected and innovative in both cases.

Haile Gerima's 1975 *Bush Mama* and Charles Burnett's *Killer of Sheep*, completed in 1973 but released in 1977, are without question two seminal films of the group. Both take place in post-riot Watts and both reveal the everyday forms of state violence that circumscribe the lives of its inhabitants. However, the two films diverge in their prescription for black empowerment. *Bush Mama* is overtly concerned with black revolution throughout the African diaspora, arguing that African revolution can be a source of African American empowerment. Gerima's heroine Dorothy actively searches for a theoretical and practical framework through which she may understand and act to change her circumstances. Stan, the protagonist of *Killer of Sheep*, on the other hand, is concerned with his family's daily survival. He leads an alienated existence—he seems to sleepwalk through his life as a slaughterhouse worker—seemingly without connection to Third World sources of support and inspiration. The two films reflect, in part, the differences in the two filmmakers' experiences. Burnett primarily wanted to represent the reality of those with whom he grew up in Watts. Gerima used his diasporic understanding of Third World revolution as a way of linking conditions in Watts to colonial conditions around the globe. Contrasting the two films raises a set of questions about how the tensions between cultural nationalism and Third World Marxism impacted the group.

Looking at these films, I am concerned with the implicit and explicit ways Burnett and Gerima situate Watts in a global field of relations. Typically, criticism of the films describes them as local portraits of a particular historical moment; they are so-called Watts films. I want to position them in a transnational field of influence and exchange showing how their use of Third Cinema practices, black cultural nationalism, and Third World Marxism enables Gerima and Burnett to critique U.S. practices of state violence and portray the devastated communities and resistant or numbed black subjects left in their wake. If filmmaking was a primary means of exploring transnational identities and their attendant tensions, it was not always so easy to visually mediate local realities and global influences. It was not always possible to visually display complex identities emerging in the spaces between and across antiracist, anti-colonial, and anticapitalist ideology and activism. The filmic subjects under consideration here may be locally specific and transnationally resonant, but the narrative evidence is often obtusely rendered.

As did the work of other U.S. Third World Leftists, *Killer of Sheep* and *Bush Mama* reposition black Americans as members of an internal colony subject to some of the same forces terrorizing Third World colonies. Both films suggest that racial segregation and discrimination are a constitutive part of the U.S. nation-state rather than structural anomalies capable of reform. Gerima's film does this quite explicitly, relocating U.S. imperialism from the periphery to the very heart of U.S. life, revealing it to be as much an internal as an external threat. In Burnett's case, Watts and its residents are so alienated, they cannot participate in a larger Third World public. This critical difference means that Burnett's film gestures toward the larger global dynamics that shape Watts, but ultimately his characters are too preoccupied with daily survival to seek or see such connections. The films' disparities reflect the two directors' differing orientations to and formations within the African diaspora. Burnett, a black American, was indeed thoroughly influenced by Third World theory and praxis, but his desire to realistically depict his protagonist Stan as Rocha's reformulated everyman ultimately renders him unable to also represent Stan as a man capable of forging concrete or imagined political alliances with Third World peoples. The very forms of oppression and alienation that plague Stan also necessarily constrict his political and cultural vision. To depict the former, Burnett must also depict the latter. Gerima, on the other hand, having recently traveled from Ethiopia to Chicago to Los Angeles, has a more concrete sense of how to bridge geographic spaces through politically committed cultural practice. That experience means that a "realistic" representation of Dorothy is not necessarily his primary concern; instead, Gerima makes *Bush Mama* into a contradictory canvas for both hope and despair.

Bush Mama, Revolutionary Mother

In *Bush Mama*, Gerima pointedly identifies the multiple state practices that construct Watts as an internal colony, indicting the agents of state violence, whether they be black or white, and then connecting that state violence to Dorothy's burgeoning consciousness. Born in Ethiopia, Gerima was influenced early on by his father, a priest, teacher, historian, and playwright who traveled with an itinerant drama troupe performing plays around Gondar. His mother and grandmother were also storytellers bequeathing to Gerima a strong sense of Ethiopia's oral traditions. His compulsion to tell stories collided with a transnational perspective that developed once he arrived in the United States and, in the critic Mike Murashige's words, "witnessed firsthand the brand of racism particular to the U.S."[62] Gerima has described his vocation this way: "A filmmaker is a story teller, nothing more, nothing less; one who provides information, one who creates and explores the vital elements and innovatively synthesizes social relationships; one who plays a role in linking not only the historical but global human experience."[63] *Bush Mama*, then, is the filmmaker's attempt to depict Watts as a microcosm of both the United States and the Third World, a site constructed by forms of violence and terrorism so destructive and brutal that armed self-defensive emerges as the only alternative.

As is also the case in *Killer of Sheep*, *Bush Mama* consists of a series of nonlinear vignettes, some of which take place inside the protagonist's own head. Dorothy, a pregnant, unemployed mother on welfare lives with her young daughter Luann. Her husband has recently been killed in Vietnam. From the film's initial frames, she struggles to support her family, maintain autonomy, and resist the state's various forms of humiliation. Her lover T. C., a Vietnam veteran, has been convicted of a robbery he did not commit because Dorothy's insistence that he was with her on the night of the robbery is insufficient proof of his innocence. As Dorothy walks the streets of Watts, stares blankly out of her window, or talks to her friends and neighbors, she simultaneously ponders her options and bears witness to the various forms of state violence visited on black Watts.

Whatever choices she makes will be in response to the violence and brutality around her. From the opening frames, this point is clear. As the cameraman Charles Burnett pans across the streets of Watts, focusing on the faces of men, women, and children going about their daily life, we hear the sounds of a helicopter overhead, police car sirens, and the sound loop of a social worker questioning, "Have you ever received noncash gifts from someone not a member of your household?"[64] The action on the street is both routine and extraordinary as the camera captures from above a scene of police frisking two black men splayed against a car. What the viewer cannot know is that the police stop is not a scripted part of the story but rather an actual incident in which Watts police stopped Gerima's crew because they had expensive camera equipment. Such harassment is clearly routine in Watts—people barely stop to watch the event—and as such serves as simply one more manifestation of Watts's internal-colony status. The bounds of fiction and reality blur as the very attempt to represent Watts summons state violence; ostensibly the image is perceived to be as dangerous as the bodies of black men automatically defined as criminals. Murashige rightly identifies this opening scene as one that conflates the act of policing black areas and the disciplining and regulating of the poor.[65]

Throughout the film, this documentary style melds with scenes of lurid surrealism as if to underline the absurd cruelties of life in Watts. For example, we learn that T. C. served two tours of duty in Vietnam because he could not find a job. Willing to die for "his country," and functioning as the literal agent of U.S. imperialism, T. C. finds himself falsely imprisoned when he returns. While waiting at the welfare office, Dorothy witnesses a horrifying scene in which a man comes down to the office angry because he's been denied benefits. Brandishing an ax, the man is clearly symbolically striking out against a corrupt system, but he has little possibility of using his weapon since no one stands nearby and he does not even attempt to enter the welfare office. Nonetheless, the black workers summon the police who drive up, issue a perfunctory warning, and shoot the man in the back before he can even respond. This scene is echoed again later when the police shoot a handcuffed man they are arresting simply because he refuses to be shoved. Men in this world are quickly dispatched—either to jail or to their deaths—as they encounter a state structure opposed to their very survival. Arrest and police murder are so commonplace that they rarely appear a reason to stop one's progress on the street, rarely a reason to express sadness or outrage.

But if black men find themselves facing the full brunt of state violence, black women fare no better. Though we do not see them murdered by the police, other state structures threaten them in equally destructive ways. For example, the welfare office, the supposed symbol of a benevolent state tending to its citizens' needs, becomes a site of psychic pacification and devastation. Dorothy is repeatedly summoned to the welfare office with promises of employment, only to sit there for hours before being told that there are no available jobs. She and the other women there are repeatedly made to fill out forms that pry into their personal lives. To receive welfare, women must deny the presence of friends or lovers who may be a source of emotional, if not financial, support. To receive welfare, they must acquiesce to various forms of state surveillance and regulation. Questions about whether one drinks, has a job, has a telephone, has children, has a lover are not only routine but can serve as alibis for state neglect. The surveyed and tightly regulated body—literalized by Dorothy's insistence on hiding her natural hair under a wig—is the price Dorothy must pay for survival; and even that offers no guarantee.

This tension leads to the central conflict of *Bush Mama*: the question of

6. Dorothy imagines an abortion. Still from Haile Gerima's
Bush Mama.

whether Dorothy will agree to abort her baby. When she seeks help at the welfare office, her black social worker tells her, "You have one daughter. You're on your way to another child. You'd better go to a doctor. . . . Now, we can do all we can to help you, but we advise you . . . [comment trails off]." Throughout the film, those bitterly ironic words echo in Dorothy's head as she listens to others tell her not to abort, as she sits in the abortion office before running out, as she fantasizes about hitting her black social worker in the head with a liquor bottle. State violence extends all the way into the womb, all the way into Dorothy's head, where her ability to mother is undermined, her right to procreate denied. The fact that Dorothy cannot afford another child because the state has falsely imprisoned the recently employed T. C. only adds insult to injury. The state's insistence that poor black women should not be mothers threatens to be internalized by them. It is worth noting, however, that Dorothy's dilemma remains firmly within the safe bounds of female reproduction; the "radical" position in this case is to assert her right to be a mother. The choice to abort is positioned as a genocidal one. For Gerima, gender seems to mean that the differential experience of state violence is psychically as well as physically devastating. For instance, Dorothy imagines being strapped to a table, at least eight months pregnant (clearly past the window for a safe abortion), with a white doctor standing between her legs, and then imagines a masked and writhing figure on a cross. In another "real" instance, Dorothy hears the pleas of a man urging a woman to "come down and hand over the baby." She goes outside to find a woman holding a crying baby on the edge of a roof. Dorothy intervenes, demanding that the woman give her the baby, saying that "then she can jump if she wants to." State violence is most immediately felt and yet invisible at the level of the individual's consciousness.

It is individual black consciousness that Gerima ultimately wants to explore. The transformation begins with Dorothy who must first recognize that the situation in Watts is not one of her own making. Dorothy moves from being a quiet, essentially nonactive presence to (in a Fanonian gesture) asserting her identity through violence. When she returns home from her first day of work to find a white police officer raping a handcuffed Luann, she instinctively uses the only weapon available to her, an umbrella, to beat him to death. The road to this act leads through several figures—T. C., who has begun to read and reflect in jail and has come to believe that it is capitalism and white imperialism that have oppressed black people; Molly, a friend who survives on alcohol and sheer toughness; and Siemie, a neighbor who asserts that collective action will lead to black empowerment. It also leads through Annie, a teenaged friend of Luann who brings news of community demonstrations and two posters that go up on Dorothy's walls, one of a black man shot dozens of times by police, the other of an African woman holding a baby and gun in her arms. Though Dorothy does not endorse any one program, she does begin to incorporate fragments of each position into her own.

As she reflects on her life, she stares at these two posters hearing T. C.'s voice saying, "They built their major wealth off our back and the wealth from Africa." She moves from seeing herself as completely removed from African liberation struggles to wearing her hair in a style mirroring that of the woman in the poster. As Murashige suggests, "The poster of the African woman works towards a recoding of what black bodies mean within representational politics. Rather than being a site of deprivation, pain, despair and victimization, this image embodies a very material form of political and social insurgency."[66] So, too, does Dorothy's act of violent resistance. In its aftermath, she is insulted and tortured by a white police officer, and so badly beaten that she miscarries. Nonetheless, she is not broken. Instead, the film concludes with a shot of her standing in front of the African liberation poster, and finally we hear her own words on the soundtrack, rather than those of others. In a letter to T. C., she writes:

> T.C. they beat our baby out of me. They wouldn't let me see nobody, not even a doctor for ten days. We got to make changes so we can raise our kids with both of us at home so things can go right. I've been blaming myself all this time 'cuz things wasn't right. I thought that I was born to be poor and pushed around and stepped on. I don't want Luann growin' up thinking like that. I can see now that my problem was a place I was born into, a place with laws that protect the people who got money, doctors and hospitals for people who got money. I have to get to know myself, to read and to study.

We all have to so we can change it so we can know how to talk to each other. Talking to each other's not easy. I know you're in jail, T.C. and angry, but most of the time I don't understand your letters. Talk to me easy T.C. 'cuz I want to understand. It's not easy to win over people like me. There's a lot of people like me and we have many things to fight for just to live. But the idea is to win over more of our people. Talk the same talk but easy T.C. You remember you used to ask why I always wear a wig all day and all night, when I eat, when I sleep. T.C., the wig is off my head. The wig is off my head. I never saw what was under it. I just saw on top, the glitter, the wig. The wig is off my head.

If Dorothy's final letter is evidence that she has emerged as a radical subject, it also functions as a critique of intellectuals. Dorothy's pleas that T.C. be patient with her are also a plea to the audience and to other artists. Black consciousness and empowerment will not be a matter of simple transmission from the vanguard to the masses; rather, it will take open collaboration, a willingness of intellectuals to be schooled by the working class as much as the reverse. *Bush Mama* ultimately tells a double narrative about Dorothy's development and the artist-intellectual's humility in the face of working-class common sense. As with much U.S. Third World Leftist film, liberation is delayed. Dorothy will spend much of her life behind bars for killing a white cop, and thus the audience can only imagine her subsequent acts of freedom fighting. Dorothy has arrived at a radical subjectivity, but it is one contained by state forces.

Killer of Sheep in the Inner City

Just a few minutes into Charles Burnett's *Killer of Sheep*, the protagonist Stan says, "I'm working myself into my own hell. I close my eyes. I can't get no sleep at night. No peace of mind."[67] In a figurative sense, Stan's words echo again and again as we watch him meander through the streets of Watts, a Watts marked by abandoned lots, jobless women, hustling men, and children whose playground is the city street. Like Stan, the viewer is forced to make sense of his oscillation between the streets of Watts, the confines of his house, and the interiors of the slaughterhouse. If Stan is the literal killer of sheep, then who or what is the metaphorical killer of the men, women, and children of Watts? As its title suggests, Burnett's film refuses to romanticize the ghetto or its inhabitants. The situation in Watts is not even explicitly shown to have international resonance, though Burnett implies that the condition of Watts is the condition for all black ghettoes.

Born in South Central Los Angeles to Mississippi migrants spurred west by the wartime boom that increased L.A.'s black population by 75 percent, Burnett spent his youth in Watts, a witness to the discrimination that isolated Watts, as well as to the dislocations wrought by the civil rights movement itself. For Watts, the civil rights movement meant increasing, if highly circumscribed, opportunity and the splintering of South Central as (lower) middle-class African Americans out-migrated, leaving, in Burnett's words, "a big vacuum in the community" just beginning to be acutely felt in the late 1960s.[68] Railroaded through an educational system that encouraged high dropout rates, Burnett graduated from high school and avoided the draft by enrolling at the working-class Los Angeles Community College. Initially interested in engineering, Burnett soon turned to creative writing and filmmaking in part to avoid the dead-end working lives of the people in his midst.[69] In 1970, he enrolled in UCLA's film department.

Killer of Sheep reveals Burnett's opposition to two dominant tendencies within the filmmaking world of Los Angeles and UCLA. For one, he wanted to give voice to a Watts community ignored by both Hollywood and UCLA's film program, but this desire took on an added dimension. He wanted to explain, in his words, "what went wrong with [the kids he grew up with]"; he wanted to explore how his peers ended up in jail, dead, or fighting in Vietnam.[70] Second, Burnett resisted the dominant forms of alternative filmmaking popular at the time because he felt they depended on formulaic and stereotyped depictions of the working class. In an interview with me, Burnett said he wanted to avoid the typical working-class narrative that pitted the boss against the workers. Those working-class characters were not familiar to him, did not look like guys in his neighborhood who were simply worried about finding and keeping jobs.

Peopled with nonactors and Burnett family members, the seventy-five-minute, black-and-white *Killer of Sheep* gives us a multidimensional view of working-class Watts. Deeply preoccupied with the ways that race and class oppression deform black lives, Burnett represents working-class people without reducing the complexities of their struggles or their flaws. Through the character of Stan—a man with two children, a loving and sexually frustrated wife, and a slaughterhouse job—Burnett outlines the dehumanizing conditions under which Stan struggles to maintain a sense of dignity if not hope. Rigorously unsentimental and unflinchingly political without endorsing any ideological stance or program, the film suggests a critique of a U.S. nation-state indifferent to the plight of black people. Not only has the promise of the civil rights era largely remained unrealized but also the ability to challenge the U.S. nation-state has also been subdued, if not destroyed. Watts is, in a very real sense, an internal colony, part of the United States and yet completely cut off from the legal protections and economic promise enjoyed by others. Unemployment, exploitation, housing segregation, poverty—these are symptoms or traces left behind by internal colonialism and as such, they are manifestations of a state violence no less pernicious for being less spectacularly visible. Here, as a matter of fact, the agents of state violence are invisible: they have been evacuated from Watts so that only their handiwork remains.

Killer of Sheep does not have a conventional plot nor does it include much dialogue. Rather, it features vignettes in the life of Stan, his wife, and their two children. In various scenes, we see Stan cashing his check at the local liquor store, rebuffing his wife's sexual advances, and passively resisting the pitch of two men who want him to join their murder-for-hire scheme. The few moments in which Stan acts on his environment are also moments of impotency (in every sense of the word). Stan's actions either result in failure or in cruelty toward his wife, his children, or the unlucky sheep he slaughters. His is a tightly bounded, circumscribed life. In contrast, the neighborhood children find ways to maintain a sense of optimism, their daily lives full of adventure and possibility as they jump rope, climb junk heaps, and wrestle in dusty, litter-filled lots.

In the space between Stan and the children's lives lies Burnett's sharpest critique. In a pivotal scene in the film, Burnett puts the song "The House I Live In" to stunning cinematic effect. Sung by Paul Robeson and written by the blacklisted writer Earl Robinson, "The House I Live In" was a Popular Front anthem extolling the virtues of racial equality and economic justice. As the lyrics of the song—"What is America to me? / A name, a map with a flag I see? / A certain word, 'Democracy'? / What is America to me?"—envelop the scene, we watch young boys playing in an abandoned lot, bricks their only available toys (see figures 7 and 8). As Robeson intones, "The children at the playground, / the faces that I see, all races, all religions. / That's America to me," we realize that the Popular Front dream of racial inclusion has been abandoned, nearly obliterated. In this scene and others, Burnett brilliantly uses black music, the linking of the African American past to the Watts present, as a way of ironically commenting on the action.

The construction of Stan's pessimism and alienation is rife with historical and political meaning. His situation underscores the limits of U.S. democracy; Stan is quite literally living a profound historical crisis. Watts stands in for a larger set of effects felt across black America. Even after the civil rights movement, black people cannot help but recognize their alien and alienated status, must understand that their citizenship is defined by restriction rather than freedom. If the slaughterhouse offers a microcosm of Watts and Watts offers a

7. Wide shot of boys playing in an abandoned lot. Still from Charles Burnett's *Killer of Sheep*.

8. Close-up of young boys playing in an abandoned lot. Still from Charles Burnett's *Killer of Sheep*.

microcosm of the United States, then black people are lambs to the slaughter. At the same time, Stan has also been positioned as an agent of the state; he is doing the work of the state: killing the sheep with whom he has so much in common. Neither he nor they can exercise much control over destiny. As in *Bush Mama*, state violence works on both the outside of the body and the inside of the mind as it is internalized and made spectacularly invisible.

Burnett's refusal of any overt political solution to the alienation and despair evident in Watts is a strategic choice that forces the viewer to explore the reasons for Stan's plight. If Burnett fails to focus the anger and frustration felt by Stan on any one target, if he fails to provide a global analysis, he does so precisely to point out that Stan and other guys on the block have run out of answers. The triumph of white domination in this case means the closing down of analysis, as well as of options. Nonetheless, a subtle critique of the

9. Stan in the slaughterhouse. Still from Charles Burnett's
Killer of Sheep.

10. Lambs to the slaughter. Still from Charles Burnett's *Killer
of Sheep*.

state lies in every frame of the film. Pans of a decaying Watts landscape and
intercuts of Stan and the helpless sheep, for example, force the viewer to
question the equation of Watts and the slaughterhouse. What or who is making
Watts a literal and metaphoric slaughterhouse? What are the forms of state
violence that hem in Stan, his family, and friends? Is Watts part of the United
States or is it located outside the bounds of its fictive liberty and justice? In
telling the simple story of Stan's everyday survival, Burnett opens up a critical
gap between the film and the audience. The viewer is then forced to do the
analytical work of which Stan seems incapable, forced in some sense to defini-
tively act when Stan cannot.

In many ways, one might think of both *Killer of Sheep* and *Bush Mama* as
films that explore the preconditions for an emergent social order, one generated by exclusion from the dominant social order. As a segment of society

positioned by the state as outside that order, Stan, Dorothy, and other Watts residents are poised to form an alternate one. In Burnett's film, the potential of an emergent social order seems nonexistent or at least of little or no value. Gerima's *Bush Mama*, however, holds out the hope that Dorothy and T. C. represent the beginning of an emergent social order that can be of eventual political use. The state has successfully contained their bodies, but not their minds. Gerima's use of surrealism and straight narrative, though, does present a ruptured style, one that may in fact undercut Dorothy's seamless trajectory toward liberation. Is her letter at the end just another hallucination? The difference in outlook has much to do with individual orientation, but it also expresses the differential influence of Third World theory on the two men. Burnett turned to African American cultural traditions—music, in particular—for inspiration and sustenance, while Gerima explicitly appealed to African revolutions as a source of inspiration, using his film as a way of gesturing toward a diasporic consciousness. Both men, however, consciously used their films to both represent and help create a black public that might serve as an alternative to U.S. state practices. *Bush Mama* and *Killer of Sheep*, to quote James Snead, "set about recoding black skin on screen and in the public realm by revising the contexts and concepts with which it had long been associated."[71] In both films, that recoding takes place at multiple levels, attacking the stereotypical representations of black Americans; resituating black communities as both subject to powerful forms of state violence and akin to Third World colonies; and opening up a space in which a new subject position, a new of form of radical consciousness, might potentially develop. Understanding that recoding requires a deep analysis of the intellectual, political, and aesthetic stakes of the period, stakes often as elusive as they are hybrid.

Coda

●

By the end of the 1970s, the emergent social order for which *Bush Mama* and *Killer of Sheep* so urgently long seemed to be receding into the distance. If objective material conditions had not changed for most communities of color, the mass social movements of the sixties and seventies had. In a few short years, the long Reagan-Bush winter would arrive. Though the FBI's COINTELPRO activities had officially ended by 1971, the legacy of fear, paranoia, and disorder left in their wake severely hampered many organizing activities. This combined with a global recession and the grappling of postcolonial nations with the exigencies of nation and state building changed the climate for all leftists. Some activists went underground, while others entered academic institutions that would give them the credentials and the institutional bases from which to continue their work. Still others channeled their energy into local grassroots campaigns and institution building in their individual contexts.

In the case of 1199, the hospital workers union went into an extended period of racial and ethnic factionalism that lasted until the late 1980s. The coalition that had made the union a powerful, progressive voice frayed under the pressure of idiosyncratic and ego-driven leadership and increasingly balkanized leftist politics. In 1989, Dennis Rivera replaced Georginna Johnson, a black social worker's assistant, as 1199's president. With his dynamic leadership and the union's activist membership base, 1199 consolidated its union power throughout the 1990s. Long an independent union, 1199 merged with SEIU, the Service Employees Industrial Union, in 1998, a move that reflected the increasing corporatization of health care. Today the union continues to be one of the strongest in the nation, with well over 240,000 members in New York State alone and vigorous organizing efforts throughout much of the Midwest and West. Rather than solely focusing on consolidating gains for its core membership, 1199 has continued to organize new segments of the industry including home health care workers, a notoriously difficult segment to reach, and has become a force in national politics. Recently, the union spent millions of dollars to register new voters and campaign for the defeat of President George W. Bush in 2004. Despite its ambitious roster of activities, 1199 continues its vigorous cultural activities. Its gallery exhibitions, in-hospital theater programs, and commitment to arts education for New York's schoolchildren remain at the forefront of worker-organized cultural activity.

Haile Gerima, Charles Burnett, and Julie Dash are the most well-known filmmakers to have emerged from the L.A. Rebellion. Gerima has directed numerous films, founding the Mypheduh Films (MFI) company in 1982 as a distribution vehicle for them. After a decade of research and fund-raising, he released *Sankofa* in 1993. The film depicts the transformation of a black American woman who is transported back in time to a West Indies plantation where she encounters the brutalities of enslavement and the rich tradition of slave resistance. Though the film lacked a corporate distributor, Gerima toured major cities with it, building a large audience by word of mouth. Currently, the director teaches at Howard University. Julie Dash continues to write and direct film and video for television, though she is most well known for the groundbreaking experimental film *Daughters of the Dust*, which earned numerous national and international awards. *Daughters* broke significant aesthetic and thematic ground, detailing the struggles of a South Carolina Gullah community to hang onto its traditions in the face of northern migration. Dash is also the founder of Geechee Girls Productions and Geechee Girls Multimedia, the latter designed to produce CD-ROM and DVD materials. Charles Burnett still lives in South Los Angeles and has written and directed over twenty feature and documentary films including the 1990 *To Sleep with Anger*, the 1998 *The Wedding*, and the 2003 *Nat Turner: A Troublesome Property*. In 1988, he won the MacArthur Foundation fellowship grant, the so-called Genius Award. Recently, the Library of Congress declared *Killer of Sheep* a "national treasure," making it one of the first fifty films to be placed in the National Film Registry.

Other U.S. Third World Leftists entered the university system. Today, Teshome Gabriel and Ntongela Masilela teach at UCLA and Pitzer College, respectively, and for many years, the late Harold Cruse taught at the University of Michigan. Angela Y. Davis, the author of numerous books including the classic *Women, Race and Class* (1981), *Blues Legacies and Black Feminism: Gertrude "Ma" Rainey, Bessie Smith, and Billie Holiday* (1998), and *Are Prisons Obsolete?* (2003), remains a committed intellectual-activist whose most recent work focuses on dismantling the prison industrial complex. Ironically, in 1994 the state university system that once fired her for being a communist appointed Davis the University of California presidential chair in African American and feminist studies, which she currently holds at UC Santa Cruz.

Amiri Baraka continues to work as a prolific poet, playwright, and essayist, and Newark, New Jersey, has remained his organizational base. A Third World Marxist since 1974, he and his family have continued their local political and cultural organizing efforts. In May 2002, those efforts were recognized when Baraka was appointed the poet laureate for New Jersey, an honor he held until 2003, when the New Jersey legislature abolished the poet laureate position. They did so in response to the outcry caused by a poem Baraka wrote entitled "Somebody Blew Up America," a reflection on the 11 September 2001 bombing of the World Trade Center that was seen as anti-Semitic. His son Ras Baraka is currently the deputy mayor of Newark; in that capacity he recently helped organize a large hip-hop convention that drew artists and activists from all over the country and brokered a gang truce between Newark's Crips and Bloods gangs.

The legacy of Third World Newsreel founders is also quite impressive. In 1977, Susan Robeson left the organization to produce the television program *Like It Is*, the Emmy Award–winning public affairs program hosted by Gil Noble still produced in New York City. After eight years with the show, Robeson left to produce a series of music documentaries before relocating to Saint Paul, Minnesota, where she has been involved in grassroots community initiatives including *Kev Koom Siab*, a weekly program focusing on the Southeast Asian Hmong community, and *Don't Believe the Hype*, an Emmy Award–winning series produced by at-risk African American youth. In 1981, Robeson also published a photographic memoir of her grandfather entitled *The Whole World in His Hands: A Pictorial Biography of Paul Robeson*. Recently, Robeson took her commitment to grassroots media education to South Africa where she trained township-based video groups so they could eventually apply to run their own broadcast channels.

Up until 1988, founders Christine Choy and Allan Siegel jointly ran Third World Newsreel, collaborating on several projects including *Mississippi Triangle* (1984) and *Chronicle of Hope: Nicaragua* (1985). These joint collaborations, as well as their own individual projects, won fellowships and awards that helped keep the organization afloat. The curator Pearl Bowser also worked with them to develop several touring exhibitions, notably the popular Independent Black American Cinema, 1920–1980, which increased Third World Newsreel's national and international profile. In her long career, Choy has worked on scores of film and video projects including the Oscar-nominated *Who Killed Vincent Chin?* (1989) and *Sa-I-Gu: From Korean Women's Perspectives* (1993), a film depicting the impact of the 1992 Los Angeles uprising on Korean shopkeepers. Currently, she is an associate professor in New York University's film and television department, having previously directed the School of Creative Media at the City University of Hong Kong. For many years after his departure from Newsreel, Siegel worked in Chicago, teaching, writing articles, and producing films. He remains committed to documenting Newsreel's impressive history and has recently contributed articles to *ARTMargins*, a journal on contemporary Central and Eastern European visual culture, and the book *Screening the City*. Currently, however, Siegel resides in Budapest, where he teaches in the intermedia department at the Academy of Fine Arts and is working on *Usti Opre*, a film and accompanying CD on Roma music in Central and Eastern Europe.

Between 1988 and 1998, the filmmaker and activist Ada Gay Griffin directed the organization. Under her leadership, the group's distribution network radically expanded with the addition of work by emerging artists including Lourdes Portillo, Charles Burnett, and Arthur Dong. In propelling forward this expansion, Griffin introduced viewers to an entirely new generation of media-makers of color. During that time, she also produced and codirected with Michelle Parkerson the extraordinary film *A Litany For Survival: The Life and Work of Audre Lorde* (1995). Rather than supporting a core group of filmmakers, Third World Newsreel now more often serves as a sponsor for independent affiliated filmmakers. Since 1998, Dorothy Thigpen, formerly of Women Make Movies, has directed the organization. Most recently, TWN commissioned short pieces that explored the impact of the 9/11 bombings on New York City's complicated race relations. The results were screened at New York University's Cantor Film Center in September 2003. Carrying on a tradition begun at that very first meeting in 1967, TWN continues to respond to contemporary crises by providing the resources and the political space for media-makers to produce counter-hegemonic cultural texts.

By any standard, the individual and collective achievements of U.S. Third World Leftists form an impressive legacy. Just as important, however, is the meaning of their presence for activists and cultural producers today. Their efforts help resituate contemporary debates around the meaning and efficacy of identity politics. The current project was propelled, in no small measure, by my sense that identity politics had become a convenient scapegoat for the Left's failures in the sixties and the Right's triumph in the late seventies. Sixties participants and critics often masked a deeply racialized critique of how identity politics killed the revolution by rewriting their own largely New Left history. These New Left revisionists implied and sometimes declared that class was always the New Left's "real" focus. This was in the face of historical evidence that Students for a Democratic Society sought to break with the Old Left, hence the *new* in New Left. This historiographic tendency seems to imagine that had identity politics not arrived on the scene, if a class-based revolution had been the one and only goal, then leftists might have won. It seems clear, however, that the forces arrayed against the Left were formidable. Confronted with a state prepared to use violence, imprisonment, infiltration, and sabotage to quell dissent, faced with a virulent backlash against civil rights, and the quiescence of organized labor and other potential allies, leftists would have needed the kind of consolidated opposition and single-minded purpose that is perhaps only possible in twenty-twenty hindsight.

Exploration of the U.S. Third World Left disputes the scholarly and popular understandings of identity categories. Often scholars of and witnesses to the sixties and seventies have held rigid conceptions of identity categories and their role in political and cultural organizing. Such reification positions identity categories and identity politics as inherently narrow and limited, blaming them for the demise of an imagined and largely imaginary terrain of utopian possibility. Instead, *Soul Power* contends that narrow analytic paradigms have obscured the ways in which identity-based activism was far from monolithic or unitary. Appeals to and descriptions of people as workers, prisoners, African Americans, or Puerto Ricans, for instance, encompassed multiple geographic positions, class locations, and racial identities. For this group of leftists, the discursive banner *Third World* described organizing that thoroughly integrated race-, gender-, nation-, and class-based critiques. If one reads identity rhetoric too literally and outside of its material context, then one misses the complex range of demands made in its name.

Rather than conceiving of identity politics in narrow, nonuniversalist terms, *Soul Power* shows how they can reflect both a group's historically specific location and its resonances with other historically specific local contexts. For example, the Black Consciousness movement leader Stephen Biko recontextualized the term *black*, borrowing associations and meanings from the U.S. Black Power era to rally nonwhite South Africans and defy the Apartheid regime's discriminatory logic. In that instance, *black* stood as both a discursively dense and a generative site producing new associations and protest strategies. If identity politics are hybrid formulations articulated through the rhetoric of singularity, then that rhetoric serves as a placeholder signaling a critical engagement with a complex social world. Rather than focusing on identity as a given label or set of labels that can be ranked, *Soul Power* offers ways of conceptualizing identity politics as an arena that relies on a sophisticated enactment of unity in difference. Identity-based discourse references a range of local conditions, a series of interconnected oppressions that might be collected under several discursive banners. From this perspective, identity politics is a field in which struggles around power, cultural representation, and discursive meaning are ongoing. People adopting or organizing under a given identity engage in a war of position that seeks to secure or change that identity's meaning even as it appears, from both within and without, to be stable and self-evident. Battles over whether *black* means queer, feminist, and/or anticapitalist indicate the dynamic meanings encompassed by seemingly unitary identities.

U.S. Third World Leftists emphasized the relation between cultural experimentation and radical politics, theorizing and enacting a distinctly new radical racial and ethnic subjectivity. These new subjectivities were not vehicles for a narrow identity politics—as some historiographers would have it—but rather constituted means for linking local racial and ethnic oppression to global patterns of Western imperialism and economic exploitation. This meant building coalitions across race, ethnicity, gender, generation, and national lines. It meant crafting a new theoretical and political language and adapting the rhetoric and tactics of Third World anticolonial movements for First World mobilization. U.S. Third World Leftists worked, thought, and moved across racial, ethnic, political, and national boundaries. Engagement with their legacy affords us an opportunity to think beyond the familiar binaries that structure most understandings of the sixties and seventies—cultural nationalism versus civil rights; race versus class; domestic versus international; political activism versus cultural experimentation. Evidence of a landscape more complicated than such convenient binaries suggest, the U.S. Third World Left displayed a remarkably pragmatic and uniquely flexible and nonsectarian vision that blurred such distinctions, rendering them less important in daily cultural and political praxis. What some critics have seen as theoretical imprecision or incoherent anarchy obscures the series of alliances U.S. Third World Leftists enacted between diverse constituencies: prisoners and college students, Cuban revolutionaries and African American writers, Puerto Rican hospital workers and Jewish pharmacists, grassroots organizers and independent filmmakers. The use of the term *Third World* by U.S. Third World Leftists described a dense ideological and political nexus as much as it did a particular geographic region or economic stage of development.

As enabling as the comparison of U.S. minorities and Third World majorities proved for U.S. Third World Leftists, it also exacted a price. The vexed modes of transnational exchange, the multiple translations and substitutions that enabled U.S. Third World Leftists to imagine a radical Third World subject and link their situation to that of their Third World counterparts came at a significant symbolic and ideological cost. Often U.S. Third World discourse and activism reduced the complexities and material realities of Third World people and their struggles to a general condition primarily defined by the fight against imperialism and colonialism and the struggle for national autonomy. That reduction papered over various class, gender, and ethnic conflicts that already defined emerging postcolonial nations. The deployment of this term, ironically, had the paradoxical effect of reinforcing the undifferentiated and exploitable identity beyond which postcolonial nations were rapidly moving.

As intellectual-activists, our work is based on the belief that deconstructing ideas, social formations, and cultural practices yields epistemological or ontological truths that have value and meaning in the material world, if only incrementally. Yet as someone who aspires to produce academic work that can tangibly impact struggles for social justice, I do not ask myself often enough when the parsing of ideas, histories, personalities, literary texts, or the never-ending quest for greater nuance hits the brick wall of political pragmatism. And how will we know when we get there? Even if we can now identify the multiple ways in which U.S. Third World Leftist theorizing "got it wrong," does that necessarily mean that their cultural practices or political organizing did not "get it right"?

The ability to imagine and articulate how and why local conditions mimic global ones builds solidarity, political projects, and empathy between radically different kinds of people. U.S. Third World Leftists believed that they could claim sameness and difference at the same time, that they could make demands on their own behalf and on behalf of others. They not only imagined that they could build connections and networks on a global scale but recognized that it was urgent to do so. In an atomized era, a historical moment defined by what Raymond Williams has termed "mobile privatization,"[1] when we imagine that our private choices have no impact on other people, this belief seems a precious and sorely needed commodity. In his reflection on forms of community and citizenship, Partha Chatterjee reminds us that unorthodox communities arise precisely when nation-states refuse to fully recognize subjects as citizens. "When the colonized refuse to accept membership of this civil society of subjects," Chatterjee writes, "they construct their national identities within a different narrative, that of the community." He continues, "They do not have the option of doing this within the domain of bourgeois civil-social institutions. They create, consequently, a very different domain—a cultural domain— marked by the distinctions of the material and the spiritual, the outer and the inner."[2] Faced with forms of organized state violence that not only refused to recognize their full rights as citizens but alienated them from the very concept of national citizenship, U.S. Third World Leftists built alternative communities that offered transnational forms of solidarity and strength. They attacked imperial practices abroad as a way of overturning the domestic forms of oppression facing them. Doing so required a certain political leap of faith, a transcendence of the outer and the inner, of the material and the spiritual. At this disturbing historical juncture, perhaps this stands as the most important lesson they offer us.

Notes

●

Preface

1 See Lipsitz 1998.

Introduction

1 Du Bois 1982, 236.

2 Von Eschen 1997, 169.

3 See, for example, Von Eschen 1997, W. James 1998, and Kelley 1990.

4 Von Eschen 1997, 175.

5 See Welch 2002.

6 Appadurai 1996, 22.

7 Cruse 2002, 152–56.

8 Examples of this tendency include J. Miller 1987, Bacciocco 1975, and Gitlin 1987.

9 When I use the term *the sixties* here, I am talking about it with all of its mythic valences, not simply as a temporal moment, but rather as a zeitgeist. It is this zeitgeist that I aim to unsettle.

10 T. Anderson 1996, 332.

11 T. Anderson 1996, 294.

12 Jameson 1984, 180–83.

13 Elbaum 2002.

14 Lyons 1976, 215.

15 Gosse 1993, 1–3.

16 Diggins 1992, 237.

17 Students for a Democratic Society 1998, 217.

18 Gosse 1996, 307.

19 I am indebted to Rachel Lee for helping me frame my argument in these terms.

20 Elbaum 2002, 62.

21 See S. Torres 2003.

22 Denning 2004, 2–3.

23 Susman 1984, 185.

24 Williams 1989, 174–75, qtd. in Denning 1996, xx.

25 See Clifford 1994; Gilroy 1993.

26 Edwards 2003, 13–15.

27 Grewal and Kaplan 1994, 18.

28 Edwards 2003, 241.

29 I recognize the fraught nature of the term *originate* given the reality of hybridity as it has been produced by the global slave trade, global capitalism, immigration, migration, forced removal, war, and so on. I use it provisionally as a way of working from rather than against a commonsense understanding of *originate* to explode it from within. What follows calls into question any simple identification of origin points.

30 Grossberg 1993, 97.

31 Gramsci 1992, 44–122.

32 Fanon 1963, 152, 203.

33 Althusser 2001, 109–10.

1. Havana Up in Harlem

1 Gosse 1993, 147.

2 Though Cruse, in fact, primarily targets black leftists who have worked with or been substantially influenced by the Communist Party of the United States (CPUSA) in *The Crisis of the Negro Intellectual*, he is also concerned with the possibility that a new generation of leftists, the black New Left, will fall into the CPUSA's orbit and repeat many of the mistakes he alleges have been made by earlier generations of black leftists.

3 Moore 1988, 59.

4 Robert Williams, in *The Crusader*, 30 July and 13 August 1960, qtd. in Gosse 1993, 153.

5 Moore 1988, 120.

6 Kelley and Esch 1999, 16.

7 Reitan 1999, 44.

8 Plummer 1998, 137–38.

9 I do not mean to suggest that Cuba was a land free of racism. Instead, I am highlighting the reputation actively cultivated by Castro's regime and the ways in which African Americans shaped and invested in that discourse. Vigorous debate on the question of Castro's treatment of Afro-Cubans continues. See, for example, Moore 1988; Booth 1976; Cole 1980.

10 Moore 1988, 62.

11 Gosse 1993, 307.

12 Moore 1988, 79.

13 Plummer 1998, 144.

14 This was not the first instance of African Americans linking antiracist and anti-colonial politics. Von Eschen 1997, for one, depicts this dual mobilization in the 1940s and 1950s.

15 Qtd. in Plummer 1998, 140.

16 Reitan 1999, 33.

17 Chanan 1985a, 83.

18 Chanan 1983, 3.

19 Fredric Jameson, foreword to Fernández Retamar 1989, ix, xiii.

20 Jameson 1984, 201.

21 L. Jones 1998, 13.

22 R. Williams 1962, 69.

23 Gosse 1993, 153.

24 Robert Williams, in *The Crusader*, 11 November and 28 November 1959, qtd. in Gosse 1993, 170.

25 L. Jones 1998, 13.

26 Kelley and Esch 1999, 16.

27 Robert F. Williams, interview by Robert Carl Cohen, 1968, Robert Carl Cohen Papers, State Historical Society of Wisconsin, University of Wisconsin at Madison, qtd. in Tyson 1999, 40–41.

28 R. Williams 1962, 51.

29 Tyson 1999, 47.

30 Dittmer 1994, 1–9.

31 R. Williams 1962, 51; Tyson 1999, 81. Tyson points out that Williams was not exactly typically working class. He had three years of college, lived in a house that his family owned free and clear, no small feat in the Jim Crow South, and was a published poet.

32 R. Williams 1962, 68.

33 Qtd. in Tyson 1999, 214.

34 R. Williams 1962, 63.

35 Tyson 1999. Tyson's account of Williams points out that individual NAACP chapters were often more radical than the central leadership. Unfortunately, the conventional view of the NAACP privileges the central office and neglects the push-and-pull dynamic between the central office and its branches.

36 R. Williams 1962, 66.

37 R. Williams 1962, 73.

38 Kelley and Esch 1999, 28.

39 Tyson 1999, 288–95.

40 Tyson 1999, 225.

41 R. Williams 1962, 69–72.

42 Tyson 1999, 232–38.

43 R. Williams 1962, 70–76.

44 Qtd. in Kelley and Esch 1999, 36.

45 L. Jones 1998, 9–10.

46 Baraka 1971, 44.

47 Baraka 1984, 3–11, 113.

48 Baraka 1984, 118; emphasis added.

49 L. Jones 1998, 12.

50 Baraka 1984, 161.

51 Gosse 1993, 53, 99, 94.

52 Benston 1978, x.

53 Gosse 1993, 1.

54 L. Jones 1998, 61.

55 Baraka 1984, 245.

56 L. Jones 1998, 32.

57 Baraka 1984, 246.

58 Baraka 1984, 166.

59 Cruse 1969, 13.

60 L. Jones 1998, 13.

61 Cruse 1984, 356.

62 Cruse 1969, 185–86.

63 Moore 1988, 7, xi. Moore argues that Castro's policy of support for African nations did not translate into support for Afro-Cubans at home.

64 Cruse 1969, 185–86, 195. Further citations for quotes from *Rebellion or Revolution?* appear in parentheses.

65 Cruse 1984, 354. Further citations for quotes from *The Crisis of the Negro Intellectual* appear in parentheses.

66 Woodard 1999, 66.

67 Cruse 1969, 104. Further citations appear in parentheses.

68 L. Jones 1998, 66.

69 Woodard 1999, 57–58.

70 Baraka 1984, 260–62.

71 Woodard 1999, 59.

72 L. Jones 1998, 210.

73 Neal 1966, 4.

74 Baraka 1968, xvii.

75 I am indebted to conversations with Robin D. G. Kelley for this insight.

76 Woodard 1999, 132, 149.

77 Baraka 1968, 298.

2. Union Power, Soul Power

1 Fink and Greenberg 1989.

2 Jameson 1991, 209, qtd. in Denning 1996, 464.

3 Sayres et al. 1884, 3.
4 For examples of this view, see Unger 1974; Howe 1970; Shostak 1969.
5 Levy 1994, 5, 107, 194.
6 Examples of this tendency include J. Miller 1987; Gitlin 1987.
7 Anderson 1996, 32.
8 Though I have borrowed the use of this term from Denning 1996, I am indebted to Fink and Greenberg 1989 for an analysis of 1199's early principles.
9 Fink and Greenberg 1989, 20.
10 Crowe 1986. Thanks to the late Moe Foner for his generosity in giving me access to this and other documents in his personal files.
11 Fink and Greenberg 1989, 25.
12 *1199 Drug News* 1956, 15.
13 Qtd. in Fink and Greenberg 1989, 24.
14 *1199 Drug News* 1956, 15.
15 Fink and Greenberg 1989, 26.
16 This amount reflects the wages of maintenance workers in 1937.
17 *1199 Drug News*, November 1958, 9.
18 *1199 Drug News*, January 1959, 3.
19 Fink and Greenberg 1989, 41.
20 *1199 News*, July–August 1959, 9; Fink and Greenberg 1989, 79.
21 *1199 News*, July–August 1959, 9.
22 *1199 Hospital News*, 8 October 1959, 1.
23 *1199 Hospital News*, 3 December 1959, n.p.
24 *1199 Drug and Hospital News*, May 1967, 17.
25 *1199 Drug and Hospital News*, April 1967, 21.
26 Fink and Greenberg 1989, 100.
27 *1199 News*, February 1972, 14.
28 *1199 Drug and Hospital News*, April 1967, 21.
29 Fink and Greenberg 1989, 13.
30 *1199 Drug and Hospital News*, April 1967, 21.
31 Fink and Greenberg 1989, 220–27.
32 Dreyfuss 1975, qtd. in *1199 News*, September 1975, 10.
33 *1199 Hospital News*, 14 April 1960, 4.
34 Fink and Greenberg 1989, 211.
35 Fink and Greenberg 1989, 113.
36 *1199 Hospital News*, 14 April 1960, 5; *1199 Hospital News*, 14 April 1960, 1.
37 *1199 Hospital News*, 14 April 1960, 5.
38 *1199 Hospital News*, July 1964, 4.
39 *Drug News*, April 1960, 5.
40 Ibid.
41 *1199 Hospital News*, August 1963, 2.
42 *1199 Drug and Hospital News*, April 1967, 2. I am referring to all three versions of *1199*.

43 *1199 Hospital News*, March 1968, 2.

44 *1199 Drug and Hospital News*, April 1967, 21.

45 *1199 Drug and Hospital News*, June 1967, 4.

46 *1199 Drug and Hospital News*, February 1967, 17.

47 *1199 Drug and Hospital News*, March 1969, 24.

48 Ibid.

49 *1199 Hospital News*, July 1964, 5.

50 *1199 Hospital News*, 30 September 1961, 1.

51 *1199 Hospital News*, 1 June 1963, 1.

52 *1199 Hospital News*, 14 April 1960, 4.

53 *1199 Hospital News*, August 1963, 2.

54 *1199 Hospital News*, 20 November 1961, 2; italics mine.

55 *1199 Hospital News*, January 1967, 11.

56 *1199 Hospital News*, February 1968, 2.

57 *1199 Hospital News*, July 1970, 1.

58 *1199 News*, June 1972, national union edition, 13.

59 Fink and Greenberg 1989, 184.

60 *1199 Hospital News*, February 1968, 7.

61 Fink and Greenberg 1989, 184.

62 *1199 Hospital News*, August 1963, 2.

63 *1199 Hospital News*, January 1967, 5.

64 *1199 Drug and Hospital News*, January 1969, 3.

65 *1199 News*, November 1956, 7.

66 *1199 Hospital News*, March 1965, 7.

67 *1199 Hospital News*, January 1964, 5.

68 *1199 Drug and Hospital News*, October 1966, 2.

69 *1199 Drug and Hospital News*, February 1967, 8.

70 *1199 Drug and Hospital News*, October 1969, 19.

71 *1199 Drug and Hospital News*, December 1966, 24.

72 *1199 Drug and Hospital News*, November 1966, 30.

73 *1199 Drug and Hospital News*, August 1967, 4.

74 *1199 Drug and Hospital News*, December 1967, 4, 8.

75 Davis and Dee 1998, 243.

76 Davis and Dee 1998, 244.

77 *1199 Hospital News*, 15 March 1964, 6.

78 *1199 Drug News*, March 1958, 8; *1199 Drug News*, April 1960, 10; *1199 Hospital News*, 15 March 1961, 6.

79 *1199 Hospital News*, April 1966, 8.

80 Moe Foner, "Ossie and Ruby and 1199," 1199 headquarters, New York, photocopy, 3.

81 Davis and Dee 1998, 313.

82 Cruse 1984, 210–11, 193–99.

83 Cruse 1984, 405.

84 *1199 News*, n.d., n.p., photocopy obtained from the files of Moe Foner.

85 *1199 Hospital News*, 11 February 1960, 1.

86 *1199 Hospital News*, April 1968, 16.

87 *1199 Drug and Hospital News*, April 1959, 5.

88 *1199 Drug and Hospital News*, December 1966, 8.

89 Fink and Greenberg 1989, 103.

90 *1199 Drug and Hospital News*, April 1968, 18.

91 *1199 Hospital News*, May 1968, 1.

92 *1199 Hospital News*, October 1970, n.p. The fifteen-story building also held rooms named for Franklin Delano Roosevelt and Eugene Victor Debs.

93 *1199 Hospital News*, July 1968, 29.

94 *1199 Hospital News*, April 1969, 3.

95 *1199 News*, January 1974, 6.

96 *1199 Hospital News*, February 1968, 2.

97 *1199 Hospital News*, July 1971, 24.

98 *1199 Hospital News*, January 1971, 17.

99 *1199 Hospital News*, November 1970, 9.

100 *1199 Hospital News*, July 1971, 15.

101 *1199 Hospital News*, May 1973, n.p.

102 *1199 Hospital News*, December 1971, 21.

103 Given the battles over Israel's status as a settler colony, it is quite likely that disagreement ensued over the event, but this did not prevent it from occurring.

104 *1199 Hospital News*, April 1967, n.p.

105 *1199 Drug and Hospital News*, April 1958, 15.

106 *1199 Hospital News*, March 1971, 11.

107 Foner 1965, n.p.

108 *1199 Hospital News*, October 1971, 8.

109 Foner 1965, n.p.

110 Martin Levin, *New York Times,* 21 March 1965, sec. x, p. 3.

111 Foner 1965, n.p.

112 *Hospital News*, April 1965, 8.

113 1199, brochure, 1199 headquarters, New York, n.d., n.p.

114 *Hospital News*, October 1971, 10.

115 1199, *Gallery 1199: Labor's Only Art Gallery*, brochure, 1199 headquarters, New York, n.p., n.d.

116 *Hospital News*, June 1967, 17.

117 Fink and Greenberg 1989, 142.

118 Moe Foner, interview by the author, New York, 9 October 1996.

119 Qtd. in Fink and Greenberg 1989, 158.

120 Fink and Greenberg 1989, 158.

121 Bobo 1998, 14.

122 *Hospital News*, March 1965, 6–7.

123 *1199 Hospital News*, January 1967, 7.

124 *1199 News*, September 1976, 41.

125 Foner 1965, n.p.

3. Newsreel

1 Allan Siegel, interview by Jackie Stewart, 1997. Photocopy of the transcript given to the author by Stewart.

2 Mekas 1972, 305.

3 Mekas 1972, 305.

4 See Lyons 1996 for a comparison of right-wing and left-wing student activists during the sixties.

5 See Renov 1987b; Renov 1987a; and B. Nichols 1980. For a more extensive analysis of Newsreel in the 1960s, see W. Nichols 1972.

6 Nichols 1972, 52.

7 Renov 2004, 5.

8 Renov 1987a, 14.

9 Renov 1987a, 14.

10 Norm Fruchter, interview by Michael Renov, 1985. Photocopy of transcript given to the author by Renov.

11 Payne 2002a.

12 Norm Fruchter, interview by the author, 1997.

13 Dworkin 1997, 67; Woolen 1973.

14 For a history of ERAP, see Frost 2001.

15 W. Nichols 1972, 52.

16 W. Nichols 1972, 53.

17 Siegel, interview by Jackie Stewart, 1997.

18 T. Anderson 1996, 179.

19 Isserman and Kazin 2004, 193.

20 Mailer 1968.

21 Riggs et al. 1991 brilliantly evokes the visual impact of these violent images; see also S. Torres 2003 for an analysis of the media's role in shaping U.S. audience views of the civil rights movement.

22 Qtd. in W. Nichols 1972, 97.

23 Siegel, interview by Jackie Stewart, 1997.

24 One notable exception to this policy is *America '68* (1968), which is credited to Norman Fruchter and John Douglas.

25 T. Anderson 1996, in particular chapter 5, "The Counterculture."

26 Siegel, interview by Jackie Stewart, 1997.

27 W. Nichols 1972, 6.

28 In a survey of several newspapers in eastern, midwestern, and western large cities, I did not find even one article about the movement. My efforts to find information on the group in New York City turned up scant coverage.

29 W. Nichols 1972, 67.

30 Payne 2002a.

31 Qtd. in Goldman 1983, 18.

32 Payne 2002a.

33 Siegel, interview by Jackie Stewart, 1997.

34 Renov 1987b, 25.

35 Norm Fruchter, interview by Michael Renov, 1985.

36 Siegel, interview by Jackie Stewart, 1997.

37 Mekas 1972, 306.

38 Payne 2002a.

39 Many of these films are no longer in circulation. In those cases, I am relying on a description of their content featured in a 1969 Newsreel film list obtained from Third World Newsreel's files.

40 Qtd. in W. Nichols 1972, 75.

41 The Columbia Strike Committee, *Why We Strike*, 1968; available at http://beatl.barnard.columbia.edu/learn/archives.htm. As I write this in 2005, Columbia University is again planning an expansion into the surrounding neighborhood. This time the proposed site is a section of Manhattanville bordered by West 125th Street on the south and 133rd Street on the north and extending from Broadway on the east to 12th Avenue on the west. The university administration appears to have learned some of the lessons from the 1968 shutdown and has formed a community advisory committee with representation from dozens of community-based organizations. Whether the result will be any more popular with city residents than the gymnasium project remains to be seen.

42 Allan Siegel, interview by the author, 1998.

43 Siegel, interview by Jackie Stewart, 1997.

44 W. Nichols 1972, 78; italics mine.

45 Renov 1987a, 14.

46 "Newsreel Footage Seized" 1969, 32.

47 Fruchter, interview by Michael Renov, 1985.

48 B. Nichols 1980, 62.

49 Renov 1987a, 14.

50 W. Nichols 1972, 61.

51 Qtd. in Newsreel 1968–69, 43.

52 B. Nichols 1980, 74.

53 Newsreel 1968–69, 46.

54 Newsreel 1968–69, 46.

55 Nichols 1972, 93.

56 *Rat*, October 29–November 12, 1969, 8.

57 Qtd. in W. Nichols 1972, 78.

58 Dziga Vertov, "Kinoks Revolution," qtd. in W. Nichols 1972, 9.

59 Newsreel 1968–69, 44.

60 Newsreel 1969. This source was obtained from Third World Newsreel files with the permission of Ada Gay Griffin.

61 Newsreel 1968–69, 47.

62 Renov 1987a, 14.

63 Siegel, interview by Jackie Stewart, 1997.

64 Renov 1987a, 13.

65 Siegel, interview by Jackie Stewart, 1997.

66 W. Nichols 1972, 155.

67 Siegel, interview by Jackie Stewart, 1997.

68 Siegel, interview by the author, 1998.

69 Wilkerson 2001.

70 Richard C. Smith to Sarah Cooper, 15 December 1988, list of films donated to Southern California Library for Social Research, Third World Newsreel files, New York City. This material was obtained with the permission of Ada Gay Griffin, former director of Third World Newsreel.

71 B. Nichols 1980, 48.

72 W. Nichols 1972, 144.

73 Fruchter, interview by Michael Renov, 1985.

74 Qtd. in Nichols 1972, 142.

75 Nichols 1972, 144.

76 T. Anderson 1996, 335.

77 B. Nichols 1980, 27.

78 Newsreel 1971a. All quotations from the film are from the author's transcription.

79 Allan Siegel, e-mail communication with the author, 24 May 2004.

80 For a more recent film on the Young Lords Party in New York, see Morales 1996.

81 A. Torres 1998, 7.

82 A. Torres 1998, 3–4.

83 Morales 1998, 210.

84 Rodriguez-Morazzani 1998, 29.

85 Guzmán 1998, 161. Guzmán recalls that Newsreel film crews accompanied the Lords to street corners where they filmed drug dealers bribing police officers. When they approached several local television networks with the proof, none would use the footage.

86 Rodriguez-Morazzani 1998, 41–42.

87 Rodriguez-Morazzani 1998, 42–43.

88 Morales 1998, 222.

89 Guzmán 1998, 157.

90 Young Lords Party and Abramson 1971, 8–9.

91 Morales 1998, 215.

92 Lao 1995, 36. For information on the massacre, see M. Lee 2003.

93 Young Lords Party and Abramson 1971, 10.

94 Morales 1998, 218.

95 Young Lords Party and Abramson 1971, 150.

96 "Young Lords Organize March to U.N." 1970, n.p.

97 Guzmán 1998, 157.

98 Pietri 1974, 1–11.

99 In their accounts of the takeover, both Guzmán and Morales deflect this intra-ethnic tension by blaming the church's exiled Cuban minister for the standoff. However, the minister clearly had the support of the congregation. See Morales 1998, 213; and Guzmán 1998, 160.

100 Lao 1995, 38.

101 Young Lords Party and Abramson 1971, 77.

102 For a reading of how the Black Panther Party fashioned an ideologically meaningful style, one that was interpreted and reinterpreted by the mainstream media, see Singh 1998a.

103 Singh 1998a, 83.

104 Guzmán 1998, 160.

105 Young Lords Party and Abramson 1971, 78.

106 B. Nichols 1980, 158

107 Lao 1995, 39.

108 "Young Lords Organize March to U.N." 1970, n.p.

109 Schwartz 1986.

110 Newsreel 1971b. All quotations transcribed from the film by the author. The film's speakers are never identified, perhaps because the filmmakers were afraid that to do so might unintentionally make them complicit in law-enforcement efforts to identify and then neutralize the organization's members.

111 Buck and Fainstein 1992, 42–43.

112 Schwartz 1993, 61–113. Schwartz's book provides an excellent history of the factors leading to the pact between Moses, reformers, and politicians that produced New York's disastrous urban renewal policy.

113 Schwartz 1993, 199.

114 "Fifty-five in State Senate Ask U.S. Aid to City Slums as Disaster Areas" 1970.

115 Cross and Waldinger 1992, 154.

116 Buck, Drennan, and Newton 1992, 92.

117 Harloe, Marcuse, and Smith 1992, 182.

118 Shipler 1969, 1, 40.

119 Qtd. in Shipler 1970, 47.

120 Harloe, Marcuse, and Smith 1992, 188.

121 "Columbia S.D.S. Calls for One-Day Strike" 1969, 30.

122 Castells 1983, 176.

123 B. Nichols 1980, 120.

124 James 1956.

4. Third World Newsreel

1 Hall 1996, 141–42.

2 Althusser 2001, 85–133.

3 The phrase *modes of oppression* in connection with this project emerged in a fruitful exchange I had with Robert Hill at UCLA's Third World Lecture Series on 17 May 2002.

4 This quotation is amended from Renov 1988, 10–12.

5 Nichols 1980, 27.

6 Choy puts the number at five, while Nichols asserts there were only four at that meeting. See Milner 1982, 21; Nichols 1980, 28.

7 Renov 1987b, 26.

8 Nichols 1980, 30.

9 Susan Robeson, interview by the author, 1997.

10 Milner 1982, 21.

11 For these conflicting accounts, see Payne 2002a; Nichols 1980, 28.

12 Nichols 1980, 31.

13 This mandate was mentioned in a position paper distributed by San Francisco Newsreel in the midst of their group's dissolution. It was obtained from Susan Robeson's personal files.

14 Milner 1982, 21.

15 Robeson and Nichols differ on the specific month and year in which the white caucus left. See Nichols 1980, 30; Robeson, interview by the author, 1997.

16 Milner 1982, 21.

17 Milner 1982, 21.

18 MacDonald 1998b, 200.

19 Ibid., 200–202.

20 Robeson, interview by the author, 1997.

21 In 1971, before Robeson joined Newsreel, she wrote a long position paper in which she outlined her intention to create a national Third World media center that would bring together black and Third World political artists to make films and operate a mobile film and sound unit that would show films in the streets to local communities. This paper was obtained from the personal files of Susan Robeson.

22 In fact, to this day Third World Newsreel continues to be run by women of color.

23 Third World Newsreel, "Act First, Then Speak," 1972,. This statement was originally obtained from Susan Robeson's personal files. There is some conflicting evidence concerning the document's moment of production. Susan Robeson wrote 1973 on the top of her copy, but when the author surveyed Third World Newsreel's files, this document was attached to Newsreel's national newsletter, entitled "Focal Point" and dated October 1972.

24 Third World Newsreel, "Organizational Principles of Third World Newsreel," 1973. This was obtained from Susan Robeson's personal files.

25 Milner 1982, 21.

26 Hall 1980, 308.

27 Singh 1998b, 479.

28 Fanon 1963, 233.

29 Newsreel, "Organizational Principles of Third World Newsreel."

30 Marcuse 1969, 51.

31 Newsreel, "Organizational Principles of Third World Newsreel."

32 Gramsci 1978, 6.

33 In the next few years, Third World Newsreel released *We Demand Freedom* (1972), *In the Event Anyone Disappears* (1973), and *Inside Women Inside* (1975). Each film elucidated the structural similarities between Third World life inside and outside the U.S. penal system. In *We Demand Freedom*, contrasting footage of U.S. prisons, Japanese-American concentration camps, and Vietnam "trace[d] the development of prison philosophy," demonstrating how "prisons have been used historically and their function today" according to an undated Third World Newsreel catalog, most likely from 1973. *In the Event Anyone Disappears* and *Inside Women Inside* explored the nascent prisoners' rights movement largely through testimonials from male and female inmates in New Jersey prisons.

34 Nichols 1980, 53.

35 Foner and Allen 1987, xiii.

36 See Robinson 1983, 308–9.

37 Kelley 1990, 13–14.

38 West 1996, 84.

39 Peery 1994, 71. Further citations to *Black Fire* appear in parentheses.

40 Elbaum 2002, 103.

41 Peery 1972, 3. Further citations to *The Negro National Colonial Question* appear in parentheses.

42 Marx 1962, 107.

43 Peery 1972, 18.

44 Peery is quoting Charles Mann, *Stalin's Thought Illuminates Problems of Negro Freedom Struggle* (1953).

45 He also sounds remarkably reminiscent of the white social scientists' essentializing project critiqued in Kelley 1997, 15–42.

46 Stalin 1934, 22.

47 Elbaum 2002, 134.

48 MacDonald 1998b, 200–202.

49 Qtd. in Nichols 1980, 35.

50 Peery 1972, 97.

51 Nichols 1980, 33–34.

52 These conditions were detailed in the 1972 McKay Report, qtd. in Bell 1985, 16–27.

53 Joseph Martin et al., "Attica: Anatomy of a Tragedy," *New York Daily News*, 4–8 October 1971, qtd. in Badillo and Haynes 1972, 27–28.

54 Bell 1985, 1.

55 Third World Newsreel 1972b. All quotations are taken from the author's transcription of the film.

56 Bell 1985, 18.

57 I am indebted to Lisa Lowe who used this phrase and sparked this insight in an 11 March 2004 e-mail.

58 For insight into the connection between the prison system and civic death, I am

indebted to Dylan Rodriguez's paper, "Languages of Death: Captive Radical Intellectuals and the Political Logic of Mass Incarceration," delivered at the American Studies Association Annual Conference, 18 October 2003.

59 Qtd. in Chanan 1985a, 180.

60 Chanan 1985a, 179.

61 M. Williams 1970.

62 There was at least one other woman named Marietta, but none of the early Third World members I interviewed could remember her last name. The group's membership tended to wildly fluctuate as money became scarce and responsibility became too great. Robeson, Choy, and Siegel were the only constants for much of the 1970s.

63 Nichols 1980, 159.

64 Robeson, interview by the author, 1997.

65 I obtained copies of several film request letters from Susan Robeson's personal files.

66 Excerpt from two-page photocopy from Susan Robeson's personal files.

67 Chanan 1985a, 75.

68 Excerpt from 1975 Higher Ground Cinema announcement from Susan Robeson's personal files.

69 Allan Siegel, interview by the author, 1998.

70 Susan Robeson, "Personal Notes," Third World Newsreel, New York, 1971, n.p.

71 Conference programs were all obtained from Susan Robeson's personal files.

72 This was obtained from Susan Robeson's personal files.

73 This was obtained from Susan Robeson's personal files.

74 Robeson, interview by the author, 1997.

75 Susan Robeson, "Personal Notes," Third World Newsreel, New York, 1974, n.p.

76 Nichols 1980, 26.

77 Ibid.

5. Angela Y. Davis

1 For an excellent introductory essay, see J. James 1998. The production of the *Angela Y. Davis Reader* has made it possible to do the much-needed critical work on Davis. Kelley 2002 also discusses Davis.

2 See Lowe 1998; Gordon 1998/1999.

3 Fanon 1963, 248.

4 A. Davis 1974, 110.

5 This quote appears in a 1970 pamphlet written by the National United Committee to Free Angela Davis, but no original source for Davis's words is given.

6 J. James 1998, 3.

7 See Kelley 1990.

8 See Stepto 1979.

9 A. Davis 1974, 82.

10 Nadelson 1972, 65.

11 Yancy 2000, 137.

12 A. Davis 1974, 103.

13 Nadelson 1972, 67, 69.

14 Nadelson 1972, 75.

15 Baldwin was scheduled to deliver a series of lectures on literature during Davis's freshman year, but the Cuban Missile Crisis prompted him to cancel most of them. However, the two did maintain contact. Baldwin even wrote an open letter in defense of Davis when she was put on trial in connection with Jonathan Jackson's fatal rescue attempt of his brother. For Baldwin's letter, see Davis et al. 1971, 13–19.

16 A. Davis 1974, 129.

17 A. Davis 1974, 129.

18 Kelley 1999, 1037.

19 I am indebted to Robert Hill for the use of the phrase *modes of oppression* in connection with Davis.

20 The logic of U.S. global domination is still dependent on distinguishing between citizens and noncitizens within the body politic, whether they are disfranchised U.S. nationals or legal or "illegal" immigrants.

21 For an interesting exchange about the student Left's goals and tactics, see "Herbert Marcuse and Theodor Adorno's Correspondence" 1999.

22 Katz 1982, 17.

23 Katz 1982, 33–34.

24 Jay 1973, 29.

25 Katz 1982, 100. For a detailed intellectual and social history of the Frankfurt School's early period, see Jay 1973.

26 Qtd. in Nadelson 1972, 102.

27 Jay 1973, 40–44. Further citations to *The Dialectical Imagination* appear in parentheses.

28 Horkheimer expands on and refines the concept of critical theory in Horkheimer and Adorno 2002.

29 Horkheimer 1972, 205.

30 Hoy and McCarthy 1994, 16.

31 Hoy and McCarthy 1994, 8.

32 Jay 1973, 61.

33 Hoy and McCarthy 1994, 9.

34 Davis et al. 1971, 180.

35 Hoy and McCarthy 1994, 23.

36 Gottlieb 1992, 18.

37 Katz 1982, 92.

38 Katz 1982, 144.

39 Kelley 2002, 2.

40 Marcuse 1969, 4.

41 Hoy and McCarthy 1994, 23.

42 Qtd. in Katz 1982, 144.

43 Kelley 2002, 9.

44 Jay 1973, 64.

45 Jay 1973, 64.

46 Pickford 1997, 254.

47 Schoolman 1980, 291.

48 Schoolman 1980, 291–92.

49 Marcuse 1969, 10.

50 Marcuse 1969, viii.

51 Marcuse 1971, 22.

52 A. Davis 1974, 120. Further citations to *Angela Davis* appear in parentheses.

53 Nadelson 1972, 119.

54 Aptheker 1999, 9.

55 Aptheker 1999, 16–21, 23.

56 Davis et al. 1971, 26. Further citations to *If They Come in the Morning* appear in parentheses.

57 For more on this, see C. E. Jones 1998.

58 Davis et al. 1971, 27.

59 See Singh 1998a.

6. Shot in Watts

1 Qtd. in George 1987, 177.

2 See George 1987, 177, and S. E. Smith 1999.

3 S. E. Smith 1999, 237.

4 Masilela 1993a, 107.

5 Noriega 2000, 101–12.

6 Snead 1995, 23.

7 Masilela 1993a, 107.

8 Bambara 1993, 120.

9 Taylor 1989a, 96.

10 Willemen 1989, 15.

11 Willemen 1989, 7.

12 Chanan 1985a, 252.

13 Masilela 1993a, 110, 6.

14 Burnett and Lane 1991.

15 Klotman and Cutler 1999, 352.

16 Masilela 1993a, 110.

17 M. Martin 1997, 273.

18 Qtd. in M. Martin 1997, 286.

19 See Guevara 2000.

20 Ntongela Masilela, interview by the author, 2003.

21 Guerrero 2000, 34.

22 Auster and Quart 1984, 8.

23 Horne 1995, 35.

24 Horne 1995, 3.

25 *Los Angeles Times*, 13 October 1965, qtd. in Horne 1995, 41.

26 Masilela, interview by the author, 2003.

27 Qtd. in MacDonald 1998a, 107; Charles Burnett, interview by the author, 2002.

28 Burnett, interview by the author, 2002.

29 MacDonald 1998a, 108.

30 Masilela, interview by the author, 2003.

31 Taylor 1986, 2.

32 Masilela, interview by the author, 2003.

33 Gerima 1989, 86.

34 Guerrero 2000, 34.

35 Young 1993.

36 Taylor 1986, 1.

37 Masilela, interview by the author, 2003.

38 Reynaud 1991, 328.

39 Snead 1995, 23.

40 Kaplan 1997, 219.

41 Taylor 1996, 233.

42 Masilela 1993a, 111.

43 Gabriel 1982; Gabriel 1985; Gerima 1995.

44 Bambara 1993, 128.

45 MacDonald 1998a, 110.

46 Masilela 1993a, 109.

47 Fanon 1963, 38.

48 Gibson 1999, 338.

49 Gibson 1999, 342.

50 Fanon 1963, 152.

51 Said 1999, 211; see also Parry 1999, 227.

52 Fanon 1963, 175.

53 Julien 2000, 159.

54 Parry 1999, 234.

55 Baldwin 1961, qtd. in Parry 1999, 240.

56 Fanon 1963, 245.

57 Fanon 1963, 238.

58 Ngugi 1972, 11.

59 Masilela, interview by the author, 2003; Burnett, interview by the author, 2002.

60 Masilela, interview by the author, 2003.

61 Masilela 1993a, 109.

62 Murashige 1997, 184.

63 Gerima, " 'Fireplace-Cinema' (Gathering, Warming, Sharing)," qtd. in Murashige 1997, 183.

64 Gerima et al. 1993. All quotations from the film have been transcribed by the author.

65 Murashige 1997, 187.

66 Ibid., 200.

67 Burnett 1977. All quotations from the film were transcribed by the author.

68 Reynaud 1991, 326.

69 Burnett, interview by the author, 2002.

70 Burnett, interview by the author, 2002; Reynaud 1991, 326.

71 Snead 1995, 22.

Coda

1 See Williams 1974.

2 Chatterjee 1993, 237.

Bibliography
and Filmography

•

Print Publications

Abodunrin, Femi. 1996. *Blackness: Culture, Ideology, and Discourse; A Comparative Study*. Bayreuth, Germany: E. Breitinger.

Ackah, William. 1999. *Pan-Africanism: Exploring the Contradictions; Politics, Identity, and Development in Africa and The African Diaspora*. Aldershot, U.K.: Ashgate.

Adler, Patricia Rae. 1976. "Watts: From Suburb to Black Ghetto." Ph.D. diss., University of Southern California.

Alexander, Karen. 1993. "*Daughters of the Dust.*" *Sight and Sound* 3 (9): 20–22.

Allen, Gary. 1967. *The Plan to Burn Los Angeles*. Belmont, Mass.: American Opinion.

Allen, Robert Loring. [1969] 1992. *Black Awakening in Capitalist America: An Analytic History*. Trenton, N.J.: Africa World Press.

Althusser, Louis. 2001. "Ideology and Ideological State Apparatuses: Notes Towards an Investigation." In *Lenin and Philosophy and Other Essays*, 85–133. Trans. Ben Brewster. New York: Monthly Review Press.

Anderson, Terry H. 1996. *The Movement and the Sixties*. New York: Oxford University Press.

Appadurai, Arjun. 1996. *Modernity at Large: Cultural Dimensions of Globalization*. Minneapolis: University of Minnesota Press.

Aptheker, Bettina. 1999. *The Morning Breaks: The Trial of Angela Davis*. 2d ed. Ithaca, N.Y.: Cornell University Press.

Arana, R. Victoria. 2002. "The Epic Imagination: A Conversation with Chinua Achebe at Annandale-on-Hudson, October 31, 1998." *Callaloo* 25 (5): 505–26.

Armes, Roy. 1995. "Culture and National Identity." In *Cinemas of The Black Diaspora: Diversity, Dependence, and Oppositionality*, ed. Michael T. Martin, 25–39. Detroit: Wayne State University Press.

Arthur, Paul. 1999. "Springing Tired Chains: Experimental Film and Video." In *Struggles for Representation: African American Documentary Film and Video*, ed. Phyllis R. Klotman and Janet K. Cutler, 268–97. Bloomington: Indiana University Press.

Association of Third World Filmworkers. N.d. "Principles of Unity." N.p.

Auchincloss, Eve, and Nancy Lynch. 1989. "Disturber of The Peace: James Baldwin; An Interview." In *Conversations with James Baldwin*, ed. Fred L. Standley and Louis H. Pratt, 64–83. Jackson: University Press of Mississippi.

Auster, Al, and Leonard Quart. 1984. "American Cinema of the Sixties." *Cineaste* 13 (2): 4–12.

Avellar, José Carlos. 2000. "From the Spontaneity of Speech to the Order of Writing: Brazilian Film From Cinema-Novo to 'Central Do Brasil.'" *Kosmorama*, no. 225: 31–40.

Axel, Brian Keith. 2002. "The Diasporic Imagination." *Public Culture* 14 (2): 411–27.

Bacciocco, Edward J., Jr. 1975. *The New Left in America: Reform to Revolution 1956 to 1970*. Stanford, Calif.: Hoover Institution Press.

Backstein, Karen. 1992. "The Cinematic Jazz of Julie Dash." *Cineaste* 19 (4): 88.

Badillo, Herman, and Milton Haynes. 1972. *A Bill of No Rights: Attica and the American Prison System*. New York: Outerbridge and Lazard.

Baldwin, James. 1961. *Nobody Knows My Name*. New York: Vintage.

Bambara, Toni Cade. 1993. "Reading the Signs, Empowering the Eye: *Daughters of the Dust* and the Black Independent Cinema Movement." In *Black American Cinema*, ed. Diawara Manthia, 118–45. New York: Routledge.

Baraka, Ameer. 1968. Foreword to *Black Fire: An Anthology of Afro-American Writing*, ed. LeRoi Jones and Larry Neal. New York: Morrow.

Baraka, Amiri. 1971. *Raise, Race, Rays, Raze: Essays since 1965*. New York: Random House.

——. 1984. *The Autobiography of LeRoi Jones/Amiri Baraka*. New York: Freundlich Books.

——. 1996. "Revolutionary Culture and the Future of Pan African Culture." In *African Intellectual Heritage: A Book of Sources*, ed. Molefi Kete Asante and Abu. S. Abarry. Philadelphia: Temple University Press.

Barnes, Denise. "Hollywood's Color Barrier." *Insight on the News*, 2 March 1998, 38.

Barrera, Mario, Carlos Muñoz, and Carlos Omelas. 1972. "The Barrio as Internal 'Colony.'" *Urban Affairs Annual Review* 6: 465–98.

Basch, Linda, Nina Glick Schiller, and Cristina Szanton Blanc. 1994. *Nations Unbound: Transnational Projects, Postcolonial Predicaments, and Deterritorialized Nation-States*. Basel: Gordon and Breach.

Bauman, Robert Alan. 1998. "Race, Class, and Political Power: The Implementation of the War on Poverty in Los Angeles." Ph.D. diss., University of California, Santa Barbara.

Beiner, Ronald, ed. 1999. *Theorizing Nationalism*. Albany: State University of New York Press.

Bell, Malcolm. 1985. *The Turkey Shoot: Tracking the Attica Cover-Up*. New York: Grove.

Belton, John, ed. 1996. *Movies and Mass Culture*. New Brunswick, N.J.: Rutgers University Press.

Benner, Erica. 1995. *Really Existing Nationalisms: A Post-communist View from Marx and Engels*. Oxford: Clarendon.

Benston, Kimberly, ed. 1978. *Imamu Amira Baraka (LeRoi Jones): A Collection of Critical Essays*. Englewood Cliffs, N.J.: Prentice-Hall.

Berman, Ronald. 1968. *America In the Sixties: An Intellectual History*. New York: Free Press.

Bernardi, Daniel. 1996. *The Birth of Whiteness: Race and the Emergence of U.S. Cinema*. New Brunswick, N.J.: Rutgers University Press.

Betsworth, Roger G. 1980. *The Radical Movement of the 1960s*. Metuchen, N.J.: Scarecrow.

Bhabha, Homi K. 1990. "DissemiNation: Time, Narrative, and the Margins of the Modern Nation." In *Nation and Narration*, ed. Bhabha, 291–323. London: Routledge.

"Black Filmmakers Win Top Awards at Festival." 1990. *Jet*, 19 February, 59.

"*The Black Scholar* Interviews James Baldwin." 1989. In *Conversations with James Baldwin*, ed. Fred L. and Louis H. Pratt, 142–59. Jackson: University Press of Mississippi.

Bobo, Jacqueline. 2001. *Daughters of the Dust*. In *Black Feminist Cultural Criticism*, ed. Bobo, 63–85. Malden, Mass.: Blackwell.

——. 1998. "Black Women's Films: Genesis of a Tradition." In *Black Women Film and Video Artists*, ed. Jacqueline Bobo. New York: Routledge.

Boesel, David, and Peter H. Rossi, eds. 1971. *Cities under Siege: An Anatomy of the Ghetto Riots, 1964–1968*. New York: Basic Books.

Bonnett, Aubrey W., and G. Llewellyn Watson. 1990. *Emerging Perspectives on the Black Diaspora*. Lanham, Md.: University Press of America.

Booth, David. 1976. "Cuba, Color and the Revolution." *Science and Society* 11 (2): 129–72.

Boskin, Joseph. 1976. *Urban Racial Violence in the Twentieth Century*. 2d ed. Beverly Hills, Calif.: Glencoe.

Bracks, Lean'tin L. 1998. *Writings on Black Women of the Diaspora: History, Language, and Identity*. New York: Garland.

Brant, Beto, et al. 1998. *Cinema Novo and Beyond*. Rio de Janeiro, Brasil: Riofilm: Prefeitura Da Cidade Do Rio De Janeiro Secretaria de Cultura.

Brehony, K. J., and N. Rassool, eds. 1999. *Nationalisms Old and New*. New York: St. Martin's Press.

Brouwer, Joel R. 1995. "Repositioning: Center and Margin in Julie Dash's *Daughters of the Dust*." *African American Review* 29 (1): 5–16.

Brun, Gustavo. 1996. "Learning While You Make Films: The True Lessons of Cinema Novo." *Blimp* (spring): 37–41.

Buck, Nick, Matthew Drennan, and Kenneth Newton. 1992. "Dynamics of the Metro-politan Economy." In *Divided Cities: New York and London in the Contemporary World*, ed. Susan S. Fainstein, Ian Gordon, and Michael Harloe, 68–105. Oxford: Blackwell.

Buck, Nick, and Norman Fainstein. 1992. "A Comparative History, 1880–1973." In *Divided Cities: New York and London in the Contemporary World*, ed. Susan S. Fainstein, Ian Gordon, and Michael Harloe, 29–68. Oxford: Blackwell.

Bullock, Paul, ed. 1969. *Watts: The Aftermath; An Inside View of the Ghetto*. New York: Grove.

Burby, Liza N. 1997. *The Watts Riot*. San Diego, Calif.: Lucent Books.

Burnett, Charles, and Charles Lane. 1991. "One on One: Charles Burnett and Charles Lane." *American Film* 16 (8): 40–43.

Burton, Julianne. 1985. "Film and Revolution in Cuba: The First Twenty-five Years." In *Jump Cut: Hollywood, Politics, and Counter-cinema*, ed. Peter Steven, 344–60. Toronto: Between the Lines.

Bush, Rod. 1999. *We Are Not What We Seem: Black Nationalism and Class Struggle in the American Century*. New York: New York University Press.

Cabral, Amílcar. 1973. *Return to the Source: Selected Speeches*. Ed. Africa Information Service. New York: Monthly Review Press.

Campt, Tina. 2002. "The Crowded Spaces of Diaspora: Intercultural Address and the Tensions of Diasporic Relation." *Radical History Review*, no. 83: 94–113.

Canby, Vincent. 1990. "Scene: Black Middle Class Home; Enter a Comic, Lost Demon." *New York Times*, 5 October.

Carby, Hazel V. 1999. *Cultures in Babylon: Black Britain and African America*. London: Verso.

Carmichael, Stokely, and Charles V. Hamilton. 1967. *Black Power: The Politics of Liberation in America*. New York: Random House.

Carson, Clayborne. 1981. *In Struggle: SNCC and the Black Awakening of the 1960s*. Cambridge, Mass.: Harvard University Press.

Carvalheiro, Manuel. 1982. "Le dernier entretien aven Glauber Rocha." *Revue du Cinéma* (October): 65–76.

Castells, Manuel. 1983. *The City and the Grassroots: A Cross-cultural Theory of Urban Social Movements*. Berkeley: University of California Press.

Cham, Mbye Baboucar. 1984. "Art and Ideology in the Work of Sembène Ousmane and Hailé Gerima." *Présence Africaine* 129 (1): 79–91.

Cham, Mbye Baboucar, and Claire Andrade-Watkins, eds. 1988. *Blackframes: Critical Perspectives on Black Independent Cinema*. Cambridge, Mass.: MIT Press.

Chanan, Michael. 1983. *Twenty-Five Years of the New Latin American Cinema*. London: Channel Four Television: BFI Books.

——. 1985a. *The Cuban Image: Cinema and Cultural Politics in Cuba*. London: British Film Institute.

——. 1985b. "The Documentary in the Revolution." In *The Cuban Image: Cinema and Cultural Politics in Cuba*. London: British Film Institute, 148–76.

———. 1985c. "Imperfect Cinema and the Seventies." In *The Cuban Image: Cinema and Cultural Politics in Cuba*. London: British Film Institute, 251–74.

———. 1985d. "The Revolution in the Documentary." In *The Cuban Image: Cinema and Cultural Politics in Cuba*. London: British Film Institute, 177–202.

———, ed. 1983. *Twenty-five Years of the New Latin American Cinema*. London: British Film Institute.

"Charles Burnett Gets Award for 'To Sleep with Anger.' " 1991. *Jet*, 4 February, 17.

Chatterjee, Partha. 1993. *The Nation and Its Fragments: Colonial and Postcolonial Histories*. Princeton, N.J.: Princeton University Press.

Cineaste. 1995. "Resolutions of the Third World Film-Makers Meeting, Algiers, December 5–14, 1973." In *Cinemas of the Black Diaspora: Diversity, Dependence, and Oppositionality*, ed. Michael T. Martin. Detroit: Wayne State University Press.

Clifford, James. 1994. "Diasporas." *Cultural Anthropology* 9 (3): 302–38.

Cohen, Jerry, and William S. Murphy. 1966. *Burn, Baby, Burn! The Los Angeles Race Riot, August, 1965*. New York: Dutton.

Cole, Johnetta B. 1980. "Race toward Equality: The Impact of the Cuban Revolution on Racism." *Black Scholar* 11 (8): 2–25.

Collins, Keith E. 1980. *Black Los Angeles: The Maturing of the Ghetto, 1940–1950*. Saratoga, Calif.: Century Twenty One.

"Columbia S.D.S. Calls for One-Day Strike." 1969. *New York Times*, March 18.

Conniff, Michael L., and Thomas J. Davis. 1994. *Africans in the Americas: A History of the Black Diaspora*. New York: St. Martin's Press.

Corliss, Richard. 1990. "To Sleep with Anger." *Time*, 22 October, 63.

Cross, Malcolm, and Roger Waldinger. 1992. "Migrants, Minorities, and the Ethnic Division of Labor." In *Divided Cities: New York and London in the Contemporary World*, ed. Susan S. Fainstein, Ian Gordon, and Michael Harloe, 151–75. Oxford: Blackwell.

Crowe, Kenneth. 1986. "Brothers in Dissent." *Newsday*, 24 November, 3.

Crump, Spencer. 1966. *Black Riot in Los Angeles: The Story of the Watts Tragedy*. Los Angeles: Trans-Anglo Books.

Cruse, Harold. 1969. *Rebellion or Revolution?* New York: Morrow.

———. [1967] 1984. *The Crisis of the Negro Intellectual*. New York: Morrow.

———. 2002. "Rebellion or Revolution? I." In *The Essential Harold Cruse: A Reader*, ed. William Jelani Cobb, 152–56. New York: Palgrave.

Cunneen, Joseph. 1992. "*Daughters of the Dust*." *National Catholic Reporter*, 27 March, 14.

Dash, Julie. 1995. "Making *Daughters of the Dust*." In *Cinemas of the Black Diaspora: Diversity, Dependence, and Oppositionality*, ed. Micahel T. Martin, 376–88. Detroit: Wayne State University Press.

Dash, Julie, and Houston A. Baker Jr. 1992. "Not without My Daughters." *Transition*, no. 57:150–66.

Dauphin, Gary. 1997. "Above It All." *Village Voice*, 4 February, 76–77.

Davis, Angela Y. 1974. *Angela Davis: An Autobiography*. New York: Random House.

——. 1981. *Women, Race and Class*. New York: Vintage Books.

——. 1998. *Blues Legacies and Black Feminism: Gertrude "Ma" Rainey, Bessie Smith, and Billie Holiday*. New York: Pantheon Books.

——. 2003. *Are Prisons Obsolete?* New York: Seven Stories Press.

Davis, Angela Y., et al. 1971. *If They Come in the Morning: Voices of Resistance*. New York: Third Press.

Davis, Ossie, and Ruby Dee. 1998. *With Ossie and Ruby: In This Life Together*. New York: Morrow.

Davis, Zeinabu Irene. 1989. "The Future of Black Film: The Debate Continues." *Black Film Review* 5 (4): 6–9, 26–28.

——. 1990. "Daughters of the Dust." *Black Film Review* 6 (1): 12–17, 20–21.

Denning, Michael. 1996. *The Cultural Front: The Laboring of American Culture in the Twentieth Century*. London: Verso.

——. 2004. *Culture in the Age of Three Worlds*. London: Verso.

Diawara, Manthia. 1990. "Black British Cinema: Spectatorship and Identity Formation in Territories." *Public Culture* 3 (1): 33–47.

——. 1999. "The 'I' Narrator in Black Diaspora Documentary." In *Struggles for Representation: African American Documentary Film and Video*, ed. Phyllis Klotman and Janet K. Cutler, 315–29. Bloomington: Indiana University Press.

Diegues, Carlos. 1994. "Black God, White Devil, and Cinema-Novo." *Positif*, no. 400: 31–32.

——. 1997. "Cinema Novo." In *New Latin American Cinema, Vol. 1: Theory, Practices and Transcontinental Articulations*, ed. Michael T. Martin, 272–74. Detroit: Wayne State University Press.

Diggins, John Patrick. *The Rise and Fall of the American Left*. New York: Norton, 1992.

Dimock, Wai Chee. 2001. "Deep Time: American Literature and World History." *American Literary History* 13 (4): 755–75.

Dittmer, John. 1994. *Local People: The Struggle for Civil Rights in Mississippi*. Urbana-Champaign: University of Illinois Press.

Dixon, Wheeler Winston. 1995. "The Practice of Theory, the Theory of Practice: The Post-colonial Cinema of Maureen Blackwood and the Sankofa Collective." *Film Criticism* 20 (1–2): 131–43.

Dreyfuss, Claudia. 1975. "Doris Turner: The Woman from 1199." *New York News*.

Dubey, Madhu. 1998. "The 'True Lie' of the Nation: Fanon and Feminism." *Differences* 10 (2): 1–29.

Du Bois, W. E. B. 1982. "The Bandung Conference" [1955]. In *Writings by W. E. B. Du Bois in Periodicals Edited by Others*, ed. Herbert Aptheker. Millwood, N.Y.: Kraus-Thomson.

——. [1903] 2003. *The Souls of Black Folk*. New York: Modern Library.

Dworkin, Dennis. 1997. *Cultural Marxism in Postwar Britain: History, the New Left, and the Origins of Cultural Studies*. Durham, N.C.: Duke University Press.

Ebron, Paulla A. 1998. "Enchanted Memories of Regional Difference in African American Culture." *American Anthropologist* 99 (1): 94–105.

"Echoes from the Past: Screenplays of the African Americans." *African American Review* 28 (2): 317.

Edwards, Brent Hayes. 2003. *The Practice of Diaspora: Literature, Translation, and the Rise of Black Internationalism*. Cambridge, Mass.: Harvard University Press.

Elbaum, Max. 2002. *Revolution in the Air: Sixties Radicals Turn to Lenin, Mao, and Che*. London: Verso.

Fairchild, Halford H. 1994. "Frantz Fanon's *The Wretched of the Earth* in Contemporary Perspective." *Journal of Black Studies* 25 (2): 191–99.

Fanon, Frantz. 1963. *The Wretched of the Earth*. Trans. Constance Farrington. New York: Grove.

———. 1965. *Studies in a Dying Colonialism*. Trans. Haakon Chevalier. New York: Monthly Review Press.

———. 1967. *Black Skin, White Masks*. Trans. Charles Lam Markmann. New York: Grove Press.

Farber, David R. 1994. *The Sixties: From Memory to History*. Chapel Hill: University of North Carolina Press.

Fernández Retamar, Roberto. 1989. *Caliban and Other Esssays*. Trans. Edward Baker. Minneapolis: University of Minnesota Press.

Ferreira, Patricia. 1993. "The Triple Duty of a Black Woman Filmmaker: An Interview with Carmen Coustaut." *African American Review* 27 (3): 433–42.

"Fifty-five in State Senate Ask U.S. Aid to City Slums as Disaster Areas." 1970. *New York Times*, 18 February.

Fink, Leon, and Brian Greenberg. 1989. *Upheaval in the Quiet Zone: A History of Hospital Workers' Union, Local 1199*. Urbana: University of Illinois Press.

Fogelson, Robert M., comp. 1969. *The Los Angeles Riots*. New York: Arno.

Foner, Moe. 1965. "Culture in a Local Union." AFL-CIO *American Federationist*, August, n.p.

Foner, Philip Sheldon, and James S. Allen. 1987. *American Communism and Black Americans: A Documentary History, 1919–1929*. Philadelphia: Temple University Press.

Foster, Gwendolyn Audrey. 1997. *Women Filmmakers of the African and Asian Diaspora: Decolonizing the Gaze, Locating Subjectivity*. Carbondale: Southern Illinois University Press.

Fousek, John. 2000. *To Lead the Free World: American Nationalism and the Cultural Roots of the Cold War*. Chapel Hill: University of North Carolina Press.

Francke, Lizzie. 1993. "Daughters of the Dust." *Sight and Sound* 3 (9): 43–44.

Frost, Jennifer. 2001. *An Interracial Movement of the Poor: Community Organizing and the New Left in the 1960s*. New York: New York University Press.

Gabriel, Teshome H. 1982. *Third Cinema in the Third World: The Aesthetics of Liberation*. Ann Arbor, Mich.: UMI Press.

———. 1995. "Towards a Critical Theory of Third World Films." In *Cinemas of the Black Diaspora: Diversity, Dependence, and Oppositionality*, ed. Michael T. Martin. Detroit: Wayne State University Press.

Garcia, Espinosa Julio. 1979. "For an Imperfect Cinema." Trans. Julianne Burton. *Jump Cut*, no. 20: 24–26.

García, Ignacio M. 1997. *Chicanismo: The Forging of a Militant Ethos among Mexican Americans*. Tucson: University of Arizona Press.

Gates, Henry Louis, Jr. 1991. "Critical Fanonism." *Critical Inquiry*, no. 17: 457–70.

Gateward, Frances K. 2000. "Challenging Racism and Sexism through Cinematic Discourse: Black Women Film and Video Makers." Ph.D. diss., University of Maryland, College Park.

George, Nelson. 1987. *Where Did Our Love Go?* New York: St. Martin's Press.

Georgakas, Dan, and Lenny Rubenstein. 1983. *The Cineaste Interviews: On the Art and Politics of the Cinema*. Chicago: Lake View.

Gerima, Haile. 1989. "Triangular Cinema, Breaking Toys, and Dinknesh vs. Lucy." In *Questions of Third Cinema*, ed. Jim Pines and Paul Willemen. London: British Film Institute.

——. 1991. "Thoughts and Concepts: The Making of Ashes and Embers." *Black American Literature Forum* 25 (2): 335–50.

——. 1994. "Filming Slavery." *Transition*, no. 64: 90–104.

——. 1995. "Visions of Resistance." *Sight and Sound* 5 (9): 32–33.

Gerstle, Gary. 2001. *American Crucible: Race and Nation In the Twentieth Century*. Princeton, N.J.: Princeton University Press.

Gibson, Nigel. 1999. "Beyond Manicheanism: Dialectics in the Thought of Frantz Fanon." *Journal of Political Ideologies* 4 (3): 337–64.

——. 2002. "Dialectical Impasses: Turning the Table on Hegel and the Black." *Parallax* 8 (2): 30–45.

——. 2003. *Fanon: The Postcolonial Imagination*. Cambridge: Polity.

——, ed. 1999. *Rethinking Fanon: The Continuing Dialogue*. New York: Humanity Books.

Gilroy, Paul. 1993. *The Black Atlantic: Modernity and Double Consciousness*. Cambridge, Mass.: Harvard University Press.

Gitlin, Todd. 1987. *The Sixties: Years of Hope, Days of Rage*. New York: Bantam.

Goldman, Debra. 1983. "A Decade of Building an Alternative Movement: How Some Marginal Groups of the '60s Sprouted into an Entire Field of Solid Institutions Spanning Production, Exhibition, and Distribution." *Independent*, 18–23 September.

Gong, Stephen. 1991. "A History in Progress: Asian American Media Arts Centers, 1970–1990." In *Moving the Image: Independent Asian Pacific American Media Arts*, ed. Russell Leong. Los Angeles: UCLA Asian American Studies Center and Visual Communications, Southern California Asian American Studies Central.

Gordon, Avery. 1998/1999. "Globalism and the Prison Industrial Complex: An Interview with Angela Davis." *Race and Class* 20 (2/3): 145–57.

Gosse, Van. 1993. *Where the Boys Are: Cuba, Cold War America, and the Making of a New Left*. London: Verso.

——. 1996. "'El Salvador Is Spanish For Vietnam': A New Immigrant Left and the Politics of Solidarity." In *The Immigrant Left in the United States*, ed. Paul Buhle and Dan Georgakas. Albany: State University of New York Press.

Gottlieb, Roger S. 1992. *Marxism, 1844–1990: Origins, Betrayal, Rebirth*. New York: Routledge.

——, ed. 1989. *An Anthology of Western Marxism: From Lukács and Gramsci to Socialist-Feminism*. New York: Oxford University Press.

Gramsci, Antonio. 1978. *Selections from the Prison Noteboooks*. New York: International Publishers.

——. 1992. "Notes on Italian History." In *Selections from the Prison Notebooks of Antonio Gramsci*, ed. Quintin Hoare and Geoffrey Nowell Smith, 44–122. New York: International Publishers.

Grant, Malina. 2001. "The Los Angeles Times Coverage of the 1965 Watt's Riots." B.A. thesis, California Polytechnic State University.

Gray, Herman. 1999. "A Different Dream of Difference." *Critical Studies in Mass Communication* 16 (4): 484–88.

Grayson, Sandra M. 1998. " 'Spirits of Asona Ancestors Come': Reading Asante Signs in Haile Gerima's *Sankofa*." cla *Journal* 42 (2): 212–27.

Grewal, Inderpal, and Caren Kaplan. 1994. *Scattered Hegemonies: Postmodernity and Transnational Feminist Practices*. Minneapolis: University of Minnesota Press.

Grossberg, Lawrence. 1992. *We Gotta Get Out of This Place: Popular Conservatism and Postmodern Culture*. New York: Routledge.

——. 1993. "Cultural Studies An/In New Worlds." In *Race, Identity, and Representation in Education*, ed. Cameron McCarthy and Warren Crichlow. New York: Routledge.

——. 2000. "Identity and Cultural Studies: Is That All There Is?" In *American Cultural Studies: A Reader*, ed. John Hartley and Roberta E. Pearson, with Eva Vieth. Oxford: Oxford University Press.

Guerrero, Ed. 2000. "Be Black and Buy." *Sight and Sound* 10 (12): 34–37.

Guevara, Ernesto. 2000. *Che Guevara Speaks: Selected Speeches and Writing*. New York: Pathfinder Press.

Guillory, Monique, and Richard C. Green, eds. 1998. *Soul: Black Power, Politics, and Pleasure*. New York: New York University Press.

Gundaker, Grey. 1998. *Signs of Diaspora/Diaspora of Signs: Literacies, Creolization, and Vernacular Practice in African America*. New York: Oxford University Press.

Guss, David M. 2000. *The Festive State: Race, Ethnicity, and Nationalism as Cultural Performance*. Berkeley: University of California Press.

Guzmán, Pablo. 1998. "*La Vida Pura*: A Lord of the Barrio." In *The Puerto Rican Movement: Voices from the Diaspora*, ed. Andrés V. Torres and José E. Velázquez. Philadelphia: Temple University Press.

Hall, Stuart. 1980. "Race, Articulation, and Societies Structured in Dominance. In *Sociological Theories: Race and Colonialism*. Paris: unesco.

——. 1989. "Cultural Identity and Cinematic Representation." In *Framework* no. 36, 68–82. London: Sankofa Film and Video.

——. 1996. "On Postmodernism and Articulation: An Interview with Stuart Hall," ed. Lawrence Grossberg. In *Stuart Hall: Critical Dialogues in Cultural Studies*, ed. David Morley and Kuan-Hsing Chen, 131–50. London: Routledge.

Hall, Stuart, and Tony Jefferson, eds. 1976. *Resistance through Rituals: Youth Sub-cultures in Post-war Britain*. London: Hutchinson.

Hardt, Michael, and Antonio Negri. 2000. *Empire*. Cambridge, Mass.: Harvard University Press.

Harloe, Michael, Peter Marcuse, and Neil Smith. 1992. "Housing for People, Housing for Profits." In *Divided Cities: New York and London in the Global World*, ed. Susan S. Fainstein, Ian Gordon, and Harloe. Oxford: Blackwell.

Harris, Joseph E., ed. 1982. *Global Dimensions of the African Diaspora*. Washington: Howard University Press.

Harris, Kwasi. 1986. "New Images: An Interview with Julie Dash and Alile Sharon Larkin." *Independent* 9 (10): 16–20.

Heale, M. J. 2001. *The Sixties in America: History, Politics, and Protest*. Chicago: Fitzroy Dearborn.

Herbert, Bob. 2004. "America's Abu Ghraibs." *New York Times*, 31 May.

"Herbert Marcuse and Theodor Adorno's Correspondence on the German Student Movement." 1999. *New Left Review* 1 (223): 123–36.

Heywood, Linda M., ed. 2002. *Central Africans and Cultural Transformations in the American Diaspora*. Cambridge: Cambridge University Press.

Hine, Darlene Clark, and Jacqueline McLeod. 1999. *Crossing Boundaries: Comparative History of Black People in Diaspora*. Bloomington: Indiana University Press.

Holden, Stephen. 1992. "*Daughters of the Dust*: The Demise of a Tradition." *New York Times*, 16 January.

——. 1997. "Literacy: A Weapon for a Slave." *New York Times*, 31 January.

Holloway, Joseph E., ed. 1990. *Africanisms In American Culture*. Bloomington: Indiana University Press.

Hollyman, Burnes Saint Patrick. 1983. *Glauber Rocha and the Cinema Novo: A Study of His Critical Writings and Films*. New York: Garland.

Holston, James. 1999. "Spaces of Insurgent Citizenship." In *Cities and Citizenship*, ed. Holston. Durham, N.C.: Duke University Press.

Horkheimer, Max. 1972. "Traditional and Critical Theory." In *Critical Theory: Selected Essays*. Trans. Matthew J. O'Connell et al. New York: Herder and Herder.

Horkheimer, Max, and Theodor Adorno. [1937] 2002. *Dialectic of Enlightenment*. Trans. Gunzeline Schmid Noerr. Stanford, Calif.: Stanford University Press.

Horne, Gerald. 1995. *Fire This Time: The Watts Uprising and the 1960s*. Charlottesville: University Press of Virginia.

"How We Did It." 1994. *Essence*. September, 40.

Howard, Steve. 1985. "A Cinema of Transformation: The Films of Haile Gerima." *Cineaste* 14 (1): 28–29, 39.

Howe, Irving. 1970. *Beyond the New Left*. New York: McCall.

Hoy, David Couzens, and Thomas McCarthy. 1994. *Critical Theory*. Oxford: Blackwell.

Hozic, Aida A. 1994. "The House I Live In: An Interview with Charles Burnett. *Callaloo* 17 (2): 470–92.

Hutchinson, Sharon, and Bruce Wiegard. 1998. "Gerima's Imperfect Journey: No End in Sight." *American Anthropologist* 99 (1): 169–71.

Isserman, Maurice, and Michael Kazin. 2004. *America Divided: The Civil War of the 1960s*. 2d ed. New York: Oxford University Press.

James, C. L. R. 1956. *Every Cook Can Govern: A Study of Democracy in Ancient Greece; Negro Americans and American Politics*. Detroit: Correspondence Publishing.

James, Caryn. 1998. "Race, Love, and the Black Proprieties." *New York Times*, 20 February.

James, David. 1987. "Chained To Devilpictures: Cinema and Black Liberation in the Sixties." In *The Year Left 2: An American Socialist Yearbook*, ed. M. Davis et al. London: Verso.

James, Joy, ed. 1998. *The Angela Y. Davis Reader*. Cambridge, Mass.: Blackwell.

James, Winston. 1998. *Holding Aloft the Banner of Ethiopia: Caribbean Radicalism in Early Twentieth-Century America*. London: Verso.

Jameson, Fredric. 1984. "Periodizing the Sixties." In *The Sixties Without Apology*, ed. Sonnya Sayers et al., 178–209. Minneapolis: University of Minnesota Press.

———. 1991. *Postmodernism; Or, The Cultural Logic of Late Capitalism*. Durham, N.C.: Duke University Press.

Jay, Martin. 1973. *The Dialectical Imagination: A History of the Frankfurt School and the Institute of Social Research, 1923–1950*. Boston: Little, Brown.

Johnson, Randal. 1984a. *Cinema Novo X 5: Masters of Contemporary Brazilian Film*. Austin: University of Texas Press.

———. 1984b. "Film, Television, and Traditional Folk Culture in *Bye Bye Brasil*." *Journal of Popular Culture* 18 (1): 121–32.

Jones, Charles E., ed. 1998. *The Black Panther Party (Reconsidered)*. Baltimore, Md.: Black Classic Press.

Jones, LeRoi. 1965. "The Revolutionary Theater." *Liberator* 5 (7): 4–5.

———. [1966] 1998. *Home: Social Essays*. Hopewell, N.J.: Ecco.

Joseph, May. 1998. "Soul, Transnationalism, and Imagings of Revolution: Tanzanian Ujama and the Politics of Enjoyment." In *Soul: Black Power, Politics, and Pleasure*, ed. Monique Guillory and Richard C. Green. New York: New York University Press.

Julien, Eileen. 2000. "*Terrains de Rencontre*: Césaire, Fanon, and Wright on Culture and Decolonization." *Yale French Studies*, no. 98: 149–66.

Kandé, Sylvie. 1998. "Look Homeward, Angel: Maroons and Mulattos in Haile Gerima's *Sankofa*." *Research in African Literatures* 29 (2): 128–46.

Kaplan, E. Ann. 1997. "Healing Imperialized Eyes: Independent Women Filmmakers and the Look." In *Looking for the Other: Feminism, Film, and the Imperial Gaze*. New York: Routledge.

Katz, Barry. 1982. *Herbert Marcuse and the Art of Liberation: An Intellectual Biography*. London: Verso.

Kauffmann, Stanley. 1992. "*Daughters of the Dust*." *New Republic*, 10 February, 26–28.

Kaufman, Anthony. 1998. "Sentimental Journey as National Allegory: An interview with Walter Salles." *Cineaste* 24 (1): 19–21.

Kebede, Messay. 2001. "The Rehabilitation of Violence and the Violence of Rehabilitation: Fanon and Colonialism." *Journal of Black Studies* 31 (5): 539–62.

Kelley, Robin D. G. 1990. *Hammer and Hoe: Alabama Communists during the Great Depression*. Chapel Hill: University of North Carolina Press.

——. 1997. *Yo' Mama's Disfunktional! Fighting the Culture Wars in Urban America*. Boston: Beacon.

——. 1999. "'But a Local Phase of a World Problem': Black History's Global Vision." *Journal of American History* 86 (3): 1045–77.

——. 2002. *Freedom Dreams: The Black Radical Imagination*. Boston: Beacon.

Kelley, Robin D. G., and Betsy Esch. 1999. "Black Like Mao: Red China and Black Revolution." *Souls* 1 (4): 6–41.

Kennedy, Lisa. 1989. "Senegal Burning." *Village Voice*, February 7, 65.

Kilson, Martin L., and Robert I. Rotberg, eds. 1976. *The African Diaspora: Interpretive Essays*. Cambridge, Mass.: Harvard University Press.

Kim, Sojin, and R. Mark Livengood. 1998. "Talking With Charles Burnett." *Journal of American Folklore* 111 (439): 69–74.

King, John, Ana M. López, and Manuel Alvarado, eds. 1993. *Mediating Two Worlds: Cinematic Encounters In the Americas*. London: British Film Institute.

Kitson, Thomas J. 1999. "Tempering Race and Nation: Recent Debates in Diaspora Identity." *Research in African Literatures* 30, no. 2: 88–95.

Klotman, Phyllis R., and Janet K. Cutler. 1999. "Interviews with Filmmakers." In *Struggles for Representation: African American Documentary Film and Video*, ed. Klotman and Cutler. Bloomington: Indiana University Press.

Kohn, Hans. 1957. *American Nationalism: An Interpretative Essay*. New York: Macmillan.

Lao, Agustin. 1995. "Resources of Hope: Imaging the Young Lords and the Politics of Memory." *Centro* 7 (1): 34–39.

Larkin, Alile Sharon. 1988. "Black Women Filmmakers Defining Ourselves: Feminism in Our Own Voice." In *Female Spectators: Looking at Film and Television*, ed. E. Deidre Pribram. New York: Verso.

Lavie, Smadar, and Ted Swedenburg, Eds. 1996. *Displacement, Diaspora, and Geographies of Identity*. Durham, N.C.: Duke University Press.

Lee, Felicia R. 1997. "Home Is Where the Imagination Took Root." *New York Times*, 3 December.

Lemelle, Sidney J., and Robin D. G. Kelley, eds. 1994. *Imagining Home: Class, Culture, and Nationalism In the African Diaspora*. London: Verso.

Lesage, Julia. 1985. "For Our Urgent Use: Films on Central America." In *Jump Cut: Hollywood, Politics, and Counter-cinema*, ed. Peter Steven. Toronto: Between the Lines.

Levy, Peter B. 1994. *The New Left and Labor in the 1960s*. Urbana: University of Illinois Press.

Lipsitz, George. 1998. *The Possessive Investment in Whiteness: How White People Benefit from Identity Politics*. Philadelphia: Temple University Press.

Long, Gerald. 1968. "Radical Media: The Newsreel." *Guardian*, 20 April.

Lovejoy, Paul E., ed. 2000. *Identity in the Shadow of Slavery*. London: Continuum.

Lowe, Lisa. 1998. "Reflections on Race, Class, and Gender in the USA." In *The Angela Y. Davis Reader*, ed. Joy James. Cambridge, Mass.: Blackwell.

Lowery, Mark. 1994. "The Making of 'Holly-Hood.'" *Black Enterprise*, December, 104.

Lyons, Paul. 1976. "The New Left and the Cuban Revolution." In *The New Cuba: Paradoxes and Potentials*, ed. Ronald Radosh, 211–46. New York: William Morrow.

——. 1996. *New Left, New Right, and the Legacy of the Sixties*. Philadelphia: Temple University Press.

Macdonald, Scott. 1998a. "Charles Burnett." In *A Critical Cinema 3: Interviews with Independent Filmmakers*, ed. Scott Macdonald, 104–25. Berkeley: University of California Press.

——. 1998b. "Christine Choy." In *A Critical Cinema 3: Interviews with Independent Filmmakers*, ed. Scott Macdonald, 196–218. Berkeley: University of California Press.

Mahieu, José Augustín. 1997. "Nelson Pereira Dos Santos, the Father of 'Cinema-Novo.'" *Cuadernos Hispanoamericanos*, no. 569: 45–55.

Mailer, Norman. 1968. *The Armies of the Night: History as a Novel, the Novel as History*. New York: New American Library.

Malcolm X. 1964. "Message to the Grassroots." In *African Intellectual Heritage: A Book of Sources*, ed. Molefi Kete Asante and Abu. S. Abarry. Philadelphia: Temple University Press.

Mander, Mary S. 1999. *Framing Friction: Media and Social Conflict*. Urbana: University of Illinois Press.

Mann, Charles. 1953. *Stalin's Thought Illuminates Problems of Negro Freedom Struggle*. New York: National Education Dept., Communist Party USA.

Marcuse, Herbert. 1969. *An Essay on Liberation*. Boston: Beacon.

——. 1971. "Dear Angela." *Ramparts*, February, 22.

Martin, Joseph, et al. 1971. "Attica: Anatomy of a Tragedy." *New York Daily News*, 4–8 October, 27–28.

Martin, Michael T., ed. 1995. *Cinemas of the Black Diaspora: Diversity, Dependence, and Oppositionality*. Detroit: Wayne State University Press.

——, ed. 1997. *New Latin American Cinema*. Vol. 1, *Theory, Practices, and Transcontinental Articulations*. Detroit: Wayne State University Press.

Marx, Karl. 1962. *Poverty of Philosophy*. Moscow: Foreign Languages Publishing House.

Masilela, Ntongela. 1993a. "The Los Angeles School of Black Filmmakers." In *Black American Cinema*, ed. Manthia Diawara. New York: Routledge.

——. 1993b. "Women Directors of the Los Angeles School." In *Black Women Film and Video Artists*, ed. Jacqueline Bobo. New York: Routledge.

——. n.d. "The Los Angeles School: An Introduction." Typescript.

Maslin, Janet. 1984. "*My Brother's Wedding* from Coast." *New York Times*, 30 March.

Masoni, Tullio, and Paolo Vecchi. 1996. "Brasile e trent'anni dal Cinema Novo." *Cineforum* 36 (1): 16–23.

McCone, John A. 1965. *McCone Commission Report! Complete and Unabridged Report by the Governor's Commission on the Los Angeles Riot; Plus One Hundred Four Shocking Photos of the Most Terrifying Riot in History*. Los Angeles: Kimtex.

Mekas, Jonas. 1972. *Movie Journal: The Rise of the New American Cinema, 1959–1971*. New York: Macmillan.

Miller, David. 1995. *On Nationality*. Oxford: Clarendon.

———. 2000. *Citizenship and National Identity*. Cambridge: Polity.

Miller, Jim. 1987. *Democracy Is in the Streets: From Port Huron To the Siege of Chicago*. New York: Simon and Schuster.

Mills, C. Wright. 1960. "Letter to the New Left." *New Left Review* 1 (5): 18–23.

Milner, Sherry. 1982. "Third World Newsreel, Ten Years of Left Film: Interview with Christine Choy." *Jump Cut*, no. 27: 21–22, 39.

———. 1985. "TWN: Interview with Christine Choy." In *Jump Cut: Hollywood, Politics, and Counter-cinema*, ed. Peter Steven. Toronto: Between the Lines.

Moon, Michael, and Cathy N. Davidson, eds. 1995. *Subjects and Citizens: Nation, Race, and Gender From Oroonoko to Anita Hill*. Durham, N.C.: Duke University Press.

Moore, Carlos. 1988. *Castro, the Blacks, and Africa*. Los Angeles: Center for Afro-American Studies, University of California.

Morales, Iris. 1998. "Palante, Siempre Palante!" In *The Puerto Rican Movement: Voices from the Diaspora*, ed. Andrés V. Torres and José E. Velázquez. Philadelphia: Temple University Press.

Morland, Carol A. 1998. *Diasporic Identity*. Arlington, Va.: American Anthropological Association, Committee on Refugees and Immigrants, General Anthropology Division.

Moten, Fred. 2003. *In the Break: The Aesthetics of the Black Radical Tradition*. Minneapolis: University of Minnesota Press.

"A Movie, Then a Book." 1997. *New York Times*, 17 October.

Murashige, Mike. 1997. "Haile Gerima and the Political Economy of Cinematic Resistance." In *Representing Blackness: Issues in Film and Video*, ed. Valerie Smith. New Brunswick, N.J.: Rutgers University Press.

Murphy, Joseph M. 1994. *Working the Spirit: Ceremonies of the African Diaspora*. Boston: Beacon.

Nadelson, Regina. 1972. *Who Is Angela Davis? The Biography of a Revolutionary*. New York: P. H. Wyden.

Nagib, Lúcia. 2000. "New Cinema under the Specter of Cinema Novo (Brazilian Culture)." *Cuadernos Hispanoamericanos*, nos. 601–2: 39–51.

Neal, Lawrence. 1966. "Development of LeRoi Jones." *Liberator*, January: 4–5.

Neverson, Yvonne. 1989. "The Artist Has Always Been a Disturber of the Peace." In *Conversations with James Baldwin*, ed. Fred L. Standley and Louis H. Pratt. Jackson: University Press of Mississippi.

Newell, Stephanie, ed. 1996. *Images of African and Caribbean Women: Migration, Displacement, Diaspora*. Stirling, U.K.: Centre of Commonwealth Studies, University of Stirling.

Newsreel. 1968–69. "Newsreel." *Film Quarterly* 21 (2): 43–51.

———. 1969. Newsreel Catalog. New York City: Newsreel.

"Newsreel Footage Seized." 1969. *Cineaste* 3 (2): 32.

Ngugi, Wa Thiong'o. 1972. *Homecoming: Essays on African and Caribbean Literature, Culture, and Politics*. London: Heinemann.

Nichols, Bill. 1980. *Newsreel: Documentary Filmmaking on the American Left (1971–1975)*. New York: Arno Press.

Nichols, William J. 1972. "Newsreel: Film and Revolution." Master's thesis, University of California, Los Angeles.

Nicholson, David, Clyde Taylor, and Zeinabu Irene Davis. 1991. "Voices." *Wide Angle* 13 (3–4): 120–35.

Noriega, Chon A. 1996. "Imagined Borders: Locating Chicano Cinema in America / América." In *The Ethnic Eye: Latino Media Arts*, ed. Noriega and Ana M. López. Minneapolis: University of Minnesota Press.

——. 2000. *Shot in America: Television, the State, and the Rise of Chicano Cinema*. Minneapolis: University of Minnesota Press.

O'Brien, Ellen. 2002. "Charles Burnett's *To Sleep with Anger*: An Anthropological Perspective." *Journal of Popular Culture* 35 (4): 113–27.

Okafor-Newsum, Ikechukwu. "Africa in the African-American Imagination: Perspectives from the Motherland." *Research in African Literatures* 29 (1): 219–30.

Okpewho, Isidore, Carole Boyce Davies, and Ali A. Mazrui, eds. 1999. *The African Diaspora: African Origins and New World Identities*. Bloomington: Indiana University Press.

Onwuachi, P. Chike. 1973. *Black Ideology in African Diaspora*. Chicago: Third World Press.

Ozkirimli, Umut. 2000. *Theories of Nationalism: A Critical Overview*. New York: St. Martin's Press.

Paranagua Paulo Antonio. 1986. "Cinema-Novo: A Cultural-Revolution on the Screen Brazilian Film since 1960." *UNESCO Courier*, no. 12: 33–36.

Parry, Benita. 1999. "Resistance Theory/Theorizing Resistance; Or, Two Cheers for Nativism." In *Rethinking Fanon*, ed. N. C. Gibson. New York: Humanity Books.

Paxman, Andrew, and Nelson Hoineff. 1998. "Global Kudos Shine on Brazil Pix—Spotlight: Latin America." *Variety*, 23–29 March, 44.

Peery, Nelson. 1972. *The Negro National Colonial Question*. 2d ed. Chicago: Workers Press.

——. 1994. *Black Fire: The Making of an American Revolutionary*. New York: New Press.

People's Cinema Commission. 1973. "Statement." Paper presented at the Third World Filmmakers Meeting, December, Algiers.

Pickford, Henry. 1997. "Critical Models: Adorno's Theory and Practice of Cultural Criticism." *Yale Journal of Criticism* 10 (2): 247–70.

Pietri, Pedro. 1974. *Puerto Rican Obituary*. New York: Monthly Review Press.

Pines, Jim. 1996. "The Cultural Context of Black British Cinema." In *Black British Cultural Studies: A Reader*, ed. Houston A. Baker Jr., Manthia Diawara, and Ruth H. Lindeborg. Chicago: University of Chicago Press.

Pines, Jim, and Paul Willemen. 1994. *Questions of Third Cinema*. London: British Film Institute.

Plummer, Brenda. 1998. "Castro in Harlem: A Cold War Watershed." In *Rethinking the Cold War*, ed. Allen Hunter, 133–53. Philadelphia: Temple University Press.

Poole, Ross. 1999. *Nation and Identity*. London: Routledge.

Pribram, E. Deidre, ed. 1988. *Female Spectators: Looking at Film and Television*. New York: Verso.

Prussion, Karl. 1965. *Communist Influence in the Los Angeles Riots: Dress Rehearsal for Revolution?* New Orleans: The Independent American.

Rafferty, Terrence. 1990. "To Sleep with Anger." *New Yorker*, 5 November, 140–41.

——. 1997. "Social Studies: 'Nightjohn' and 'Suburbia.'" *New Yorker*, 10 February, 84–86.

Redding, Judith, and Victoria Brownworth. 1997. "Zeinabu Irene Davis: A Powerful Thang." In *Film Fatales: Independent Women Directors*. Seattle: Seal Press.

Rego, Cacilda M. 1991. "Cinema-Novo and the Question of the Popular." *Studies in Latin American Popular Culture*, no. 10: 59–73.

——. 1997. "Cinema Novo: For a Popular Cinema in Brazil." Ph.D. diss., University of Texas, Austin.

Reid, Mark A. 1991. "Dialogic Modes of Representing Africa(S): Womanist Film." *Black American Literature Forum* 25 (2): 375–88.

Reitan, Ruth. 1999. *The Rise and Decline of an Alliance: Cuba and African American Leaders in the 1960s*. East Lansing: Michigan State University Press.

Renov, Michael. 1987a. "Early Newsreel: The Construction of a Political Imaginary for the New Left." *Afterimage* 14 (7): 12–15.

——. 1987b. "Newsreel: Old and New—Towards an Historical Profile." *Film Quarterly* 41 (1): 20–33.

——. 1988. "Imaging the Other: Representations of Vietnam in '60s Political Documentary." *Afterimage*, 16 December, 10–12.

——. 2004. *The Subject of Documentary*. Minneapolis: University of Minnesota Press.

Reynaud, Bernice. 1991. "An Interview with Charles Burnett." *Black American Literature Forum* 25 (2): 323–34.

Robeson, Susan. 1981. *The Whole World in His Hands: A Pictorial Biography of Paul Robeson*. Sacramento: Citadel Press.

Robinson, Cedric J. 1983. *Black Marxism: The Making of the Black Radical Tradition*. London: Zed.

Rocha, Glauber, and John Davis. 1997. "History of Cinema Novo." In *New Latin American Cinema*, vol. 1: *Theory, Practices, and Transcontinental Articulations*, ed. Michael T. Martin. Detroit: Wayne State Press.

Rodney, Walter. 1996a. "How Africa Developed before the Coming of the Europeans Up to the Fifteenth Century." In *African Intellectual Heritage: A Book of Sources*, ed. Molefi Kete Asante and Abu S. Abarry. Philadelphia: Temple University Press.

——. 1996b. "Towards the Sixth Pan African Congress: Aspects of the International Class Struggle in Africa, the Caribbean, and America." In *African Intellectual Heritage: A Book of Sources*, ed. Molefi Kete Asante and Abu S. Abarry. Philadelphia: Temple University Press.

Rodriguez, Dylan. 2003. "Languages of Death: Captive Radical Intellectuals and the Political Logic of Mass Imprisonment." Paper presented at Annual Meeting of

American Studies Association: Violence and Belonging, Hartford, Conn., 16–19 October.

Rodriguez-Morazzani, Roberto P. 1998. "Political Cultures of the Puerto Rican Left in the United States." In *The Puerto Rican Movement: Voices from the Diaspora*, ed. Andrés V. Torres and José E. Velázquez. Philadelphia: Temple University Press.

Rohter, Larry. 1990. "An All-Black Film (Except the Audience): 'To Sleep with Anger' Wins High Praise But Misses Its Target." *New York Times*, 20 November.

Rule, Sheila. 1992. "Director Defies Odds with First Feature, 'Daughters of the Dust.' " *New York Times*, 16 January.

Rustin, Bayard. 1966. "The Watts 'Manifesto' and the McCone Report." *Commentary*, March, 29–35.

Safford, Tony, and William Triplett. 1983. "Haile Gerima: Radical Departures to a New Black Cinema." *Journal of Film and Video* 35: 59–65.

Said, Edward W. 1999. "Traveling Theory Reconsidered." In *Rethinking Fanon*, ed. N. C. Gibson. New York: Humanity Books.

Sayres, Sonnya, et al., eds. 1984. *The Sixties without Apology*. Minneapolis: University of Minnesota Press.

Schein, Louisa. 1999. "Diaspora Politics, Homeland Erotics, and the Materializing of Memory." *Positions* 7 (3): 697–725.

Schiff Frederick. 1974. "Brazilian Film and Military Censorship: Cinema Novo, 1964–1974." *Historical Journal of Film, Radio and Television* 13 (4): 469–94.

Schoolman, Morton. 1980. *The Imaginary Witness: The Critical Theory of Herbert Marcuse*. New York: Free Press.

Schwartz, Joel. 1986. "Tenant Power in the Liberal City, 1943–1971." In *The Tenant Movement In New York City, 1904–1984*, ed. Ronald Lawson, with Mark Naison. New Brunswick, N.J.: Rutgers University Press.

——. 1993. *The New York Approach: Robert Moses, Urban Liberals, and Redevelopment of the Inner City*. Columbus: Ohio State University Press.

Scoble, Harry M. 1967. *Negro Politics in Los Angeles: The Quest for Power*. Los Angeles: Institute of Government and Public Affairs, University of California.

Segal, Ronald. 1995. *The Black Diaspora*. New York: Farrar, Straus and Giroux.

Seshadri-Crooks, Kalpana. 2002. " 'I Am a Master': Terrorism, Masculinity, and Political Violence in Frantz Fanon." *Parallax* 8 (2): 84–89.

Seton-Watson, Hugh. 1978. *The Imperialist Revolutionaries: Trends in World Communism in the 1960s and 1970s*. Stanford, Calif.: Hoover Institution Press.

Shepherd, Verene A., ed. 2002. *Working Slavery, Pricing Freedom: Perspectives from the Caribbean, Africa, and the African Diaspora*. New York: Palgrave.

Shiel, Mark, et al. 2003. *Screening the City*. New York: Verso.

Shipler, David. 1969. "The Changing City: Housing Paralysis." *New York Times*, 5 June.

——. 1970. "New Housing Chief Would Rebuild Slums to Draw Middle Class." *New York Times*, 7 January.

Silber, Irwin. 1969. "Film: Tools for Organizing." *Guardian*, 20 December.

Simons, Jon. 2002. "Aesthetic Political Technologies." *Intertexts* 6 (1): 74–97.

Singh, Nikhil Pal. 1998a. "The Black Panthers and the 'Underdeveloped Country' of the Left." In *The Black Panther Party Reconsidered: Reflections and Scholarship*, ed. Charles E. Jones. Baltimore: Black Classic Press.

——. 1998b. "Culture/Wars: Recoding Empire In An Age of Democracy." *American Quarterly* 50 (3): 471–522.

——. 2004. *Black Is a Country: Race and the Unfinished Struggle for Democracy*. Cambridge, Mass.: Harvard University Press.

Smith, Anthony D. 1988. *The Ethnic Origins of Nations*. Oxford: Blackwell.

Smith, Suzanne E. 1999. *Dancing in the Street: Motown and the Cultural Politics of Detroit*. Cambridge, Mass.: Harvard University Press.

Smith, Valerie. 1988. "Reconstituting the Image." *Callaloo*, no. 30: 709–19.

——, ed. 1997. *Representing Blackness: Issues in Film and Video*. New Brunswick, N.J.: Rutgers University Press.

Snead, James A. 1995. "Images of Blacks in Black Independent Films: A Brief Survey." In *Cinemas of the Black Diaspora: Diversity, Dependence, and Oppositionality*, ed. Michael T. Martin. Detroit: Wayne State University Press.

Solanas, Fernando, and Octavio Getino. 1997. "Towards A Third Cinema: Notes and Experiences for the Development of a Cinema of Liberation in the Third World." In *New Latin American Cinema*, vol. 1, *Theory, Practices, and Transcontinental Articulations*, ed. Michael T. Martin. Detroit: Wayne State University Press.

Sonnenberg, Ben. 1992. "Ashes and Embers." *Nation*, 20 January, 64–67.

Spalding, Sophie. 1991. "Watts '65: To the Rebellion and Beyond." M.A. thesis, University of California, Los Angeles.

Sragow, Michael. 1995. "An Explorer of the Black Mind Looks Back, But Not in Anger. *New York Times*, 1 January.

Stalin, Joseph. 1934. *Problems of Leninism*. New York: International Publishers.

Staples, Robert, et al. 1977. "A Symposium on Roots." *Black Scholar* 8 (7): 36–42.

Steady, Filomina Chioma. 2002. *Black Women, Globalization, and Economic Justice: Studies from Africa and The African Diaspora*. Rochester, Vt.: Schenkman.

Stepto, Robert B. 1979. *From Behind the Veil: A Study of Afro-American Narrative*. Urbana: University of Illinois Press.

Stevens, Maurice E. 2003. *Troubling Beginnings: Trans(Per)Forming African American History and Identity*. New York: Routledge.

Stoltze, Frank. 2004. "The LA County Jail's Woes." Radio report on station KPCC, Los Angeles.

Storey, John. 1998. *An Introduction to Cultural Theory and Popular Culture*. 2d ed. Athens: University of Georgia Press.

Students for a Democratic Society. 1998. "Port Huron Statement." In *America in the Sixties: Right, Left, and Center*, ed. Peter Levy, 44–46. Westport, Conn.: Praeger.

Susman, Warren. 1984. *Culture as History: The Transformation of American Society in the Twentieth Century*. New York: Pantheon.

Tajima, Renee. 1991. "Moving the Image: Asian American Independent Filmmaking, 1970–1990." In *Moving the Image: Independent Asian Pacific American Media Arts*, ed. Russell Leong. Los Angeles: UCLA Asian American Studies Center and Visual Communications, Southern California Asian American Studies Central.

Taubin, Amy. 1998. "Close to the Edge." *Village Voice*, 21 July, 120.

"Taut Family Thriller 'To Sleep with Anger' Boasts Ensemble Cast." 1990. *Jet*, 29 October, 58–60.

Taylor, Clyde. 1982. "'Salt Peanuts': Sound and Sense In African/American Oral/Musical Creativity." *Callaloo*, no. 16 (October): 1–11.

——. 1985a. "Black Writing as Immanent Humanism." *Southern Review* 21 (3):7 90–800.

——. 1985b. "Third World Cinema: One Struggle, Many Fronts." In *Jump Cut: Hollywood, Politics, and Counter-cinema*, ed. Peter Steven. Toronto: Between the Lines.

——. 1986. "The L.A. Rebellion: A Turning Point in Black Cinema." New American Filmmakers Series, Exhibitions of Independent Film and Video, program narrative no. 26. New York: Whitney Museum of American Art.

——. 1987. "After Winter: Sterling Brown." *Black Scholar* 18 (4–5): 50–51.

——. 1988a. "The Paradox of Black Independent Cinema." *Black Film Review* 4 (4): 2–3, 7–19.

——. 1988b. "We Don't Need Another Hero: Anti-theses on Aesthetics." In *Blackframes: Critical Perspectives on Black Independent Cinema*, ed. Mbye Cham and Claire Andrade-Watkins. Cambridge, Mass.: MIT Press.

——. 1989a. "Black Cinema in the Post-aesthetic Era." In *Questions of Third Cinema*, ed. Jim Pines and Paul Willemen. London: British Film Institute.

——. 1989b. "The Future of Black Film: The Debate Continues." *Black Film Review* 5 (4): 7, 9, 27–28.

——. 1990a. "The Colonialist Subtext in *Platoon*." In *From Hanoi to Hollywood: The Vietnam War in American Film*, ed. Linda Dittmar and Gene Michaud. New Brunswick, N.J.: Rutgers University Press.

——. 1990b. "Light from Darkness." *Areté* 2 (5): 54–57.

——. 1991. "The Re-birth of the Aesthetic in Cinema." *Wide Angle* 13 (3–4): 12–30.

——. 1993. "The Ironies of Palace-Subaltern Discourse." In *Black American Cinema*, ed. Manthia Diawara. London: Routledge.

——. 1996. "New U.S. Black Cinema." In *Movies and Mass Culture*, ed. John Belton. New Brunswick, N.J.: Rutgers University Press.

——. 1998a. "Conclusion: But Is It Art?" In *The Mask of Art: Breaking the Aesthetic Contract—Film and Literature*. Bloomington: Indiana University Press.

——. 1998b. "*Daughters of the Terreiros*." In *The Mask of Art: Breaking the Aesthetic Contract—Film and Literature*. Bloomington: Indiana University Press.

——. 1998c. *The Mask of Art: Breaking the Aesthetic Contract—Film and Literature*. Bloomington: Indiana University Press.

——. 1999. "Paths of Enlightenment: Heroes, Rebels, and Thinkers." In *Struggles for Representation: African American Documentary Film and Video*, ed. Phyllis R. Klotman and Janet K. Cutler. Bloomington: Indiana University Press.

——, ed. 1973. *Vietnam and Black America: An Anthology of Protest and Resistance*. Garden City, N.Y.: Anchor.

Third World Newsreel. N.d. *The Higher Ground Cinema Statement of Purpose.* New York: Third World Newsreel.

———. 1972. *Act First, Then Speak.* New York: Third World Newsreel.

———. 1973. *Organizational Principles of Third World Newsreel.* New York: Third World Newsreel.

Thompson, Ben. 1994. "*Sankofa.*" *Sight and Sound* 4 (7): 53–54.

Tomashoff, Craig. 1992. "American Playhouse: Daughters of Dust." *People Weekly,* 27 July, 11.

Torres, Andrés V. 1998. "Introduction: Political Radicalism in the Diaspora—The Puerto Rican Experience." In *The Puerto Rican Movement: Voices from the Diaspora,* ed. Torres and José E. Velázquez. Philadelphia: Temple University Press.

Torres, Sasha. 2003. *Black, White, and in Color: Television, Policing, and Black Civil Rights.* Princeton, N.J.: Princeton University Press.

Treviño, Jesús Salvador. 1982. "Chicano Cinema." *New Scholar,* no. 8: 167–80.

Tyler, Bruce Michael. 1983. "Black Radicalism in Southern California, 1950–1982." Ph.D. diss., University of California, Los Angeles.

Tyson, Timothy B. 1999. *Radio Free Dixie: Robert F. Williams and the Roots of Black Power.* Chapel Hill: University of North Carolina Press.

Ukpokodu, I. Peter. 2002. "African Heritage from the Lenses of African-American Theatre and Film." *Journal of Dramatic Theory and Criticism* 16 (2): 69–93.

Unger, Irwin, and Debi Unger. 1974. *The Movement: A History of the American New Left, 1959–1972.* New York: Dodd Mead.

Van Deburg, William L., ed. 1997. *Modern Black Nationalism: From Marcus Garvey to Louis Farrakhan.* New York: New York University Press.

Vernon, Robert, and George Edward Novack. 1965. *Watts and Harlem: The Rising Revolt in the Black Ghettos.* New York: Pioneer.

Von Eschen, Penny. 1997. *Race against Empire: Black Americans and Anticolonialism, 1937–1957.* Ithaca, N.Y.: Cornell University Press.

Walters, Ronald W. 1993. *Pan Africanism in the African Diaspora: An Analysis of Modern Afrocentric Political Movements.* Detroit: Wayne State University Press.

Ward, Brian, ed. 2001. *Media, Culture, and the Modern African American Freedom Struggle.* Gainesville: University Press of Florida.

Watson, James Milton. 1973. "Violence in the Ghetto: A Critical Comparison of Three Theories of Black Urban Unrest." Ph.D. diss., University of California, Los Angeles.

Watts, 1980: Fifteen Years after the Riot; A Series of Articles Reprinted from the Los Angeles Times. 1980. Los Angeles: Los Angeles Times.

Waugh, Tom. 1985. "In Solidarity: Joris Ivens and the Birth of Cuban Cinema." In *Jump Cut: Hollywood, Politics, and Counter-cinema,* ed. Peter Steven. Toronto: Between the Lines.

Welch, Rebeccah E. 2002. "Black Art and Activism in Postwar New York, 1950–1965." Ph.D. diss., New York University.

West, Cornel. 1996. "Race and Social Theory: Towards a Genealogical Materialist Analysis." In *The Year Left 2: An American Socialist Yearbook,* ed. Mike Davis, Michael Sprinker, and Fred Pfeil. New York: Verso.

White, Armond. 1997. "Sticking to the Soul." *Film Comment* 33 (Jan./Feb.): 38–41.

Wilentz, Gay Alden. 1992. *Binding Cultures: Black Women Writers in Africa and the Diaspora.* Bloomington: Indiana University Press.

Wilkerson, Travis. 2001. "Hasta la victoria siempre." *Senses of Cinema,* no. 17 (Nov.– Dec.): n.p. (online journal).

Willemen, Paul. 1989. "The Third Cinema Question: Notes and Reflections." In *Questions of Third Cinema,* ed. Jim Pines and Willemen. London: British Film Institute.

Williams, Bruce. 1995. "A Cinema in Search of Itself: Meta-filmic Trends in Cinema Novo." *Encruzilhadas/Crossroads,* no. 4: 49–51.

——. 1999. "To Serve Godard: Anthropophagical Precesses in Brazilian Cinema." *Literature/Film Quarterly* 27 (3): 202–9.

Williams, John. 1995. "Re-creating Their Media Image: Two Generations of Black Women Filmmakers." *Black Scholar* 25 (2): 47–57.

Williams, Patrick. 1996. "Imaged Communities: Black British Film in the Eighties and Nineties." *Critical Survey* 8 (1): 3–13.

Williams, Raymond. 1992. *Television: Technology and Cultural Form.* Middletown: Wesleyan University Press.

Williams, Robert F. 1962. *Negroes with Guns.* New York: Marzani and Munsell.

Woodard, Komozi. 1999. *A Nation within a Nation: Amiri Baraka (LeRoi Jones) and Black Power Politics.* Chapel Hill: University of North Carolina Press.

Woolen, Peter. 1973. *Signs and Meaning in the Cinema.* Bloomington: Indiana University Press.

Woolford, Pamela. 1994. "Filming Slavery: A Conversation with Haile Gerima." *Transition,* no. 64: 90–104.

Wright, E. Assata. "From the Continent: A Return to the Past." *Black Film Review* 8 (1): 24–28.

Xavier, Ismail. 1993. "Eldorado as Hell: Cinema Novo and Post Cinema Novo; Appropriations of the Imaginary of the Discovery." In *Mediating Two Worlds: Cinematic Encounters in the Americas,* ed. John King, Ana M. López, and Manuel Alvarado. London: British Film Institute.

——. 1997. "The Humiliation of the Father: Melodrama and Cinema Novo's Critique of Conservative Modernization." *Screen* 38 (4): 329–44.

Yakir, Dan. 1980. "The Mind of Cinema Novo: Interview with Diegues, Carlos." *Film Comment* 16 (5): 40–44.

Yancy, George. 2000. "Interview with Angela Y. Davis." In *Women of Color and Philosophy: A Critical Reader,* ed. Naomi Zack, 135–52. Malden, Mass.: Blackwell.

Yglesias, José. 1985. "*Cinema Novo X 5: Masters of Contemporary Brazilian Film.*" *New York Times Book Review,* 13 January.

Young, Cynthia. 1993. "Integrationist Fantasy and Interracial Desire in *Guess Who's Coming to Dinner* and *Jungle Fever*." Research paper, Yale University.

———. 1998. Interview with Allan Siegel. *Artists and Influence*, February, n.p.

Young, Deborah. 1999. "Adwa: An African Victory." *Variety*, 20 December, 60.

"Young Lords Organize March to U.N." 1970. *Guardian*, 31 October, 7.

Young Lords Party, and Michael Abramson. 1971. *Palante: Young Lords Party*. New York: McGraw-Hill.

Ziarek, Ewa Plonowska. 2002. "Introduction: Fanon's Counterculture of Modernity." *Parallax* 8 (2): 1–9.

Online Publications

"Documentary Filmmaker and Community Activist Susan Robeson to Speak and Serve as Artist-in-Residence." 2000. www.mtholyoke.edu.

Julie Dash Filmography. 2002. geecheetv/Julie.html.

Lee, Morgan. 2003. "Mexican Government Had More than 360 Snipers at 1968 Massacre, Federal Investigator Says." Associated Press, 1 Oct. Lexis-Nexis.com.

Payne, Roz. 2002a. "Early History of Newsreel." Roz Payne's Archives, www.artvt.com/newsreel/roz_photos.htm.

———. 2002b. "A List of Many of the Early Members of Newsreel." Roz Payne's Archives, www.artvt.com/newsreel/roz_photos.htm.

———. 2002c. "Sixties Archives." Roz Payne's Archives, www.artvt.com/newsreel/roz_photos.htm.

———. 2002d. "Video and Film Listings." Roz Payne's Archives, www.artvt.com/newsreel/roz_photos.htm.

Savio, Mario. 1964. "Mario Savio's Speech before the FSM Sit-In." Regents of the University of California. www.fsm-a.org/stacks/mario/mario_speech.

Third World Newsreel. "Third World Newsreel." twn.org.

Williams, Maxine. 1970. "Why Women's Liberation Is Important to Black Women." scriptorium.lib.duke.edu/wlm/blacklib.

Unpublished Interviews

Burnett, Charles. 2002. Interview by the author. Los Angeles, 29 October.

Foner, Moe. 1996. Interview by the author. New York, 9 October.

Fruchter, Norm. 1985. Interview by Michael Renov. New York City, 18 June.

———. 1997. Interview by the author. New York, 14 September.

Kelley, Robin D. G. 1999. Interview by the author. New York, 20 August.

Masilela, Ntongela. 2003. Interview by the author. Claremont, Calif., 23 February.

Robeson, Susan. 1997. Interview by the author. New York, 3 November.

Siegel, Allan. 1997. Interview with Jackie Stewart. Chicago, 29 July.

———. 1998. Interview by the author. New York, 12 February.

Newsletters

Various issues of the following newsletters were consulted in the writing of *Soul Power*. Specific references are given in the notes.

1199 Drug News

1199 Drug and Hospital News

1199 Hospital News

1199 News

1199 News. 1976. "Working in Hospitals: Then and Now." September.

Film and Video

Anderson, Madeline. 1971. *I Am Somebody*. New York: First Run/Icarus Films. VHS. Videocassette.

Angry Voice of Watts. 1966. Chicago: Films Incorporated. Videocassette.

Burnett, Charles. 1977. *Killer of Sheep*. New York: Third World Newsreel. VHS. Videocassette.

———. 1991. *America Becoming*. Alexandria, Va.: PBS Video. VHS. Videocassette.

Dash, Julie. 1983. *Illusions*. New York: Third World Newsreel. VHS. Videocassette.

Gerima, Haile. 1982. *Ashes and Embers*. Washington: Mypheduh Films. VHS. Videocassette.

———. 1993. *Child of Resistance*. Washington: Mypheduh Films. VHS. Videocassette.

———. 1993. *Bush Mama*. Washington: Mypheduh Films. VHS. Videocassette.

———. 1994. *Imperfect Journey*. New York: First Run/Icarus Films. VHS. Videocassette.

———. 1995. *Sankofa*. Washington: Mypheduh Films. VHS. Videocassette.

Larkin, Alile Sharon. 1982. *A Different Image*. New York: Women Make Movies. Videocassette.

Morales, Iris. 1996. *Palante Siempre Palante! The Young Lords Party*. New York: Third World Newsreel. Videocassette.

Newsreel. *Columbia Revolt*. New York: Third World Newsreel. Videocassette.

———. 1971a. *El pueblo se levanta*. New York: Third World Newsreel. Videocassette.

———. 1971b. *Rompiendo puertas*. New York: Third World Newsreel. Videocassette.

Riggs, Marlon T., et al. 1991. *Color Adjustment*. San Francisco: California Newsreel. VHS. Videocassette.

Tambellini, Flávio R., et al. 1995. *Terra estrangeira*. Brazil: Istoé Novo Cinema. VHS. Videocassette.

Third World Newsreel. 1972. *Teach Our Children*. Ed. Christine Choy and Susan Robeson. New York: Third World Newsreel. Videocassette.

Index

tion, 23–24. *See also specific filmmakers* (i.e., L.A. Rebellion; Newsreel; etc.)

Fink, Leon, 55, 60–61, 63–64, 67, 74, 96

Firestone, Cindy, 98

Fishman, Marvin, 103, 105, 110–11

Foner, Moe, 55, 59–62, 64–65, 67, 69, 81, 84, 92–93, 95

Ford, Gerald, 164

Foundations of Leninism (Stalin), 162

Four Women (1975), 213

FPCC (Fair Play for Cuba Committee), 19, 24

Frankfurt School philosophy, 192–99, 208

Freedom Dreams (Kelley), 197

Friedman, Steve, 151

From Spikes to Spindles (1976) (Choy/ Third World Newsreel), 150, 175

Fruchter, Norm, 103, 105, 109–10, 113, 120, 151

Fuentes, Carlos, 25

Fuller, Buckminster, 151

Gabriel, Teshome, 217, 225–26, 232, 246–47

Ganda, Oumarou, 225

Gandhi, Mohatma, 199

Garbage (1968), 110

García Espinosa, Julio, 23–24, 218

Garvey, Marcus, 43, 63

Gaye, Marvin, 209–13

Geer, Will, 81

Gerima, Haile, 4–5, 213–16, 219, 222, 226, 232–39, 246. See also *Bush Mama* (1979)

Gessner, Peter, 119

Ghana, 8

Ghettos: Davis on, 206; likened to Third World colonies, 49–50, 207. *See also* Watts

Gibson, Kenneth, 52, 227

Gibson, Richard, 19, 25, 29

Gillespie, Dizzy, 90

Ginsberg, Allen, 8, 32

Godoff, Elliot, 55, 59–62, 64–67, 69

Gold, Tammy, 122, 139

Golpeandos en la selva (1967), 119, 177

Gonzalez, Gloria, 125

González, Juan, 125, 128

Goodman, Andrew, 69

Grain, The (1967), 104–5

Gramsci, Antonio, 227

Grant, Bev, 103, 122, 139

Grant, Mikki, 89

Graves, Milford, 51

Greenberg, Brian, 55, 60–61, 63–64, 67, 74, 96

Gregoria, Rose, 92

Gregory, Dick, 81

Grewal, Inderpal, 11

Griffin, Ada Gay, 248

Grossberg, Lawrence, 12

Guerrero, Ed, 223

Guess Who's Coming to Dinner (1967), 223

Guevara, Ernesto "Che," 23; films on, 119; influence on U.S. Third World Leftists, 8; as mythic figure, 33–34; writings of, 9. *See also* Cuba; Cuban Revolution

Guttiérez Alea, Tomás, 23–24, 219

Guzmán, Pablo, 125, 129–30

Haley, Harold, 202

Hall, Stuart, 103–4, 146, 153

Hamilton, Charles, 157

Hammer and Hoe (Kelley), 157

Hampton, Fred, 166

Hanoi, martes 13 (1967), 119, 173, 177

Hansberry, Lorraine, 44, 83

Harlem, and Cuban Revolution, 21–25

Harrington, Michael, 93

Harris, Harold, 63

Harrison, Hubert Henry, 2

Hasta la victoria siempre (1967), 119

Hayden, Tom, 58, 151

Haywood, Harry, 157

Hegel, G. W. F., 193–94

Cynthia Young is an associate professor of English and director of the African and African Diaspora Studies Program at Boston College.

A portion of chapter 1 was published as "Havana Up in Harlem: LeRoi Jones, Harold Cruse, and the Making of a Cultural Revolution," *Science and Society* 65 (1) (spring 2001): 12–38. A portion of chapter 4 was published as "Third World Newsreel: Third Cinema in the U.S.," in *Ethnic Media in America: Taking Control Book 2*, ed. Guy Meiss and Alice A. Tait (Dubuque: Kendall/Hunt Publishing, 2005), 31–59. A synopsis of chapter 5 was published in *Revolutions of the Mind: Cultural Studies in the African Diaspora Project, 1996–2002*, ed. Dionne Bennett et al. (Los Angeles: CAAS Publications, 2003), 3–10.

Library of Congress Cataloging-in-Publication Data

Young, Cynthia
Soul power : culture, radicalism, and the making of a U.S. Third World left / Cynthia Young.
p. cm.
Includes bibliographical references and index.
ISBN-13: 978-0-8223-3679-2 (cloth : alk. paper)
ISBN-10: 0-8223-3679-0 (cloth : alk. paper)
ISBN-13: 978-0-8223-3691-4 (pbk. : alk. paper)
ISBN-10: 0-8223-3691-x (pbk. : alk. paper)
1. African Americans—Politics and government—20th century. 2. Minorities—United States—Political activity—History—20th century.
3. African American political activists—History—20th century. 4. African Americans—Intellectual life—20th century. 5. Radicalism—United States—History—20th century. 6. Social justice—United States—History—20th century. 7. Anti-imperialist movements—Developing countries—History—20th century. 8. Developing countries—Politics and government—20th century. 9. United States—Politics and government—1945–1989. 10. United States—Race relations—Political aspects—History—20th century. I. Title.
E185.615.Y58 2006
303.48'21724008996073—dc22 2006010448